NO FIXED ADDRESS

Donald Robertson co-founded and published the music magazine *Roadrunner* (1978-83), and was the inaugural editor of *Countdown Magazine* (1983-86). His previous books include *On Tour with INXS* (Music Sales 1986), *Roll Over Beethoven: Contemporary music education for secondary schools* (Fairfax 1987), *Rock Around the Clock: Careers in the Australian Music Industry* (Ausmusic 1992) and *The Big Beat: Rock Music in Australia 1978-83* (Roadrunnertwice 2019). In a 25-year public service career between 1988 and 2013, he was variously publisher, manager media and public relations and digital publisher at Australia's media and communications regulator.

NO FIXED ADDRESS

THE STORY OF AUSTRALIA'S TRAILBLAZING ABORIGINAL ROCK'N'REGGAE BAND

DONALD ROBERTSON

Roadrunner twice

This edition published in 2024 by Roadrunnertwice
Sydney, New South Wales, Australia

www.roadrunnertwice.com.au

First published 2023 by Hybrid Publishers, Melbourne, Australia.

ISBN: 978-1-7635371-0-1 (paperback)   978-0-646-88385-4 (E-book)

This publication was supported by the History Trust of South Australia's South Australian History Fund.

Cover design: Jim Paton. Front cover photograph by Ian de Gruchy.

Important note: Aboriginal and Torres Straits Islander readers are advised that this book contains the names and images of people who have died.

British Library Cataloguing in Publication Data.
A catalogue record for this book is available from the British Library.

Type used in this book: TT Livret, Metafora and Gill Sans.

You can't change the rhythm of my soul
You can't tell me too what to do
You can't break my bones by putting me down
or by taking the things that belong to me

We have survived the white man's world
and the horror and the torment of it all
We have survived the white man's world
and you know you can't change that

—Bart Willoughby, 'We Have Survived'

CONTENTS

PART 3: THE AUSTRALIAN MUSIC MACHINE (1981–84)

PART 4: OVERSEAS TOURS (1984–88)

EPILOGUE

APPENDICES

NOTES

INDEX

When No Fixed Address showed up in the mainstream music industry in the early '80s, they pretty much kicked the door open. They shook everyone up because they not only broke through but they stuck around; they held their ground and demanded attention. They were here to stay.

Coincidentally, in May 1981 the great reggae man Bob Marley died. He was also a breakthrough artist, coming from the ghetto to the mainstream, and many people felt that loss very deeply. NFA with their own brand of Australian reggae helped to ease the pain for many people at that time.

No Fixed Address's presence in the mainstream music industry in Australia changed the algorithm – people working in all areas of the industry had to come to terms with Aboriginality at close quarters. Every interaction brought change, making it an easier fit for other Aboriginal performers to inhabit the space. Their ongoing presence changed the conversation in the rock scene forever by introducing Aboriginal concepts into the mix. They were creating the environment for change and all that would flow from that. I'm not so sure that the music industry changed that much, as it is a money-making machine. It was more that Aboriginal performers now knew their own value, and that the audiences knew what to expect from them (as there had been no Aboriginal people on the scene since Jimmy Little in the '60s).

NFA played the mainstream music industry circuits on the east coast, getting bookings through Harbour in Sydney and Premier in Melbourne – just check out their gig lists. They worked hard like most bands playing those circuits, but they had to contend with much more than any of those other bands could imagine.

The change that happened in their wake instigated more change as other Aboriginal performers showed up in the east coast music scene. Us Mob, who were more for Metalheads, had also featured in the movie *Wrong Side of the Road* and played a few gigs around Sydney after the release of the movie. Then along came Warumpi Band and Coloured Stone from Central Australia, changing things up again as they too hooked into the mainstream circuits.

Like Frank Sinatra, NFA broke through with some help from the shadowy side of life; they had to, they had no choice, nothing else was available to them. Things changed after that and by the '90s there was much more tour funding available through the government. Yothu Yindi, Archie Roach and Ruby Hunter became household names with chart-topping hits. Performers like Kevin Carmody and Tiddas also experienced commercial success and were very big in the alternative scene.

They were followed by Gurrumul in the 2000s with huge hits and much international recognition, while back at home, the Pigram Brothers from Broome were wowing audiences on the festival circuit and getting strong airplay on the alternative airwaves. Today, Aboriginal performing artists are found in many genres. Acts like A.B. Original, Emma Donovan and the Putbacks and Thelma Plumb, all exciting artists, are excelling in their specific genres.

More power to Aboriginal musicians everywhere who are bringing our stories to the world – may you all live on in the music that you make. VIVA NFA.

– Maxine Briggs
Victorian Aboriginal woman of Taungwurrung and Yorta
Yorta Nations
Lighting engineer in the No Fixed Address crew, 1980-82
Chairperson, Songlines Music Corporation 1994-95
Events Manager, Koori Arts Collective, 1992-97
Koori Librarian, State Library Victoria from 2008

INTRODUCTION

I was living in Adelaide and editing *Roadrunner* magazine when I first met No Fixed Address. A bunch of young Aboriginal musicians at the University of Adelaide's Centre for Aboriginal Studies in Music (CASM), bouncing around Adelaide from gig to gig, they were about to start filming a movie, *Wrong Side of the Road*, loosely based on their lives and experiences, and songs from their demo tape were getting strong airplay on Adelaide public radio station 5MMM-FM.

They sounded like nobody else in my experience and they were the first band in a long, long time to send shivers down my spine. I got to know them and, as they didn't seem to have a manager, I tried to help them out. I found them some gigs, took Don Walker from Cold Chisel to see them one night – which resulted in a support slot on one of Chisel's national tours – and when the combination of the magazine and the band got too much, I introduced them to Redgum's manager, Chris Gunn, who took them under his wing. And off they went to (some) fame and (I suspected, not very much) fortune in the Australian music machine of the 1980s. But they left their mark.

As Graeme Isaac, co-producer of *Wrong Side of the Road* and its soundtrack album points out, No Fixed Address was the first Indigenous band to be playing mostly original material in a contemporary idiom with songs about their own lives – years before Warumpi Band or Yothu Yindi. 'They were trailblazers for these bands in an Australian music industry that wasn't quite ready for them, and never really allowed them to fully realise or capitalise on their talent,' he says.

Wrong Side of the Road was an eye-opener for both black and white audiences. White audiences could hardly believe the casual, everyday racism that was portrayed – racism that, if anything, was toned down for the big screen. On the other hand, Indigenous audiences could hardly believe seeing the struggles they faced in their daily lives being acted out. 'Can they really say that?' they whispered wonderingly. But all agreed about the freshness and power of the music, the original Aboriginal reggae of No Fixed Address and the hard rock stomp of Us Mob.

In some ways, says Isaac, the film's biggest achievement was in legitimising the idea of an urban Aboriginal community and identity. 'At the time, for most white Australians, urban Aboriginals were seen as inauthentic, not really "Aboriginal". When we went to school in the 1950s and '60s, we were taught that Aboriginals were a dying race; so, in the '70s and into the '80s urban Aboriginals were seen as these poor souls on a journey of assimilation. Until the political protest movements of the era – the land rights movement, the tent embassy, the bicentennial protests etc. ... began to turn that around. And of course, No Fixed Address (along with Jimmy Chi and Kuckles in Broome, CAAMA in Alice, the Black Theatre Movement etc.) were a significant part of that new positive assertion of identity.'

~

Both No Fixed Address and Us Mob were stalwarts of the Rock Against Racism concerts of the early 1980s, but after *Wrong Side of the Road* their paths quickly diverged. Us Mob struggled in Sydney and broke up after they couldn't work out why they were running on fumes during a sold-out outback tour. No Fixed Address based itself in Melbourne and proceeded to clock up thousands upon thousands of kilometres crisscrossing the country on the booming Australian pub rock circuit. A highlight was the headline spot at a Rock Against Racism concert in Brisbane, part of the Indigenous protests against the 1982 Commonwealth Games.

After signing a recording deal, No Fixed Address's debut release *From My Eyes* was launched by future Prime Minister Bob Hawke and the band performed the title track on

Countdown, the first Aboriginal band to appear on the iconic ABC-TV program.

There were downs as well as ups. The band's record label folded. There were disagreements, even fights. Members came and went as the grind of the road took its toll, and the band was down to a three-piece when it went to play in England in 1984, becoming the first Aboriginal band to mount an overseas tour. Warmly received by English audiences as well as the notoriously anti-Antipodean music press, the band attracted a number of high-profile admirers, from dub poet Linton Kwesi Johnson to Led Zeppelin guitarist Jimmy Page.

No Fixed Address broke up in 1985 but reformed two years later, and the distinctive drone of a didgeridoo underlined their messages in song when they ventured behind the Iron Curtain in 1988 on a white-knuckle tour of Eastern Europe. The stress told, however, and on their return, they broke up again.

~

The band reunited for a handful of performances in 1996 and has got together intermittently to perform ever since. Acknowledgement of their ground-breaking role came slowly; but it came. In 2008, the version of 'We Have Survived' from the *Wrong Side of the Road* soundtrack was added to the National Film and Sound Archives' *Sounds of Australia* collection, the sounds that 'make up Australia's history, the sounds that are among the most important to our collective memories as Australians'. In 2011, the band, along with fellow CASM outfit Coloured Stone, was inducted into the National Indigenous Music Awards Hall of Fame. In 2013, *Wrong Side of the Road* was fully digitally restored by the National Film and Sound Archive and in 2016, No Fixed Address was inducted into the South Australian Music Hall of Fame. Then in July 2020, the City of Adelaide said the fifth home-grown music artist to have a city laneway renamed in their honour – following Cold Chisel, The Angels, Paul Kelly and Sia – would be No Fixed Address.

I was delighted at the news and delved back into my *Roadrunner*-era scrapbooks to see what I had kept about the band. I found a draft schedule for the 1980 Cold Chisel tour and some press clippings about a 1981 Royal Charity Concert attended by Prince Charles at Adelaide's Festival Theatre. I sent these on to the band's guitarist Ricky Harrison and out of the resulting conversation I asked if anyone had ever written their story. He said no – and would I be interested? I said I would, if everyone would be happy to participate.

Harrison gave me contact details for the band's remaining original members Bart Willoughby, Les Graham and John John Miller and they all thought it was a worthy project. As well as sharing their memories, they put me in touch with others who were around and involved with the band. Graeme Isaac was incredibly helpful in providing me with leads to people who could contribute to the story. Then, when I went to Adelaide for the opening of No Fixed Address Lane I met their manager Michael Fisher. Michael subsequently put aside his dream of writing a book about No Fixed Address and generously shared his thoughts, memories and insights about the nitty-gritty of managing an Aboriginal band in the 1980s, as well as providing me with access to the remarkable archive he had collected and preserved. My sincere thanks to Michael and Graeme for their contributions to this book.

~

One of the things that struck me as I spoke to people, particularly white people, about those days in the late 1970s and early '80s, was the shock they experienced when they were first confronted by the blatant racism against Aboriginal people. It's a sad commentary on Australia that the racism and other issues that No Fixed Address wrote and sang about so powerfully in their songs are still with us today.

One can only hope that initiatives like the Uluru Statement from the Heart, with its call for a constitutionally enshrined First Nations voice to parliament, along with a Makarrata

Commission to supervise a process of agreement-making between governments and First Nations, and truth-telling about our history, bears some fruit.

Because, as Henry Reynolds puts it in the conclusion to *The Other Side of the Frontier*, his masterful account of Aboriginal resistance to the European invasion of Australia:

> If we are unable to incorporate the black experience into our national heritage we will stand exposed as a people still emotionally chained to our nineteenth century British origins, ever the transplanted Europeans.[1]

It was Easter 1982. No Fixed Address were on the road, driving back east from Perth, heading to Alice Springs. Although they'd been impressing audiences and slowly building a live following in Adelaide, Melbourne and Sydney for a couple of years, the release of the film *Wrong Side of the Road* the previous November had brought the group to the attention of the national media. A drama about 48 hours in the lives of two Aboriginal bands, No Fixed Address and Us Mob, it had won the Jury Prize at the 1981 Australian Film Institute Awards and had been playing to capacity audiences on the independent film circuit.

Four shows to packed houses on Cold Chisel's Summer Offensive tour in December 1980 had opened the eyes of No Fixed Address to how big things could be. Supports to Ian Dury and the Blockheads (November 1981) and The Clash (February 1982) had just put the group in front of a whole new audience of Australian punk and new wave music fans. The soundtrack album to *Wrong Side of the Road*, with six tracks from each of the two featured bands, had received solid airplay on alternative radio across the country and sold well over the summer. They had management in the form of Mick Pacholli, publisher of *tagg* (the alternative gig guide) magazine; had a music publishing deal with Michael Gudinski's Mushroom Music; and after signing with hip Melbourne independent label Rough Diamond, had just completed recording tracks for a mini-album. The producer was David Briggs, former guitarist with Little River Band, who was fresh from doing the honours on Australian Crawl's five-times platinum debut *The Boys Light Up*. No Fixed Address were a young band that was definitely going places in the Australian music scene. But the difficulties of being young Aboriginals were never far away.

'We'd had trouble in Perth,' says guitarist Ricky Harrison. 'We had about twenty gigs booked and thirteen of them were cancelled when the promoters found out we were an Aboriginal band. Cold Chisel were in town as well and helped us get some gigs.'

'They got to Perth and I had all these gigs booked,' says Mick Pacholli. 'Two grand a gig. And all the Italians over there said, "These are blackfellas – we're not putting 'em on."

'I said, "What didn't you understand about Australia's premier Aboriginal rock band? What is wrong with you people?"

'"We're not putting them on."

'"Well, that's a big slice of my budget. You're leaving me stranded."'

Local promoter Kenn McMillan managed to cobble together enough replacement gigs to cover costs. But the episode – which closely mirrored an incident of discrimination depicted in *Wrong Side of the Road* – left a sour taste.

The cancellation of the gigs was just the first setback on the trip. While in Perth, drummer Bart Willoughby broke his right arm. While he could still get up on stage to sing, the band's two recently engaged percussionists, Joe Geia and Billy Inda Cummins, had to cover for the lack of drums. For the final show of the Perth run, which was filmed by ABC-TV's *Rock Arena*, local drummer Reg Zar was drafted in.

When the Perth engagements were completed, the touring party loaded up their two cars and equipment truck and set out on the next leg of the tour, to Kalgoorlie. From there it would be the long trek across the Nullarbor Plain to Ceduna, South Australia and then up to Alice Springs. But at 1:30 am on Tuesday, 13 April, on the Eyre Highway 20 kilometres east of Norseman, disaster struck.

'I was in the lead car, with our roadie Angelo DiCarlo, who was driving,' recalls Ricky Harrison. 'His mouth was going a hundred miles an hour. Maxine Briggs was in the back seat. She did our lights. Also back there was Joe Hayes, our bass player and his wife, Jean. Behind us was the truck with the PA and drums and our amps and guitars. Then behind them was the second car. Like a convoy.

'So, we're going down the road and there's this car coming towards us, in the middle of the road. There's a ditch on the side of the road, so we couldn't go off the road. Angelo just managed to scrape past it. Then in the rear-view mirror I just saw this ball of flame, like a bomb had gone off. The car had gone straight at the truck and the truck had driven over the top of the car and exploded.'

Edward Claude Love [Woody] was driving the truck with John Parker [Car John] and Les Graham [guitarist] next to him in the cabin. 'Woody was saying to me the guy wouldn't turn his lights down,' Graham recalls. 'I just knew straightaway, he's asleep or he's ... I didn't think about him being pissed, I really thought he was asleep. Driving over the Nullarbor is so far, it's so easy [to fall asleep at the wheel]. I reached over and pulled Woody towards me. Car John was in the middle. It was instinct, just natural instinct. We were all hugging together like a big ball, so we were too big to go through the front window. Otherwise we would have been splattered out through the front window from the impact.

'Then the car come into us. It came in so hard it threw us up in the air. We flew up and our petrol tanks blew up. We went up in a mushroom, like explosives, like a bomb. This is amazing; it didn't put the truck on the side, it put us on the roof. It actually flipped us right over on the roof. Then it slid down the road while we were still in the cabin. There was the most endless screeching noise. I can never forget it. It was just continuous, this noise. The back of the truck was scraping on the bitumen. I know it was a matter of seconds but it was just forever, that noise. I was waiting for it to stop but it wouldn't. It all happened in slow motion. Even the sound.

'The truck was in flames while we were still inside it. When it stopped we got out through the front window. The windscreen was gone. When we got out there were flames everywhere. That car went completely underneath us. It pulled the front end out of the truck. The two front wheels were on the side of the road. It came out from underneath the back of the truck and we had a car behind us and they had to do a lot of swerving to miss it.'

The driver of the car died in the vehicle and his two passengers were hospitalised for weeks. Woody, Car John and Les Graham sustained minor injuries and were held overnight in hospital for observation but were not detained.

'The truck exploded in Norseman,' says Mick Pacholli. 'I didn't know where any of the band was. Les rings me, I say, "Where is everyone?" "I don't know." "Well, you better find them because we've got a gig in three days, mate." I said, "Is anyone [in the band or crew] dead?" They've gone, "Nope." "Well, we're doing the fucking gig," I said. "I've already been down to Troy Music. I've got brand new guitars coming up boys, Bart's got a new drum kit. Just make sure the band's there." And he did.'

It was hard enough being a rock band on the road in Australia in the 1980s. Being a black band just added another degree of difficulty. A lot of the time, No Fixed Address really must have felt they were on the wrong side of the road. But not only did they survive; they persevered. And they endured. This is their story.

PART I

CENTRE FOR ABORIGINAL STUDIES IN MUSIC

(1977–80)

| NIGHT DRIVE TO MORWELL

It was a hot start to 1979 in South Australia. The heatwave began on New Year's Eve, and for the next two weeks, maximum temperatures of at least 45°C were a daily occurrence at places such as Marree and Oodnadatta in the north of the state. The extreme heat also reached further south: at Port Augusta the mercury topped 44°C on five days. While Adelaide did not have that many days of extreme heat, 42°C on 4 January was the highest temperature for 11 years.

It was summer holidays for the students at the Centre for Aboriginal Studies in Music (CASM) at the University of Adelaide. Towards the end of the month, Les Graham[1] was out one night having a drink with his brother Boots [Albert John Kelly]. 'My mother lived at Murray Bridge,' says Graham. 'We were heading back there and he was going to drop me off at my mother's place. His wife Sylvia was Ricky Harrison's sister. I was pretty well intoxicated and I ended up going to sleep in the back of the car. It was a station wagon.

'When I woke up, I woke up in Melbourne. And I had to drive because my brother was up all night driving. I didn't know my way through Melbourne but I followed the signs showing me which direction and that. I was 18, 19 years old, first time I had to drive in a big city like Melbourne. Anyway, we ended up going back to their place in Gippsland – Morwell. And that's when I met Rick.'

~

Ricky Harrison had been playing in a teenage cover band called Black Satin in Morwell for two or three years but had given it up the previous year because 'it wasn't going anywhere'. Nicky Moffatt, who would later join No Fixed Address, was the bass player.

'Nicky was like my little brother,' says Harrison. 'My dad and his dad were brothers. So, we're first cousins. I used to go down to his house. He had some friends who had some equipment. So, we started a band and used some of their equipment and got our own. We used to rehearse at the back of his parents' house in Margaret Street. We had this little three-piece thing set up, bass guitar, guitar amp, guitar and drums, and a mic. His mum bought us a mic. My mum bought me a guitar and Sammy ... not sure where we got the drums from.

'We sat there and rehearsed, and we used to play our own songs and did a lot of covers. A lot of country songs back then. A bit of Eagles. Then *Countdown* come on and we started listening to other bands. I bought The Angels album, *Face to Face*. We used to do a few covers from that album. That was the stuff I liked to get into. AC/DC was a bit too heavy for us [laughs]. But The Angels were perfect for what we were doing. We used to do, "Take a Long Line", "(Take Me Away To) Marseille", "Be with You". A few Eagles songs and some old Jim Reeves songs as well.'

Harrison had just come back from a funeral when he met Les Graham. 'They said to me Les is starting a band,' Harrison recalls. 'And Les told me he'd read one of the songs I'd written. Because I'd have these sheets of paper all over the room.'

'Rick showed me this pile of songs he'd wrote,' says Graham. 'A big pile of them. And I said, "What are you doing?" And he said, no, nothing. And I said, "Why don't you come with us? Come back to South Australia with me and join up, we're looking to put this band together." So, we all agreed.'

Graham had been in a band at CASM, but two of the members had left at the end of the year, leaving just guitarist Graham and drummer Bart Willoughby. Harrison's cousin Tony Mullett played bass a bit so he was roped in as well.

'We hitchhiked from Morwell,' says Harrison. 'Les went ahead and we ended up picking him up along the way and we ended up in Spencer Street station. He called Auntie Leila [Rankine] and she was able to get him a fare on the train over to Adelaide, but because me and Tony weren't students we had to hitchhike over from Melbourne.

'First lift we got took us all the way through to Adelaide.

The guy pulled up, he had a little thing on the back of his F100 or whatever it was, a little house, like camper thing. It looked like he'd put it together himself. Anyway, he opened the door and looked at us and said, "Where are you jerks going?" [laughs]. And he goes, "Come on, get in," and he goes like sixty kilometres an hour all the way; sometimes he hit eighty [laughs]. We left about six in the morning and got to Adelaide about eight at night.

'We went looking for where my sister Bobbi Yates used to live and this guy came out with a rifle. Threatened us with a rifle. First day we got there. I think it might have been Unley or somewhere round there. It was our first time in Adelaide. We ended up staying at a hostel on South Terrace. So, the next day we went and met up with Les at CASM. We didn't meet Bart till later.'

Harrison thought it was a bit strange the Centre for Aboriginal Studies in Music was in a house. 'It was really weird,' he says. 'It wasn't like any college I'd ever seen. First time I'd ever been to a college anyway. I saw how structured everything was, like there was one of the rooms where I had my saxophone lessons but basically it was a house and people would be playing the violin in the bathroom and another one in the common room. There was a bit of space there but it was a bit squishy.

'But the thing was, it had an officialdom about it. There was Auntie Leila and Big Ben, Ben Yengi. From Kenya or somewhere around that area [Sudan]. He was the administrator and Auntie Leila was the administrator. I talked to her and she seemed like one of the aunties from back home. Spoke that same way. It was nice meeting Ben. It was the first time I'd met a fella from overseas, a blackfella. It was really surprising because he was an African fella working at CASM. He was just like the rest of us in a way; he was into the music. He loved playing the bongos and the congas. He was actually teaching us how to make the ones they made in Africa out of cowskin.'

As the student year got under way, one of the classes that

made a big impression on Harrison was the tribal singing led by the Pitjantjatjara elders from Indulkana. 'Oh yeah, it was part of the curriculum,' he says. 'You had to do tribal singing. Mr Baker was the Head man. We'd all sit around in a circle there and the tribal people would sing a song, and they'd really get right into it. Then they'd turn around and everyone is singing then he'd stop the class and point his finger at you and go, "You, boy, sing!" and you'd try to sing and he'd tell you, "No, no, do it this way, this is how Aboriginal people sing. This is how your people used to do this a long time ago. This is how they sang their songs. This is what their songs were more than likely about."

'It made you feel really good inside. It's like saying to me, you're an Aboriginal person. This belongs to you. As it belongs to everybody in a way. That history, that language that's theirs, is still there. My language, you've got to read it from books. All the old people could speak it, but when we moved from the mission [Lake Tyers, in East Gippsland] back in 1965, I was about five years old and I lost contact with our people in a lot of ways. Going from learning how to make boomerangs ... they'd all sit around back on the mission when I was a kid making artefacts and stuff and painting and telling me the stories about what they were doing and the history of why they were making it.

'It was interesting because they had this big chunk of wood shaped like a boomerang and they had a vice that they held it in and they used to cut slices off this big chunk of wood and all the men would take credit and they'd be sandpapering and painting.

'So, when we moved from there, that was gone. I ended up going to school. When we moved to Morwell there were only allowed to be three Aboriginal families in a town, three black families. So, we went to white school. Which was all good, you know. Really good people. I didn't really come across any racism at school.'

Harrison didn't have high expectations about CASM. 'I

went in there wanting to learn an instrument,' he says. 'To learn how to read music and become a college student, and from experience, as a student band we might get a couple of gigs around the city. Which was all I wanted to do, go to college and do a few shows around the city. Because at the time, I'd already finished playing. But in the end the songs that I wrote turned out really well. "The Vision", the one that I wrote when I was sixteen, that was the first original song that we put together.'

In 1978, Graeme Isaac was sharing a house in Melbourne with Steve James, who the previous year had played in Adelaide coffee shops with CASM staffers Matt Bienstock and Leigh Hobba. On a visit to Melbourne, Sherree Goldsworthy met Isaac and they took up together. Goldsworthy was working at the South Australian Media Resource Centre (MRC), part of the creative hub scattered around the east end of Rundle Street. Founded in 1974, the MRC provided an equipment base and the space for filmmakers to work on their projects, network with others and attend seminars and screenings.

Under the benevolent gaze of the state Labor government, by the end of the 1970s a loose network of alternative and community arts groups had sprung up in Adelaide.[1] Many of the artists who visited the state during the biennial festival of arts liked what they saw and the network was continually being invigorated by interstate talent. 'That was the thing about Adelaide,' says local artist and filmmaker Margaret Dodd. 'Everybody connected. That was just the sort of town it was. We coalesced around the Media Resource Centre, the Women's Art Movement, the Experimental Art Foundation and then all the Trotskyists, the Maoists, [Flinders University Professor] Brian Medlin.'

After her trip to Melbourne, Goldsworthy returned to Adelaide where she and her young son were living in one of two adjoining workers cottages in Little Grenfell Street, Kent Town. When word that Matt Bienstock was leaving CASM at the end of the year filtered through the grapevine to Goldsworthy, she rang Isaac in Melbourne and suggested he call Leigh Hobba.

'He rang up and said, "Is there a place?"' recalls Hobba. 'Because he was really thinking of coming over if there was a job at CASM. I was able to get him a job and he was able to take it from there. Came in as guitar tutor and the whole thing.'

'In those days it was all very word of mouth,' says

Goldsworthy. 'It was all about connections. He was certainly here because of me. I think the story is "boy from Melbourne meets girl who works at the Media Resource Centre, comes over, gets a job at CASM and things start."'

'I lived next door to Sherree,' remembers screen-printer Mark Thomson, 'and actually for a whole lot of reasons, I went over to Melbourne with Sherree and brought Graeme back to Adelaide, and they moved in next door. I just remember things fell into place remarkably quickly. It was kind of intriguing.'

'All the building blocks were there,' confirms Bienstock. 'A lot of groundwork had been done. The guys at CASM were used to playing with each other and some of them were really good on their instrument. Others were at the beginning stages of learning. Graeme came over to Adelaide and in the crisscross, I ended up buying Graeme's amp off him and taking it back to Melbourne. I started using it playing in bands in Melbourne and Graeme started working with the guys.'

~

In the early 1970s, Isaac had been a member of the Australian Performing Group, a collective of artists based in the Pram Factory in Melbourne's inner-city suburb of Carlton. After Captain Matchbox Whoopee Band, Australia's favourite dope-smoking jug band, experienced one of their many break-ups in late 1975, lead singer Mic Conway joined with the APG and began rehearsing a political circus show.[2] As a side venture, Conway and Isaac formed a jazz-swing group called the Vipers. After the line-up expanded, Conway changed the band's name to Matchbox, to reconnect with the Whoopee Band's sizable fan base.

Under the banner of Soapbox Circus, Matchbox and the APG mounted several productions and recorded a live album, *The Great Stumble Forward* in 1976. Isaac's final involvement with Matchbox was as part of the Soapbox Circus alternative pantomime *Smack in the Dacks: The Undone Panto*. Billed as an 'All new Xmas rock'n'roll spectacular', the show ran from 17

November to 24 December 1977 at the Pram Factory.

'When I left the circus, I played with a couple of jump blues bands,' says Isaac. 'But after a while I tired of playing in pubs where people would cheer like crazy when you played like crap and then next night when you played really well, no-one took any notice.

'But more fundamentally I realised that I was never really going to develop the chops of the people that I really admired musically, like for instance, Andy Baylor. They had all been prepared to sit in a bedroom for six hours a day and just get their chops together. I was never going to do that. It was the social aspect of the music, and the connection between the music and the audience that engaged me.'

Arriving at CASM was a real eye-opener. 'I had never met any Aboriginal people and I just found it a window into a new world,' says Isaac. 'There was such a mixture of people there. Teenagers and also adults; people of different ages and coming from different places and for different reasons. Some with real musical talent and others with no great talent for music, but with aspirations to do all sorts of other things in their lives. And all of them had stories to tell and things to say.

'And the woman who ran it, Leila Rankine, was one of these matriarchal community figures that I soon learned are so common in Indigenous communities and often their backbone. A quiet but immensely strong woman with committed social values and a determination to build a school for Indigenous youth that would make a difference. And the school's administrator was an African guy named Ben Yengi who was also a drummer.

'The school operated from a building on the edge of Adelaide University. A little building with salt damp, in Finniss Street just down the road from the British Hotel in North Adelaide. And I felt it was really being used as a fish bowl for the ethnomusicology students to have access to these Indigenous elders who had come down from Indulkana. Pitjantjatjara men and women, senior figures, who would come down and teach their traditional singing.'

It was apparent that there were a number of threads operating simultaneously at CASM. The ethnomusicology and western classical orchestral threads had been part of the program developed by Dr Catherine Ellis that led to the establishment of the Centre. But what was starting to emerge was a contemporary creative thread. This was naturally of most interest to Isaac.

'I am not sure, at that time anyway, that there was that much interest on the part of the university in the school functioning in a really meaningful way for the urban Aboriginal community, which was how Leila wanted it to be,' he says. 'It was a slightly uncomfortable arrangement.

'But then the presence of these senior traditional people was also important for the urban students there. Even if they were not Pitjantjatjara and even if they were distant from their own traditional background, I think it was very valuable for them. Certainly, it was important to Leila.

'In the '70s, and even for enlightened types as Cath Ellis must have been, the idea of an urban Aboriginal culture and identity was not imagined or understood by those outside of that community. You can see it in her idea of what the Centre would be – it would teach Western orchestral and choral music to these urban waifs along with the traditional music they had lost contact with. Outside of the traditional stuff there was no vision of music as an expression of contemporary urban or at least post-mission Indigenous identity.

'I never met her and don't know the circumstances of her withdrawing from involvement with the Centre, but I think it probably had something to do with the tension between her original intentions and the way the Centre was evolving. Certainly, amplified instruments and rock'n'roll would have been a bridge too far. It wasn't Leila's sort of music either; her music was the music of the world of the mission, closer to the musical world that Cath Ellis might have conceived of as being "Aboriginal". But Leila recognised that rock'n'roll and electrified country music was what that generation wanted and so she supported it and fought for it. And was very proud of it.'

The university hadn't signed up to the idea of a school of rock either. 'The idea from the university's point of view about what musical education was going to be was very old school,' says Isaac. 'I mean orchestras, people learning clarinet, choral groups, ensembles, all that sort of stuff. I mean, it was just weird – the idea that kids like Bart or Les – and they were just kids then, just sixteen or seventeen – the idea they would be interested in "ensembles".

'But they would all turn up every day, because there were a couple of guitars kicking around along with a drum kit, and they could get paid a student's allowance, and they were in a place where they could do the things they wanted to do. It was a safe environment, and Leila Rankine had a lot to do with that; and in fact her sister, Veronica Brodie, was a student there. Leila and Veronica really ran the show. Veronica was meant to be a student there, but she carried a similar authority in the place to her sister by virtue of her personality.

'But in terms of its facilities, they had nothing. The building had salt damp, there were no practice rooms. The year before they had managed to get a drum kit in there. Leigh Hobba had managed to get that along with a couple of guitars and an amp. But very little. With Leila and Ben's help I was able to get a little bit more gear in there. A bass amp, and maybe a bass guitar, a small PA and a couple of other things, and to get an additional room in a next-door building to set up as a practice room, a band room. Because that's what they needed more than anything. A place to work.

'I very quickly saw that all right, I can give a few guitar lessons, but what these guys need is ... the best way they will learn is by performing. And they have already got their own thing going; they just need the resources and they need the framework. And they need a bit of help to actually play together as a band. So, I wanted to encourage them to write their own songs and to help get their show on the road.

'They were playing covers, but Ricky already had "The Vision". But he was playing it as sort of rock and roll. Or really like a blues, I think it might have been. It wasn't reggae. I don't know how this came about but I started turning them on to reggae.'

'The Vision' was really powerful, Bart Willoughby recalls. 'The words were really powerful. The tune was original. When we first did it, it was a blues song. Then one of our teachers came along and said, "Why don't you change it to a reggae beat?" And we went, "Ah. That'd do." So, we were trying to work out a bass bit and then we just swept it all completely around. Instead of on the beat, we changed it to an offbeat. We could actually do that because we were really getting influenced by Bob Marley.'

At Finniss Street, the new band was putting a set list together and rehearsing in preparation for some public performances. The line-up was Les Graham and Ricky Harrison on guitars, Bart Willoughby on drums, Tony Mullett playing bass and John Newchurch on lead vocals. 'I got Ricky and Tony over and we put this band together. But we didn't have a name for it,' Graham recalls.

One of the staff at the Centre, Chester Schultz, had written a dramatic musical. Performed by the South Australian Churches of Christ Youth Choir, it premiered at the University of Adelaide's Scott Theatre on 30 March 1979. 'He ran a play called *No Fixed Address* at the Adelaide University, an ensemble kind of play,' says Graham. 'We just asked him if we could use that name. Well, he was more than pleased, so we adopted the title.'

On the Easter holiday weekend, No Fixed Address played at the 1979 National Aboriginal Country Music Festival. The fourth event of its kind, it was held at Meyer Oval in Taperoo, a coastal suburb in Adelaide's north-west. The festival attracted more than five thousand people and featured musicians and dancers from all over the country.

'The Indigenous country music festival was also a national competition,' says Graeme Isaac. 'Which would be endless father and daughter acts singing, "Me and Bobby McGee", stuff like that.'

Leigh Hobba and Ian de Gruchy produced a small book and cassette about the 1979 festival.[1] The cassette includes 'Vision', by No Fixed Address (sung by John Newchurch). While the version is rough compared with what was later recorded, it still sounds fresh and new, with an inherent power that stands in stark contrast to the reedy warblings of Sheena D'Angelo ('Blanket on the Ground') and Debbie Williams ('Take Me Back to my Homeland') and the other country offerings.

Les Graham, Ricky Harrison and Bart Willoughby at the Aboriginal Country Music Festival, Taperoo, SA, Easter 1979.

Photo by Ian de Gruchy.

On Easter Monday, No Fixed Address played their first proper gig, bottom of the bill at a Nunga Community social at Kilburn Hall. Nunga Community was an Aboriginal Australian Rules football club based in the north-west suburbs of Adelaide that held socials and cabarets for the Aboriginal community. CASM supplied the musical equipment for the night and one of the road crew was Ronnie Ansell, later the bass player in Us Mob.

Isaac explains, 'This idea of Indigenous bands playing rock and roll was a whole new thing – let alone reggae and original stuff, not covers. There was a gig at the Nunga Football Club social. They were playing support to a white band that was headlining, a country band, needless to say.

'No Fixed Address were really cooking and the crowd was into it and dancing away, but the Nunga Football Club committee were very upset because they were a bunch of crusty old blokes and they didn't like it. They wanted their country band. And they said, "We paid this white band to come, we've paid them lots of money, so they have to play", right?

'So, they basically pull No Fixed Address off the stage to get the white band to come on. And the crowd is getting restless: "Where is the music, what's going on?" And the guy from the committee was saying, "Can you just leave your drum kit there and your bass there? And your amps?"

'The white band got up and started using the gear. And playing. Because the crowd was baying, they wanted action, you know, all charged up. And Ronnie Ansell was a pretty fiery sort of bloke and he said, "Fuck that." So, he walked onstage and just started taking the gear off. While the white band is playing. And then all the others joined in and they were just taking … you know … the hi-hat going, the bass amp, and this going and that going.

'So, while the band is playing, their gear is disappearing off-stage and their sound is getting more and more disjointed. And then the bouncers moved in and it just turned into a free-for all. I saw someone about to get into Ronnie, and I ran in to try and pull him out of the way, and then I got a chair over the head and came to outside the hall sometime later. I got a bit of credibility out of that with the guys. Yeah, I took one for the team; stood me in good stead that did too.'

Ricky Harrison has a slightly different recollection of the incident. 'That was my first date with Laurel Wilson. We were outside sitting in the car when everything started. It fucked my date up. But anyway, I saw Ronnie bringing stuff out of the back door so I jumped out of the car. Graeme and Bart were standing there and I was trying to block their view so they couldn't see who was in the car. The next minute this drunk bouncer, Harradine, came out with a chair. Bart had his back to him and he was talking to Graeme. I could see Harradine start to swing the chair and I shouted, "Duck, Bart, duck!" He ducked and Graeme copped it.

'Ronnie started taking the equipment off. That's when it all started. The band that was playing, they continued playing while they were taking the drum set off. In the end, he just had the snare and the hi-hat. That's all you need. That's what Ronnie thought anyway! Apparently, they were fighting inside before over that. Harradine tried to stop them and Ronnie tuned round and said, "Fuck off, that belongs to CASM. They can use their own equipment." You could see what was going to happen so I went out into the car then.'

The following weekend Bob Marley and the Wailers played two nights at Adelaide's Apollo Stadium on their only visit to Australia. Pre-tour concerns about over-zealous drug squads busting the tour party for the carriage and consumption of marijuana proved unfounded and the tour was a huge success. Reggae was in the air.

~

Bart Willoughby had been a straight-ahead hard rock fan as a young teenager. 'When I was growing up, Suzi Quatro was doing her thing,' he says. 'I hated it when she was going out with her lead guitarist. Bastard! [laughs]. My first album was Deep Purple. That blew me away. I listened to heavy metal and country and western and rock and Creedence Clearwater. Deep Purple blew me away and Creedence Clearwater too.

'Then one day Graeme said there was this movie coming out, *The Harder They Come*. For a year where I was staying, I was watching music clips and all that. Bob Marley would pop up. This was the early stages. When he'd pop up, I'd just turn the TV down and wait three minutes then turn it up again. And then, Kiss ... (sings) 'I wanna rock'n'roll all night' [laughs]. That's what I was into. When Bob Marley came on, I just turned him over. I didn't understand it.

'When I went to *The Harder They Come*, I think I smoked a joint and I was right up the front. They had an hour and a half of Bob Marley live first. So, this time I couldn't turn him off. And I couldn't get up and leave the room because I was right up the front and there were all people around and I was stoned and I just sat there and had to watch it. And after the first couple of minutes I thought, "What's the bass player and drummer doing?" I was just spellbound. And that's when my whole life changed. Just right then and there.'

The next day Willoughby went out and bought all the Bob Marley and Jimmy Cliff albums he could find.[2] 'The most mind-blowing music. You listen to bloody, "I wanna rock and roll all night", it's bullshit rhythm. Where you've got this other thing where the rhythms are just broken up and they start again more or less. No, it's deeper than that. I've never felt this deepness before. The bass was just like an awakening. The bass was deep. The drums were like spiritual, beyond spiritual. There were all these things happening at once. I thought it was the coolest version of how to play music ever created. And I still believe that.'

~

Former neighbour Mark Thomson was visiting Graeme Isaac at his house in Westbury Street, Hackney when he met Bart Willoughby for the first time. 'Bart turned up on a Sunday morning. He must have been sixteen or seventeen. A kid, you know? And he'd just got out of the lock-up. He'd been in the cells. And he'd been hit by the cops in the kidneys, with a phone book. He was so matter of fact about it. And it was just, that's what happens; "Ow, it's really sore, ow, it's really sore!"

'Those guys lived an interesting sort of life in that … they're young guys just looking for places to stay and they had some family stuff but they were just on the loose generally. They're just looking for an interesting life and CASM represented a fantastic opportunity for them.

'Graeme is an extremely good guitar player. I remember being astonished by this guy just whipping out some Django Reinhardt stuff and playing that style of music. And so, Graeme had his guitar lying around the place and he was playing while Bart was there. Bart's lying down not feeling too well. Graeme was trying to teach me how to play Django Reinhardt's "Topsy", which is one of the classic swing jazz tunes.

'And Bart, who was lying there, said, "Oh, that's interesting, what kind of music is that?" Bart had never heard swing or Django Reinhardt or anything. And I'm there, laboriously trying to do this stuff, with Graeme showing me, and Bart picks up a guitar. And within about five minutes, he is trading swing guitar riffs with Graeme. I was like, "Alright, that's a musician, right, thank you sir."

'I mean he's never heard this music before. He's like, "That's fantastic, that's really interesting," and so, he was just kind of a musical blotter. And I knew he was a drummer, but here's this guy, he could play guitar as well; "Oh, that's a really interesting chord, man, that's sounds amazing."'

Bart Willoughby remembers really expanding his musical vocabulary in that period. 'With the bass I could play on-beat and offbeat,' he says. 'I could play on-beat or offbeat or both together. I could play funk too, because I was playing percussion. My hands are getting really strong. Holding drumsticks and going up and down is giving me the slapping. The back of my hand and the middle part was giving me the slap on the bass. The percussion's giving me the perfect rhythm to be playing rhythm guitar. I'm just getting better because of the technique on the bongos. Drums and piano, my hands are going all different levels and fingers. The other guys, Les is just playing lead and Ricky's playing simple chords. A, B, C, D, E, F, G. I'm learning other things from my teacher. I'm really going somewhere.'

THE ADELAIDE ABORIGINAL ORCHESTRA

The Centre for Aboriginal Studies in Music grew out of the work of University of Adelaide academic, Dr Catherine Ellis. As an ethnomusicologist, Ellis looked at music within culture and music as a reflection of culture. The story of how she sought to understand, preserve and revitalise Australian Aboriginal musical culture is an intriguing one. It is also crucial in understanding how a place as curious as the Centre came to be.

After completing her Bachelor of Music degree at the University of Melbourne, in 1957, Ellis took a position as a research assistant to Professor TGH (Ted) Strehlow at the University of Adelaide.[1] Ted was the son of Carl Strehlow, a missionary at the Lutheran mission in Hermannsburg (Ntaria), west of Alice Springs in Central Australia. Ted grew up speaking Aboriginal language and was initiated into Arrernte tribal customs.[2] Ellis was given the opportunity to begin her studies of Aboriginal music by transcribing Strehlow's song tapes collected in Central Australia.

Ellis started visiting Aboriginal communities to record interviews with people about their music and cultural practices. After extensive fieldwork in detribalised areas, she switched her focus to Aboriginal groups living in the far north-west of South Australia, where tribal music and culture were still largely intact.

Ellis resolved to do what she could to revive interest in Aboriginal musical traditions, not only in the tribal areas but also among urban Aboriginal people. She conceived an ambitious scheme, which she called the Program of Training in Music for South Australian Aboriginal People. It operated in two locations: Indulkana, in the Pitjantjatjara lands; and Port Adelaide, an urban area with a significant Aboriginal population.

In Port Adelaide, Ellis leveraged off an existing music program at the Sunday Friendship Club in the Dale Street

Mission Hall. The club was a place where members of the Aboriginal community could meet, socialise and learn crafts and other skills. One of the people involved in the music program was Ben Yengi, a Sudanese student at Salisbury Teachers College. When Ellis explained her ideas to Yengi, they immediately resonated with his feelings about his own tribal traditions and he was keen to participate in any way he could.[3] The urban program was named the Adelaide Institute of Narrative and Music of Aborigines (INMA). The acronym reflected the Pitjantjatjara word *inma* (oral tradition) and chimed with the name of the Intalkanya Inma Centre in Indulkana.

With the assistance of her husband Max, a lecturer at Adelaide's Flinders Street School of Music, Ellis established a program of music lessons for Aboriginal children at the Dale Street Mission Hall. The children received instruction in flute, clarinet, trumpet, trombone and violin.

While in the main the youngsters were less than enthusiastic participants, often hiding to avoid the lessons or mucking up when they got there, the program attracted the interest of influential members of the Aboriginal community. Prominent among these were sisters Leila Rankine and Veronica Brodie and their friend, Cherie Watkins. The three women became founding members of the Adelaide INMA Committee, with Leila Rankine as chair.

From the classes, 12 Aboriginal children were selected to form the original Adelaide Aboriginal Orchestra, with Max Ellis as conductor and some of his students from the Flinders Street School of Music as tutors. From that small beginning, the training orchestra developed and flourished.

Meanwhile at the Intalkanya Inma Centre, Pitjantjatjara elders Minyungu Baker and Billy Mungie agreed to come south to Adelaide to present some of their non-secret songs to school and university students. The sessions with students, which focused on songs about birds and animals, were a big hit. During Writers' Week at the 1972 Adelaide Festival of Arts, headlining American beat poet, Allen Ginsberg, took time out from chanting William Blake poems on the University of Adelaide's Barr Smith Lawns to take in one of the performances. Ginsberg was so impressed, he invited the elders onstage at his recital at the Adelaide Town Hall.

~

The early 1970s was a period of rising activism among Aboriginal people. Hopes of positive changes had been high following the May 1967 referendum that amended the Australian constitution to give the Commonwealth the power to make laws for Indigenous people.[4] However, when Prime Minister Harold Holt died in December 1967, his progressive ideas of improving the lot of Aboriginal people were not matched by his Liberal Party successors. The Gorton and McMahon governments were quite content with the status quo and blocked initiatives for land rights, non-discriminatory legislation and more autonomy for communities, much to the frustration of many Aboriginal people.[5]

The 1971 judgement in the long-running Gove land rights case catapulted the issue of land rights into the national spotlight. The case had begun in 1963, after traditional lands of the Yolngu people in Arnhem Land were sold without consultation to Nabalco, a bauxite mining company. Traditional owners subsequently made several attempts to have the land returned, including submitting bark petitions to Federal Parliament asserting their ownership of land. When Justice Blackburn of the Northern Territory Supreme Court ruled against the Yolngu on the grounds that native title was not part of Australian law, campaigns to change the law increased.[6]

On the eve of Australia Day/Invasion Day 1972, Prime Minister Billy McMahon announced a major change in Aboriginal policy. McMahon jettisoned the assimilation stance that had prevailed since the 1940s and adopted the integration approach proposed in South Australia by Don Dunstan ten years previously. Assimilation proposed all persons of Aboriginal blood or mixed blood would live like other white Australians do. Integration, on the other hand, envisaged Aboriginal people coming into the community as a group and retaining their physical and cultural identity.

McMahon made no concession on the issue of land rights, however. Instead, he announced a new system that rejected granting independent ownership of traditional land to Indigenous people in favour of 50-year general purpose leases for Indigenous communities – providing they could demonstrate a social and economic use for the land and excluding any mineral and forest rights. An Aboriginal tent embassy was set up outside Parliament House in Canberra on 26 January 1972 to protest McMahon's announcement, and in the Federal election later that year, Aboriginal policy was a hot political issue.[7]

The establishment of the tent embassy energised Aboriginal people and organisations across the country to push for increased recognition and responsibilities. In South Australia this change in mood was keenly felt among the key Aboriginal participants of the INMA program. The program was only accredited by the University of Adelaide as part of Catherine Ellis's research work. With the support of the Aboriginal Arts Board (part of the federal Australia Council for the Arts), the Adelaide INMA committee began to press for better official recognition within the university. It wanted the program accepted as a legitimate teaching establishment. In this way, the training program could continue and Aboriginal students who were not qualified in the usual way would have access to university staff and facilities.

A special meeting was convened at the university on 16 October 1974 to consider the future of the INMA program. More than 30 people attended and all the forces that combined to create the Centre for Aboriginal Studies in Music were represented. Crucially, four tribal elders came down from Indulkana to share their views on the program and its future.[8]

All the university officials expressed their in-principle support for the program, but noted the many issues in fitting it into the existing university structure. In response, Leila Rankine was particularly strong in pressing for assurances that if the program was endorsed, the Aboriginal elders would be accepted at the same level as European teachers; the program would continue as a doorway for other Aboriginal students wishing to enter the university; and Catherine Ellis's role in the program would be officially recognised.

Consultation and conversations continued over the summer, and in April 1975 the university council, taking into account a commitment of financial assistance from the Aboriginal Arts Board, established the Centre for Aboriginal Studies in Music. Catherine Ellis was appointed head of the Centre and Ben Yengi was engaged as administrator. The university recognised knowledge gained through tribal education and granted the status of visiting lecturers to the tribal teachers.

From the University of Adelaide's viewpoint, the Centre for Aboriginal Studies in Music provided an opportunity for ethnomusicology students to interact with authentic tribal musical culture in the form of the Pitjantjatjara elders. The Aboriginal community viewed the granting of lecturer status to the elders and their payment by the Aboriginal Arts Board as recognition of the elders' authority over their tribal music and traditions – and their right and responsibility to pass knowledge of it on to younger generations. And the Central Methodist Mission, which had been involved since the start of the program, saw the Centre as a continuation of its Aboriginal community development program.[9]

The Adelaide Aboriginal Orchestra moved to a large first floor space in Twin Street, with Max Ellis continuing as conductor and students from the Elder Conservatorium taking on the role of tutors. The composition of the orchestra had begun to change after it moved from Port Adelaide. Instead of local schoolchildren, the Central Methodist Mission started referring teenagers from the wider Aboriginal community. Many of these had been caught in the all-too-common downward spiral of children's home, foster home, dropping out of school, living rough, petty crime and juvenile detention. Once they were accepted into the program, the welfare of these troubled teens became a major focus for Ben Yengi and Leila Rankine. In her biography, Leila's sister Veronica Brodie recalled how Leila got to love her work at the Centre. 'She became the chairperson, the mediator, the auntie, the mother and the counsellor to all the students there.'[10]

By 1977, CASM had provided tuition to around 90 Aboriginal students. While some only stayed a short time, half had participated in courses for at least a year and the Centre was able to present full-length concerts as well as lunchtime programs. These performances drew on the orchestra as well as a smaller ensemble of more experienced students, tribal performers, non-tribal singers and solo instrumentalists.

But some of the young urban Aborigines were starting to chafe at what they saw as the restrictive instrumental base and repertoire at the Centre. They wanted to see an increased emphasis on the music they were listening to, popular music. They wanted lessons in electric guitar added.

While Ben Yengi was no great fan of rock'n'roll, both he and Leila Rankine were of the view that the music students should be given the opportunity to learn the instruments of their choice and develop the music they wanted to create and play.

The discussion about reconciling the need for a rigorous educational policy with the desire to give students a bigger say about the program raged through 1977 and was often heated.[11] In the end, the majority of the CASM management committee agreed with Yengi and Leila Rankine, and in early 1978, the changes were implemented. Catherine Ellis took study leave in 1978 to research the work of the Centre and while she remained on the management committee, both she and Max

Ellis stepped back from active involvement in the Centre.

The university found new accommodation for the Centre in a cottage it owned on the far side of its North Adelaide sports fields. Riddled with salt damp in the walls and with no soundproofing, 77 Finniss Street was far from ideal. Bathrooms and showers doubled as practice areas and percussion students had to practise in an outhouse in the backyard. But somehow, they made it work.

Veronica Brodie's daughter Margaret Brodie lived through the tumult as a student. 'The funny thing is, we didn't have a lot in there, but it was operating,' she says. 'The showers, they were little rehearsal rooms [laughs]. I don't know if we were excited to learn something new or to come away from those broken families; break that trend and learn something new. We got direction out of it, in life. I don't think we've ever looked back. It's taken us out of that stigma, that broken-down family stuff. CASM was just like a family to us.'

~

When CASM moved to Finnis Street in early 1978, Ben Yengi and Leila Rankine hired Leigh Hobba to replace Max Ellis in the role of conductor. 'When Leigh came in, it became different, a different generation of music,' says Margaret Brodie. 'The jazz, the swing, all of that came into CASM. I remember learning "In the Mood", Glenn Miller, on the alto sax. Difficult piece to play.'

In 1970, Leigh Hobba had been a founding member of Adelaide's Moonshine Jug and String Band. The acoustic band, which included John and Rick Brewster, added Bernard 'Doc' Neeson in 1971 and played covers of early jazz and jug band music around Adelaide campuses and coffee houses. After leaving the band, Hobba was a musician around town and a student at the Elder Conservatorium. After graduating in 1975, Hobba began working with experimental sound, video, performance and installation art, and was heavily involved with Adelaide's Experimental Art Foundation. The EAF was established in 1974 by a small group of Adelaide artists and theorists to both encourage new approaches to the visual arts and to promote a philosophy of art as socially/politically active.

One day Hobba came across an intriguing newspaper advertisement. 'They were looking for a conductor for the Adelaide Aboriginal Orchestra,' he says. 'I applied for it and I got the job. What I inherited started as a ... field study lab, I suppose in a way, with Dr Catherine Ellis. Cath had this kind of strange idea. Her methodology was that there were various stages towards this sort of state of Nirvana, that you could reach through music. She used to talk about people like Ravi Shankar, and people who were transcendent musicians and had got there through music. That was one of the themes she ran through the philosophy of the place.'

In a 1982 article, Ben Yengi stressed that staff and tutors at the Centre had to be so careful with the students because, 'Life for most students who come to the Centre has been an infinite process of frustration, pain and intimidation from authority figures'.[12] Kid gloves were obviously very much a part of how staff had to operate.

'Yeah, you had to be really honest and you had to give yourself to the place, that's for sure,' says Hobba. 'I think I was there two or three years and it felt like a lifetime. I just became so involved in it, and that has continued right through my life really. I was very much into it and Leila Rankine was also much like my mother. We were very close, we had lots of adventures and intense times. But I inherited this thing that was classically based, this orchestra, and obviously there were kids in there, like Bart Willoughby, who were completely lost in this thing. I inherited this orchestra with very hybrid players and it was obvious that that was not going to cut it. So, I was able to get in other tutors and shift it into smaller ensembles, ensembles of people's interests.'

Bart Willoughby was the first member of No Fixed Address to go to the Centre for Aboriginal Studies in Music. At this point, it's worth taking a step back to recount how that came about.

Willoughby was already a full-time student when Leigh Hobba arrived at the Centre. 'He was about sixteen or seventeen. He was young,' Hobba recalls. 'He was shy, he was reluctant. And he was having nightmares about his time in McNally.'

The McNally Training Centre was a state government youth detention centre in the Adelaide foothills. When Willoughby's nocturnal activities as a member of a street gang landed him in strife with the law, he got locked up. While in McNally, he encountered art school graduate Matt Bienstock, who had answered an ad looking for artists and musicians to work on a special program at the Centre.

'Everybody at McNally wanted to learn guitar,' says Bienstock. 'Everyone wanted to learn how to play music, so I became a music tutor for this limited term program. But one of the people who stood out was Bart. He didn't say he wanted to play guitar so much as he said he wanted to learn music. Throughout the entire time I spent with him there, which was quite a few months, he kept indicating that he had a lot of music in him, and he didn't know how to get it out. He also spoke about these voices in his head which were, in his estimation, responsible for him doing some of the things which found him at McNally in the first place.

'Then one week I went up there for my regular sessions and he was gone. And maybe a week or two later, I got a call from CASM and they asked if I wanted to come down. Bart had offered my name as a recommendation to present contemporary western music as part of the curriculum.'

Bart Willoughby believes Bienstock had a hand in steering him to CASM. It could have been as simple as telling someone at McNally about his natural musical talent.

'I think he talked to the staff,' says Willoughby, 'and then the staff went and checked to see to if there was such a thing as an Aboriginal college for music. That's when they let me out early and I had to go to CASM and church for one year straight. I wasn't allowed to skip. So, I went to church and I went to CASM, where I fell in love with music.'

Before the decision was made to release him into the community, Willoughby was allowed to visit CASM. Under supervision. 'When I first went to CASM I was handcuffed with two coppers,' Willoughby recalled in 2000.[1] 'That's when I first met Veronica [Brodie] and all the kids. They were kids then. Auntie Veronica said, "Can you take those handcuffs off?" Because they were standing with me with the handcuffs on while I'm sitting down having a lesson. She had to plead with the coppers to take the handcuffs off. They took the handcuffs off and stood behind me.'

~

Under the conditions of his early release from McNally, Willoughby was living with his father. 'Within six months I had bought myself a drum set and had that where I was staying with my father,' he says. 'I just practised every day to Creedence Clearwater. That used to blow me away. All those songs I played. Drummed to them. He was cooking food at the place and I'd be practising every day. I went from drums to piano. By the time I got to CASM I was getting better on drums, bass and guitar and I could muck around on the piano.'

The orchestra wasn't really Willoughby's bag. 'Leila would have to go and grab him and pull him in and sit him down on a kit and get him to play with us,' says Leigh Hobba. 'He was not engaged until other younger musicians came into the Centre and he was able to express himself more fully with them. He would play drums in this so-called orchestra, but then I remember him being equally happy just sitting in his room playing guitar. And everyone in the ... I call it the orchestra, which is a crazy name for it, but that's what I inherited, and everyone was reading music, they had dots in front of them whereas that wasn't Bart. He didn't need that and was probably self-taught.'

One thing Hobba did teach Bart Willoughby was how to play the didgeridoo. Hobba brought his didgeridoo to the Centre and Willoughby was immediately interested.

'I had a didgeridoo,' says Hobba. 'I got one from Maningrida, in central coastal Arnhem Land, as a gift. Then I guess I was just around with it, playing it at the Centre. Bart must have just gravitated into it then and wanted to play it, which was kind of typical of Bart. I never studied the didgeridoo as an Aboriginal instrument. No, I just studied it for my own reasons, but I did teach Bart. When I say I taught Bart, I taught him how to breathe. I taught him how to get a sound out of it and have a sustained circular breath.'

'Leigh Hobba was the musical conductor and we just clicked straightaway,' Willoughby later recalled.[2] 'I was this bad little boy and he was this genius who ... he gave me something. And he went out of his way to give it to me. So, I stayed at his place, he was the one who gave me my first jam. He could play anything: flute, saxophone, piano, drums ... but he couldn't play percussion. That's where Ben Yengi comes into it. He'd always make African drums and I'd get lessons about all these different rhythms and where they come from. At the same time, I'm getting taught by this genius whitefella, who actually taught me how to play didge.'

As well as being the Centre administrator, Ben Yengi was a performer, a dancer, a percussionist and a drum maker. 'He made different drums,' says Willoughby. 'Big drums, little drums, fat ones and thin ones. I'd come in every week, because I would be the first one in college and Ben would have a new drum outside of the room there waiting for me to notice it. I'd walk in and start playing it. And he'd tell me what sort of beat I was playing. The spirit of it, the language of it. He would say, you can play with your hands, you can play with your fingers. He taught me how to use my fingers and the middle of my hand

and then the base of my palm, you know, boom. It's not just boom, boom, boom, it's the whole hand.'

And the Pitjantjatjara elders were there giving classes too. 'Ben Yengi and them traditional fellas were like the weirdest combination in the world,' says Willoughby.[3] 'You've got Ben Yengi, he's African and he speaks Pitjantjatjara ... These guys, they go out and there's all this chaos out there and they come back and they're just smiling. I just loved 'em. The old fellas knew who I was because of my face. They don't tell you. They're just very spiritual people. You have to work things out yourself. They knew more than me anyway. When they looked at me ... they wouldn't look through me because you could feel that. It was something different. It was more knowing. I'm starting to work it out now. They're smarter than they look, in their sense of understanding. In the way they understand. There's a lot more than meets the eye with those people in the bush. I didn't think it was important at the time but it definitely helped me as a person, helped my career.'

'What did the elders do at CASM?' I asked Willoughby.

'They would do bird singing,' he laughs. 'Singing the birds. An ancient story about the birds singing.'

~

Things really started to look up for Willoughby when budding guitarist Les Graham joined the Centre. Graham grew up in a place called Three Mile, an Aboriginal community three miles outside of Tailem Bend, 90 kilometres south-east of Adelaide. 'We weren't allowed to be in the city,' says Graham. 'That was my upbringing there. I got brought up kind of traditional. When 1967 came, with equal rights, my mother got a house in Murray Bridge.

'I used to watch [ABC-TV music program] *Countdown*. I always liked Hush. People used to tell me I looked like [guitarist] Les Gock. Also, because I had long hair. So, there was a band with Asians in it and there was also an African band, I can't remember their name. But I thought, "How come there's no Aboriginal band?"'

When he rang the University of Adelaide, Graham was just wanting to get professional help to help him play his guitar. 'I didn't know anything about CASM or anything like that. They asked if I was part-Aboriginal and I said yeah, and they directed me to CASM.'

The Centre wasn't quite what he expected. 'The first thing they did was throw an acoustic guitar at me and give me a chord progression and started doing orchestra stuff. And I'd never seen that in my life. I might have seen it on TV or something. I never thought I'd be sitting in the middle of an ensemble, playing a guitar. It sharpened me up. On the rhythm section and that. Bart was the drummer. Then Bart and me started playing together.'

'Les had just got out of jail too,' says Willoughby. 'We met and just clicked. He was a relation of all them kids: the Rankines. So, he was coming through that way. I was coming through ... I had nothing. From the West Coast, but they knew I was taken away and I could go that way or that way. He was country and western based, I was rock'n'roll, so when we jammed together, we knew all the songs. Les said, "Do you want to start a band together?" And I said, "Yeah."'

After jumping in the deep end with their first two public performances over the Easter weekend, the next adventure for No Fixed Address was a regional tour. As part of the South Australian youth festival Come Out 1979, a large party of staff and students from CASM visited Port Lincoln and Ceduna in early May.[1]

The group spent seven nights in Port Lincoln, conducting sessions on video and drum-making, as well as music workshops on guitar, saxophones, flutes and recorders, before travelling to Ceduna on Saturday, 12 May. That night No Fixed Address, Mr. X and the X Men, Raw Deal and the ensemble played for the locals.

'Mr. X was the name we gave to Buna Lawrie's band, later to be called Coloured Stone,' says Graeme Isaac. 'They hadn't thought of a name for themselves at that time and we had to call them something. But they were already singing "Dancing in The Moonlight", which went on to be Buna's signature tune, which he continued to sing with his band on the road for the next thirty years.'

Raw Deal was a blues band featuring Isaac and Billy Harrison on guitars, Ronnie Ansell on bass and Wally McArthur on drums.

'The boys were really frightened in Ceduna,' Sherree Goldsworthy recalls. 'I can't remember if it was the No Fixed boys or Us Mob. I think it was the No Fixed boys. They were shit-scared, because they were uninitiated. But they were really well received. Fantastic gigs, really exciting. The community got out and did the dancing. It's funny to remember, but the old ladies [Leila Rankine and Veronica Brodie] went on the tours as well. The CASM tours. It was like having your granny around. Very funny. Everyone really respected them.'

Isaac adds, 'Ceduna was the place that was the furthest we travelled from Adelaide when we were going out to play these community gigs. Out on the edge of the Nullarbor. And Ceduna was the place that was the closest to a more traditional community, because the audiences in Ceduna were coming into town from the old missions surrounding it, like Koonibba. Often though, people would be very shy, especially women. The young girls would hang back. People would hang back and wouldn't come into the hall, but they would be listening from outside, and the brave ones would come inside and they would sort of hang there. Only the bravest would come down the front and dance.

'And I remember Bart coming in and saying, "Oh, I just met my mother outside." I remember just being blown away. I mean, you JUST MET YOUR MOTHER? I was a middle-class boy from Melbourne and this just blew me away. As he tells it, he was taken at the age of two. He had an ear infection, very common for Aboriginal kids, and they took him off to the hospital and just never brought him back. So, he was basically institutionalised from that age.'

~

Despite the positive reception to the fledgling band, things for No Fixed Address were still a bit unstable. 'After that, things weren't going so well, so when we got back from holidays, it was like Bart was ... No Fixed Address had split up,' says Ricky Harrison.

Les Graham had been arrested for drink driving. It wasn't his first offence and he had been sentenced to a prison term. 'I was going and giving Les guitar lessons in a prison somewhere for a few weeks,' says Graeme Isaac. 'I think it was Yatala. And he was saying all the other guys were jealous because he got guitar lessons and they didn't.'

'Yeah, I was in there for three months,' Graham confirms. 'That's when I learned how to play lead guitar.'

Things could get rather hairy very quickly for young Aboriginal boys out on the town, and both Margaret Brodie and Sherree Goldsworthy stressed the importance of the support the students received outside the Centre as well as within its walls.

'There is also a women's thing behind this,' says Goldsworthy. 'There was Veronica [Brodie] and there was Auntie Leila ... all these women supporting these blokes. When they'd get into trouble, they'd be the ones who'd bail them out or they'd be the ones who'd make them breakfast. Or provide the house for them to sit around and sing at.'

'Alcohol was pretty rife back then,' says Margaret Brodie. 'Auntie Leila had a three-bedroom house with a sleepout at the back of it. That house became a home for a lot of them. Even for myself. She had a heart of gold. It was about food; it was about sleeping. There was never a day when her house didn't have a bed for you or a feed on the table for you. She was like mum to all of us, I suppose.

'If there was anything happening outside of CASM that drew the police in, Auntie Leila and Ben and my mum would all go and speak on that person's behalf. One student got arrested and the police came in and spoke to Ben and Leila and it was a really smooth takeover. There was no argument about it or resisting arrest or anything. The police really worked with CASM at the time, and Ben and Auntie Leila were the spokespeople.'

After Les Graham went to prison, John Newchurch and drummer Wally McArthur approached Ricky Harrison about keeping the name No Fixed Address. 'The band split up,' Harrison recalls. 'Les was in jail; Tony Mullett went back to Morwell; Bart, he ended up joining the blues band with Ronnie – Ronnie Ansell. So, when I got back, John and Wally said, "We'll keep the name and we'll keep playing and we'll get Duckie [Donald Taylor] to play bass." Wally played drums and Carroll Karpany, he played lead guitar. So, we were this heavy metal No Fixed Address that played around town. So anyway, after about a month or so of it, I figured it wasn't my cup of tea.'

One of the dates the heavy metal No Fixed Address played was 'Operation Public Disorder' at the Port Adelaide Town

Hall on Saturday, 21 July 1979. The event was organised by the Australian Cultural Association, and No Fixed Address headlined a four-band bill that included Mr. X, Raw Deal and blues/boogie veterans Mickey Finn. The name was undoubtedly provocative and, to press home the point, the event poster featured an unsmiling member of the South Australian police force with a guitar slung around his neck and wearing buttons saying 'GROG' and 'FOOD'. It's quite likely the police regarded this as an open invitation to attend. Which they did in some force.

Police presence was a feature at many early gigs as it provided an opportunity to look for people who had warrants out for their arrest. 'The gigs in the town hall and in places where people could drink were often on pension day, which also meant a bigger turnout, more grog, and a more highly charged atmosphere,' says Graeme Isaac.

The night was later recreated for the opening scenes of the film *Wrong Side of the Road*. As well as attending the original gig, Mark Thomson played the part of a policeman in the movie. Writing in *Roadrunner* on the film's release in November 1981, he gave an account of the 1979 event:

> It's a siege. The police outside and us inside. The doors are all locked and we've got a wanted man. The mostly black crowd is here for a dance organised by the Australian Cultural Association, a Maoist activist group. The bands are stopping and starting. Whilst people stand on tables to make speeches calling alternatively for order or action. The crowd had earlier ejected two policemen who grabbed Barry [not his real name], a friend of mine, on the way out.
>
> Handcuffed, he escaped from the paddy wagon and came back into the hall. The police reacted by calling reinforcements

---

Opposite page: Operation Public Disorder handbill, 21 July 1979.

Artwork by Eddie Hughes.

INDEPENDENCE ROCK
PRESENTS
OPERATION PUBLIC DISORDER
WITH
NO FIXED ADDRESS
MICKEY FINN
RAW DEAL
MR. X
GROG
FOOD
PORT ADELAIDE TOWN HALL
SAT. 21st. JULY
8p.m. $3.00
aust. cultural association

and surrounding the hall. Inside, pandemonium reigned. There were conflicts between different factions of the black people and tension over whether the white Maoists had acted as provocateurs. It was uncertain whether we should hand over Barry to the cops and get on with the entertainment or whether we should hold out.

Barry was surrounded by drunks trying to get his cuffs off. They succeeded in breaking the chain that held the two halves together. Unfortunately, in doing so, they closed the ratchet lock closer together, causing his hands to swell up and go blue. It was decided that he should be smuggled out with one of the bands through the lightly guarded side door.

Barry casually got in the back seat of the car, wearing a heavy overcoat to cover his wrists and carrying a bass.

He sat playing the bass in the back, obviously not handcuffed to the several idle policemen about. Billy, a guitarist from an early band, grabbed me and said, "You do the talking." The driveway was blocked with two or three police cars, their lights flashing.

Billy brazenly blew the horn and after a cursory glance at our faces, and "We're with the band, we want to move our stuff", the police cars moved. As we drove out down Port Road we cheered and yelled. We took Barry to Billy's cousin's place nearby and hid him in the shed.[2]

'The Australian Cultural Association was a bunch of people in Adelaide who were kind of like the fun Marxists, the fun Maoists,' says Thomson. 'Quite a few of them came from Whyalla and some of them are still down there, Port Adelaide way. They put on a series of these kind of events, dances, and there was a really interesting anarchic element to it. This was when the Sex Pistols were all the go, and so they were harnessing a good deal of that. Which was a little bit out of the line of politically correct culture as far as the more severe Maoists went. These were kind of bad boys.

'They were pretty organised. I helped them. At the time I was running this political screen-printing studio place and they printed all the posters and stuck them up and I helped them print them. We'd do runs of four or five hundred posters for them. And so, they had an interesting presence about the place, and they put on ... I can't remember, it was at least four or five events, I think. But the Port Adelaide one was the big one where things got a bit stroppy, and somebody got arrested and handcuffed.'

Bart Willoughby relates how he escaped the chaos that night. 'I remember when the cops busted the Town Hall, what the movie was made about. A lot of blackfellas was going, "No-one gets in the door", and closing the door and the cops were on the other side pushing, and so you had the blackfellas stopping the cops from pushing it. And then for one second, one minute, I grabbed my woman who had my baby at the time and the blackfellas stopped pushing and I opened the door and I walked past the blackfellas with this girl I had and I walked past the coppers who all stopped pushing and they were all looking at me and as soon as I get to the footpath a cab pulls up. It all happened in less than five seconds. I walked through this little corridor that was made for me in these five seconds. Everybody stopped, the blackfellas stopped, the cops stopped, I walked past, the cab pulls up, I get in and go home. Then they all turned back and went about their business [slaps hand, laughs].'[3]

The reinforcements that arrived when the situation reached an impasse were members of the Special Tasks and Rescue (STAR) Force, the police tactical group of the South Australia police. The STAR Force would also take a heavy-handed interest in an ACA gig featuring No Fixed Address the following year.

'I'VE BEEN HASSLED BY THE COPS NEARLY ALL OF MY LIFE'

Back at the beginning of the year, in the week after Ricky Harrison and Tony Mullett hitchhiked from Melbourne to join CASM, SA Premier Don Dunstan sensationally resigned, citing ill health. The resignation, on Thursday, 15 February 1979, ended the Dunstan era that had reshaped South Australia from a conservative backwater into the most progressive state in the country.

Speaking in Sydney six months previously, Dunstan said, 'Naturally we're proud that it was South Australia that paved the way in advancing Aboriginal, women's, homosexual and consumer rights, and we have made our constitution the most democratic of any Australia state'.[1]

The state into which Harrison and Mullett arrived was, in many respects, very different for Aboriginal people than the one that Bart Willoughby and Les Graham had been born into almost 20 years previously. But in other respects, as the scenes at the Port Adelaide Town Hall would demonstrate five months later, it had hardly changed at all.

At the dawn of the 1960s, the legal framework that applied to Aboriginal people in South Australia was harsh and repressive. The impositions placed on Aboriginal people by the South Australian *Aboriginal Affairs Act* 1934–1939 (which operated until 1962) were not unusual across Australia. The SA Aboriginal Protection Board could remove Aboriginal people to reserves; force them to move their camp from the vicinity of a town; or declare a town off-limits to those who didn't work there. On the order of a magistrate, the Board could take possession of a person's property. There were detailed rules about relationships between Aboriginal and non-Aboriginal people. The Board was the legal guardian of every Aboriginal child under the age of 21, and a child under 18 could be declared a 'state child' and removed to a training institution.

In 1961, the SA Department of Aboriginal Affairs expressed its policy of Aboriginal assimilation in the following terms:

> ... that all Aborigines and part-Aborigines are expected eventually to attain the same level of living as other Australians and to live as members of a single Australian community enjoying the same rights and privileges, accepting the same responsibilities, observing the same customs and influenced by the same beliefs, hopes and loyalties as other Australians.[2]

Despite this aspirational statement, Aboriginal people remained a dispossessed and excluded minority. In 1960, there were just over 7,000 Aboriginal people in South Australia. Around half were part-Aboriginal. The population fell into three main categories: tribal Aboriginal people in the Pitjantjatjara lands in the far north-west; some part-Aboriginal people in Adelaide and the southern towns; and the rest, the majority, in Aboriginal missions, reserves, on cattle stations or as fringe-dwellers on the outskirts of towns.

Aboriginal people comprised the lowest socio-economic group in society, suffering profound disadvantages on just about every measure – income, housing, education, health and life expectancy. Many had become institutionalised – less able to think and act independently – after prolonged periods in a children's home, juvenile detention or an Aboriginal reserve or mission.

The Liberal Country League government of Sir Thomas Playford introduced a bill in 1962 to liberalise some of the provisions of the *Aboriginal Affairs Act*. On behalf of the Labor Party, Don Dunstan successfully extended the scope of the proposed changes and argued forcefully against the policy of assimilation. Instead, he said, a policy of integration should be adopted.[3] His arguments were accepted and South Australia, alone among the states, moved its policy settings away from assimilation.

As Attorney-General and Minister for Aboriginal Affairs in the 1965–68 Labor government, Dunstan pushed through further reforms. He introduced legislation that enabled the transfer of Aboriginal reserves and other Crown lands to the newly-created Aboriginal Lands Trust.[4] The Trust continues to operate today and holds title to 65 properties covering more than half a million hectares. The Aboriginal communities of Koonibba, Point Pearce, Raukkan (formerly Point McLeay) and Yalata, among others, are on Trust land. Related amendments enabled Aboriginal reserves to elect councils to run the affairs of the community and for cooperatives to be formed to run businesses, including mining businesses. And finally, anti-discrimination legislation was passed that made it an offence to refuse admission to premises (including licensed premises), refuse to provide a service, or let a house or dismiss a person from employment on the basis of race, skin colour or country of origin.

These may seem small steps today, but in the mid-1960s they were close to revolutionary and attracted strong criticism from vested interests. In practice, enforcement of the anti-discrimination law proved problematic. And moreover, looming over the everyday existence of Aboriginal people was the shadow of the police.

The relationship between the police force and Aboriginal people at the start of the 1970s was steeped in mutual hostility. The establishment of an Aboriginal/Police Steering Committee in 1972 was an acknowledgement of the problem and the creation of an Aboriginal/Police Liaison Committee in 1975 was another step forward.[5] But despite the repeal of much of the discriminatory legislation and the establishment of these committees, on the ground victimisation by the police and the criminal justice system continued virtually unabated.

Aboriginal people were disproportionately arrested for trivial crimes, such as drunkenness, vagrancy, indecent language and disorderly conduct. Once arrested, they were much more likely to denied bail and to be convicted. Then, once convicted of minor crimes, they were much more likely to receive a high fine, to be sent to jail and to be given a longer sentence. In 1972, Aboriginal people made up less than 1 per cent of the South Australian population but made up a quarter of male prisoners admitted to prison.[6] This figure had not changed by 1979.

A 1978 study of race relations in Ceduna found that while the legal framework had changed, Aboriginal people were still subject to crippling discrimination. The report concluded:

> ... that racial discrimination exists in the area on a scale that can only be described as total because it affects practically every aspect of Aboriginal existence and totally conditions the Aborigines' role in the community ... [C]onsistent comments made by the Aborigines themselves presented the picture of a people living in fear of white oppression, haunted by the spectre of police harassment and brutality, [and] resentful of white dominance ...'[7]

For white people, coming face to face with this all-pervasive racism and police harassment was often shocking. Leigh Hobba recalls his reaction. 'There were some intense times when the bands were on the road, or when they were playing. Anything could happen. I just remember thinking, the best thing you could be in that situation with those people, would be to be a lawyer. Just the sort of stuff they had to put up with, the day-to-day shit, the sickness and the troubles in family and the racism that was just like a seeping pus, you know.

'You travel with them on a bus somewhere and you can just feel the tension that those people had to live with day by day. It was quite powerful and palpable. The difficulties of their life. So, they would come to CASM and they would sit down, and they would find some kind of safety there. And if music was a reason for allowing that to happen, well, that was just great. That was like the element, you know, that allowed that sort of safety and structure in their life, apart from giving them a bit of money. There was a community of trust in there. It was a safety net for a lot of people.'

If you didn't have a lawyer with you, it could help if you knew one. In the mid-'70s, Aboriginal activist Gary Foley was a senior lecturer for the Community Organisations Course at Melbourne's Swinburne College of Technology when he took a team to a football carnival in Adelaide. One of the players was Henry Thorpe, future drummer with Hard Times, an Aboriginal band whose members attended CASM in the early '80s.

'During the footy match, Henry got pinched by the local coppers for smoking a joint,' Foley recalls. 'And I was madly trying to get him out of jail that night, out of the cells and the coppers wouldn't budge and I wasn't prepared to bring my bus of students back to Melbourne until he was on the bus. And so, in the middle of the night, I rang up Elliott Johnson, who was a QC I knew from when I had helped in the early establishment of the Aboriginal Legal Rights Movement in Adelaide. He was one of the people who helped to set it up and I had stayed with him while we were setting it up. And so, I rang him up in the middle of the night and he appeared at the police station with me and magically, within ten minutes, Henry was on my bus and we were on our way back to Melbourne.'

8   RUGBY STREET

Peter 'Pedro' Butler arrived at CASM in mid-1979. 'I was in Perth at the time,' he says. 'I had to leave Perth, for reasons I won't go into. And my father had told me, he said there's a music college here. He said, "There's a couple of blokes over there, Ronnie Ansell's one of them. He's one of your relations from Alice Springs." He said, "Do you want to come over and have a look, see what you think?" So that's what I did. I left Perth and came back to Adelaide and went down to the college and met up with these guys. Then I ended up enrolling in the college itself.

'The first or second day I went in there, I met up with Ronnie and Wally McArthur. They virtually convinced me to come to the college. They were already involved in the thing. I had a jam with them and that was the beginning of the band. They said, "Yeah, you're the bloke we want."

'I'd just gone in there to have a look, to suss the place out. And they said, "Do you want to have a jam? Because we're looking for another guitarist." So, I said, yeah, I'll have a jam, so I picked a guitar up and that was it. That was the beginning. "You'll do."'

Originally from Tasmania, Butler had grown up in Alice Springs and Port Augusta. His father bought him a guitar when he was eight or nine and he had aunties and uncles that played. One of his aunties was a country and western singer who wrote her own songs.

'I was fascinated by the way she put these songs together,' he says. 'Even though it was just three chords and a heap of words, I used to find it fascinating how she used to do it.'

The new band, with Carroll Karpany from the heavy metal No Fixed Address also on guitar, took the name Us Mob and started rehearsing. Butler had some original 'bits and pieces' that started taking on a fuller form. 'Because I had the other guys in the band, it was easier to get those ideas out,' he says.

'In a musical sense. Rather than me sitting there strumming away on the guitar, I had these other accompaniments that made it easier for me to envisage ... it made it easier for me to write the song. When I did start writing songs, they just came along ... it just seemed to happen without me putting too much thought into it.'

Us Mob started performing at shows organised by CASM. 'That was part of our training as well, to go out and perform,' says Butler. 'And we started doing a few shows around but we didn't do a lot of shows because there weren't many places around where Aboriginal bands could go and play.'

Heading out of town for a gig in Whyalla, 385 kilometres north of Adelaide, Us Mob was involved in a serious car accident. The car was being driven by Duckie Taylor, who had been drinking.

'We were on our way to do a show in Whyalla. I can't remember exactly what the venue was,' says Butler. 'We ended up having a head-on collision, halfway between Port Augusta and Whyalla. And Duckie was driving. Ronnie and myself ended up in the hospital and they let us go later on. Which probably wasn't a good idea at the time because Ronnie was still suffering from concussion. But we ended up still playing that night. We ended up playing the show. We were very lucky, actually, to walk away from that one.'

Duckie Taylor was convicted of drink driving and sentenced to two months in prison. As he was going in, Les Graham was getting released. They waved to each other in passing.

'Les got back and I thought, "Oh no, he's gunna get back with Bart and they're gunna form this great band."' Ricky Harrison laughs. 'So, I grabbed Bart and said let's go and grab Les. So, we went down to meet him at the station and off we went over to Morwell to find Tony [Mullett], because he'd gone back to Morwell. And of course, he had a kid so he stayed.'

~

Settling on a bass player for No Fixed Address was proving problematic. Duckie Taylor would have been an option, but he was inside. Ricky Harrison recalls the conundrum. 'So, we went back and we're sitting around in CASM, thinking maybe we'd go out as a three piece with me playing bass,' he says. 'John John rocked up then, knocked on the door and there he was and Bart says, "Hey, John John, come here, come here ducka, come and play bass." And John John says, "Aaaah, yeeeah, yeeeah." He comes in and starts playing and it was like, this is what was missing [laughs].'

'Tony left and I then thought, oh shit, what are we gunna do?' says Bart Willoughby. 'And the others said, why don't you grab John John because you've been teaching him bass? And I said, "Nooo ..." but anyway he joined the band and that was the beginning of No Fixed Address.'

John Miller, universally known as John John, was the younger brother of Shane Miller, the drummer in Mr. X, the band that became Coloured Stone. He was also Bart Willoughby's first cousin. 'His mum and my mum are sisters,' says Miller. 'Buna Lawrie [from Coloured Stone]'s mum is a sister too. Three sisters. All musical folks. The thing about all them, my mum and all the sisters, was singing and playing the guitar. And I don't [laughs]. My mum was a singer and a guitar player. She used to play the guitar at Fowler's Bay, a town near Eucla, near the West Australian border. Near Yalata mission, up that way. She used to play the guitar in the old stockman's houses. Old farmers' houses. Big rocks for walls, they'd fill them in with cement. There were holes in the walls. She'd play the guitar and the snakes would stick their heads out when she played the guitar. She'd go down and play on the beach. On the seaweed.'

Shane Miller was already at CASM when John John left Ceduna for Adelaide. 'I was searching for what I needed to do,' he says. 'I got a lift to CASM because Coloured Stone were there too. They were called Mr. X Band.

'Me and Shaney made a band called Burnt Toast. We were just messing around. We were playing Cars music; you know

The Cars? My brother, he got sick, he couldn't keep drumming. He had very bad bronchitis. I joined No Fixed … I didn't actually join them, I just played bass because they had no bass player. I was playing bass with the other band and the orchestra. The big orchestra with the trumpets. I just filled in playing bass. Their bass player was in jail, I think.

'They only had one song, "The Vision". Then I came along and he was in jail so I just filled in and ended up playing with them. When we started playing, we only played a couple of times and we were packing the pubs out. I said, "Hey, what?" We were packing the places. I didn't realise we were so good. Just didn't realise it.'

Veronica [Vonnie] Rankine was Leila Rankine's daughter. She had been learning flute and saxophone at the Centre, and after asking Ricky Harrison if she could join the line-up, she started rehearsing with the band around this time.

'She was my first cousin,' says Margaret Brodie. 'Like Bart, she was another one who thought outside the box. She had the music in her for reading and for playing by ear. Even though she wore a hearing aid.'

~

Graeme Isaac had been schooling the band on the mechanics of reggae. 'One of the things you have to do in a band and especially in reggae, of course, is that you don't play all the rhythm on one instrument, everyone plays their part. It's quite spare; sparse and spare. It doesn't have great requirements technically in terms of … you don't have to be a virtuoso. What you have to do is to play less and not more. It's the spaces in the music that make it, in a way.

'And sitting back on the rhythm also. Sitting back, not pushing. Most everyone's sitting back. The bass player is holding the beat, and the drums are sometimes a little behind that, and then the guitars a bit further behind there … it's the spaces, you know? What I showed Les how to do was to leave that offbeat rhythm guitar to Ricky and for the lead guitar to play little licks around.

'So, I began to show them how to break the rhythm of the song down and arrange it, but they very quickly grabbed the ball and ran with it by themselves. And then Bart turned up with, I think, "We Have Survived". That was the next song we worked on actually, yeah. Very quickly followed by "Black Man's Rights".'

Ricky Harrison was also bringing new songs to the band. 'When we were first starting off, that's when Graeme Isaac came in and changed rhythm to reggae from punk rock,' he recalls. 'And he helped out with "Street Fighter" to help get us started. After that, we started writing our own songs and putting it together. I would go to the other guys and if I didn't have a bass line, then John John would put a bass line on it, or Bart. I would have the musical structure there. Like with "Pigs", when it goes into the musical part, I'd done all that and I had the bass line, but it was missing the bit at the end. That's where Bart comes in and he goes, "Well, we'll finish it off like this – why don't we just sing 'Pigs leave our people' at the end of the song?" There was always a point where Bart would come along and help out. Or John John would help out with a bit of bass here. Les did his own thing. I couldn't play lead anyway. He was more putting his lead guitar down. Just following what I did. So, I would sit there with Les and he would say, "I can't play till I hear the words to the song, the melody of the song." I'd sit there with a guitar and we'd go over the melody of the song. Some of the songs anyway. Or we'd just rehearse it and I'd sing the song and Les would listen to the melody and put his own bit down there.'

~

As well as the music program, with his contacts in the art world, Leigh Hobba set up an art program. He used to take the students across to the art studio at the University of Adelaide once a week, with artist Margaret Dodd as art tutor. Dodd was well known for her ceramics of FJ Holden cars. She had also made an experimental film called *This woman is not a car.*

'Leigh was a friend and asked if I'd be interested in doing some art classes at CASM,' Dodd remembers. 'Ben Yengi wasn't particularly interested but Auntie Leila was keen. She was writing poetry and running the show.'

Dodd was also playing drums in an all-female band called Foreign Body. 'I started playing drums in 1977 when I went back into the Rugby Street house,' she says. 'There was a drum kit. My boyfriend was playing drums in one room and taught me, roughly. I went and got lessons after that. Then Foreign Body came up.'

Dodd's Rugby Street house in the inner eastern suburb of College Park became a something of a Mecca. There were some empty rooms in there – and a drum kit. Bart Willoughby needed somewhere to stay and moved into Dodd's house. 'Bart brought in his friend Steven Auricht (aka Jug, later Ken Hampton) and the story of the film was woven around Steven's search for his parents, who we found during the filming in 1980,' says Dodd.

'There was a night when Bart and Jug worked on a song in the kitchen into the wee hours. They came and woke me up to play it to me. I turned on an old ghetto blaster and recorded it over some taped music. It was "Sunrise". Bart was brilliant. He was an amazing person to have living in the house.'

Graeme Isaac recalls Willoughby writing there. 'Bart was living at Margaret's place and I remember he used to, I guess,

---

Opposite above: Bart Willoughby, Ricky Harrison and Pedro Butler at Rugby Street, College Park, SA, 1980.

Photo by Margaret Dodd.

Opposite below: Ricky Harrison, John John Miller and Bart Willoughby rehearsing at Rugby Street, College Park, SA, 1980.

Photo by Ian de Gruchy.

in a sort of echo of his time, his years of incarceration, he used to close all the blinds, turn all the lights and heaters on, every electrical appliance on, and then he would write: "We have survived, the white man's world" and all these incredible songs. But that's where he was living at the time and I'm pretty sure that's where he wrote that song.'

Willoughby confirms the unconventional environment that unlocked his creative juices. 'I used to write songs with the stereo on and the TV on and the radio on and I'd be writing just strumming on the acoustic guitar while all that chaos was going on. Still today, I don't know how I did that. All I know is people would say, "How do you start writing?" and I'd just go, "I dunno." Maybe I was just used to the chaos, because of the way I was brought up. Chaos was where I could get it all together.'

~

Things were starting to get interesting at the Centre, Graeme Isaac remembers. 'They were starting to write these great original songs, starting to arrange, to understand how to arrange their own material. Starting to get on top of electronic gear, amps and all that sort of stuff … you know … how to get a fat guitar sound, how to set up foldback, how to avoid a microphone feeding back; starting to get their stagecraft skills together. And then of course, you've got to have some gigs. So, then we started setting up gigs, initially within the Aboriginal community … the Nunga Football Club Social, or a gig at the Aboriginal Task Force. And as soon as they did, there were all these other young musicians from around the place – actually a little bit older than them – who wanted to come and join. And they were all more experienced musically.'

When Duckie Taylor got out of prison and went back to CASM, the No Fixed Address line-up was settled, with Les Graham and Ricky Harrison on guitars, Bart Willoughby on drums, Veronica Rankine on saxophone and backing vocals, and John John Miller on bass. 'I thought to myself, well, that's my own fault because I maybe would have been part of the band,' says Taylor. 'It didn't worry me because they needed a sound engineer and I put my hand up for that and just started on a little 6-channel mixing desk, because we were only doing gigs around Adelaide.'

No Fixed Address and Us Mob started doing some pub gigs on the rock'n'roll circuit in Adelaide. Some of the first of these were Us Mob supporting Redgum at a 5MMM gig at the Tivoli Hotel on 18 October 1979, and No Fixed Address supporting The Immigrants at the Norwood Town Hall the following night.

'Their sound was sometimes rough as bags,' says Isaac. 'It was hard to get them sounding good live because it was a while before they had their own sound mixers, and as they were coming on as supports to other bands, they never got proper soundchecks or a proper mix set up. But there was something really exciting about them. There was an energy about them, and also, you can feel they were writing ... this was really new, what they were doing. They were writing songs about their own lives but in the contemporary idiom. There'd been plenty of Aboriginal bands around the place but they were all country bands.'

One gig that stands out in Graeme Isaac's memory, for all the wrong reasons, was a 1979 end-of-year dance for students attending the Aboriginal Task Force. The task force was a pathway for Indigenous Australians to gain tertiary qualifications from an accredited academic institution. It was developed within the South Australian Institute of Technology and funded by the Department of Aboriginal Affairs. The dance was at the city campus of the institute, on the corner of North Terrace and Frome Road.

'So here you had students from an Adelaide University Indigenous music centre playing on campus for other Indigenous university students, with the gig being busted up by the police dog squad and closed down,' says Isaac. 'In the early days when bands from CASM went out to play at Indigenous events, the police were invariably there. This business of Indigenous bands was a new thing and generated a lot of excitement, so the police were naturally curious. But they turned up this night with the dog squad. On a university campus. For no apparent reason. It was such complete overkill. Hanging around with the guys as I had over the previous year, I had seen a lot of this before, but this really shocked me.'

PART 2

WRONG SIDE OF THE ROAD

(1980–81)

Graeme Isaac thought No Fixed Address was ready to demo some of their original songs. While there was a rudimentary recording set-up at CASM, Isaac was looking for something a bit more sophisticated. He found it via Philip Roberts, a sound engineer and producer who had recently arrived in Adelaide from London.

'He had quite a pedigree,' says Isaac. 'He had worked at some famous studios in London, including Basing Street Studios. Producing reggae and African music. He was born in Rhodesia and left because he couldn't hack the system. That was before Rhodesia became Zimbabwe. And then he was in South Africa producing music with African artists. Then he went to London and he was working with reggae bands there.'

Basing Street Studios was established by Island Records owner Chris Blackwell, and many of Island's artists recorded there, including notably, Bob Marley and the Wailers and Jimmy Cliff.

Roberts had played in one of Rhodesia's top groups, the Otis Waygood Blues Band. The band relocated to South Africa in 1969 and toured around Europe in the early 1970s, before moving to London in 1976.

'We got some West Indians into the band and started doing kind of reggae feel numbers,' says Roberts. 'I had written a bunch of original material and there was a group called Pat and the Remels that was like a lover's rock, rock steady band and they had a manager called Dixie who had bought a song from me. So, we went to Basing Street to make the single which was called "Several Reasons".

'You know if I had told anybody I was working at Basing Street, that's what I meant. That I was in there producing my song for Dixie, over a couple of weeks. I knew my way around the studio, and I was trying to get a new career going in Adelaide, so I was probably lying [laughs].'

Working out of EMS Studios in Hindley Street, Roberts had produced an album, *Everything I Am* for Bruce Wellington, that was nominated for a Golden Guitar Award at the Tamworth Country Music Festival. 'I guess I started to get a little bit of a reputation,' he says. 'I was doing some live music mixing as well for some bands.'

Roberts was managing Greenhill Studios, a small eight-track studio owned by original Cold Chisel bass player Les Kaczmarek. 'Graeme came down to have a look at it and we got to talking. We just got on really great and he took me around to the Centre for Aboriginal Studies in Music. So, we went there and I started listening to No Fixed Address.'

In October 1979, Isaac and Roberts decided to record some demos with the bands from the Centre. 'With recording No Fixed Address and the other bands we tag-teamed it really,' says Isaac. 'Working with them in the studio to get the songs into shape. We'd get into the studio and we ... I'd be in there trying to pull the best out of them and keep the guitars in tune, and he'd be behind the control desk getting it down, you know ... And when they heard what a bit of production could do to their sound, some reverb, some delay, some dub mixing, that moved them on another step down the road. The dub mix of "The Vision" which Phil did for the film was possibly the first reggae dub mix done in Australia. I can't think of anything like that done earlier.

'Phil brought a lot to their sound which then went on to further develop their playing. Especially Bart, who started adding his own percussion bits into his playing, and Les who Phil showed how to shadow the bass line with heavy reverb to give a dub feeling to his playing. Together with the lyrics, these things were both part of what gave the band such an original sound.'

Mark Thomson was an interested bystander in the studio. 'It was so nice to hear them through a studio monitor,' he says. 'I remember being struck by how fantastically percussive Bart's drumming sounded, in a proper studio, properly recorded.

It was like, wow; it was everything his drumming promised. When you saw them play, that was what would really stick out ... this kind of masterful drum technique. The way he played was quite mesmerising.

'Bart was a musical sponge and it was beautiful to watch. He finally got to the studio, and I thought, "Yeah, that's good, that's great that it's got to that point." So pleasant. But they were not necessarily using great gear. The bass guitar was kind of still sounding like a giant rubber band and things like that.'

Isaac had rustled up some money for the initial recordings. 'We had some money from the school. I can't remember where we got it from initially, maybe it was from the Aboriginal Artists Agency,' he says. 'As Phil was managing the studio, he also had the elbow room to put his own time into it.'

The first No Fixed Address song recorded at the October sessions was Bart Willoughby's 'From My Eyes', written about his experience of being locked up in solitary confinement at the McNally Training Centre. Also recorded were three of Ricky Harrison's songs, 'The Vision', 'Darkness of Day' and 'Street Fighter', plus one uncredited number, 'There Was a Time'. Us Mob recorded 'Suicidal Contemplation' and 'Sweet Juice of Love'.

'After our initial recordings we started trying to get record company interest, particularly for No Fixed Address,' says Isaac. 'We got money to do more demos, I think from Warner Brothers. We also had a meeting with CBS. But in the end the recording companies in Sydney just wouldn't come at it. They saw it as a marketing problem, merchandising a black band to a white "market". I think it was someone from Warners who said of No Fixed, "if only we had a white band with that gimmick"!

'Somewhat of a contradiction because that WAS the concept! It was an Indigenous band playing reggae, you know. Anyway, so we said, "Well, bugger you. We'll just ... we're just going to do it anyway. We'll make a film."

'So, I contacted a filmmaker friend, Ned Lander, who I'd known from Melbourne. I rang him up, and I played him a couple of tracks of No Fixed Address over the phone. I said, "Listen, this is … we have to tell this story!" And so, he jumped on a plane and flew straight down … and that's basically how the film project started.'

Ned Lander's friendship with Graeme Isaac dated back to Melbourne in the early 1970s. 'Graeme was in the very first film I made which was … oh, 1973 or something like that,' says Lander. 'Which was being funded by the Experimental Film and Television Fund. Bert Deling and Fred Schepisi and other assessors decided to give me the funds as a very young person to go off and make an experimental film. And Graeme was one of the actors and I met him through a friend who was involved with the Pram Factory theatre in Melbourne. I wasn't a member of the Pram Factory or involved in their productions directly. I was like a fellow traveller or a "friend" of the Pram Factory.'

In the mid-'70s, Lander had moved to Sydney and enrolled in the Australian Film and Television School. When Isaac got in touch, Lander was in the process of getting kicked out of the school. 'He had done two years; he was in his third year,' says Isaac. 'But at that time in the film school, you had to spend the first couple of years watching other people's films, not making your own. And he started trying to make his own and it seems this was not the right thing to do.'

'Graeme had visited me in Sydney while I was at the film school,' says Lander. 'And then I sort of left the film school to go and make a documentary.'

The documentary was *Dirt Cheap*, about the land rights battle that was going on around uranium mining in Arnhem Land. 'I'd spent quite a bit of time in Arnhem Land, going back and forth up there over a couple of years,' says Lander. 'We'd been researching it for several years and then went up there for a while. I'd just come back from making that film and Graeme is on the phone playing a first rough recording of one of Bart's songs … now which one exactly, I can't remember.

But I remember it sounded pretty good. I mean we were all listening to quite a lot of reggae at that time.

'And this was a lovely reggae sound and he said come down, come down and so I did. I jumped on a plane and came down and went straight to a gig that night. They were struggling to get their gear together that night as they always were at that time because they didn't have any equipment; a minimal amount of equipment was being shared by three bands. I thought the bands were great, the words and songs were terrific. We immediately got together with the bands and people involved with the bands and started talking about making a film.

'It took me a while to get my head around what was really going on. I had spent quite a lot of time in the bush with people who spoke language and who still had direct kind of cultural practice happening and stuff like that.

'And I was down in Adelaide with people from all different sorts of backgrounds – who had come down from Alice, people who'd grown up more in the city. It was sort of funny, it was back to front. I was starting to get some kind of sense of what life was like for Aboriginal people who were living mainly in the city; having spent a lot of time in the bush with Aboriginal people to start with. You immediately got that sense of how many different experiences of being an Aboriginal in Australia there were.

'And there is a bit of ... I don't know if it's apocryphal or not ... but there is a bit of a story that Graeme wanted to get a record made and at some point, it occurred to him that if we made a film, the music would all get recorded. So that was a way to get a record made. A very elaborate way to get a record made.

Lander continued: 'But you know, I think he was probably very interested in both recording the music, properly in a studio, but also quite seriously interested in the many stories that he was hearing and learning from the people that he was teaching.

'And this is pre– the term "Stolen Generations", this is pre– "black deaths in custody", so this is pre– a number of those big things that gave names to bits of history that were pretty awful.'

'The script was basically sown together from the stories and experiences of the bands themselves, and of family and friends,' says Isaac. 'I had spent the previous year working with them and some scenes, like the opening scene of the gig at the Port Adelaide Town Hall, came straight from those experiences. If I was uncertain about what would happen in a certain situation in a scene, I was writing I could go and ask them what they would say or do. And Ned did in-depth biographical interviews with everyone as well which opened up yet more story ideas.'

'I've got a very strong sense of sitting down and listening to these life stories unfolding,' says Lander. 'These very young people ... they were still kids in a way, but they had been through so much by that stage already. Particularly Bart, but probably all of them. Bart obviously has that classic institutionalised background, from a very young age.'

10   'IMAGINATION INVOLVES BEING IN DANGEROUS POSITIONS'

Bart Willoughby's journey from an Aboriginal mission in the far west of South Australia to a juvenile detention centre is a depressingly familiar one for members of the Stolen Generations.

Between 1900 and the early 1970s, large numbers of Indigenous children were systematically removed from their families. Taking young children out of their family and community environment meant they lost the opportunity to learn about their traditional culture. Putting them in situations where they were only taught about mainstream white Australian culture advanced the cause of assimilation. Not only were children removed for alleged neglect, they were removed to attend school in distant places, to receive medical treatment and to be adopted out at birth.

Willoughby was born at Koonibba Mission, 50 kilometres west of Ceduna, on the edge of the Nullarbor Plain. 'I was there for about three years,' he says. 'I'm a twinless twin. My brother passed away when I was about three. My father was born in Ooldea. My grandfather and grandmother are from that Maralinga area. After being rounded up and put in a boys' home he [Bart's father] ended up being taken down to Yalata and setting up in a reserve there. That's where he bumped into my mother who was a Mirning woman.'

As a young child, Willoughby developed an ear infection and was taken to hospital in Adelaide. And did not return. He was in hospital for a year or so, then was moved to a children's home.

'My sister told me: you were snatched from your mother's arms,' he says. 'That's were my chaos began. By the time I was three, I was getting smacked on the back of my hand by this weird nurse in Semaphore. Because I couldn't eat the food. I remember that clearly today, because that's how much it hurt.

When I get put inside the cot with all the other fifty kids, I can still remember the looks on their faces. They're crying and they're really scared.

'You become institutionalised. You accept it. You make your own fun. There's no TV around, so you use your imagination a lot. There were about six of us in a boys' room and I used to tell them stories. They were all older than me. That's where the stories came from. The imagination wasn't interfered with. It just flowed naturally. So, if I was in the boys' home and came out with these outrageous stories about the war or whatever, by the time I finished they'd be all asleep. So, I think I went from there to dreams. When you're a kid, you demand that you dream this and you do. I think that's to do with the imagination being allowed to flow freely like that. The homes had your flesh, but they didn't have your soul. And imagination involves being in dangerous positions.'

When Willoughby was around nine, purely by accident he ran into his sister. 'I went and stayed with her and my other sister at this other home,' he says. 'I ended up with my sisters in a children's home. I had a beautiful time with my sisters.' Willoughby also reconnected with his father at this time.

Things were about to take a turn for the worse, however. 'I was about eleven or twelve,' says Willoughby. 'I started to become boyish, you know, doing boys things. Started going to town. Hanging out with the guys. It was like being a rebel. You just took things. To be a man. Till they realised I was doing this thing. It was a kids' home and I was growing up, so I had to leave. I had to go to a boys' home. It was only when I went to a boys' home and left my sisters that I picked up bad techniques.'

Willoughby was moved to the Salvation Army Boys' Home on Fullarton Road in Kent Town. Its sister home, Eden Park at Mt Barker in the Adelaide Hills, featured prominently in the 2017 report of the Royal Commission into Institutional Responses to Child Sexual Abuse. The Royal Commission found the Salvation Army did not protect young boys from being abused while in its care from the late 1950s to the early

1970s. Willoughby recalls new arrivals being lined up at the Kent Town home and the superintendent taking his pick. 'I'll have you, you and you.'

'I was only in there for months but it was enough to change your whole life. Just right there,' says Willoughby. 'The SA government hasn't even talked about that. This is in plain sight and they still did whatever they wanted.

'My room was at the back. There would have been about 20 kids, boys. We used to have tyre games. You get a tyre from a car. Six guys hide around a corner and they're all bigger than you. You've got to make it from A to B and these guys are hidden everywhere. So, you have to get that way before you get hit. And if one hit ya, they'd all hit ya. You could end up ... dead. If your head was in the wrong position. It had that much force, it could take your whole head off. But it was the game, you know? I'd never get caught. But guys who were slow ended up in hospital. Broken legs. It was boys. Rough. I remember one guy got chucked in the pool, a little boy, and the other guy laughing at him. If it wasn't for me jumping in, he would have drowned.'

The boys from the Kent Town home attended Norwood Primary School and marched together to the school each day. They received daily religious instruction from the Salvation Army officers in charge of the institution and were required to say daily prayers. On weekends they attended church and Sunday school, again marching as a group to church, three times every Sunday. At school Willoughby was a restless pupil.

'I'd be tapping, tapping at my desk,' he remembers. 'I drove my science teacher crazy. He actually swore at me. It's really hard to get teachers to swear, yeah? I made him lose it. Just through tapping. "Why do you come here tapping all the time?"'

Willoughby started spending more and more time in town, eventually running away from the boys' home and living on the streets. 'Because at the boys' home it's chaotic,' he says. 'You've got this Salvation Army bloke, he's bashing boys. It's like he's a demon. You'd always wake up scared. Shitting yourself.' But living on the streets and sleeping rough was no picnic either. 'Would have been a year and a half, two years. I'm talking about no money. One pair of clothes. So, it was pretty hard for that one and a half years. I always slept by myself. I would find the darkest spot where no-one goes at night time and wedge myself in there. The spots that society forgot. And it's everywhere. Slept in all the parks in Australia. No big hassle. When I first started off it was a bit freaky. You try to work out ways to keep yourself warm. Newspaper and tin. You work out these ways to keep yourself warm and dry. You become really good at it.'

Willoughby may have been on the streets, but he wasn't alone. 'I bumped into the wrong guys,' he says. 'I was in a gang, one of the biggest gangs in Adelaide – the Goodwood Mob. We were the boss. We could go anywhere, get away with anything. And it was a multicultural gang. Black, white, Italians, skinheads. We were the toughest. There must have been one thousand five hundred of us. But the core of the gang was the blackfellas. We were the best fighters out. We were in the same boys' home so it was really close-knit. We were the gang that controlled the gang. And it just started off by boys being at school. We all liked each other and from that we became the biggest gang in Adelaide. Which was important in them days. If you were a weak gang you were bashed up and never heard from again. If you're a strong gang you're top of the earth. No-one can muck with you; your back is always protected. So, it wasn't dangerous. The only dangers that came from anywhere was the police.'

Violence was part and parcel of being in the gang. 'We would fight other gangs,' says Willoughby. 'If you couldn't find a gang to bash up, the last resort was to find something to bash up. And at the end of the weekend there was always someone that got bashed up. We had a mate who used to start fights. He'd say, "What are you looking at?" The bloke will say,

"Nothing." Then he goes (slap), "Don't call me nothing." It was his knockout punch. It was pretty crazy. No-one was safe when we were all together.'

Willoughby was living a Jekyll and Hyde existence; going to school during the day and roaming the streets at night. 'We'd go snowdropping, take people's clothes. Milk rounds, wake up at night take everybody's milk money. You could make twenty-five bucks, or maybe a bit more. It was a lot for a kid who's got nothing. Then we got into housebreaking. I became a perfect thief, because of the way I was brought up. I was light. I could do whatever I want. I started climbing when I was real young. Because I could climb, I was doing maybe twenty houses a week. It's a rush, isn't it? Getting caught and not caught. It's like your hormones are completely alive. It's a buzz. It's an energy.'

Willoughby's nocturnal activities eventually landed him in strife with the law. 'At first, they gave me a warning, because I was a kid,' he says. 'That urged me on more rather than scaring me. There were kids badder than me. I was the quiet achiever. I always made friends with everybody. I always found it easy. I had no hassle.'

But like so many before him, Willoughby's luck ran out and he slid from institutional life into the clutches of the criminal justice system. 'I got myself in trouble,' he says. 'When I was on the run, the wild started coming out. So, I took off and it built up so every place I was at, the coppers were ten minutes afterwards. So, I was always ahead of the police. So, I got sick of it and gave myself up. I walked down the police station. They locked me up. I think I would have been most wanted at the time.'

~

Willoughby was sent to McNally Training Centre. The centre provided secure residential care for boys between the ages of 15 and 18 who had been sentenced by the Juvenile Court. Education Department teachers ran classes at the centre and boys were trained in trades and crafts and worked on the attached farm.

Accommodation at McNally was broken down into units, each of which housed 12 to 18 boys. There was also a security section for boys whose behaviour required them to be separated from the other residents. This included a solitary confinement cell known as the Cabin. The Cabin was used for potential absconders, boys with behavioural problems and boys who were distressed.

A 1973 report to the Director of the SA Department of Community Welfare described accommodation at the centre as a series of 'locked units of incarceration'. Boys in the security section were 'locked up under grossly anti-therapeutic conditions' and boys on remand were 'bewildered and bored', as well as feeling 'anxiety and apprehension due to ignorance about their fate'.

Juveniles were usually committed to McNally for two years or until they turned 18. Once they had completed a program of training, many were released into the community under the supervision of a probation officer for the rest of their sentence.

'When I went into the lock-up it became more easier,' he says, 'because you had your mates there. There were too many blackfellas. My best mate who I grew up with in boys' home and childhood, he was in there too. We're like two tigers, not one individual. If you've got another mate, you're ten times stronger. If you've got another mate, you're a hundred times. You can get someone beaten up just on your say.'

Willoughby was released into the care of his father after about eight months. His father tried to tell him about his ancestry, but the words fell on deaf ears. 'I couldn't understand what he was talking about,' says Willoughby. 'He'd be saying you're related to such and such ... all I had was just this gang, and loyalty within this gang was the only love I was ever taught. I was already amongst my people. And they explained I was too far away. Too far gone, in other words. Traditional people were people that had a home. Street people were people that didn't have a home.'

Willoughby's father was staying at an alcohol rehabilitation centre in Adelaide's north-east suburbs. 'It was sort of a Christian place,' he says. 'My father was giving up alcohol so they'd have their sons stay there. To help his father. So, I stayed there to help my father give up alcohol. I'd be sitting at the table with my father and there would be about ten other old guys from all around Australia. I was only young. They'd start talking. Or take their teeth out, false teeth out and put them in a jar, and eat. And all I can hear is "clack, clack, clack, clack". Anyway, that was making me laugh. I'd be sweating and trying to hold my laugh but I couldn't. And they'd see me and start laughing. And the other young fellas would be laughing. Quite a few times they couldn't finish their food because I'd make 'em all laugh. I'd look up and one of the old fellas would look up and he'd look like he was cross-eyed and I'd start laughing. One of the old fellas would be about to put something in his mouth and something would slip out and the way he'd look at me, that would make me laugh. They'd tell me stories that would make me laugh. It became that bad that they told me to go in the lounge room and eat, which I did so I could watch TV too, I'd watch cartoons. Then something would happen and I'd start laughing in there and they'd start laughing and "What the ...?"

'They were great years. The best years of my life. Listening to them old fellas telling stories. My father was a full blood. He couldn't speak English properly so I had to really listen to what he was trying to say. I didn't know I was a full blood because I'd been in homes all my life. Raised by white people and it's very difficult to relate to that full bloodness even if you are one. You would look in the mirror and see you were black. It was weird, weird shit.'

While living with his father, Willoughby had been running with the gang again. And got caught again. And was sent to

McNally for a second stint. But this time he had something to focus on. 'When I got into music it gave me another energy,' he says. 'Without violence. Without a threat on your life. And it's to do with attitude. I wanted to be a rock'n'roll star. I'd had enough of that crazy life. And music gave me that change. "We Have Survived" was like me saying, I have survived the streets. So, it's a street song more than it's a bush song.'

Through her positions on the boards of the Sydney-based Aboriginal Arts Board and Aboriginal Artists Agency, Leila Rankine became aware of a music program being run in New South Wales by a maverick character called Gil Weaver. Weaver's program, which went under the banner of the Children's Free Embassy, took young bands out on tour to perform music for local kids in regional areas. In many respects it was like CASM's visits to Port Lincoln and Ceduna. It sounded like a good opportunity for No Fixed Address to spread their wings over the summer. Bart Willoughby says Weaver came down to Adelaide to discuss it with CASM.

'He gave us this bit of paper,' Willoughby recalls. 'We were sitting around laughing. "No drinking, no fighting, no smoking dope." We'd never had a contract that *precise*. I think it was his experience with other black bands who had really fucked up, got drunk, had a fight. He might've had a difficult time with other black bands.'[1]

Arrangements were made for No Fixed Address to join the Children's Free Embassy on a two-week tour of northern New South Wales, leaving from Sydney in the week after Christmas 1979.

~

Gil Weaver was a returned serviceman who had worked across outback Australia in the 1950s as a jack of all trades. In his journeys, he had become keenly aware of the injustices suffered by Aboriginal people as wards of the state.

Later, as a single parent of four in Sydney in the late 1960s, Weaver faced the prospect of putting his children into state care. Mindful of his outback experience, he joined the crusade for financial support for single parents.

Weaver became part of a larger lobby group though the setting up of an improvised centre for 60 to 70 latchkey kids in a condemned house on two acres out the back of Macquarie

University in Sydney. Word soon spread that kids were having fun, making cubby houses out of scrap materials and they started coming in buses, first white kids from Ryde and Ultimo, then black kids from Redfern. The centre developed into a kids' holiday home, with makeshift learning programs.

When the campus house was demolished, Weaver organised camping trips and weekends away in the country. In the towns they passed through, local kids wanted a piece of the action, asking for a band, a dance or something.[2]

Thus began the music program of the Children's Free Embassy, a non-profit, community organisation that gave young people from disadvantaged backgrounds the chance to involve themselves with a group of touring performers. Some of these tours simply consisted of bands playing a series of concerts and dances, while others involved participants learning skills in the areas of music, dance, production, lighting and theatre electronics.

~

In 1976, Alec Morgan was living at a friend's place in Balmain when, unannounced, Gil Weaver arrived on the doorstep. Morgan had recently returned to Sydney from London where he had been working in the thriving alternative theatre scene. At the invitation of the newly formed Addison Road Community Centre in Marrickville, he had started a theatre project for schools to teach students about other cultures. The innovative project involved Greek and Turkish shadow puppets and word of its success reached Weaver though the community arts grapevine.

'He asked me if I wanted to go out on this tour they did,' Morgan remembers. 'I thought it was a great idea, to get out of Sydney and have a look at the countryside and that was my first connection with the Aboriginal communities.

'Gil lived out the back of Macquarie University. I remember this double-decker bus. It was back roads, really open fields. There was this rundown old weatherboard house. And he had all these vehicles hanging around. He'd always have his trousers hanging down. His face was like a beat-up face. To us, he was much, much older. Incredible guy. One of those Aussie, unique, eccentric characters who pushed his way through everything. Luckily there was a community arts section that supported him, but most people were horrified.

'Gil would take these kids from Redfern, kids getting in trouble with the law and take them out to communities where they could actually get a bit of culture. So, we went up the coast, the east coast, places like Cabbage Tree Island, and then it went across. The main area it went across to was Moree, Brewarrina and Bourke. Gil gave me a van. He said, "Here's a van, go around and do some shows." I had to do it at night. I had to put up a tent and I had a light behind the screen for the shadow theatre.

'The stories, the Turkish one ... they connected with it. I didn't realise at the time, the main character Karagöz is a poor, underdog character who goes out to get his daily bread and runs up against police and welfare and bureaucracy, and it was quite comic.'

One of the major community leaders Morgan met through Gil Weaver, was Essie Coffey. Coffey had settled in Brewarrina with her husband Albert 'Doc' Coffey in the 1950s. The couple raised 18 children there, ten of them adopted, and Coffey became a driving force in the town's Aboriginal movement, earning herself the affectionate title of 'Bush Queen of Brewarrina'.

'Essie was such a charismatic dynamic personality,' says Morgan. 'People gravitated towards her. She was politically involved as well. With the Aboriginal Legal Service and standing up for rights in that area.

'Essie had a band, mainly country music and rock. They'd team up with Gil and part of it was that Gil would always bring out a band or two and pick up bands along the way. So, it would be this rather strange motley troupe that would arrive in town and they would hold dances. They'd hire a hall in the town and hold a dance. So, music was huge.

'Walking into a community like that with Gil really was opening a whole new world. In a really positive way. I don't know how he did it. He just kept going. I'm surprised he went for so long. He always looked like he was going to topple over. Any second, this guy is going to really fall apart any second. What's holding him up? Looks like a couple of bits of barbed wire tied around him and a bit of bloody tin here and there stapled to him. You think he's gonna fall apart but he just kept going.'

~

When the New South Wales tour with Gil Weaver was booked in, Graeme Isaac asked his former partner Janie Conway and her brother Mic (who had played with Isaac in Matchbox) if they would organise some dates for the band in Melbourne on the way. After leaving Carlton darlings Stiletto in 1977, Janie Conway was fronting her own outfit Scarlet. She remembers the first meeting vividly. 'When I met No Fixed Address, it was like a portal opened into the real-life experience of what it was like to be Indigenous in Australia,' she says. 'They were the ones who opened me up to it. And from then on in, there was no turning back. It began a journey that was incredibly important in my life. But they started it. And they were so young. I think John John was too young to be playing in a hotel.

'My first meeting with them, I don't know whose place it was, but Ned Lander, the film maker, was there. He'd asked my brother and I if we would get them some gigs. A Latrobe University gig was part of it, I'm pretty sure ... Christmas Hills and the Martini's gig as well, but I'm not sure how we actually did that. Anyhow, I went to meet them and they were staying at this place where Ned was as well, and when I was introduced to them, they were so shy. Graeme had been teaching them and had been saying he had this terrific band. I didn't think much about it. On the strength of that, I was helping them get these gigs. I met them and they were so shy and I was like, "Oh dear. Oh my God. Are they going to be able to perform? They're so shy."

'At that time, I understood very little about the protocols with Indigenous people and meeting and how you don't just leap on people you meet in the Western way. When I saw them at Latrobe Uni – and in my memory that was the first one I saw – they just were magic. They transformed into this amazing band. Right from the get-go, the audience was up and dancing and having a wonderful time, and I was greatly relieved.'

The band played at a weekend festival at Christmas Hills, 45 kilometres north-east of Melbourne, on the weekend of 15 and 16 December. Les Graham remembers the crowd reaction. 'That was thirty-five to forty thousand people. I went sick when I seen the crowd. I didn't know if they were going to throw things at us. I didn't know what was going to happen. They cheered us on. We did three encores after that. They wouldn't let us leave.'

Skyhooks was the headlining band on the bill. 'We were the first Aboriginals they ever talked to in their lives,' says Graham wonderingly. 'It's not that they were racist, it's just that they were like kinda scared.'

After playing a gig supporting Reuben Tice ('Eltham's version of the Grateful Dead'[3]) at Eltham Town Hall, the band finished up their stint beside the Yarra with a headline slot at inner-city nightspot Martini's in Carlton.

Mark Thomson, writing in *Roadrunner* magazine, said local musicians were predominant in the crowd at Martini's, with former Daddy Cool guitarist Ross Hannaford, 'even being moved to say that he's been trying to write a song like "From My Eyes" all his life'.[4]

Through Les Graham, the band had obtained their first manager, Danny Haveron, a partner in Adelaide's biggest second-hand record store Umbrella Music. Haveron called Mick Pacholli, a mover and shaker on the Melbourne music scene. He asked Pacholli if he would keep an eye on the band, in case they ran into any issues with venue owners or promoters.

Pacholli recalls getting a phone call from Les Graham telling him that the venue owners at Martini's were refusing to pay the band. 'Don't worry, just get out of there, I'll sort it out,' Pacholli told him. The next day Pacholli sent one of his staffers, a young Irish girl, around to Martini's to 'rip them another arsehole'. Which she duly did and collected the band's money.

With that taste of the big, bad Melbourne music scene fresh in their mouths, it was time to jump in their cars for the first of what would be many trips up the Hume Highway to Sydney.

~

On 29 December 1979, the Children's Free Embassy Christmas Tour left Sydney and headed north. Travelling under the banner of the Teenage Roadshow, the latest edition of Gil Weaver's caravan featured three bands: Waldo's Wedding (keyboard-based progressive rock), Transaction (heavy rock), both from Sydney, and No Fixed Address. A three-tonne truck carried the 1000-watt PA system, sixteen microphones and a disco and light show. The road crew consisted of thirteen from the Children's Free Embassy and three from South Australia.

Ian Chambers, the vocalist with Waldo's Wedding, remembers the start of the tour vividly. 'The first morning, the bands and crew, never having met, assembled in Kempsey's Nirvana Caravan Park cafe, each sitting in their own group at separate tables, waiting on Gil Weaver to advise the day's plan. The three bands were being nonchalant but were definitely scoping each other out ... with the two sets of urban Sydney boys not having a clue of how to even say hello to a formidable-looking group of Indigenous South Australians. It was like we were frozen in amber to the point of feeling awkward and ridiculous.

'Putting us all out of our misery, Bart Willoughby stood up, walked over to the Waldo's Wedding table and proceeded to lay out a set of matchsticks in the form of a puzzle ... by moving

Ricky Harrison, John John Miller, Bart Willoughby and Les Graham, Eltham Town Hall, Victoria, December 1979.

two matches, turn this into this, etc. I'd seen the puzzle, so I let my bandmates have a shot, but I was in awe of this gesture ... it was the best icebreaker ever ... and the beginning of several weeks of laughter, kinship and wonderful experiences.

'The three bands on that tour could not have been more different, but the combination somehow worked and our audiences were often very appreciative, even if a little bewildered initially. That first gig, on New Year's Eve at the Burnt Bridge Aboriginal Mission, I regard as one of the high points of my life. The three bands delivered their sets, with the other bands watching and listening. Being a fan of Jimmy Cliff, I immediately fell in love with No Fixed Address. Their original songs were as strong as the covers they chose. They were tight, melodic and a joy to experience.'

'Our first gig was at Kempsey,' Bart Willoughby recalls. 'A blackfella mission. Gil kept us last because we were the only black band there. He kept us last because we were playing to blackfellas. And it was New Year's Eve. So, he put the other two bands on. And he hadn't seen us play. And after, when we finished playing, he shoved the bloody contract out the door and bought us a dozen beers. He was totally blown out.'[5]

All the bands were travelling in their own cars. Chambers had keyboard player Steve Wood as passenger in his 'little Datsun'. 'We'd left the caravan park in daylight but we returned from the gig well after midnight, in near pitch-blackness,' remembers Chambers. 'Steve and I exited my car with the intention of bunking down in a cabin provided. Steve noticed something and drew my attention ... as we approached, we could make out large dark shapes covering the cabin, including the door. Well over a dozen of the biggest huntsman spiders I'd ever seen, quite literally two hand-spans across, which we later dubbed "Kempsey face-huggers". Steve looked at me and said, "What'll we do?"... "Dunno"...

'We stood there contemplating our demise for a few minutes when Bart arrived. "What's going on?" he asked. "Small spider problem." I pointed towards the cabin. "What'll we do?" he says. Steve and I looked at each other and I turned to Bart and said, "Your people are close to the Earth, don't you have some way of dealing with this?"

' "Not me, man ... I'm scared of spiders!"

'The three of us busted a gut laughing.

'I had some mosquito repellent which seemed to do the trick and we were able to bunk down, if a little uneasily. I can confirm dubbing Bart the "one-bar radiator". Bart generated so much heat when he slept, I was surprised he didn't glow in the dark.'

~

There was a hand-written tour itinerary, but according to Chambers it deviated from the moment the bands arrived in Kempsey. The itinerary lists both Crescent Head Surf Club and Burnt Bridge Mission on 31 December, possibly as alternative options. 'Crescent Head was rescheduled,' says Chambers, 'so

New Year's Eve was definitely at Burnt Bridge and further gigs were added or rescheduled during the tour.' For the first week of January, the itinerary also lists dances at the Nambucca Heads Surf Club and the Coffs Harbour Youth Club, and then an outdoor concert at Evans Head.

'On that tour we played in some beautiful beachside locations, often in surf clubs,' says Steve Wood. 'I'm not sure whether the boys from No Fixed Address had limited surf experience but I do recall that they always went in wearing their black jeans. On one occasion I was sitting watching the ocean with them and they were "winding me up" with stories of people being tracked down to receive "blackfella justice" on the streets of Adelaide. They may have also mentioned kangaroos hopping down the streets, I'm not too sure, but I do recall them falling apart laughing after I took them seriously.'

'As the shows progressed and the bands got familiar, we'd request our favourite songs from each other,' says Chambers. 'And considering how "unconventional" Waldo's Wedding could be, their love for our stuff still boggles my mind.'

Wood has many happy memories of the tour. 'As we were all thrown together, we tended to watch each other's sets,' he recalls. 'For my part I was particularly struck by Bart's performance. He seemed to have a special "magic" about him. He was totally at home in the dual role of singer and drummer, and seemed a very natural talent. He was also a very charismatic and captivating front man (even from behind those drums), as well as one heck of a funny and likeable guy. Les was also a very strong and powerful character but more cool and distant. He seemed to observe things more cautiously. John John was funny; Ricky was quiet and Veronica was just a lovely spirit. I was the keyboard player in my band and Bart and I confided that we really liked each other's playing. One afternoon before the evening's performance in an old hall, we organised a jam with me playing an old beat-up piano, Bart on drums, our bass player Con Apokis and possibly some others whom I have forgotten, cruising through some well-known reggae numbers.'

It wasn't all sweetness and light, however. Wood recalls one incident that left a sour taste in their mouths. 'Travelling between towns, we all stopped in at a roadside pub to grab some lunch. We went up to the bar and the proprietor said, "I'll serve you blokes but your mates are gonna have to stay outside." I don't recall the conversation that ensued but suffice to say that they got an unambiguous "response" from the tour's organiser Gil Weaver, but never again our business! It was my first taste of this sort of racism.'

The second week of the tour found the bands in Ballina, where on Wednesday, 9 January they appeared at the Ballina Shire Promotion Association's annual Mardi Gras (*Northern Star* 11 January 1980).

'We played one night at this festival in Ballina,' says Willoughby. 'Then two days later we played at this hall. We turned up at the concert and there was this row that went into the street, three rows full of all these white people and they were all coming to see No Fixed! So, the name started flitting around then. The energy was just pure fun. We all loved doing it.'[6]

Janie Conway was also in Ballina for the fun. 'The biggest memory I have is of sitting out on the rocks at Ballina,' she says. 'It was probably between soundcheck and gig. The venue was very near the rock wall where we sat. There's a big line of rocks … it's not a pier but it stops the water coming in. We sat out on the end of the rocks and I swear that Bart called the dolphins in. He was doing something and all of sudden there were dolphins all around us. That's all I can say. And I really, really witnessed it and that man has some kind of magic, which I can't really explain except in Indigenous terms. A very, very intuitive, extraordinary person. As they all were.'

~

There was more to come. Ricky Harrison takes up the story. 'Gil ended up taking us down to Canberra. He got this tip-off that they were having this big function at Parliament House. So, he goes, "Come on guys, we're going over here, to the Parliament House." So, we rocked up with all the equipment and set up, and there's all these politicians around and we started playing "Black Man's Rights" and all our songs to the politicians there. And I met Gough Whitlam! [laughs]. Yeah, it was amazing. I thought, wow. So anyway, Bob Hawke was there too around that time. Anyway, it was good to get out of the rain and get some food and stuff and a few drinks. Gil Weaver is just one of those people.'

The event was a reception to celebrate the release of a book, *It's coming yet: - an Aboriginal treaty within Australia by Australians,* published by the Aboriginal Treaty Committee. It was launched by ex-South Australian premier Don Dunstan at the National Press Club on 17 January 1980. Dunstan used the occasion to criticise the South Australian government's proposals to allow mining on Pitjantjatjara tribal lands, saying the moves amounted to 'cultural genocide' (*Canberra Times*, 18 January 1980).

The Parliament House reception was a star-studded political affair. The *Aboriginal Arts Board Newsletter* (January 1980) reported:

> Back in Canberra, the Children's Free Embassy attended the launching of a book on land rights. No Fixed Address had been invited to play and their performance really impressed Charles Perkins [then deputy secretary at the Department of Aboriginal Affairs], who was there among a number of VIPs including EG Whitlam and D Dunstan. All of them learned something, not just that No Fixed Address are top performers, but that the Children's Free Embassy is about the most exciting and useful youth program in Australia and that it is unique in the way it uses the arts to fight a particular social battle.

Perhaps not everybody who was there that night learned something. In episode 5 of *Pop Movie* (1986), Ray Argall's ABC-TV series on music in Australia, Gil Weaver said, 'I took an Aboriginal band to Canberra and they played reggae. Some bloody idiot of a politician gets up and says, "Oh, I thought they were going to be doing something cultural." What the fuck do you think they're doing? To them, that's important!'

~

Back in Sydney, No Fixed Address was booked to play an outdoor concert on 26 January (Australia Day/Invasion Day), at the Mount Druitt Shopping Centre with five other bands, including Waldo's Wedding.

'That tour was one of the great experiences of my life but I'm sad to say it ended on a fairly disappointing note,' says Steve Wood. 'The last scheduled date was to be an open-air event in a civic square out west of Sydney in Mt Druitt. As we readied ourselves for the day's performance, some local "lads" decided to start messing with the equipment at the mixing desk. Needless to say, the road crew of mostly "no nonsense" mainly Indigenous young men did not take kindly to their actions. An all-out brawl ensued which led to the event being cancelled. Afterwards I think we all had a pizza and a couple of drinks.'

That wasn't the end of the drama. Bart Willoughby fell in a fountain and gashed his arm quite badly. Ian Chambers takes up the tale. 'They wrapped the wound in a towel and I drove Bart and Les to the nearest casualty. We got Bart into a cubicle and, after some routine questions, waited for someone to clean and stitch the wound (hoping there was no major damage). It was taking some time and Les began to get more agitated the longer we waited, questioning staff and asking for someone to attend to his friend, mostly being met with "as soon as we can", etc. The more agitated Les got, the more amusing Bart seemed to find it. "He's a human being, not a fucking piece of meat!" That set Bart off laughing ... the more profanity Les used, the more Bart laughed, to the point of hysterics. The guy bleeding profusely was in danger of laughing himself to death.'

Veronica Rankine, Les Graham, Ricky Harrison, Bart Willoughby and John John Miller, Mt Druitt, NSW, January 1980.

Photo by Carol Ruff.

When the members of No Fixed Address arrived back in Adelaide from their interstate adventures in February 1980, the landscape had changed. While officially they were all still students at CASM, both Leigh Hobba and Graeme Isaac had left the staff. And Ned Lander and Isaac had something to share.

The pair had spent time at Hobba's Carey Gully house in the Adelaide Hills over the summer of 1979–80. 'Graeme and Ned came up and bunkered down there and put the [film] script together,' says Hobba.

Carey Gully was a beautiful place, Lander remembers. But there were ... distractions. 'I think South Australia was a reasonably sort of liberal state in Australia at that time,' he says. 'And I think you could probably grow things legally in the backyard and things like that. And so, I think a certain amount of writing time might have been lost in the process [laughs]. Look, we were making it up as went along in terms of how to put this film together. It wasn't like we had no idea about film craft or no idea about story telling or any of that, but we knew we wanted to do something that had a very different feel to it.

'We were always looking to build on the reality of their experiences and trying to create a road movie. We wanted to make a movie that young people would want to go to see rather than something worthy. We wanted to make a movie that was entertaining and really "of the moment", I guess.

'And films like Jimmy Cliff's *The Harder They Come* ... that was a big inspiration. So, we were drawing on multiple inspirations. We were also drawing on the kind of traditions of some of the English filmmakers, like Ken Loach who made *Poor Cow* and many, many other brilliant films. Ken Loach did that thing of workshopping and working from people's lives and then working with actors and creating drama. And then on the other hand, there is the Jimmy Cliff ... guns and gangster elements. And music obviously being a central thing.

'I mean, both Graeme and I grew up with schooling of, "Aborigines were a proud and noble race who lived a long time ago." Having been brought up with his kind of total myth, and to be surrounded with this kind of music and lifeblood and energy ... it was really challenging, and it was something that you want to get involved in helping to bring to life on screen.

'We were also dealing with the fact that there were two bands, Us Mob and No Fixed Address. We were trying to find a way to tell a story of two bands on the road. It's hard enough to make the film about one band on the road, let alone two!

'We made life incredibly hard for ourselves,' Landers continues, 'but it wasn't an option to start telling people they have to pretend they were all in the same band or something like that. That's the sense in which it is documentary, in that we were not there to impose classic film form on the world that we had been allowed into.'

Pedro Butler from Us Mob remembers Isaac and Lander sitting down and pitching the whole thing to the bands. 'And we said, "Aw yeah, that sounds okay." But when it came to putting in our different stories, I wasn't real sure about that. But they managed to talk us into it. It would add to the narrative of the whole thing if we could look at individuals' stories and how it all tied in. At the end of the day, I could see how that would have worked. So yeah, they sold us on that and that's how we got going on that.'

'And there were also people around the bands whose stories were woven in,' says Isaac. 'For example, Jug who was part of the No Fixed Address road crew had been adopted out as a child, and at the time of filming was in the process of trying to find his birth mother. Les ended up playing that story out in the film, even though it was not his story, because we thought it was an important one to tell. At the time it was a story pretty much unknown outside the Aboriginal community, and this was before the term "Stolen Generations" came into general usage.

'But then Bart's flashbacks in the film to his time at a juvenile boys' home were straight autobiography. And other scenes such as the roadside bust were dramatic imaginings of events that could easily have happened in real life. So, the stories in the film came from a variety of sources, but the spine of it was this journey of two bands on the road over two days – "48 hours on our side of town" as the film's by-line said.'

When Isaac and Lander emerged from Hobba's Adelaide Hills hideaway, they had enough of a script to apply to the Australian Film Commission for funding. The initial pitch was for a short film on 16mm. 'The Film Commission assessors came to Adelaide to do the assessment,' Isaac recalls. 'We all met with them together, but they knocked us back. Their principal problem was, "It's a nice idea, but who's going to play the parts of the guys in the band?" They couldn't get their brains around the idea that they would essentially play themselves, play out their own experiences or the experiences of family and friends ... the idea that the film would be somewhere in between documentary and drama. This was problematic for them.'

It was quickly decided the rejection could not, would not, be accepted. 'This wasn't part of the picture, it wasn't what was going to happen in our minds,' says Lander. 'So, we got Pedro, Ronnie and Wally I think, the Us Mob boys, maybe Carroll was in there ... I can't remember exactly ... into my little, very, very old, very, very beaten up, very rusty, Fiat 124 station wagon, which I'd bought for about two hundred dollars and had been working on ever since. A very, very underpowered little car, which we then proceeded to drive straight across to Sydney, from Adelaide to Sydney, obviously at some totally inappropriate hour of the night, driving nonstop.

'And finally getting to the top of the Blue Mountains and the car was clearly very, very sick. I think we limped into the outer suburbs of Sydney and stopped and somebody had a look at the car and decided that the entire oil sump was full of petrol –

we were in a bomb. We were driving literally – not a figurative bomb, an *actual* bomb and somehow or another some friends came and picked us up and we went back to houses in Sydney. And then we proceeded to just turn up at the Film Commission and talk our way in as a group, as a wild group, and explain that they just made the wrong decision, and that there had been a mistake and they'd made the wrong decision [laughs].

'And, believe it or not, there was the lovely Curtis Levy, a famous documentary filmmaker ... Curtis had made films in communities, particularly in remote areas, and he got it, and championed us through the Film Commission and we got the first funding. Which was something like thirty-nine thousand dollars or something like that, or twenty-one thousand dollars. It was a tiny amount of money to make a feature film and I think we told him that it was going to be a forty-minute film rather than a feature film, because it just sounded so ludicrous to make a feature film for that much money. Then we basically used that to shoot the film, which meant we didn't really have any money to finish the film.'

~

The eleventh Adelaide Festival of Arts kicked off on 8 March 1980. For the first time, film was included as a major element of the official festival program, and a week of Australian films produced during the 1970s was presented. One of the themed days was 'Images of Black Australia', where the films shown included *My Survival as an Aboriginal* and *Robin Campbell Old Fella Now*.

My Survival as an Aboriginal was a documentary set in and around Brewarrina in north-west New South Wales. It was directed by Essie Coffey and produced by Coffey, Alec Morgan and Martha Ansara. In her curator's notes about the film on the *Australian Screen* website, Romaine Moreton observes:

> Essie Coffey's passion for her culture and her stoic dedication to her people is tangible in this film. As a charismatic, dedicated woman, she invites the audience into her community. And

while she brings to the fore the hardships endured by her community, she is continually focused on the power and richness of traditional knowledge and skills, and the power of her cultural connection to land. In this, Coffey not only raises issues of the impact of colonisation on Indigenous peoples, but also offers a solution by way of continuing cultural practice.[1]

The documentary had its genesis in *Backroads* (1977), the first feature film by director Phillip Noyce, which followed the escapades of two chancers, one white and one black, as they careened around north-western New South Wales in a stolen 1962 Pontiac Parisienne.

Noyce had persuaded Aboriginal activist Gary Foley to play the black lead, with the agreement that Foley would monitor the black content and could 'rewrite his content if he thought it was bullshit'. Many of the early scenes in the film were shot in the Aboriginal settlement of West Brewarrina, known as 'Dodge City', and featured Essie Coffey and members of her family.

Martha Ansara, like Noyce an active member of the Sydney Filmmakers Co-op, was second assistant director on the shoot, which Noyce later described as 'a pretty weird experience because there was frequently a lot of tension between the white and the black members of the crew and cast, and there wasn't a lot of money'.[2]

'There was a bit of fight over some things in *Backroads*,' Ansara confirms. 'And I said to Essie, don't worry, we'll just make our own film. And as it happens, we did. And she was the boss of the film. And I'd also worked with Alec Morgan. We were producers of *My Survival* ... Essie was also a producer. She definitely got the money.'

Margaret Dodd remembers the strong connections between the film communities in Sydney and Adelaide. 'People like Ned Lander, Martha Ansara, Margot Nash, all those filmmakers had just been at the film school in Ryde, AFTS [Australian Film and Television School]. And we, a delegation from the South

Australian Media Resource Centre, went over there, in about 1976. So, we knew all those people. And we were criticising, becoming more politically aware. It was the beginning of that way of looking at our lives, recognising racism. And also, recognising the need for Aboriginal people to be making films themselves.'

'There was a strong connection between Adelaide and Sydney,' says Alec Morgan. 'You could get the train overnight. It was a great journey and still cheap and you could get a berth overnight. So, I'd been to Adelaide a couple of times. I'd been to the 1976 festival and done a show then.'

~

During the 1980 Festival of Arts, No Fixed Address and Us Mob played a free event in Adelaide's busiest shopping strip, Rundle Mall. *Rocking Nungas*, which ran from 1–4 pm on Sunday, 9 March, was headlined by Essie Coffey (described as 'Filmmaker and Country and Western singer from NSW') and also included African drum band Black Fire.

After the festival, Coffey stayed in Adelaide for a further three months. Margaret Dodd remembers her saying she just needed to get out of Brewarrina for a while. 'She'd been staying not far from the British Hotel, in North Adelaide. She needed a break from Brewarrina. She needed somewhere to stay so she came to my place for about three months. They were making the film at the time.'

Bart Willoughby and Jug were also living with Dodd, whose College Park house was a haven for creative spirits. 'Rugby Street was just one of those places where everybody went at one time,' Dodd laughs. 'So, if Bart is living at my place, then you've got Ricky, you've got Duckie, you've got John John, Pedro, you've got the lot really. And Jimmy Chi up the road and all the rest of them. They were all there at one time or another, in and out, staying or not staying, playing or practising or whatever they wanted to do really.' While in Adelaide, Coffey did some recording at Greenhill Studios with Graeme Isaac and Phil Roberts, backed by members of No Fixed Address and Us Mob.

Ned Lander acknowledges the important role Coffey played in establishing the atmosphere of trust essential for effective cross-cultural collaboration in making the film. 'Essie came down and spent time with the boys, with the members of the bands and also, not to be forgotten, Veronica Rankine, who played saxophone in No Fixed Address, and Gayle Rankine who was in the film. We would just do things like go out camping on the weekend together with some of the people from the band and Essie, who was older and wiser than all of us. Not necessarily talking all that much about filmmaking. We did from time to time, but it was more about bringing everyone together. Building that sense of trust and then building that sense of common purpose.

'That process of coming to some agreement about the way you'll work together, it's very important. We did a lot of workshopping before starting to make the film. We did a lot of workshopping about people's lives and then starting to write the script and then starting to rehearse that script and then starting to shoot it. Sometimes we moved characters around, you know, somebody would play someone else. It was hard because some people were wanted at the time by the police, or people needed to have some sort of privacy around their real-life circumstances. So, sometimes one person's story will be played by another person in the band.'

~

There was a strong educational element to the rehearsals during the preproduction period. 'We wanted to get everyone familiar with the process of filming,' says Isaac. 'Because even though the film was built on documentary foundations, built out of the real-life experiences of members of the band and their families and their friends and so forth, it was shot like a drama. A lot of it was hand-held in long takes, which you do in a documentary, but all shot like a drama, in the sense that

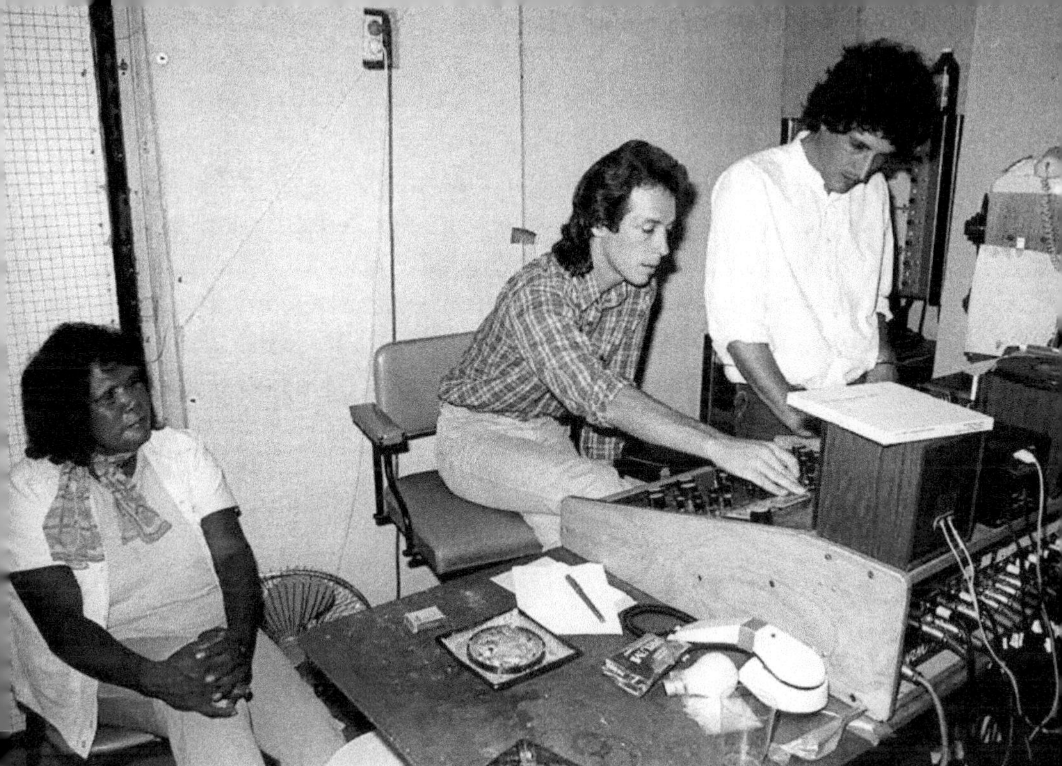

Essie Coffey, Graeme Isaac and Philip Roberts, Greenhill Studios, SA, March 1980.
Photo by Ian de Gruchy.

you shoot, let's say, a wide shot of the scene, the first half of the scene or whatever, and you stop, and you move the camera, and you play the scene again.

'You get coverage, and then in the editing room you cut the shots together, so we needed to show them how this all works. And we also wanted them to get used to seeing themselves on screen and to relax with the camera. We did it with video; we got some video gear from the Media Resource Centre and we were shooting these improvisations. Taking elements of the script or scenes close to the script and playing them out in improvisation. Shooting and then re-shooting the scene from another angle. So, they could really understand what the process was. Which was all completely new to them obviously, but they were all used to busking their way into a pub with no dosh and they were all able to hustle, they were all street wise. So, they came to understand the process very quickly.'

'The reason they wanted to do that obviously was because none of us had been on TV before,' says Pedro Butler. 'It was a whole new kettle of fish for us all. To try to act out these scenes but to be as realistic as possible. We weren't trained actors. Even when I look at the film, that comes across. I remember saying to Ned, maybe it would have been better as a documentary rather than a feature film. They already had ideas of what they wanted to do. I was no filmmaker, so I just said, whatever you guys reckon is fair.'

While preparations were being made for the shooting of the film, No Fixed Address (and to a lesser extent, Us Mob) continued to perform live. In the April 1980 edition of *Roadrunner*, Mark Thomson described a late summer No Fixed Address gig:

> It was a warm night and the barbecue garden at Adelaide's Angas Hotel was almost full. In a corner of the concrete yellow lit 'garden', No Fixed Address, Australia's only Aboriginal reggae band, are beating out a pulsing reggae tune, much to the evident joy of the leaping crowd. It's a new sight to see a mixed black and white crowd enjoying an Aboriginal band.
>
> As the night progresses and the garden fills up, the band work out their much acclaimed originals. Drummer Bart Willoughby plays a brilliant piece of reggae drumming, complete with those distinctive rimshots, whilst singing:
>
> > Sitting in the sunlight
> > with my head towards the sun
> > Suddenly there's a cloud above me
> > Blocking out the sunlight from my eyes ...
> > – 'From My Eyes' (Bart Willoughby).
>
> Although instrumentally the band is strong, it's lyrically that they really shine. Many of the songs reflect the rough and tumble of the lives of Australian Aborigines. The traditional concerns of Jamaican reggae lyrics have much in common with the direct experiences of these local songwriters. This is the strength of the band – the fact that existence is a struggle in a white-dominated society. While white bands only struggle in order to find something to write about other than love and boredom, the members of No Fixed Address have lots to write about.[1]

As well as printing posters and writing the occasional article for *Roadrunner*, Thomson was presenting a world music show on 5MMM. Through Graeme Isaac he got copies of some of the demos No Fixed Address had been recording and started airing them on his show. Once they were dubbed onto cartridges, others at the station started playing them.

Thomson was also playing guitar in a ska-reggae band. 'I was in the Jumpers, making out I was a musician,' he says. 'Playing rhythm guitar and yelling a lot. Not singing. And I did all the graphics. I did a lot of the organisation too. We played with them [No Fixed Address] because we were really the only two reggae bands around and we did at least three to four gigs together. We would alternate. They would do a set, we would do a set, they would do a set, or the other way around. But they were the best, I mean they were good. They were just better than us. There was this real sense of them being a coming thing, though. There were lots of people fascinated by them. Hanging around with them, you got insights into what urban Aboriginal life was like.

'Because I knew Graeme well, I heard the stories. There were lots of family dramas and so forth ... people getting into strife and their sickness and bad health and stuff like that. It was shocking at times, just thinking, wow, this sort of day-to-day life ... people's day-to-day life was dominated by more powerful things than us happy-go-lucky whitefellas in the '70s and '80s. For us, life was pretty good. Not a lot to complain about. Whereas you see these guys' lives were, fuck ... there were some mighty big things wading in. The relationship with the police for one ... it was kind of bad.'

~

No Fixed Address and Us Mob had been making demos of original material and were starting to record backing tracks for the film at Greenhill Studios. 'No Fixed Address were a good band,' says Philip Roberts. 'It became apparent to me that they were a live band, and instead of doing it in the way that one might have done it at that time, I tried to get them to play live in the studio. They were in one room because there were no vocal booths and that sort of thing in that studio. So, it had a pretty live feel and then we would overdub if required ... not that they were brilliant at overdubbing. I don't think John John was capable of starting like ten bars into the song and just doing two lines or something. I think they all had to start from the beginning and do it again.

'It wasn't helped by the fact Bart used to sing and play the drums. I don't recall whether we ever took him into a vocal booth later and said, "Yes, sing that again." But I don't think so. You know, I think his singing was led by what he was playing. So, that was really interesting and that was good.

'It was called Greenhill Studios and that's why the track "Greenhouse Holiday" came about. Bart wrote it while we were looking for some extra songs to get an album full of material. "I'm going to the greenhouse where they grow the stuff"; because there was a lot of weed in the scene back there. In those days, I think it was the thing to do to smoke a lot of weed and so, we did that.'

Fortunately, there was no weed in evidence on the night that members of the local constabulary paid a visit. 'I remember the door, the reception of Greenhill Studios, bursting open and three armed cops coming in with their guns levelled,' says Roberts. 'And I said, "What the fuck?" Because I had been, if you like, an activist liberal in South Africa where I'd been at university and I said, "What are you doing sir?" "Oh, there's a car outside with out of state plates, mate." I said, "So, and ...?"

'And what they'd obviously done, was seen three black guys going into the building and burst in with their guns drawn. And I couldn't believe it. I said, "Get the fuck out of here. You're on private property. Unless you've got a warrant. This is a band; they're doing a recording. Now, go away." You know, I was pretty mouthy; more so than I probably should have been in a way.

'And then, in the following weeks when they were recording, every time we drove up to North Adelaide we'd be stopped by the police. I've got stopped more times by the police in that week or two recording with No Fixed Address and with Us Mob than ever in my life before or since; including in South

Africa, and in Zimbabwe. So, I think just as a political take on the times, I think it's worth mentioning that I got stopped, that car was forever being ... I'd say, "Yes?" They'd go, "We just want to check your indicators, mate" and everything. "Fuck off, I mean, really?"

'All right, I probably didn't say fuck off. The band members would just sit there; they were used to this. This happened to them no doubt all the time. To me, that was a revelation.'

Roberts also experienced problems with service of alcohol while in black company. 'I went into a North Adelaide hotel or bar,' he says. 'I may have been with No Fixed Address or it may have been with Us Mob. Went up to the bar. I said, "Okay, I'll have five schooners of lager," and the guy said, "No, sorry, mate." I said, "What?" He said, "We can't serve those boongs ..." I said, "Listen, do you even know the law? Do you know that you are obliged to serve those guys over there?"

'And I started and I think there was Wally from Us Mob and he said, "Nah, Phil, leave it man, let's just go." I said, "No, you fucking put those beers down here or I will report you to the police. I will report you to the police." And they didn't even realise; it was that year or the year before that they had brought in the thing, that you couldn't discriminate.

'Possibly people forget about those days but the idea of refusing them a drink in a public bar – not because they're drunk or anything else, because they were black; they just walked in and they were standing at the pool table. I couldn't believe it and so I felt as a Zimbabwean who lived in South Africa for three years, this was equally fascist behaviour as I'd ever experienced there. It was unbelievable. So, I know what they were talking about. You know, "We have survived the white man's world." I could see what they were talking about.'

In late May, No Fixed Address made their second visit to Melbourne. After two weeks of shows, the final gig was bottom of the bill to Mi-Sex and James Freud's Radio Stars at Latrobe University, where they played to a crowd of 3000. Bart Willoughby recalled the reaction to what was fast becoming their signature tune, 'We Have Survived'.

'When we were playing in Melbourne, I just noticed some of the people's reaction – like, "What's this black dude doing telling us what to do?" Some looks like that, you know? But when the song finished, most of the crowd really cheered. It was great.'[1]

The next night, the band was back in Adelaide supporting legendary American bluesman Taj Mahal at the Arkaba Top Room. Taj gave Willoughby a poster that carried the inscription, 'To The Best Black Band In Australia'.

~

In mid-June, the entire student group from CASM went to Noonameena, on the Coorong southwest of Meningie, for a music camp. On Friday, 20 June 1980, No Fixed Address performed 'We Have Survived' and 'From My Eyes' to staff and students at Murray Bridge High School, then joined Us Mob and Coloured Stone for an evening cabaret at Murray Bridge Town Hall (*Tjunguringanyi*, vol. 7 no. 2, 1980).

The following night, Saturday, 21 June, No Fixed Address played at the Australian Cultural Association Basement on Port Road, Hindmarsh with The Jump and The Bad Poets. Margaret Dodd took Bart Willoughby and Jug there in her VW Kombi and recalls the police swarming all over it looking for defects.

'The Australian Cultural Association was an "old school" trade union organisation which somehow managed to get a liquor licence for its premises on Port Road, to the consternation of the more conservative neighbouring businesses,' says Harry Butler, editor of Adelaide fanzine *DNA*. 'The walls were festooned with anti-Bob Menzies posters and so forth. A number of gigs took place there in early 1980, as bands which were unable to play in regular pub venues (e.g. punk and new wave groups) constantly sought out alternative performance spaces.'

'We played at this punk rock festival at The Basement,' Bart Willoughby recalls. 'About three hundred people. Black and white. Punk rockers. Bikies. Very well-educated blackfellas to poor people. The coppers came. The cans started flying. They couldn't bust the place because they had to come through this little door and it was chock-a-block with people throwing cans and bottles.'[2]

Tim Nicholls, drummer in headlining band the Bad Poets, thinks the ACA had been refused a liquor licence for the night but decided to go ahead anyway. 'Normally you would send some cops in to shut it down but they sent the STAR Force,' he says. 'There was a staircase down, no windows, long skinny room. A stage away from the door and a bathroom out the back. We're playing away and suddenly there's a ruckus at the top of the stairs. There are about ten policemen done up in riot gear coming down the stairs. My feeling was they weren't expecting any trouble. You've got a mix of Aboriginal people and punks and the glasses and bottles just started flying. The police are pushing in and they're whacking people. One guy I know went for a cop with a glass or a bottle and hit him in the face with it. I'm sitting behind the drums and suddenly they're all on stage and kicking the shit out of our lead singer, Jade, and it was just total chaos. She was really quite badly hurt. She went down and they kept kicking her. I'm not sure how she got out of the place because there was only one way in and out. And then they started farming people out.'

'Around two dozen people were arrested,' says Butler, 'although it was the white punk kids who were grabbed and bashed, while the Indigenous musicians weren't too badly harassed (for a change).'

'I ended up in a paddy wagon with about eight other people and I think almost everybody had drugs on them,' says Nicholls. 'They were all going, "What the fuck are we going to do?" Some guy, I can't tell you who it was, said, "Give them to me," and he ate the lot. About three hours later when we're all in the cells down at Port Adelaide, they had to put him in a different cell because he was just tripping off the moon. People had given him speed and acid and I've no idea what happened to him.

'About six or seven in the morning they let everyone out that they couldn't pin an individual act of violence on. But the guy who glassed the cop, he was in really deep shit. I think he got a seven-year sentence.'

~

It was around this time that I met and introduced myself to No Fixed Address. I'd seen the band play on the Adelaide pub circuit and heard their demos on 5MMM, where I was presenting two shows. I was very impressed.

It was high time to do a major story on the band for *Roadrunner*, I decided. One Saturday night in late June, I ran into Les Graham at a party and arranged to meet the band the following day. This is the introduction to my cover story in the August 1980 edition:

> On a cold, windy Sunday afternoon about a month ago, I hopped on my bicycle and pedalled the couple of miles to Westbury Street, Hackney, one of the inner eastern suburbs of Adelaide. I was going to interview the members of No Fixed Address, an Adelaide-based Aboriginal reggae band that had been creating quite a stir in Adelaide's small musical community.
>
> My first impression of the band, confirmed and strengthened by subsequent encounters, was of something possibly unique and undeniably powerful – a black Australian band playing original songs about themselves and their people. And although reggae is not a music native to this country (what form of contemporary music is?), No Fixed

Address have taken to it like a duck to water and USED it to get their message across. No Fixed Address look and sound like nobody else in my experience and they are the first band in a long, long time to send shivers down my spine. When they perform *We Have Survived (The White Man's World)*, the song that ends their set, it's as if a whole people are speaking out with pride and defiance, qualities that are not often heard from this country's original inhabitants.

For a whole lot of reasons, political, historical and musical, No Fixed Address is probably the most important new group in this country today. The voice that they speak with has been too often suppressed in the last two hundred years. It's about time it was heard.[3]

While that story was in preparation, No Fixed Address set off on their third trip to Melbourne. Although bedevilled by truck and PA problems, Ricky Harrison wrote in *Tjungaringanyi* that the tour was a positive learning experience:

One of the best things to come out of the tour was that people helped us out when we were struggling to make the best of what we had. Like the support we got from the FM station 3CR who gave us a lot of airplay and advertised our 'gigs' for us, and the Tagg Magazine who helped set up the 'gigs' and advertise them as well – Thanks.

Hard Times, the support band at the final show at Carlton nightspot Hearts, were the local community band in Fitzroy. They had played the inaugural Victorian Rock Against Racism concert at Storey Hall, Royal Melbourne Institute of Technology on 30 March 1980, with Matchbox, Lucky Dog, Sweet Jane and Bam-bu, and in Fitzroy, they played any community event that was happening.

The Hard Times line-up in mid-1980 was Peter Rotumah on vocals and guitar and three brothers from Morwell; Ian Johnson (bass guitar), Henry Thorpe (drums) and the youngest member, Wayne Thorpe (guitar), who had played with Ricky Harrison in Morwell band Black Satin. The band had started

No Fixed Address, Adelaide CBD, 1980.

Photo by Ian de Gruchy.

out playing covers but gradually added original material. '"Only a Few" became one of our main songs,' says Wayne Thorpe. 'Then "Stand Up and Fight for Your Rights", "Yellow Is Our Sunshine" – that was talking about the flag. Those were the three main ones at that time.

'We'd cater for the community. Back then, the pubs shut at 10 o'clock. So, we'd time our music set. We'd cater for the elders first. We'd start about 8 o'clock, play the country and western old-style for the elders. By 10 o'clock, the pubs would be shutting so a lot of the younger, rowdy mob would turn up. The elders would drift off home, some of them, and we would go into the rock'n'roll and the blues and that sort of louder music and play on till midnight.'

In early 1981 Hard Times packed up and went to Adelaide to enrol at CASM. 'I'm not sure how that came about,' says Wayne Thorpe. 'Being the youngest one, I was not a decision-maker in the band. I just jumped on board and followed the older brothers. Peter Rotumah could have been talking to No Fixed Address about CASM.' It seems highly likely.

~

In 1979 and 1980, Janie Conway joined a collection of female performers on a national tour. One of the songs she performed was Ricky Harrison's 'The Vision'.

'Hearing that song, "The Vision" … it just haunted me,' she says. 'The music haunted me. The lyrics were amazing. Looking back and thinking about those lyrics now, there's such a story of colonial oppression of Indigenous people. The images and the poetry of the lyrics that Ricky wrote and the poetry of the music as well, I really, really … I just loved it. So, I started singing it.

'At the same time as I started performing "The Vision", I was on this tour with Margret RoadKnight, Jeannie Lewis, Jan Cornall and Elizabeth Drake called *All Together Now*. When we went to Adelaide, I invited No Fixed Address along to the concert.'

Presented by 5MMM and the SA Public Radio Collective, *All Together Now* was staged at the Freemasons' Hall on North Terrace on Friday, 25 July 1980.

'I drove to the concert,' Conway remembers. 'I was either driving to the concert or maybe it was home from the concert that night. I know Bart was in the car; I think some of the others from the band were there too. We were in this car and the police pulled up alongside. And everybody in the car kinda froze and went, "Oh no. We're in for it now." And sure enough, the police pulled them over.

'I had never, ever seen police degrade people by their manner and their actions and their speech in my life ever before. I'd never seen it. I was angry, but I could see that they were just being very quiet and very good. Particularly Bart. They'd singled him out. And they kept calling him "boy" all the time. It was just shocking. Then they pulled me to one side and they didn't actually say these words but this is what they meant – "What's a nice white girl like you doing with these guys?" And I was like, "Well. I've just taken them to this concert where I've been performing. See over there ... [Conway pointed to her name on a poster] That's it. That's my name, that's me. And I'm doing one of their songs. So, I wanted them to see that." And they shrunk back from me. I don't know what they thought about me at that point. But when I was able to validate my personality or something ridiculous like that ... I felt really weird, because it was like my white privilege helped. It helped on the day and they didn't do any arrests. They were trying to goad one of them into talking back so they could arrest them for something or other. I could see it. It was so overt and so open. And then their attitude towards me because I was with them.

'Whatever I did, the police understood that it had importance and that, plus the fact that they weren't able to rile any of the others into talking back, meant they let us go. I've been in similar situations since then but that was my first actual experience of it. I was so angry about it for a long time afterwards. But it did teach me that when you're not interacting with it, it's hard to believe that anyone would do that. But they did. And right in front of my own very eyes. From my eyes, so to speak. I got a real lesson in what it was like.'

~

The previous month, Cold Chisel had hit town to play two nights (Friday 20 and Saturday 21 June) at Adelaide's premier rock spot, the Arkaba Top Room. The band's third album *East* had been released at the beginning of the month and was roaring up the charts. I hadn't interviewed the band before, but loved the album, and in the week leading up to the dates, I arranged for keyboard player and main songwriter Don Walker and singer Jimmy Barnes to be studio guests on my Friday evening 5MMM show *Rockzine* – a hour-long round up of music news and new releases. The interview went off without a hitch.

Cold Chisel next came to Adelaide on 8 August to play a show at Thebarton Town Hall. The August edition of *Roadrunner,* with No Fixed Address on the cover, was just back from the printers, and sometime on that Friday, I ran into Don Walker and showed him the magazine. He was immediately intrigued by my decision to run a cover story on an unsigned and relatively unknown Aboriginal band. I told Walker that No Fixed Address were playing a late spot that night at Hartley College in Magill. 'Would you like to go and check them out?' I asked. The timing was tight, but as Magill was only 25 minutes by car from Thebarton, doable. I think we caught three or four songs after the Cold Chisel show.

While the characteristically taciturn Walker didn't give too much away on the night, I am convinced that No Fixed Address's support slot on Cold Chisel's Summer Offensive tour six months later can be traced to that night in Magill.

15   COOKIE MONSTER

Once Ned Lander and Graeme Isaac secured funding from the Australian Film Commission, things moved up a gear. Through their networks and particularly contacts in the Sydney Filmmakers Co-operative, the duo started assembling a rather impressive production team.

'Many of the crew were filmmakers in their own right, mainly with a documentary background,' says Isaac. 'They were all working for $100 a week! Alec Morgan was the cook. Pat Fiske was the boom swinger; she went on to make a whole string of highly regarded documentaries on her own.'

'We had the fabulous Louis Irvine as cinematographer and Pat Fiske and Lloyd Carrick on sound and they were enormously supportive in helping us to work out how we could actually do things with no budget,' says Lander. 'You'd beg, borrow and steal locations and wardrobe and cars and everything else.'

The vacant Aboriginal Women's Home at 50-64 Sussex Street, North Adelaide was made available to the producers. When people started coming in, they moved into the hostel, which had been reconfigured as a living and working space. 'Pedro [Butler]'s father was a big knob in the Aboriginal Child Care Agency,' says Sherree Goldsworthy, 'in fact I think he ran it. We got that hostel and we all lived in there. It had bedrooms. We put the editing suite downstairs and we'd show the rushes there and there was a kitchen and we cooked and did all that.'

'I'm trying to remember some of the people that were in that hostel,' says Pedro Butler. 'It was a full-on turn-out. It was pretty chaotic. There were people around all the time. You can imagine getting a whole heap of blackfellas together and putting them into a place. It was hard trying to coordinate it all too. I don't think they really realised at the time how difficult that whole thing was going to be for them.'

'Well, they all moved in. They thought it was great,' laughs Isaac. 'Meals laid on and everyone giving them all this attention.'

'It was a very hectic time,' agrees Goldsworthy. 'You're looking for money; we didn't get all the money that Graeme asked for. I think some of the crew may have worked for deferred wages, share of profits, whatever you want to call it. Because everybody got the vibe. It was so exciting.'

By the time Alec Morgan got there from Sydney, the hostel was pretty much set up. 'I probably first met No Fixed Address by the fact these guys wandered in and tried to raid the fridge. I would stand in front of the fridge and they were pissed off with me because I'd say, "No, you can't just come in here and eat what you want." It was always a constant with those guys. They would come back from the pub or somewhere and they'd try to get into the fridge. Because we were on such a tight budget, I couldn't let them. That's how I got the name "Cookie Monster". From a curly-headed young smarty-arse Bart who was always smiling and making remarks. Us Mob were older, so I related to them a bit more. They were lovely guys. The two bands kept to each other. There was a lot of rivalry between them.

'I don't know how I cooked there, but I did. The kitchen was a little bit off from the main entrance, just to the side. I think people got the vibe that you weren't going to get any food when you came in, but you'd get good food when lunch came, or breakfast or dinner. But I went out on location and I think I had a little van, with a trailer and a two-burner cooker. They'd try to raid the fridge all the time. I'm not sure if we put a padlock on it. It was chaos.

'The dining room was off to the right of the kitchen. I would be cooking for crew and the bands and quite often Leila Rankine and her family. I always had to cook a lot more because you never knew who was going to turn up. There was that community sense that people wouldn't go hungry.'

'I think we ended up starting to shoot the film with about a third of the final budget in place, which you can't do these days,' says Lander. 'But I think people were really surprised at what they saw as we started making the film. It's a window into a world people hadn't seen.'

Filming Wrong Side of the Road. Bart Willoughby, Ricky Harrison and publican.
Photo by Carol Ruff.

'We were playing the action of the scenes in the sequence as written, but mostly the cast weren't learning lines,' says Isaac. 'They were ad-libbing, you know, but around the action of the scene as we had planned together. Except for some scenes that involved white actors, and in some specific scenes like the road bust which required more precision in coverage. A mixture of scripting and improvisation, but around an action that we all knew was predictable in its course.'

'There were moments where the whole madness of how film gets made, how it gets made in bits, somehow struck a comedic note for a lot of the guys,' says Lander. 'I remember they were very fascinated with the idea of continuity. Like someone might walk through a door in one T-shirt and come out the other side of the door in another one, because you'd shot them on different days and they'd changed their shirt and we hadn't spotted it because we didn't have a continuity person.'

'They were kids, and they used to muck around like kids too,' says Isaac. 'Like we had to get their clothes off them at the end of the day for continuity purposes for the shoot, so they used to think this was terribly amusing and hide stuff and say, "Ah." They never really worked out what it was all about until half, three quarters of the way through. I remember Les saying: "Why didn't you tell us that in the first place?" "Well, I fucking tried to, Les!" But they were kids. Well, the guys in Us Mob were older, but the No Fixed Address guys were so young.'

'I do remember Us Mob had a fight between two of them,' says Morgan. 'They came back from the pub, they were probably drunk and one of them said, "Don't hit me in the face, I'm on camera tomorrow" [laughs]. So, they took it seriously.'

'It started off pretty chaotic,' Bart Willoughby recalls. 'You've got all these whitefellas from Sydney, and all these blackfellas from Adelaide. The fellas from Sydney have a perspective and the people from Adelaide have a different perspective and these people from Sydney are literally travelling to another dimension. So, there's going to be a few clashes. The professional side of it is we've got to make this movie and we might have to go through a lot of shit to get this through. So, there was a lot of chaos, but we all understood what the whole thing was about. I think I punched a cameraman in the eye. But not the one he looks through [laughs]. I think it was a joking around kind of thing. Yeah, I was drunk, I might have slipped.

'I worked out there's more drugs, sex and rock'n'roll in bloody making films than the bloody rock'n'roll industry. Chris Haywood [renowned Australian actor, who played a policeman in the film] ... the first time we met him we had a dozen beers and I took him out and I think I stopped him getting bashed up twice. I think I had to carry him home, me and the drummer

Filming *Wrong Side of the Road*. Chris Haywood, Pedro Butler and Ronnie Ansell
Photo by Carol Ruff.

out of Us Mob, who's passed away now. Yeah, it was pretty chaotic.'[1]

'It might sound like we just sat back and filmed what was happening,' says Lander. 'That's not what happened at all. There were call sheets, there were scenes to be shot each day, there was stuff to do each day, that was pre-planned.'

'To coordinate all that together, making sure people were going to be there when they needed to be there, that was a nightmare for them guys,' says Pedro Butler. 'We were doing our stuff but knowing we had to turn up at certain times. Some of the stuff was actually shot at the hostel. Bart's scene, when he was in the training centre, that was shot there. We would get in cars and go where we needed to go. When we had to travel to Port Augusta, that was a bit of a nightmare for those guys, getting everyone organised. Making sure we were all gonna be where we had to be, on time.'

'Ned was pretty laid back,' says Morgan. 'Ned would be the last one wandering down for breakfast in the morning. He's pretty calm and cool, Ned. I only saw him get upset once, with this old white guy who couldn't deliver his lines after about fifty takes. Graeme was more an organiser of things as well. Things went pretty smoothly, given the lack of money and the huge amount of people there. I was impressed with Ned's handling of the whole situation. That calmness helped. He never got flustered very much. He just went with it, which was good directing.'

'It was a bit trying for Ned sometimes,' says Ricky Harrison, 'because being young fellas, sometimes we'd be messing around, joking around and he'd say, "You've gotta be serious here, cut it out." And we'd be pissing ourselves laughing. Because we'd never done a film before and we didn't know what to expect. And we got to know Ned a bit more and where he was at and how he went around doing things and using the cameras. It wasn't just a role; it was learning about how they did things on the set. In that way, we learned a lot from Ned.

'John Scott was the editor. He used to splice the rushes when they came in. He used to get the white chalk out, same with the recording studios back then, they'd put a white line down where you're going to cut the film. So, there was always heaps of film sitting on the floor. It was like watching a movie, except it was people you knew.'

'I remember John saying how difficult it was,' says Morgan, 'because people would just wander into the edit room and sit down and start telling him how to cut the film. And he'd never seen these people before. But I'd been with Gil Weaver and Essie Coffey on the roadshow and it wasn't as chaotic as that was. At least there was some organisation.'

'I went out on shoot quite a bit,' says Sherree Goldsworthy, 'but I stayed back and set the rushes and did the nightly screenings with John Scott. We got equipment from the SA Film Corporation and put it into the hostel. Everyone was helpful, there was lots of assistance. Once you're making a film and it's beginning to look credible, they're all helpful. We got a lot of support. A lot of pro bono. A lot of help and support from the SA film community.'

'Amazing time. Amazing time,' says Willoughby. 'It was the first time blackfellas and whitefellas worked together. It wasn't that they were shooting the community, which was us. The community was the movie. And I don't think there's ever been a movie like that ever since. Where the community's making the movie.'

The pressure did take its toll, though. 'Graeme and I were going through some hard times because it was just impossible trying to maintain a normal relationship,' says Goldsworthy. 'I had a child, a five-, six-year-old child. It was really strained to run a relationship while trying to run fucking No Fixed Address and Us Mob – and make a movie.'

Principal shooting was wrapping up by 30 September 1980. It was Ricky Harrison's 21st birthday. The crew organised a birthday party for him at the hostel and Alec Morgan baked him a cake. That evening No Fixed Address played with Uruguayan folk singer, guitarist, composer, and political activist Daniel Viglietti at the Union Hall, University of Adelaide in a fundraiser for the Committee for the Reconstruction of Nicaragua.

The final scenes were shot over the weekend of 8 and 9 November at the Point Pearce Aboriginal Community on Yorke Peninsula. No Fixed Address and Us Mob played a concert for the community, which was filmed for the movie.

~

Reflecting on the film, Ricky Harrison says, 'With a story like that I thought it was just going to be shown around probably ... I always had this thought in my head on a lower level of thinking. Back then when you're Aboriginal you see these things as community sort of things. To me it looked like that. Because it was too powerful; it was too Aboriginal, contemporary Aboriginal. Here's these people talking about what's happening and I can relate to it and I'm thinking, Jesus, this is what was happening back home. And it was really confronting for me. Because – you can't put this on film, can ya? Or can ya? [laughs]. Because of the songs we were writing, it made it more sort of easy to understand. It's not about being racist or being nasty, it's about showing people what it's like to live as an Aboriginal person, an urban Aboriginal person. It was a snapshot of 1980, that's how Aboriginal people were back then.'

'Manager' is too strong a word, but as well as doing *Roadrunner* and my 5MMM radio shows, in October 1980 I was helping No Fixed Address find gigs and was the point of contact when Cold Chisel's manager Rod Willis called. Willis offered No Fixed Address the support slot on four key dates of the upcoming Cold Chisel Summer Offensive tour. Gulp. 'Hey Rod, thanks, leave it with me, I'll get back to you.'

It helped that at the time *Roadrunner* was based in a shed out the back of the offices of G&S Management Services in King William Street, Kent Town. The firm provided financial and accounting services to Dirty Pool, Cold Chisel's management and booking agency. G&S provided the same support to Redgum and their manager Chris Gunn, and – way down the pecking order – *Roadrunner*.

Born out of a Politics and Arts project at Flinders University, Redgum was a political folk band with a strong Australian accent. The band's original songs hit a nerve with Adelaide audiences, and they recorded an album at the ABC that became a bestseller for Sydney folk label Larrikin Records. *If You Don't Fight You Lose* contains one of the best songs ever written about the Festival City, 'One More Boring Night in Adelaide'.

In late 1980 Redgum had signed a tape lease deal with multinational label Epic Records and released their second album *Virgin Ground*. Chris Gunn quit his job at the ABC to devote himself to management duties. The four band members also decided to go full-time professional.

The Cold Chisel dates offered to No Fixed Address were the opening night of the tour, at the University of New South Wales Roundhouse; a pub gig at the Family Inn in Sydney; Melbourne Showgrounds; and an outdoor show at the University of Adelaide. The fee offered was $500 per gig, all PA and lights supplied. When I put the offer to the band, I don't think there was any hesitation. With the benefit of Chris

Gunn's advice, fill-in dates in Melbourne and Canberra were organised, logistics were coordinated through G&S and the tour was locked in.

'No Fixed Address were doing something with Chisel,' says Redgum's front man, John Schumann. 'I remember thinking, "That's great, that's really good for them." Now Redgum had accounts with [airlines] TAA and Ansett. And a hire car account, which was a bit hard to get. I was one of the signatories on the accounts because I was a teacher and had a good credit rating and all that. I remember Chris Gunn came to me and said we need to get [No Fixed Address] a truck and we need to get them two hire cars for the tour. I just remember thinking, "Oh man, this could just go to fucking shit."

'I'd had nothing to do with Indigenous Australia apart from feeling all the left-wing – but absolutely genuine – things about the injustice, the immorality. On the other side, in those days there were blackfellas belting around the outback in these fucked-out cars and they would leave them there or they would roll them. It wasn't many years before that I had gone to the bush with two mates in a 1963 Ford Thames van. We went into the outback for three months. I wrote the song "The Last Frontier" about that. "There's a corrugated highway running north from Port Augusta/Lined with ratted cars that didn't rate a tow." Let me tell you, the ratted cars were more often than not blackfella cars that had rolled or fucked-out and they had just pushed them off the side of the road. So, I saw that, and that was really my only engagement with Indigenous Australia.

'I distinctly remember thinking, "You've gotta do this," but I remember saying to Bart or John, "You better not fuck these cars over." Because we had a really good reputation. We were the lefties, but we were responsible. I figured we could say as much as we liked about capitalist Australia as long as every other piece of our life was clean. We pay our bills, so fuck you. And I just saw this whole thing unravelling. I'm not sure that Avis or Budget or Thrifty, whoever it was, had any idea that their cars were going out with a blackfella band. I just do remember thinking, "This could all go to shit and if it's gunna go to shit it's gunna go to shit with my name on the contract." But it was all cool. It turned out great.'

Cold Chisel was the hottest band in the land at the time. Despite taking two months off in April and May to record *East*, the band had clocked up 122 gigs for the year prior to the start of the Summer Offensive tour. All across the country – from Sydney to Newcastle, to Brisbane, to Rockhampton, to Cairns, to Mt Isa, to Darwin, to Alice Springs, Perth, Whyalla, Adelaide, Broken Hill, Bendigo, Melbourne, Albury, Wollongong and back to Sydney – Chisel had been packing them in.

While Don Walker told me he doesn't recall seeing No Fixed Address play in Magill in August 1980, he does say, 'I strongly suggested to Rod and the Cold Chisel guys that we should take them out on the next tour.'

'Don Walker was the force that wanted the band on,' Willis confirms. 'No-one objected. It was, "Hey, yeah. Really cool, great idea." There was a definite social reason behind it and Don was driving it. I think the band saw themselves as outliers and Aboriginal people as outliers. We saw a lot of Aboriginal kids in Adelaide coming to shows. On the peripheral. They [the band] welcomed it.'

~

In the last week of November, the No Fixed Address touring party jumped into Redgum's hire cars and truck and headed to Sydney for the opening night of the Cold Chisel tour. Speaking to Stuart Coupe in the Sydney *Sun-Herald*, Bart Willoughby said saxophone player Veronica Rankine 'left the band recently'.[1] In fact, Veronica had become pregnant, so it was impractical for her to continue with what was fast turning into a nationally touring band.

Things got off to a rocky start in the Harbour City. 'I remember at the Roundhouse, we went to go to the back door,' recalls Willoughby. 'To go and do soundcheck. And the bouncer said, "What are you doing here?" And we said, "We're the band." And he said, "No you're not." And we said, "Yes, we are." And he said, "No you're not." And we said, "We have to do our soundcheck." And he said, "Well, you're not coming in here." So, we waited on the side there. And as Cold Chisel were walking past, Jimmy Barnes noticed us and came over. "What are youse doing here?" "That fella won't let us in." Jim Barnes went up and sacked him straightway.'

'Chisel were different,' says Les Graham. 'They were brought up with Aborigines. I knew Jimmy Barnes. He used to hang with my first cousin. They went to school together.'

'We'd never seen bigness,' says Willoughby. 'This was big. The highest level. At the Roundhouse, there were about six thousand people and half of them were bikies and skinheads. As we were going upstairs to the stage, Les, John and Rick were stopped. They were shitting themselves. I was at the bottom and I just pushed really hard. Forced them on from the back on to the stage. And as I pushed, they all got onto the stage and it was really quiet. I went "one, two, three". I think the first song was "From My Eyes". Then we did "The Vision". Then a couple of other songs. Then we did "We Have Survived". But after the first song, there was a big clap. And we keep playing. They just liked it. I think it was because we were playing it right, and they'd never heard that. And as we went along, they wanted more. And the crowd was saying, do one more, and Jim Barnes was on the side of the stage saying, "Yeah, do one more!" I think they weren't all bikies; I think they were Vietnam veterans. But what we didn't know was that we were the first band not to be canned off stage. Because every band that backed up Cold Chisel got canned off stage. Except us! [laughs].'

'The thing I remember most,' says Ricky Harrison, 'is we were sitting up there at the Roundhouse, me and John John. Les and Bart had disappeared – they always had their own place. Sitting on the second floor looking down at Cold Chisel playing. The guys brought in a couple of boxes full of grog and we're sitting there watching 'em play, and by the end of the show we went back inside and we thought, "Oh no, we've drunk all the grog." So, Ian Moss comes in and I go, "Brother, you're the best guitarist ever, but by the way we've drank all your grog" [laughs]. And he turns around and looks at me and wipes his face with a towel and tells the tour manager, "Go and get some more grog" and they brought four boxes full. So, we sat there and partied and had a good time.'

All the members of Cold Chisel were impressed. 'When they saw the band, they really liked the band,' says Rod Willis. 'They liked that they were different. And what they were attempting to do and probably the subject matter that they were singing. Seeing this white audience that was there for "Khe Sanh", see them warm to this band. Because they were really good players. The crowd really responded to them. I don't ever remember them not going down well. They fitted like a glove.'

Don Walker recalls the night vividly. 'I seem to remember there were three and a half thousand university students at the Roundhouse, and for them No Fixed Address might have been a band from Mars. I don't think there was any consciousness in those days on campuses anywhere of Indigenous issues. The most recent Indigenous music had been Jimmy Little in the '60s, before they were all born. No Fixed Address transfixed that crowd. They looked alien. They were not playing rock and roll. They were playing a powerful mutation of reggae, and every line of Bart's lyrics was searing through the PA at them. I'm getting all emotional remembering it.'

In Michael Lawrence's *Wild Colonial Boys*, Walker relates what happened immediately afterwards. 'Our support band No Fixed Address were nearly kicked out of the Roundhouse soon after they walked offstage – after wiping out three and a half thousand people.'[2]

What happened?

'I remember Jimmy [Barnes]'s missus going off at some racists in the bar,' says Ricky Harrison. 'Then us being stopped from going into the band room. Security didn't believe that we were the support band.'

Matt Bienstock, the band's former music tutor from CASM, attended the concert with his brother Sam, as guests of No Fixed Address and Cold Chisel. 'I knew that the guys were having some trouble with the bouncers, the security,' he says. 'And I had attempted to try and say, "Well, look, these guys … this is No Fixed Address. They're in the band, there's the poster, there's their name, there's their picture." And they were like, "Yeah, well, we have our orders, fuck off." And I tried to stay around and that was pretty much the last thing I remember. But I know the next day my brother and I woke up with fairly sore heads. We'd had a bit to drink, but it wasn't the booze. You know, a bottle of booze doesn't punch you in the stomach.'

Sam Bienstock remembers Chisel's management and the band being very apologetic. He had some doctor's bills and the security broke his glasses. Both bills were immediately refunded – no questions asked.

~

A fortnight later, back in Adelaide and again on Redgum's tab, No Fixed Address headed out of town in a hire car and truck to reconnect with the tour. This time Les Graham also took his own car, a 1960s Holden Monaro. First, the band travelled to Melbourne for a headline show on Saturday, 13 December at Collingwood's John Barleycorn Hotel. They then drove up to Sydney for a support slot the following Tuesday with Chisel at the Family Inn, Rydalmere.

The next date on the tour was in Melbourne two nights later. Chisel were heading straight there, but No Fixed Address was booked in to play a Wednesday night gig on the way, at the Australian National University in Canberra.

The morning after the Family Inn show, Chisel offered a lift to Canberra. No Fixed Address still had to get their cars to the capital, so Les Graham drove one and one of the crew the other. Everyone else climbed on the bus.

'I remember them sharing our van on a long drive west from Sydney,' says Don Walker. 'And that's the first time we really got to know each other. Through them we got to meet the guys in Us Mob, and I think we did gigs with them too.'

'So, we did the tour with Cold Chisel, but we didn't follow them,' says Bart Willoughby. '"Nah, you're coming on the bus with us." So, we toured with Cold Chisel in the same bus as them. And the guys would say, "No, put No Fixed Address live on again." And we'd go, "No – we want to hear Cold Chisel play" and they'd say, "No, we don't want to hear us, we want to hear you play." And we were like, "Wow, freaky."'

'As far as I know, No Fixed Address were the first band playing Indigenous political music,' says Walker. 'I could be wrong. There could easily have been a lot of stuff going on that I wouldn't know about. Coloured Stone, the Warumpis, the work that the Oils did and Yothu Yindi all came later.'

Phil Roberts was still in Adelaide and doesn't recall how it transpired, but he got the message that the band needed someone to do live sound at the Canberra gig. 'It was a university student gig. They played in a big hall,' says Roberts. 'They were very well received and everything, and then we had to drive to Melbourne.

'In fact, we were running late for the Chisel gig, the big gig at the showgrounds and we're running so late that I was driving. We had two cars and I was driving. Les had a Monaro or something. He was into revved cars and I was driving that and the only thing I could think of to do was to put my foot flat because we were running very late and these guys had no concept of what was happening. They were used to just getting to the gig when it was time to arrive.

'But we were going to be late for our spot so I put my foot down and just put it flat on the floor and drove for about three hours with my foot flat, and then the motor broke up. When we were about twenty minutes outside Melbourne, the car, it just flattened, it just burnt. It fucked his engine completely. A fact which he's never forgotten to this day. In fact, when I was in Adelaide, Graeme invited me to go to the night when they got put into the South Australian Music Hall of Fame. It was the first time I had seen Les since that time and before we had a chance to say anything, I said, "Les, I'm really sorry, I blew up your car." Because I knew that would have been on his mind. And he said, "It's all right, brother." By then he'd forgotten. But for a long time, he figured I owed him a car and I figured, well, he owed me for getting them to the Cold Chisel gig. So, we had to be towed. For the last twenty minutes, we were towed by the second car going about eighty miles an hour. So, that was pretty fucking … you know, that was a nightmare!'

The Melbourne show was at the Woodfull Pavilion at the Melbourne Showgrounds. 'And then the Cold Chisel gig of course, was … you know these gigs,' says Roberts. 'What happens is that their mixer, their sound man does the settings for their mix. And they'd leave their mix on those channels for their soundcheck and then they'd make marks for those and then they'd bring them down. I think it was before they were automated. They'd bring them down and say, "Okay" and then they put them up a very little bit, so that the support band doesn't get the kind of oomph that, you know … they weren't going to allow the support band to be as loud or as clear as the other band. So, I remember having to hassle with that, big time, because we hadn't got there in time for a soundcheck and so they came on and I just had to whack up the bass. Do this, do that, big time, in a hurry.

'I think they went down very well. From what I remember, I think people really liked them. I think they were a bit bemused at first, what these guys were doing but you know, they had very winning personalities and I think people gave them a big reception which was good. So, yeah, that's all I really remember, getting there extremely late and the copious amounts of cocaine that were being hoovered up backstage. The Cold Chisel road crew used to lay out these long, six, eight-inch lines on the table backstage. Bam, bam, bam, bam. And

Supporting Cold Chisel, University of Adelaide, 20 December 1980.

Photo by Eric Algra.

---

every time there was a guitar solo or something, Jimmy Barnes would rush backstage and hoover up a line and then if there was an encore, they all came out and hoovered up a line and then went back on stage. It was a nightmare, but I don't recall No Fixed Address becoming involved in that. Good for them.'

Three down and one to go and it was back to South Australia for the last of the support spots. With Les Graham's Monaro out of action, at least some of the band climbed on the Chisel tour bus for the trip home. They lobbed into Adelaide on Friday afternoon and Jimmy Barnes invited Bart Willoughby to come with him to see a band at the Arkaba Top Room that night. It also gave Willoughby the chance to check out the venue No Fixed Address would be playing the following night – they were booked into the late slot there after they had played the Chisel concert.

'Jimmy Barnes said, come and check this band from Sydney,' says Willoughby. 'It's a new band. So, Jimmy took me to the Arkaba. They have a DJ where people walk in to check out the band, a little DJ box. So, me and Jimmy Barnes are hanging out in there. And this young band that comes from Sydney pops out. Jimmy goes, check this band out. They're called Midnight Oil. They came out and they were a punk band more or less. Or sounded like punk. Even if he wasn't singing, he was still yelling. It didn't sound out of tune. And don't forget, I'm used to listening to Suzi Quatro and she's screaming really loud. Same with Slade. That singer was really loud too.'

After a daytime high of 37C, it was a warm and balmy Saturday night beside the River Torrens for the show on the Barr Smith Lawns at the University of Adelaide. After playing, Ricky Harrison remembers sitting on the lawns among the crowd watching Cold Chisel play. 'It was the first time playing with Chisel in Adelaide. The thing that sticks out was it was a home town gig with one of the best bands around. Veronica [Rankine] was with us then. She played that show.'

Harrison acknowledges the boost the Cold Chisel dates gave to the band. 'It was good; they really looked after us. They gave us the opportunity to perform before audiences that we never would have at that stage. Helped to introduce us.'

Bart Willoughby thinks their acceptance by the Cold Chisel crowd was reflective of people at the time approaching things with an open mind. 'We were thinking,' he says. 'That era then, the Australian people were thinking. They're not blocked in their minds. Yeah. '74, '75, Vietnam's finished. Suddenly from '75 to the '80s we're all thinking. So, I think it was a time when people could actually think about stuff and everybody's listening. So, it was a pretty amazing time.'

~

Once the Cold Chisel tour had finished, I asked Redgum's manager Chris Gunn if he would be interested in taking No Fixed Address under his wing. He was agreeable and when I put it to the band members, they accepted the offer.

'Redgum was going to be the key band [for Gunn],' says John Schumann. 'There was always going to be other people he was going to pick up along the way, although he was always circumspect in what he told me. Because I was of the view that there was more than enough to do with Redgum without having our management focus diluted.

'So, Chris was offered a room at G&S Management in Kent Town, with Phil Gerlach and Greg Stephens. He really didn't want to work from home anymore. This was where Chris decided he was going to branch out a bit. Redgum were on the way. Then No Fixed Address came.'

With the extra workload this entailed, Gunn approached Mary Stutters to join his management agency. Stutters had been running fundraising gigs for public radio station 5MMM, but after run-ins with the women's collective there was looking to move on. 'Chris picked me up because I'd worked with bands in a practical way,' she says. A bonus was that Stutters had worked on *Wrong Side of the Road* as a production assistant, so she and the members of No Fixed Address knew each other.

Attending a protest for land rights in Tamworth, Madeline McGrady spotted someone shooting with a video camera. 'I said, "Oh that looks interesting!"' she told NITV in 2018.[1] 'And I had a go right there. From then on, I was hooked.' After moving to Sydney, McGrady quickly connected with the Sydney Filmmakers Co-op and the Indigenous creative community in Redfern. With five children, and no money for film school, McGrady worked full time while she learned her craft.

'My daughters were around and they'd heard of this band called No Fixed Address,' she says. 'They'd been to Adelaide and had gone to see some art shows and bands and stuff. I got to meet them [No Fixed Address] a bit later, when they were stepping out and came to Sydney. The other band, Us Mob, came as well. They were doing it pretty tough and they didn't have anyone to back them or anything. Us Mob stayed with me for a few weeks when I was living in Canterbury. They were just looking around to do some work. Didn't have any support or network. But No Fixed Address – everybody was talking about them at the time.'

McGrady had been one of the key people in the formation of Sydney's Rock Against Racism Committee in late 1980. 'I was at the cinemas up in Paddington one day and these two young guys came in to see me,' she recalls. 'They said they were suffering a lot of racism. They were young guys, around twenty, twenty-one. It was in their workplaces as well. They didn't know where to go or what to do. So, I said, come back next week and we'll have a meeting. I met with them first for the next few weeks. Then I called some other people in, down the track. And basically, that's how it all started. We had a fantastic breakthrough with the bands. We didn't think at that time that we'd get the support that we did.'

Taking its cue from the successful Rock Against Racism concerts in Melbourne, the Rock Against Racism Committee started planning a Sydney event. The committee was chaired by Tiga Bayles who had established an Indigenous arts agency called Murri Jama and was in the process of setting up the Indigenous radio station Radio Redfern.

One of the (white) members of the Rock Against Racism Committee was Peter Gray, a sometime band manager and concert promoter from Brisbane who had been politicised by the anti-Vietnam War movement and the anti-apartheid protests over the Springbok rugby tour. 'Rock Against Racism was a combination of music with the political, so in this sense it was a good fit for me and where I was at in the early 1980s,' he says. 'The Rock Against Racism Committee was a hundred per cent Aboriginal controlled, primarily by the Watson family, particularly Tiga Bayles. His mother, Maureen Watson, and his brother, Johnny Bayles, attended meetings from time to time and were always present in the background, stepping forward to help in various ways. Madeline McGrady was the other major influence in the Rock Against Racism Committee.'

The first Sydney Rock Against Racism concert took place in the Sydney Town Hall on 26 January (Australia Day/Invasion Day) 1981. It was advertised as 11 hours of music (with ten bands) and ran from 11 am to 11 pm. No Fixed Address and Us Mob were joined by Redfern legends Black Lace and a bunch of non-Indigenous bands (Un Tabu, Motoco, The Singles, Street Level, The Joe Casey Band, Metro and Teenie Weenie).

Janie Conway was there helping out. 'During 1979–80, I moved up to Sydney,' she says. 'I only lasted a couple of years because I found the music scene in Sydney much more disparate. I got involved in Rock Against Racism through Peter Gray. He asked me if I could do band liaison. There were ten bands on that line-up and there was nowhere for the band members to go and tune up or do anything. So, being a musician, I quickly organised a space for them. Then my job was to go around and ask permission for them to be filmed. I started to think, "I can help Rock Against Racism do this a lot better. They just don't know about organising concerts and I do." So, I can help. That's how I got involved.'

The concert was filmed and recorded (as were all the Sydney Rock Against Racism shows) and seven hours of footage is deposited in the National Film and Sound Archive. The set by No Fixed Address included a clutch of original songs – 'Feel So Lonely', 'Fight for Your Rights', 'From My Eyes', 'Get A Grip' and 'Greenhouse Holiday'. In contrast, Us Mob's set was peppered with covers, including Van Halen's 'Ice Cream Man', Jimi Hendrix's 'Purple Haze', Bachman Turner Overdrive's 'Let It Ride', Chuck Berry's 'Little Queenie' and 'Honky Tonk Woman' by the Rolling Stones.

Madeline McGrady's motivation for filming the concert (and the two others later in the year) was clear. 'I wanted to record it, for the future of our kids. That's basically what I did it for. If I had a camera, I would record everything and everyone. I've still got heaps of stuff in my shed! For the next generation. I would have loved to have seen a film come out of that. It was so hard because we didn't get any support from government or anybody at the time. But it was just a great time and a great experience. Helping to break down those barriers of racism was part of it as well.'

Us Mob decided to make the move to Sydney. 'There was more opportunity at that stage in Sydney than there was in Adelaide,' says Pedro Butler. 'We knew it was going to be difficult because as soon as you say you're an Aboriginal band, it was difficult getting shows. We ended up playing a lot of rallies, political rallies and stuff like that.'

After initially staying a few weeks with Madeline McGrady and her family, Us Mob based themselves in Glebe. 'That was the in place,' says Butler. 'There were a lot of musos around there. [Cold Chisel bass player] Phil Small just lived round the

----

Opposite: Bart Willoughby, Festival Theatre, Adelaide, 10 February 1981.

Photo by Eric Algra.

corner in Glebe Point Road. I met up with this sheila who lived in a house with a couple of the Sunnyboys. We started getting around and getting to know a few people. Took a while to get into the circle of things.'

There may have been more opportunity in Sydney, but it was an incredibly competitive scene. A scan of the gig guides of the time shows that on any Friday or Saturday night, there were more than 150 venues and more than 200 bands – including all the big names of the time. It was difficult to get a break for any band.

'Unless you had a record out so people would recognise you, it was a struggle to get anywhere at that time,' says Butler. 'Towards the end, we started getting shows at a few of the pubs. Bondi and places like that. But there wasn't a great deal of those. Tiga Bayles was managing us at the time and them guys, their whole thing was political. We couldn't escape that political side of things. We were caught in that and it was difficult trying to separate yourself from that side and just be musos playing rock'n'roll.

'At the same time Ronnie [Ansell] was very up front with the Aboriginal side of our thing, the injustices and that sort of stuff. We had to say something about our situation, but we didn't want to get pigeon-holed. But we did anyway. That was just the way it was going to be. An Aboriginal band, you sing a song like "Genocide", you've automatically put yourself into that mould.'

~

Back in Adelaide, No Fixed Address was one of the six finalists in the 5SSA-FM Summer Search talent contest held at the Festival Theatre on 10 February. Stephen Hunter, writing in the *Advertiser*, was perplexed at the outcome.

> The bass player who accepted the winner's cheque for Safari Set at the recent Summer Search competition had reason to be humble.

Few people could believe his band had won the prize, just minutes after No Fixed Address had won the crowd with a crisply performed set of brilliant originals that sounded streets ahead of any other band.[2]

'That Battle of Bands where we came second,' Bart Willoughby remembers. 'The crowd went for us but ... first time we saw a little bit of prejudice, I think. Or rigged. I think more rigged.'

No Fixed Address may not have impressed the judges, but they did impress someone in the audience. Shortly afterwards, Chris Gunn received an invitation for the band to appear at a Royal Charity Performance to be held at the Festival Theatre on 23 April during the visit of the Prince of Wales to Adelaide.

~

Bart Willoughby with didgeridoo, Festival Theatre, Adelaide, 10 February 1981. Photo by Eric Algra.

Once filming had finished in November 1980, Ned Lander and the rest of the Sydney-based crew headed back to the Harbour City. Graeme Isaac followed in early 1981, by which time the film had found its name. *Wrong Side of the Road* was one of the songs Pedro Butler had written for the film and Isaac says it almost picked itself. 'We had originally wanted to find a title that was not identified with a particular band, but it was such a strong and appropriate title that we could not go past it.'

In Sydney, Isaac and Lander had to hustle for the funds to complete the movie. 'We only went into the shoot with the budget for a short film and were only shooting on 16mm,' says Isaac. 'So, we blew the budget out shooting to feature length. Spent all of our post-production money, which was labs, sound editing and everything else ... that was where a lot of the budget was in those days, because it was film, not digital. Laboratory processes were very expensive.'

'We had to go to find the money to finish the film,' says Lander. 'That was quite a complicated process. John Scott did an extraordinary job of editing the film because it was chaotic making it and it didn't always conform to the script perfectly. Trying to make it all make sense ... some people would probably argue it still doesn't make sense ... it was a big job. We finished everything in Sydney, although John was assembling scenes from the very beginning of shooting. We were constantly doing things like putting little scenes together to show people to keep trying to ... keep the money coming in.'

Isaac and Philip Roberts remixed the film soundtrack and accompanying album at Studio 301, in Sydney. 'The engineer for the final mix was Chris Curtis, Christo,' says Isaac. 'He was really the gun engineer at Studio 301, which was the top recording studio in Sydney. His contribution was really significant.'

When the final mixes of the songs on the *Wrong Side of the Road* album were completed, Phil Roberts played them to the two bands separately. 'I remember presenting them to the two bands. It was different. You know, I took them along to Us

Mob and played them their mixes on an occasion when they were tripping on acid. Oh God. And I had to play them their album, which could have gone either way. Anyway, I played it and yeah, they thought it was really good. They played it really loudly and afterwards the one guy [Ronnie Ansell] says to me, "Roberts, you're fucking lucky." Because he would have beaten the shit out of me if I hadn't got it right! He had already broken my ribs by that stage on the filming.'

'They're new Royal showmen with a message in song', ran the page three headline in Adelaide's morning newspaper on 22 April 1981. Underneath was a photo of No Fixed Address – the four members standing, with Les Graham propped on his guitar and Bart Willoughby leaning on a didgeridoo and holding a pair of drumsticks. Willoughby told the *Advertiser* the band had no wish to offend Prince Charles by singing about the plight of Aboriginal people at the Royal Charity Performance the following night, '... but I hope he learns something from our words. We would like him to understand a bit of our message.'[1]

The royal tour was first flagged in June 1980, ostensibly for the Prince of Wales to open the 50th anniversary convention of the Apex Clubs of Australia. But interest in the visit was turbocharged when, on 24 February 1981, Buckingham Palace announced the engagement of the heir to the throne to Lady Diana Spencer.

After visiting New South Wales, Victoria and Tasmania, Prince Charles was met at Adelaide airport on Thursday, 23 April, by the State Governor Keith Seaman before being whisked off to Government House on North Terrace. Security around the Prince was tight, with large numbers of uniformed police and members of the STAR Force in evidence. On the short walk down King William Road to the Festival Theatre, the Prince mingled with crowds before running a gauntlet of about 40 demonstrators supporting Bobby Sands, a member of the Provisional IRA on hunger strike at the Maze Prison in Northern Ireland. Sands was leading the protest against the withdrawal of political status for convicted paramilitary prisoners.

After a reception at the Festival Theatre, the Prince settled into his comfy seat for the evening's entertainment. Hosted by actor and singer Barry Crocker, the line-up included the David Atkins Dancers, pop songbird Christie 'Goosebumps'

Rocking the Royal, April 1981.

Photo by News Ltd/Newspix.

Allen, dancer and choreographer Sir Robert Helpmann, the indestructible Julie Anthony, crooner Kamahl and opera singer June Bronhill.

Backstage at the theatre, No Fixed Address were allocated two dressing rooms near to the stage. The band members were just settling in to the larger one of the two when one of June Bronhill's entourage poked his head through the door.

'He asked us if they could use the dressing room next to ours, to put their stuff in,' says Les Graham. 'Her dressing room was over the other side of the Festival Theatre and ours was closer to the stage. We had two rooms, but we were only using one, so we said, "Yeah, no worries."' Shortly after 9 pm, as the band was preparing to go on stage, two Federal Police officers entered the No Fixed Address dressing room. A sum of $200 had gone missing from June Bronhill's room. Did the band know anything about it? No.

The band then went on stage and performed 'Black Man's Rights'. When they finished and came off, they were met by two police detectives. The detectives proceeded to search the band's dressing room, against the express wishes of tour manager Linda Samson and Mary Stutters from the band's management agency.

'I was shocked at what went down,' recalls Stutters. 'I did actually speak briefly with June [Bronhill] and she just seemed like a complete bloody fruitcake. I mean, who in the world would bring that amount of money into a concert, for crying out loud? But it really was an outrageous accusation and the police behaved in an appalling way.'

The police allegedly found Ricky Harrison's name tag in the room that was gifted to Bronhill and detained and searched him in the band's dressing room. One of the police commented, 'We could have made it a lot harder. We could have dragged him offstage.' The police's attitude changed once the forced search of the dressing room yielded no sign of the money, however. As they beat a hurried retreat, one of the detectives said, 'It's obvious the complaint is unfounded. You probably won't hear from us again.'

As a result of the backstage incident, the band missed the curtain call for all the performers. 'We were waiting at the side for our name to be called and it wasn't called,' says Les Graham. 'Because they thought we were dishonest. We were destroyed.'

Eventually Festival Centre ushers managed to extricate the band members and escorted them to the reception for artists in the Festival Banquet Room. 'But at the after-party, Prince Charles wanted to meet us,' says Graham. 'He asked why we didn't take a bow at the end. He asked where we were all from. And he was really interested in the didgeridoo.'

June Bronhill later found the 'missing' money. 'She found the money in a drawer,' says Graham. 'And there was a small item in *The Advertiser* saying she'd found it. But we were accused, and the cops were called and it was all over the papers.'

~

The royal theme continued when No Fixed Address headed to Victoria the following week as support to management stablemates Redgum. Including a not-so-subtle plug for their current album, the flyer for the tour opened:

> Redgum, with the nation of Australia and its media, have been affectionately observing the mating dance of The Prince of Wales.
>
> Like loyal Australians, Redgum are delighted by his choice, and note with pleasure he will soon cultivate virgin ground.
>
> In keeping with the general delirium of the Commonwealth's celebrations, Redgum proudly and loyally announce The Royal Engagement Tour.

The run of dates opened with a special 3CR Mayday concert at Melbourne's Dallas Brooks Hall on Friday, 1 May, with Margret RoadKnight also on the bill with the two bands. That same night the Royal Charity Performance recorded the previous week was screened nationally on the Seven network.

Previewing the program in Melbourne's morning newspaper *The Age*, television critic Rita Erlich described some of the performers and performances ('nicely-groomed' compere Barry Crocker; *Countdown's* Queen of Pop Christie Allen, looking 'very respectable'; and Sir Robert Helpmann with an 'amusing' talk about South Australia's impact in arts and entertainment), before turning her attention to No Fixed Address.

> It is curious to find how everything is tailored to the variety formula. The Aboriginal group, No Fixed Address, sings about the need to fight for rights and the audience applauds as politely as if they had presented a number from *The Sound of Music*. No Fixed Address is very different from the other performers on the show, with an enclosed style, as if they would be playing the same way even if there were no audience.[2]

John Schumann always felt the combination of the two bands was an ill-fitting one. 'I didn't think that Redgum's crowd, who were basically middle-class lefties, were going to respond to [No Fixed Address's] music,' he says. 'Ideologically and politically, it was a good fit. Lyrically and musically, it wasn't. And I never liked support bands anyway. I was always worried that someone was going to take our schtick and do it better. It wasn't a conscious thought; just a vague unease with support bands. But we were meticulous that everything we had, they had. Dressing room, beer, lights, PA – we were never one of those bands that said, "You can't use the drum riser." I just thought that was shit.'

The relationship between No Fixed Address and Chris Gunn would not prove to be a long-lasting one. 'Chris had the contacts and the skills but I don't think he had the emotional connection with them,' says Mary Stutters. 'It was a bit like me too. I was ten years older than them. They were always nice and pleasant to me, and I hope I did the right thing by them in terms of the gigs I organised for them. But they were a bunch of lads. So, I did what I had to do to make sure they got the work and they got paid rather than be their mate.'

'I do remember them being at the gigs, but I never really bonded with any of them,' says Schumann. 'It was just like two different worlds. It wasn't any reluctance on either side of the equation, but when I look back now, we had no idea what their lives were like. Backstage it was very polite but there was no brotherly engagement.'

By the winter of 1981, No Fixed Address was performing a clutch of Ricky Harrison's songs that were, in his description, angrier than Bart Willoughby's, 'more in people's faces; in the punk style'.

'When we started off, we were doing covers and Bart wrote the first political song, "From My Eyes",' says Harrison. 'I think I wrote "Stand Up" after that. That was my first political one. To me, when I look back, Bart wrote from his perspective as a Stolen Generations incarcerated in the white man's system. Mine are more about black people's struggles on the outside, about the hardships we faced living everyday as Aboriginal people.'

Harrison had experienced racism growing up as a teenager in his hometown of Morwell, but it wasn't until he moved to Adelaide and joined CASM that the realisation dawned that the practice was so widespread.

'I thought it only happened in Morwell … in Victoria, because other people in Melbourne experienced racism,' he says. 'But when I got to Adelaide, I started listening to other people's stories as well. They were still experiencing racism over there. I found this was happening all over Australia, not just us in our country.'

When Harrison was a teenager, he had attended a camp where for the first time he heard white people talking about land rights and how Aboriginal people should have land back. 'I thought, right, white people are the ones pushing for this, not so much Aboriginal people. They're trying to help Aboriginal people and Aboriginal people haven't got the mindset to do all this. But of course, I never heard what happened in '67 or the tent embassy in Canberra. That was all kept from us. I

Opposite Ricky Harrison.

Photo by Carol Ruff.

heard some stuff but the press was calling them radicals and all this. It wasn't something they put on TV and spoke about it in glowing terms like these people in the camp were talking about.

'When I went to Adelaide there were these blackfellas who were pushing for the same things these white people had been talking about. Land rights and all this. That we have all these rights and racism was a really bad thing, and no, we don't have to endure all this shit. People like Auntie Leila [Rankine] and Auntie Vonnie [Veronica Brodie]. And seeing what Mulla [Basil Sumner] was doing and his brother, out in the community and doing stuff. I ended up going to one of the meetings at the community centre in Wakefield Street. Just seeing everyone coming together and talking about the future and what they wanted to do. And I could see all these organisations around. In Morwell there's only one. And basically, when I went to Melbourne, I would just be hanging out at the pub. Whereas in Adelaide they were a lot more organised. A lot of people were into Aboriginal rights.'

Not only were Aboriginal people more organised and active, but there had been almost a decade of a state government, the Dunstan Labor government, that was sympathetic to Aboriginal issues.

'Dunstan, yeah,' says Harrison. 'It was really strange to see some white guy basically pushing for Aboriginal rights. It was a big thing for me. It made me feel more comfortable too, about writing songs. Usually, you would shy away from stuff like that because of the consequences and all that. I guess when you know the government is behind you and they're willing to stand up for Aboriginal rights, it makes things a lot easier to put down on a piece of paper and talk about ... basically I was just talking about things that were happening to me and how I felt about it. And it came out angry because I was angry. It wasn't about surviving or being black because I knew that. And I knew that we had survived; it was more, "I'm gonna get you and this is how I'm gonna get you. Youse are a bunch of cunts" [laughs]. Talking to the federal government, the people who were the main actors, the racism rants and all this, it was in response to all that.'

Harrison finally had the environment in which he could express or articulate his anger. 'Yeah, that's right,' he says. 'Because we had that support, not only from Auntie Leila but from the tutors, Graeme Isaac and that. And when Ned [Lander] came along and Phil [Roberts], they were really keen on getting all the music and the words recorded.'

How Many Voices (Ricky Harrison)

You stand up and you talk about the great country we live in
Then you stand up and speak about your so-called justice
Then you stand up and you rave about what's right and what's
  wrong
Does it make you feel so proud to be white?

How many voices have spoken out?
How many times did we have to shout?
How many backs have been turned?
How many years have we learned?
How much longer do we have to fight against racism

You speak about the land of your ancestral heritage
You speak of how they fought
How they struggled and died
You speak of the torment and hardship and the pain
Yet you laugh at black people doesn't it make you feel ashamed

How many voices have spoken out?
How many times did we have to shout?
How many backs have been turned?
How many years have we learned?
How much longer do we have to fight against racism

Then you listen to black people with closed ears
Of how we were murdered for over 200 years
You seem to ignore our doubts and our fears
But you know that I'm black and my people are still here

'How Many Voices' was a song inspired by Harrison's experience working as an apprentice gardener for the council in Morwell. 'The people that I worked with had a lot of ignorance about Aboriginal people,' he says. 'They basically didn't know anything. The guy that I worked with, he was Dutch. He was our boss, looking after the apprentice gardeners. He was in the Dutch army and he got locked up by the Nazis in a camp in Holland. He thought Australia was a really good place to be. He didn't have anything good to say about Aboriginal people. How he saw things and from what he was told, he thought they were lazy black people who did nothing. That the government was trying to help us and trying to do everything right by us.

'He came in and was talking to me and this other apprentice, Ross. We were sitting in the room behind the toilets there. This is outside so there's all my people scattered at the back of the park, beyond this wall. That's where they all drank. And I'm sitting there thinking, "No, the reason we drink in the park is because we can't get into the fucking hotels." Even today they sit in the park. They don't want to go in the hotels because of the racism that used to happen.

'I remember in the '70s I used to go in there, when I was working as an apprentice gardener and they'd go, "We're not serving you." And I'd go, "Why not?" And they said, "Because one of the Abos fucked up in here. So, you're not allowed to drink in here anymore. Because you're an Abo" [laughs bitterly]. And that was like, "Bullshit!" Those bouncers were really bad too. One of them punched my sister in the face, broke her teeth. They had a really bad attitude towards Aboriginal people in the pub. They let us in eventually. Someone complained. They went to the legal service back in the '70s. And brought up the

Anti-Discrimination Act. In the '80s they were still doing the same thing. Getting people locked out of the pubs.

'That song "How Many Voices" is written about that sort of era. How people stand up and talk about how great their country is when Aboriginal people are being treated like shit. Mum always told me, "We own this country. This is our country. This belongs to the Gunai people. It doesn't belong to the white man." We were all locked up in the missions and kept away from everything while they stole our land. That's where I come from. That's where the angriness comes from. We're still experiencing this racism and all this, but it was like a propaganda thing, I guess. Like Nazis were using propaganda to make the Jews look like they were the rich people, they owned a lot of businesses. Same as the Aboriginal people. They owned all the land and the wealth of the land and still today we can't get any of it. So, they were trying to give us the mindset that we were bludgers, living off the white man. That he owned everything and was basically God. That attitude towards us that we were basically nothing compared to them. That black people were shit. And that's how I grew up, trying to overcome all that crap. But I knew from what Mum was telling me that it was all lies anyway.'

All Because (Ricky Harrison)

Talk about a black man but you wouldn't know all the shit
  that's been laid on us
And you speak about unity but you don't even know the
  meaning of humanity

But do you know why we feel so useless
Do you know why we have to live so
Do you know why we are so sceptical
Do you know why we are political

All because what the white man say go
All because what the white man say go
All because what the white man say go

You crap about politics but you wouldn't even know all the
  danger your government put you in
And you rave about security but you don't even realise your
  insanity

But do you know why we feel so useless
Do you know why we have to live so
Do you know why we are so sceptical
Do you know why we are political

All because what the white man say go
All because what the white man say go
All because what the white man say go

Talk about a black man but you wouldn't even know if your ass
  is burning
When you learn about reality then you'll know just how a black
  man feels

But do you know why we feel so useless
Do you know why we have to live so
Do you know why we are so sceptical
Do you know why we are political

All because what the white man say go
All because what the white man say go
All because what the white man say go

'"All Because" is very much about the same stuff as "How
Many Voices",' says Harrison. 'It talks about "white privilege"
they call it nowadays. I changed the words, because in the
beginning I was talking about white purity and how people
see themselves as being in this environment where the
government protects them against everything. But at the

same time, they're only in it for themselves. When you look at what's happening overseas, I think that's more "Stand Up" as well. That environment, the nuclear age as well, the Cold War. I didn't actually come out and say it, but you rave about security, but you don't realise the danger the government puts you in. It's talking about uranium and stuff like that. The way I put the words together, it was more about us being left out of the whole political agenda. We didn't have a say in what was happening in the government or what was happening in Australia. We were left out of all the decision making.'

~

Harrison recalls the band performing 'Stand Up', on their Northern NSW tour in January 1980. 'In the song, instead of it being "Stand up black brothers/Let's fight for our rights/And not be taken in by lies", originally, I was singing, "Stand up black brothers/Let's fight for our rights/And not be taken in by whites" [laughs]. I was playing it at some bikie place, in someone's back yard practising. As I was playing it this bikie walked back in with this funny look on his face and I thought, "Hang on, that must have freaked him out" [laughs]. We used to hang out with bikies back then. Les's friends. So, anyway, I changed the words to "lies", to make it a bit less confronting for audiences. But it would have had the original words when we toured Northern NSW. I think I changed it after that.' Harrison also changed 'black brothers' to 'black people' in more recent times.

Stand Up (Ricky Harrison)

In the year '79 the law had come to pass
By the government ministers mining on black land
For the taking of uranium the price is too high
Robbing black people then how the hell will we survive

Stand up black people and let's fight for our rights
And not be taken in by lies
Stand up black people lets show them how it's done
Then the world will know that we are one and all

They talk about the invasion of Afghanistan
Yet they themselves invade on black land
They'll listen to whatever racists demand
They don't care if you're a Blackman

Stand up black people and let's fight for our rights
And not be taken in by lies
Stand up black people let's show them how it's done
Then the world will know that we are one were all

'There was a lot of anger in my words. They were coming out and sounding to me like I was being racist [laughs]. And I didn't want to do that because I'm fighting against that. In the words, I'm being that. That's what I felt like and that's why I changed my words in the songs as I went along. I didn't want to freak too many people out. They're more for them to listen to and try to understand where we were coming from. So, when I wrote a song, I kept that in the back of my mind.'

~

While Harrison would sometimes tweak the words to his songs if he felt they were coming on too strong, that wasn't the case with the lyrics to his angriest and most confrontational song, 'Pigs'.

Pigs (Ricky Harrison)

They kick you off the streets
They tell you they keep the peace
They watch you like dogs on heat
Unjustifiable police

You gotta watch yourself
You gotta protect yourself from the pigs

They're always on the move
They call them the boys in blue
They'll kick you in the head
Until they kick you dead

You gotta watch yourself
You gotta protect yourself from the pigs

They're always on the prowl
They're trying to get you now
They'll follow you around
Until they get you down

You gotta watch yourself
You gotta protect yourself from the pigs

They're always on the bust
They're people you shouldn't trust
They love to watch you fight
They don't respect your rights

Pigs leave our people
Pigs leave our people
Pigs leave our people
Pigs leave our people

'When it came to the police, it was a different story. Because I know that with the pigs, the police, they deserve everything that they get because they're up front about everything and they're always in your face. Whereas with white people generally, they weren't always like that. It was only those few that were running things mainly that had that really bad attitude. So, the police, I saw them all as basically being the same. But also, with the magistrates too. They were really racist, had racist attitudes. When you go before the court, you're guilty regardless. Doesn't matter what you say. Because the cops make up their own story anyway. The judge believes the cops.

'You go before the judge and you stand there and the judge says ... even here in Morwell when I was doing my apprenticeship, I was sitting on the bus with one of my mates and he pushed me off my seat. There was a cop on the bus. So, we both got in the shit. The next day in court, the judge said, "I'm going to make an example of you for your people" and all this. It's got nothing to do with my people. Joe just pushed me out of my seat on the bus and that was it. I got probation. I was only seventeen then. He was like, "You're a representative for your people." I was no representative for nobody. Because I worked on the council, they would all see me there, the only blackfella working on council and I was supposed to be a representative for my people and be this role model. Pig's arse. I was just working and that was it as far as I was concerned. It had nothing to do with my people. But this magistrate took it that way and, "You're a role model so I'm going to put you on probation and if you fuck up, you'll go to jail." And for what? Because my mate pushed me off my seat on the bus? I was really pissed. Make an example of me, for what? For doing nothing. Anyway, we both got locked up, but because I was Aboriginal, they said, "We'll give you two years jail if you muck up again." So, it's not just the cops, it's the magistrates as well.

'Back in the '90s, early 2000s, the magistrate down here in Morwell, he was pretty good. He had a compassion for Aboriginal people, I guess. It was really something. It was a bit different for me to see. He was down the pub drinking with blackfellas. When I went before him at the Magistrates' Court, he just looked at me and said, "I'll just put you on probation." For a year, six months or something. I'd been drink driving. So, I just did my work thing, community service, there was nothing he was worried about. Any past things I'd done were not even on the agenda. I had a little bit of a record, but not much. Mainly stealing cars [laughs]. When you're young, it's like stealing the horse, the white man's horse [laughs]. It's like an initiation for blackfellas. A lot of the older youngfellas did that. They would steal a car to prove their manhood. Like stealing a horse back in the old days. When I think about it now, it's like "Oh my God, did I used to do that?" Because I own a car now and I hope nobody steals my car [laughs].

'Anyway, we got past all that, eventually. And that's one of the reasons I changed my name. Because they were looking for me in Victoria. We used to get into a lot of different activities when we were young to stuff the system up, to get back at the system, to try to even the score. To make us feel better about ourselves and knowing they're going to suffer for it. Nothing too heavy. Maybe just break into a shop or something. Smash the window up and steal some smokes [laughs].'

Harrison adopted the name Chris Jones in 1981, around the time of No Fixed Address's appearance at the Royal Charity Performance in Adelaide. His car stealing exploits almost had major consequences down the track. But by that time, he didn't go by the name Ricky Harrison anymore.

In Sydney, post-production on *Wrong Side of the Road* was almost complete when Graeme Isaac and Ned Lander ran into a last-minute financing problem.

'We managed to raise the additional funds we needed to complete post-production at feature length and to blow up from 16 mm to 35 mm to allow for a proper cinema release,' says Isaac. 'In those days at least, you could get away with breaking the rules as long as in the end you had something good to show for it. And we knew that we did. Film making is a bit more bureaucratic now, but they were the cowboy days.

'So, we had to hustle, we had to get a good film cut that was going to be strong enough for the film to win its own way through. It nearly didn't actually. It nearly got closed down for another reason but yeah, that was a difficult time.

'We ran into a ... this is a fairly arcane issue to do with film financing, but the system, the regulatory framework for film investment, changed in 1981. That's when they introduced the 10BA tax incentives. And we'd made commitments to and contracted with an investor on the basis of that previous regulation. And they [the Film Commission] said, "Well you can't," and we said, "But, but we are contracted and we're obliged, and that was the legislation at the time," and they said, "Well, too bad, you have to, otherwise we are going to stop you from releasing the film." But then the film ... I think it might have even been completed at that stage, but it hadn't been released and they were threatening to injunct the film ... and then it started getting all these really good notices. There were previews.'

'In those days you had to have a screening before June 30 to secure the tax funding,' says Lander. 'We were still fine-tuning the final edit, but we somehow made a print. And we wanted to keep that screening very, very low key, as the official premiere had to be in Adelaide with the community. So, we had this little outdoor screening. I flew up to Townsville ... I had Aboriginal friends up in Townsville and we took a print and arranged a very makeshift screening with the local Aboriginal community in Townsville.

'We explained this was like a sneak preview screening. The official premiere would be in Adelaide, but we have to have this screening. And we said we were really thrilled that they could come along and watch it and tell us their reaction. We played the film and there was this very, very strong reaction, and then I remember at the end of it, this older Aboriginal guy coming up with tears in his eyes. And just giving me this big hug and saying how great he thought the film was. Then he proceeded to take off his shirt and started showing the scars from the different beatings he'd had from the cops. And just that sense of someone having their reality affirmed by this film ... it's very powerful. And there was a sense that this is all over Australia. This is going to acknowledge and affirm the experience that Aboriginal people have had all over Australia at that time.'

'But the clincher was when the film got a nomination for Best Film at the AFI Awards,' says Isaac. 'And that was against *Gallipoli*, right, and this was a film made on the ... not even on the catering budget of *Gallipoli*. So, at that point they had to embrace the film. They also needed the success. You can break all sorts of rules ... well you could then, as long as you came up with the goods, that was the thing.'

Lander recalls: 'Oddly enough, *Gallipoli* was being post-produced in the same place in Sydney that we were working. So, you had this beautifully crafted iconic film about the founding story of European Australia, of the nation, as they call it, in *Gallipoli*. And *Wrong Side of the Road*. They just couldn't have been further apart. But what people were responding to, and I think why it was nominated – it didn't win obviously, but it won the Jury Prize which wasn't always given at that time; it was something that they decided to do – it was acknowledging how unusual this thing was. And the energy it brought and the alternative vision that it brought and the alternative view of Australia that it brought.

'There had been indications of that sort of thing, I mean, obviously a significant forerunner to it was Phil Noyce's film *Backroads*, in which Gary Foley is brilliant and I suppose gave us a sense of what was possible. But the difference with something like *Wrong Side of the Road* was that whole frame of reference was within that Aboriginal community – apart from the odd skirmish with a bureaucrat, or a copper or what have you, but basically the frame of reference was within the community.'

~

The AFI Awards ceremony was held at the Regent Theatre, Sydney on 16 September 1981 and televised live on ABC-TV. *Wrong Side of the Road* was nominated for best film alongside *The Club*, *The Winter of Our Dreams* and eventual winner *Gallipoli*. No Fixed Address and Us Mob were also nominated for best original music score and Us Mob performed on the night. The award for best music score ultimately went to Grahame Bond and Rory O'Donoghue for *Fatty Finn*.

The star-studded audience included Mel Gibson, Grahame Bond, Richard Neville, Jonathan Coleman, Jacki Weaver, Wendy Hughes, John Hargreaves, Rebecca Gilling, Phillip Adams and US filmmaker Robert Altman (*Australian Women's Weekly*, 14 October 1981).

The nominations were obviously a boost for the film, but it was a bit of a moment too for the AFIs. 'I think it was a bit of a shock to the AFI to have such a strong Aboriginal contingent turn up,' says Lander. 'And shockingly even then as we walked in, as we walked into the cinema, one of the security guys ran

---

Leila Rankine, Wrong Side of the Road Adelaide premiere, Trak Cinema, Toorak Gardens, SA, October 1981.

Photo by Ian de Gruchy.

WRONG SIDE OF THE ROAD

up to Auntie Leila and Auntie Veronica, and tried to push them off the red carpet saying that this was an invite only event. Yeah, and you know, they were in the film and it was nominated for best film. But it was a great night in the end.'

'I remember at the AFI Awards, the big guest that year was Robert Altman,' says Sherree Goldsworthy, 'who made *M~A~S~H* and all that stuff. And all us filmy types were going, "Ooh, Robert Altman, Robert Altman, ooh." And I just remember looking over at one point and there's Bart with his arm around Robert Altman cracking on. Robert Altman was asking to meet them. They didn't know who he was, they didn't give a fuck, they're like, "Yeah, bro' ..." It was really funny. They were the people; we were the people that everyone wanted to be around because we were the happening young thing. When the award was announced there was lots of shouting in a way that there wasn't for any of the other awards. It was very exciting.

'It was a very grandiose thing. We were laughing and shouting when the film got announced. It got the Jury Prize, but it got more claps than the main film. It was a fabulous ceremony and the boys didn't give a shit. They were there. They didn't know what it was. It was fantastic, it was great. They were shouting and carrying on. It was real underdog made good. It certainly had the vibe up. At the after-party everybody wanted to know those boys, because they were genuinely the real thing. They weren't *Gallipoli*.'

The Adelaide premiere of *Wrong Side of the Road*, at the Trak Cinema in Toorak Gardens in mid-October, was a celebratory event for CASM as well as those involved in the making of the film. Prominent among the attendees were Leila Rankine in a specially designed *Wrong Side of the Road* dress and daughter Veronica with her baby son.

Bart Willoughby told Peter Parkhill how he felt when he first saw the completed film. 'It's a weird feeling. I felt like a rock star. I felt we achieved what we set out to achieve. I felt like I was on top of the world. I felt this is the way you keep going up. But I always felt sorry for my mates who I left on the streets. How they would be.'[1]

When it was released, *Wrong Side of the Road* upset the South Australian police force. The police had assisted in the production and were disturbed to see the portrayal of police behaviour in the film. This would have ramifications down the line.

~

By 1981, CASM had 27 full-time students as well as 15 part-timers. And while the members of No Fixed Address and Us Mob were no longer enrolled, Buna Lawrie and his bandmates in Coloured Stone were still there, and two new bands had joined: Kuckles from Broome, Western Australia, and Hard Times from Melbourne.

Ned Lander and Bart Willoughby, Wrong Side of the Road Adelaide premiere, Trak Cinema, Toorak Gardens, SA, October 1981.

Photo by Ian de Gruchy.

Joe Geia was another Aboriginal musician who gravitated to CASM after hearing about No Fixed Address, Us Mob and *Wrong Side of the Road*. 'I was a storeman on Palm Island,' he says. 'I didn't live on Palm Island, but one of my cousins who worked for the council gave me a job there in the store. I was a storeman when I heard about *Wrong Side of the Road*. Knowing that there was a music school down in Adelaide ... I'd written a few songs before then and those songs were written around Brisbane, Palm Island, Cairns. Anyway, I had this package of songs and I just wanted to touch up my music by enrolling at CASM because *Wrong Side* ... portrayed two bands coming out of Adelaide. CASM was a hub where these two bands were from. They were Nunga bands.

'I decided I wasn't going to be a musician on Palm Island unpacking groceries off the barge, so I made my way down to Alice Springs. You can't go anywhere without money, so I waited there for a while then I started hanging around the CAAMA [Central Australian Aboriginal Music Association] radio station in Alice Springs, meeting people there, people like Freda Glynn who was the administrator there. She got me onto one of their first compilations called *Rebel Voices*. I think that was the first ever cassette that CAAMA made. They were only in a little demountable at The Gap at that time, next to a big radio tower. They've grown since then. I liked the place. There was a Pitjantjatjara news reader. Reading news in Pitjantjatjara. Language was fluently spoken there. I was right in the midst of it all. All of that urban cultural practice.

'Around the middle of 1981, I made my way down to Adelaide. I got in contact with the people at CASM, Leila Rankine and Ben Yengi. They said, "You've come at the wrong time. We're in the middle of the year. If you want to enrol, you've got to wait till next year." I thought, "Oh well, I'll hang out here in Adelaide for another six months."

'I started hanging around a place called the Aboriginal Sobriety Group. Moogy Sumner was the administrator there. There was a very small office, but they had this big hall and at the very back of the hall was a kitchen. I had this idea: "Do you ever have the idea of having a soup kitchen or cooking for the parkies? [Indigenous public place dwellers][2]" He said, "If you want to do it, you can do it." So, I started cooking some stews and things like that for the parkies. It wasn't only for parkies. I was starving myself. There was this kitchen there with all these facilities, so I thought I'll cook them a feed and I'll have a bit myself.

'A couple of months must have gone past and No Fixed Address came back from a tour. There were times I would stroll down to CASM, bump into people there, hang out with them here or there. I bumped into Bart and introduced myself.'

Bart Willoughby remembers the day clearly. 'One day I was at the college. There was no-one there. I was at the front. A blackfella walked in with a didge. He took one look at me and I took one look at him. CASM was like two big rooms and he walked down and walked all around. I knew there was no-one there. He came back and said, "Oh, do you know where the Kuckles blokes are?" I said, "Yeah, shit." I grabbed him. He asked what my name was. I think he knew. Anyway, we ended up going to where the Kuckles fellas were and we had a jam and drank and I liked the way how comfortable rhythmically he was.'[3]

~

By this time, No Fixed Address had come to a crossroads. They felt that they couldn't base themselves in Adelaide anymore. It just wasn't practical for a nationally touring band. Where was it to be instead – Sydney or Melbourne? Their erstwhile manager Chris Gunn was in Sydney, but with Redgum demanding more and more of his attention, No Fixed Address was feeling a little neglected. Us Mob was based in Sydney too and were finding it a hard slog in the Harbour City. Another major problem was the decline in the number of Sydney venues.[4]

In Melbourne, Mick Pacholli, who had been organising their gigs there for several years, expressed his interest in taking on an increased role. As well as bigger and better tours, Pacholli held out the promise of recording and publishing deals. The band decided to move to Melbourne.

No Fixed Address played three Adelaide gigs in the dying days of October. On Thursday 22nd they were at the Hindley Street nightspot Sinatras (which closed the following month; the latest in a spate of Adelaide club fire bombings). The following night and a week later on Friday, 30 October – in what was billed as their 'Final Adelaide Appearance' – they played at the Governor Hindmarsh Hotel on Port Road, Hindmarsh.

On the same night No Fixed Address played their farewell Adelaide performance, *Wrong Side of the Road* opened at the Opera House Cinema in Sydney. The NSW Minister for Aboriginal Affairs Frank Walker remarked on the irony of it being shown at Bennelong Point, 'where all the troubles of the present-day Aborigines began almost 200 years ago' (*Sydney Morning Herald*, 2 November 1981, p. 1).

'It had a release in each capital city,' says Ned Lander. 'Sylvie Le Clezio, who was a publicist and film distributor, a solo operator, released the film together with the AFI and so it went into the Opera House in Sydney, the Longford in Melbourne. These were like six week runs. It got quite a good run and very good houses. And then similarly, independent cinemas in Adelaide and Perth and Brisbane and so on. All of the releases got good press coverage and great reviews. Interesting reviews and reasonably good audiences.'

Geraldine Brooks in *The Sydney Morning Herald* found it a 'gutsy, chilly film', writing:

> The black bands, Us Mob and No Fixed Address represent the strong positive resurgence of Aboriginal culture and pride. The film deserves to be widely seen. It is one of the few opportunities that white people will ever get to see and understand what it costs black people to hang on to that pride in a society intent on ripping it away from them.[1]

The simmering undercurrent of violence between white society and Aboriginal people was not lost on some reviewers. John Lapsley in Sydney's *Sun-Herald* wrote:

> Road movies have a strong tradition of wheeling their heroes through unfriendly countrysides peopled by maniacal yokels whose chief aims are death and destruction. ... In *Wrong Side of the Road*, the victims are two Aboriginal rock bands, Us Mob and No Fixed Address. And the redneck yokels are us.[2]

Dougal Macdonald in *The Canberra Times* concurred:

> It is difficult to be totally objective about a film that deals as forcefully with a major rift in Australian society as this one does. ... The film has power to send you out of the theatre feeling highly disturbed and perhaps even dismayed by the magnitude of the mutual enormity the film demonstrates.[3]

Looking back at the film in the context of its times, Marcus Breen highlighted its importance as the seed bed for the blossoming of Aboriginal rock music in the 1980s and beyond.

> This docu-drama launched Aboriginal rock music into the public domain. Its uncompromising examination of the treatment of black musicians in the bands Us Mob and No Fixed Address was a challenge to white Australia, whose perceptions of Aboriginal music and people had been restricted to the sounds and images of tribal Australians. Here was a story of urban Aboriginal Australia, with the vicious teeth of racism cutting deep. Here also was a delightful insight into the new generation of Aboriginal and black consciousness regenerating itself through rock music.
>
> The remarkable music, combined with the unquestioned politic of the film, pointed towards the explosion of Aboriginal aspirations that developed in the late 1970s and exploded into full view with the election of the Hawke Labor Government in 1983, two years after *Wrong Side of the Road* was released.
>
> In the years since this film was made, the subsequent use of popular music as a source of empowerment for Aborigines indicates that the film marked a significant turning point in Australian film and musical history.[4]

'But the other really significant thing that happened,' says Lander, 'was that a couple of Aboriginal people borrowed a 16 mm copy of the film and showed it to communities all over NSW into the Northern Territory. It got a lot of screenings in communities, outdoor screenings.'

The film tour came about because the NSW Premier's Department had granted the Sydney Filmmakers Co-op $7600 in 1980 to provide a specialised film distribution project for Aboriginal communities in New South Wales, to be operated by Aboriginal people. Madeline McGrady and Johnny Bayles came to the co-op in June 1981 with a proposal that they run the project as part of a National Employment Strategy for Aborigines training scheme. McGrady and Bayles subsequently toured a print of *Wrong Side of The Road* to communities in Wee Waa, Dubbo, Moree, Armidale, Inverell and Tamworth (*Filmnews*, 1 June 1982).

Nearly 40 years on, McGrady remembers the tour with great fondness. 'They'd never seen any live bands anyway,' she says. 'That was one of the reasons that really stirred me to take the film out to communities. You live out in bush areas; you think it's just being black or white. You face racism every day of your life out there. In everything you say and do. So, it was good for them to see that side of it. In music as well, they suffer that.

'They just loved it. I still want to do it. Because nothing much has happened in between. They don't get the opportunities to see that kind of stuff. It really had an effect on them. You'd be sitting up there till 12 o'clock at night after a screening. They just wanted to talk. It really, really gave them a lift. Seeing what the bands did at the time.'

McGrady was a big fan of No Fixed Address. 'I thought they were the greatest band that ever hit the country at the time. People are still talking about them out there in the communities. They got recognised really quick because of the work they put in at the time.'

Not everyone was happy about the film being shown to Aboriginal people, however. Under the headline 'Police claim film will stir racial problems', the Sydney *Daily Telegraph* (16 July 1982), reported:

> The NSW Police Association has protested to the Education Minister over high school students being shown a film about Aborigines. The association claims the film, *Wrong Side of the Road*, exaggerates police violence against Aborigines. The film

was shown at Walgett, in north-west NSW. The association fears racial tension in Walgett could worsen because of the film.

Both Graeme Isaac and Ned Lander were struck by the reaction of audiences when the film came out. 'What I remember is the completely different responses of a white and a black audience,' says Isaac. 'Black audiences would laugh a lot. They would laugh at all this stuff, like when Bart would say to John, "Ah, you bun nose," and all that stuff. White audiences would be very uncomfortable and the black audiences would hoot with laughter.'

Lander adds: 'But equally there were moments like the bureaucrat telling Les's character that he can't reveal information about his birth mother, other than that she was Aboriginal from the north of the State and not married. And white audiences laughed – at the bureaucrat, not at Les – and probably a lot of white people have also been humiliated in some way by a government bureaucrat. It's a strange laugh, it's a kind of an ashamed laugh, an awkward and embarrassed laugh, but they laughed. They laughed out of recognition and embarrassment at that moment, at what's happening to this kid who just wants to find his family. No Aboriginal people laugh at that point. It's just not at all funny for them because they are identifying with Les.'

'But it was really warmly embraced by Indigenous communities all around the country,' says Isaac. 'They regarded it as their film. And I think in the bush, it was taken as almost like a morality tale about the dangers of young people going to the city and the sort of problems they could end up in. But for urban Aboriginal people it was like a vindication. They would say, "Yes that's our life, that's what it's like if you're in our shoes."

'And the by-line to the film was "48 hours on our side of town". That was the whole idea, to just try and give a sense of a ... to give a white audience a window into a world that they couldn't enter, and for a black audience to give them a sense of ... not vindication. Confirmation, yeah that's to say, yes that's how it is.'

~

On reflection, Graeme Isaac acknowledges that the film was a compromise in some respects. 'I think as a story, as a film, it was in places a bit clunky in some aspects. I mean, it had too many characters, what have you, eight main characters. That is a lot for a conventional drama. But there were two bands, and it was a story coming out of a time and real place, portraying the lives of real people. You had to be true to that. And also, there were so many stories that needed to be told and issues that had to be aired. Especially at that time, when there were no films about the urban Aboriginal experience. When even the idea of an urban Aboriginal identity was challenged by many white Australians, who saw them as somehow inauthentic and passing off.

'So, in a way, the film had a certain obligation to be carrying all of this extra stuff, which is not baggage that normally a film has to carry. So, I think there was a compromise in a way, in terms of what the narrative strength or clarity or power of the film could have been. But it had this other quality, that it came from somewhere real. And of course, there was the music.'

PART 3

THE AUSTRALIAN MUSIC MACHINE

(1981–84)

In November 1981 the live music scene in Melbourne was pumping. The gig guide in the Rhythms section of the *Age Weekender* on Friday the 6th listed shows by (deep breath) ... The Aliens, Australian Crawl, Beargarden, Beat Detectives, Broderick Smith's Big Combo, Cheks, Dead Can Dance, Dear Enemy, Goanna Band, Jo Jo Zep and the Falcons, The Kevins, La Femme, Little Heroes, Little Murders, Lucky Dog, MEO 245, Mickey Finn, Mike Rudd and the Heaters, The Orphans, Russell Morris and the Rubes, The Stockings, Uncanny X-Men, Wendy and the Rocketts and Young Homebuyers. In addition, Moving Parts, The Radiators, Sunnyboys and Tactics were down from Sydney for the week. Despite such fierce competition, the combination of the *Wrong Side of the Road* film (which opened on 13 November) and a string of live performances earned No Fixed Address the Rhythms 'Pick of the Week'.

The band landed right in the middle of the action, at Macys, in Her Majesty's Hotel, Toorak Road, South Yarra. *Wrong Side of the Road* opened at the Longford just up the street.

'Macys was where all the bands stayed,' recalls Bart Willoughby. 'Sherbet, Real Life. So, when you were there, you come back from the gig and there would be people everywhere. Rooms down the end there and there's a big party happening with all these different bands coming from different gigs. And they finish all at the same time. And there would be gigs starting at 1 am going to 3 am that we all waited for down in St Kilda there.'

They may have been the new kids in town, but Ricky Harrison wasn't going to take any shit from the Macys' crowd. 'That's where we met the Models,' he remembers. 'Me and Bart, we were walking up past their room. Sean Kelly, the lead singer, he was a real smartarse, a real dickhead. He was drunk and his mates were in there and he said something, I don't know if he was being racist or what, I can't remember what he said, but I wanted to smash him. Bart grabbed me and said, "No, no, no, don't go punching him. He's a Model" [laughs]. You had some of those bands that tended to be a bit, I dunno, dickheads I suppose.'

Musically, what did No Fixed Address bring to the party? Fortunately, there is a recording. The band's first performance after moving over from Adelaide was at the Prince of Wales Hotel on Fitzroy Street, St Kilda on 2 November. It was broadcast live to air on community radio station 3PBS-FM, which had its studios in the same building. The master tapes survived and were released as a limited-edition CD and digital download in 2016. The CD brought back fond memories for Adelaide writer Robert Brokenmouth, who reviewed it on music website i-94bar.com.

> The reason this release only gets its [4 and a half] beer bottle rating is for the songs – not the memories. Certainly not for the sound – whoever did this was either having difficulties or not paying attention. The bass doesn't dominate like a liquid hot night in Adelaide, somehow to the fore and in the background at the same time; the guitar seems cleaner than I remember it, the pace seems slightly faster (though that could be time playing tricks) and, perhaps Veronica Rankine wasn't playing that night as I can't hear her sax. Overall the recording is so squeaky clean it lacks the intimacy the band and the songs deserve.
>
> But despite this ... is it any good? Fuck, come on. They're young, gifted and Aboriginal, talent rising off them like heat waves. NFA had an intimate, natural grasp of reggae and bent it to their will (astonishing given their age), and there's 14 cracker out-of-time original songs here and they move and groove like a long, slow fuck in the twilight.
>
> Caution: wheezy old man story ahead ...
>
> Steve, Fred, Paul and me would go down the Governor Hindmarsh, long before its marvellous refurbishment a couple of decades back, and we'd see all manner of bands: The Lounge, Systems Go, Drum Poetry, No Fixed Address. We'd heard NFA on 5MMM FM radio (they'd put out a demo tape)

and we were duly impressed, not least by their extraordinarily natural ability to weld reggae into something more modern and relevant.

In an era where there were a lot of bad and iffy bands out there … for a while there (perhaps late 79 – the memory is a tad hazy – but certainly) during 1980, it seemed like we went every time NFA played.

They were really good, had a soft/strong groovy vibe to them, a lyrical and wraparound throbbing bass sound critical to their sound (John John Miller), a smart drummer who knew how to spread his beat around the kit and use cymbals properly – who was also that rare beast a drummer whose vocals actually worked – no, hang on, Bart Willoughby had one of those marvellous, yearning cracking voices you hear once in a decade if not less frequently.

Oh, and two guitarists, Leslie Lovegrove Freeman [Les Graham] and Ricky Harrison, who filled things in beautifully, and Veronica Rankine who played (from memory, occasional, sax). The entire band was the next best thing to a work of art.

But back to the hear [*sic*] and now … it's great to hear these old classics. 'Green House Holiday', 'Get a Grip', 'Give It Up', 'Black Man's Rights' and all the rest. Fabulous. I remember wondering how many covers there were in the set and being told either 'one' or 'none' – the only cover is 'Pressure Drop' and that opens the disc. The rest are originals, smart, sharp, credible songs which frankly deserve to be covered by younger bands, a place in the sun and numerous slots in films.[1]

~

Bart Willoughby remembers the band were in a happy place at the time. 'We're not getting drunk or getting stoned, we're performing and loving what we're doing. And I think the people could see that. And also, we're playing original music that no-one's ever heard really. And we're not sounding like what the record company wants bands to sound like. We're just creating our own music, which might have melted into the rock'n'roll industry in some form of … a different outlook or a different way of playing. Like, the other musicians would not copy us, they'd just use our technique. And it would be hidden in their technique. So, if we weren't there, they wouldn't find that technique. "Saturday Night" is a perfect example of Cold Chisel listening to us playing reggae.'

The *Wrong Side of the Road* soundtrack album came out a week later, on 9 November. 'We didn't go back to any of the majors [major record companies],' says Graeme Isaac. 'We'd already spent the money recording and packaging, so we decided to go with EMI Custom, with Daymon Wynters: a Māori guy. Nice bloke he was. It was still in the days when you had reps going round the shops with albums. It was a whole different ball game. The difficulty was that the record company [EMI] was going to push the product they were most invested in, so their reps were going to be pushing what they could sell the most units of. This was part of the jeopardy of going with an independent release.'

The album came in an attractive package. A black, yellow and red cover, with the title of the film, a black and white still shot of the police outside the Port Adelaide Town Hall and the names of the bands in flowing script, opened up to a gatefold of the song lyrics printed over a backdrop of the Aboriginal flag. The sleeve insert contained photos from the film of the five members of No Fixed Address and the four members of Us Mob. The back cover listed the six songs from No Fixed Address on side one and the six from Us Mob on side two.

From the first line of the opening track – 'You can't change the rhythm of my soul' – to the walking bass, scratching rhythm guitar, subtle didgeridoo and echoes and effects of the closing number 'The Vision (Version)', side one announced the recording debut of an original voice in Australian music. The musical and vocal elements – the bass guitar steadily tracing the path, the chopping and scratching rhythm guitar, the high clean lead guitar buttressed with echoes and effects, the skittering and patterning drums, the tapping percussion, the occasional hint of didgeridoo, Bart Willoughby's clear distinctive voice and Ricky Harrison's echo enhanced vocals –

were all beautifully balanced in the mix. And on top of this musical framework, the lyrics ranged from the political ('We Have Survived' and 'Black Man's Rights') to the poetic ('The Vision') and the cheerful ('Greenhouse Holiday').

Us Mob's contribution was much more hard rock verging on heavy metal and, worthy as it was, seemed dated in comparison to the originality on display on the other side of the disc.

Although it hardly set the charts on fire (peaking at #67 on the Kent Music Report), the album sold steadily over the following months and achieved solid airplay on triple J in Sydney and public (community) radio nationally (including 2SER Sydney; 2XX Canberra; 3CR, 3PBS and 3RRR Melbourne; 4ZZZ Brisbane; 5MMM and 5UV Adelaide; 6NR and 6UVS Perth; 8CAR Darwin and 8CCC Alice Springs).

'Black Australia Records was simply a vehicle for releasing that one record,' says Graeme Isaac. 'The bands weren't tied in any way if they wanted to do anything else. They retained their own publishing. The deal was that the returns would be split equally among all band members, with me and Philip [Roberts] included as if we were band members. But the reality was that all the money went to them. Every now and then one of them would ring up and say he was a bit short and could he have an advance. Community radio picked it up, particularly "We Have Survived", "Black Man's Rights" and Us Mob's "Wrong Side of the Road". And "We Have Survived" went on to be the anthem of the land rights movement of the 1980s, into the '90s. It certainly made its impact. Even now, at political rallies, "We have survived" is a slogan or a political statement; an assertion of black resilience.'

~

Wayne Thorpe, guitarist with Hard Times, recalls the impact No Fixed Address made in the local Aboriginal community. 'Every time they would come to Melbourne, I would hear the excitement in the people, the Aboriginal people of Melbourne, wanting to go there and support No Fixed Address. They were well received over here. Being the first black band being recorded, professional recordings, people really started to recognise them and support them. Those lyrics resonated with the people. We didn't hear that sort of stuff in the cover songs. A lot of the covers might touch on some issues that we're going through, but No Fixed Address and Hard Times hit straight at it with our original songs. We're telling it as it is. That's why it resonated with so many Aboriginal people.

'If there's one saying in our communities, early days, it's "Ahh, can you say that?" "Can they do that?", you know? That's a reflection from the early mission days when you weren't allowed to say things, you weren't allowed to speak your language, you can't challenge the authorities otherwise you'll get your rations taken, you'll get your children taken away, you'll get locked up, all this sort of stuff. And so, when young black bands are coming out singing it as it is, singing it with confidence and power, that resonated with the Aboriginal communities. "Yes, that's right, that happened to us." That's how the people would respond. "Sing it brother!" And when there's a few beers under your belt, you start to sing out a bit louder. But you really feel it, whether you're drunk or not. You're really feeling it, because it's true lyrics.

'And at that time, we had survived. We had survived the massacres, the missions, all that Stolen Generations. We had survived. And I remember when they were singing about the pigs, the coppers. The police coming in and they'd start to sing that song, change straight into that song. That resonated with people. That was taking the authorities on. That's the sort of thing that helped them be successful. Not only in blackfellas' eyes but in the eyes of all nationalities. Because people had an awareness of what Aboriginal people had been through and that's why they were there supporting No Fixed Address and Hard Times in the first place. And when No Fixed Address would be singing them lyrics, they'd be looking around and checking the response. So that was a great learning for everyone.

'Reggae was hot at the time. Bob Marley and Peter Tosh and all different musicians like that were really coming out at that time. And to see a local band of this country singing our own songs with that genre of music was a revelation for a lot of people. A lot of people had heard the rock'n'roll, the country and western, and the blues, but reggae was fresh at the time. No Fixed Address were taking it on. Even the name of the band. People would be hearing the name of the band and they'd be going, "No Fixed Address?" "Yes, they've got no fixed address. They're still struggling in this day and age." From the name of the band, from the lyrics they were singing, the music, it just all resonated. And then the reaction of the crowds. It just lifted the members of the crowd. And then that gets attention. In the pubs it was predominantly mixed crowds when I was there. I have seen different concerts and venues where there weren't so many white people there, but a lot more of all nationalities there. And you see them cheering and you go, "Hey, look at this!" These fellas are really having an impact here.'

~

Shane Howard, lead singer and principal songwriter with Goanna Band – which was fresh from their big break supporting James Taylor on his September 1981 Australian tour – recalls his first impressions of the new boys in town. 'So, I'm going to see No Fixed Address play and like so many Melburnians, I'm completely blown away. Because you go, we haven't seen Aboriginal people do that before. We haven't seen a black Aboriginal band play music with attitude. This isn't cabaret. This is politically confronting music. "Pigs" and "Victims of the stupid system". It's in your face.

'I remember when I first saw those early shows, particularly around Fitzroy and Melbourne, the Aberdeen [Hotel], which was a big haunt for No Fixed Address, the Central Club, lots of non-Aboriginal people just being completely nonplussed. Stunned really by the power of that band. It was a really powerful outfit and sure, there are reggae influences but there's something else going on and it's a uniquely Aboriginal band and a uniquely Aboriginal sound. Something new is happening. Everyone that saw them in those early days realised that. And we hadn't seen that before. Maybe in Adelaide people did. But in Victoria we hadn't. We're talking about middle-class people in mainstream pubs and clubs.

'I think that period in Adelaide, that time, and CASM, are central to a kind of explosion of Aboriginal music. George Rrurrambu from Warumpi Band, he said to me, it was when he saw No Fixed Address that he said, "That's what I want to do."

'They came crashing into middle-class Australia and it changed everything. Really. The inspiration for Yothu Yindi, the inspiration for everything starts there. I mean, you've got to give respect to Buna Lawrie and Coloured Stone, who were probably going even earlier. But in terms of having an impact beyond their local reality, I can't think of any other bands.

'I think "tip of the spear" is an appropriate term. I mean, lots of people have forgotten that and lots of people come to Aboriginal music through Yothu Yindi. Some came earlier through Warumpi Band, some through Yothu Yindi, some through Archie [Roach], but really, you've got to go right back, hey? This is confrontational music in the pubs of middle-class Melbourne. Which is for me where they really take off. I know they're cutting their teeth in Adelaide, but they bring it to Melbourne, they're in the music industry from that point.'

~

On a ten-day camping trip to Uluru the previous year, Howard had stumbled upon an *inma*, a traditional Aboriginal dance ceremony. The experience and the contrast with what happened when he returned to Alice Springs was the inspiration for what later became Goanna's signature song, 'Solid Rock'. ('Band' was dropped from the group's name when they signed to WEA Records).

'I just happened to be there at a time when people from Amata were renewing their connection to Uluru,' says Howard.

'This was the early days, there's no resort, there's no Yulara, it's pretty basic. It's all dirt roads out there. I got a train from Melbourne to Adelaide then a train, the old Ghan, up to Alice Springs and then a bus. I had a little tent. I camped out there, near where the Mutitjulu community is now, at the old campground. Things were pretty basic. It was considered public, the *inma*, and someone had put a sign up at the toilet and shower block saying, '*inma*, other side of the rock'. So that's how I ended up being there.

'I hadn't really experienced that deep cultural reality before – because it had been so interrupted, brutally interrupted by colonisation – until I went to Uluru. And then I saw *inma*; I heard the songs; I heard the language; I saw the dance; I saw the *jukurrpa*; I heard the songs and the stories being told; and it impacted on me in a really powerful way. It was an undeniable experience. And then to go back to Alice Springs and hear people, non-Indigenous people speak about Aboriginal people in such abusive terms. I had already started the song at Uluru, "Out here nothing changes/Not in a hurry anyway." And that first part of the song is just a very gentle and beautiful expression of that cultural landscape. But then it has to deal with the hard-edged reality of colonisation, which happens half way through the song. Going back to Alice Springs shapes the last verse of that song. The biggest transformative moment of that song is, "Standing on the shore one day". As a whitefella, it gives people who are not Aboriginal an Indigenous perspective as to what colonisation feels like, when the aliens come, or the Romans come. It's experiential really. It's not academic.'

Howard completed the song and it was incorporated into Goanna Band's set. 'So, we're back in Geelong,' he says. 'It must be 1980. We've just started to make inroads into Melbourne, as a band. I think we've even relocated to Melbourne. We're doing it pretty tough but we're starting to gather a following. And then we come back to Geelong to do a gig at the Eureka Hotel and that's where we connect with Billy Cummins. In the bar. He's at Deakin Uni, down from North Queensland. So that's our first connection, with Billy. He's in the bar drinking while we're doing soundcheck and he hears "Solid Rock". And he says, "That song!" And I say, "Oh yeah." And he says, "I play didge. I've got one at home." And I say, "Do you wanna play it? Tonight?" And he says, "Yeah." And that's kind of how that starts. Billy starts touring with us. Once we've done that show in Geelong, Billy starts doing more shows with us. But I reckon that's early 1981.

'So, then it's Billy who then introduces me to Bart. And that's how I connect to No Fixed Address. I meet them with Billy in the latter half of 1981 and they're deeply suspicious of ... "Who's the whitefella?" But I had Billy there as an entrée. And then Billy goes on to join No Fixed Address. He tours with us, does the James Taylor tour but then goes on and says, "I really want to join No Fixed Address." It was hard to let Billy go; he was such a great spirit but that's what he wanted to do so we weren't going to hold him back. It built our connection to No Fixed at that point. For me anyway. And then with Bart, that's really where our friendship began and that's gone forty years.'

~

With the *Wrong Side of the Road* album in the shops and the film on the screens in Sydney, Melbourne and Adelaide (where it opened at the Trak Cinema on 20 November), No Fixed Address took a run up the Hume Highway to Sydney for a major Rock Against Racism concert. The concert coincided with the start of the Australian tour by British funky funsters Ian Dury and the Blockheads. No Fixed Address was already booked to support Dury and co in Melbourne the following month.

Four years after bursting onto the scene in 1977 with the remarkable *New Boots & Panties* album, Ian Dury's latest platter was again a solo effort. Recorded at Compass Point Studios in the Bahamas with ex-Bob Marley and the Wailers rhythm section, Sly Dunbar and Robbie Shakespeare, *Lord Upminster* was unfortunately rather a lacklustre affair. In between those bookends, Ian Dury with the Blockheads had hit some dizzy heights with the singles 'What a Waste', 'Hit Me with Your Rhythm Stick', 'Reasons to Be Cheerful (Part 3)', 'I Want to Be Straight' and the album, *Do It Yourself.* Their second album together, *Laughter,* had its moments, but not many, and when it failed to sell, Dury had left the cheeky UK independent Stiff Records and signed with multi-national Polydor Records.

In the wake of *Lord Upminster*'s bellyflop, the Blockheads had to all intents and purposes disbanded after a tour of Spain in September 1981. But when Zev Eisik and Michael Coppel from Australian Concert Entertainment (ACE) approached Dury with an eye-watering proposition for an Australian and New Zealand tour, Dury accepted with alacrity. After a bit of argy-bargy over payments, Dury persuaded the band to accompany him as well.

The opening dates of the tour, titled Lord Upminster's Antipodean Progress, were at Sydney's Capitol Theatre on 21 and 22 November. The entourage was ensconced at the touring rock stars' establishment of choice, the Sebel Town House in Kings Cross, to where, after one of the sell-out shows, Mr Dury returned and headed straight for the bar. 'He'd got it into his head how badly the Australians had treated the Aborigines,' co-manager Andrew King told Dury's biographer Will Birch. 'It was getting late and there was a group of businessmen in the corner. Ian ranted at them, "You killed the fucking Abbos [*sic*], you cunts!" and started lobbing gob at them, little realizing this was a harmless group of Swedish mining experts.'[2] Dury had to be removed from the scene by tour manager Roy Jordan. The Sebel banned Dury and the band for life.

~

On the evening of Lord Upminster's second Sydney show, 800 metres up George Street, a crowd of 3000 packed into the Rock Against Racism concert at the Sydney Town Hall. The concert ran for five and half hours, from 5.30–11 pm, and featured five black acts: Us Mob, Un Tabu, King Cobra, No Fixed Address and the Aboriginal and Islander Dance Company. 'I don't mean to be rude or nothing,' says Les Graham, 'but the crowd sat down for all the other acts until No Fixed Address got up, then they all stood up. When we played, they just partied. We never realised how famous we were getting.'

'Big crowd, yeah,' recalls John John Miller. 'They had cameras and everything. We were on fire, man. I didn't realise. It passes real quick.'

Madeline McGrady was one of those wielding a camera. 'Somebody said, "You won't get people to come and see black bands." And I said, "Well, we're going to give it our best shot." We worked so hard setting up and I went home about 3 o'clock in the afternoon and I came back at 5 to the Town Hall and there were queues of people going for miles. I just couldn't believe it. We had the greatest time. I think we made something like forty thousand dollars. That was big money at the time. People came and provided food. It was just a fantastic time. But the question is, "Did we break down some of that racism?" I think the people in Sydney were really, really supportive at the time. In that era, in that time, we did. We certainly got a lot of support from people.'

~

This Sydney visit marked the debut of lighting engineer Maxine Briggs with the band. Briggs, a Victorian Aboriginal woman of Taungwurrung and Yorta Yorta nations, had trained in theatre lighting and cut her teeth working in leagues clubs, doing school productions, kids shows, pantomimes, theatres and with a number of alternative bands handled by Lobby Loyde's Sydney management agency SCAM.

In the lead-up to the release of *Wrong Side of the Road*, No Fixed Address had played a few gigs in Sydney and the word was out. 'People were talking,' says Briggs. 'A few people would say, "Have you seen this band? Have you heard of them?" So, when their movie came on at the Opera House Cinema, I went along. I was completely captivated, of course. I said to Mick Pacholli – who was producing *tagg* mag at the time and was part of the network that brought them to Sydney – I said to him, "I'm really interested in working with them. If they need a lighting person when they come over, I'm putting my hand up now, okay?"

'Because I hadn't met any of the guys in the band before, I had to be interviewed for the job. One day there was a knock at the door and there stood Rick and Leslie. I was given a cross-examination on my family history and obligations, my cultural affiliations and my cultural practice. Whether I could do the job or not didn't seem to be the issue, or maybe that was already established by other means. Anyway, I got the job, maybe 'cos I was identifiable as a Victorian Koori. It was a great job and I loved it.'

Briggs was starting to feel a certain isolation out there in the music mainstream and really felt she was much more in her element when she hooked up with No Fixed Address – especially when she discovered another Victorian Koori in the band. 'We were from different places but everyone is connected some way or other, the bloodlines, the songlines, the totemic system, trade routes ... it's complicated.'

At the time, Maxine Briggs and sound engineer Katie Yeowart were working as a team. 'She'd been working with the Go-Betweens but they had stopped working so she came down to Sydney from Brisbane,' says Briggs. 'When No Fixed Address came to town, they didn't have any crew at all so Katie and I became their crew for a while, but that didn't last long. For some reason Duckie, the band's sound guy from Adelaide, couldn't come over with the band but did turn up eventually. So, Katie and I had to part company, which was sad for me. It was great to be working with another woman in rock'n'roll. The music industry was a lily-white, man's world in those days. It was even hard for the Māori musos to get anywhere in their own right – and they were everywhere, in so many Australian bands.'

~

With the Melbourne support on the Ian Dury and the Blockheads tour not until 10 December, the band headed back to Adelaide, and bass guitarist John John Miller fell into a world of pain. This was Miller's account of what happened in Hindley Street, as told to *Nunga News*.

> It was on the 4th December 1981. We ... arrived in the city about 9.00 p.m. got off the bus at the corner of King William Street and North Terrace. Then [name redacted] and I walked down Hindley Street, went to the Overway Hotel and had a look inside; was there for about fifteen minutes. Then we walked back up Hindley Street and we turned down a side street walking down. Then we stopped. [Name redacted] and I were talking to each other and this wog came out of nowhere behind me and said to me, 'What are you doing, trying to steal my car?' I said I wasn't and then he said, 'I'll fix you up, you black bastard'. He then jumped into his car and pulled out a small pistol. When I seen him pull out a pistol from his car I ran up the lane and as I turned the corner there was a copper there, he grabbed me by the hand and said, 'What are you running from?' I told the young policeman that the wog was after me with a gun. When I told ... that, he took me back where I ran from. As we got to the laneway, another policeman grabbed me ... He was choking me and I couldn't breathe. I tried to pull away that's when he grabbed my right hand and twisted it behind my back then they took me to the police car. The police were standing there holding me that's when they began asking me my name and address which I gave. Then the police officer ... tried to throw me into the police car and I said I can get in the car myself which I did. As I was about to lift my legs up to jump in the car one of the policemen tried to close the door on my legs so I pushed the door open so I wouldn't get my legs caught in the door. Then I said to the police officer, would you like me to close the door for you. Then the police officer said yes. Then I was taken to the city watch house. I asked the police officer what I was arrested for the police didn't tell me why I was arrested, they didn't say anything.

> When I was in the city watch house [another] police
> officer ... said to me, 'yeah, I hear your song on the radio'. I asked
> him which song was it. He said, 'Black, black, blackman song'.
> I said I'll get them for all this. He said, 'You black bastard and
> where is them old wati's man with a bone to bone us.' I then
> said, 'I am going to get you by the law'. Then the policeman ...
> said, 'You are not going to remember what happened tonight
> because I am going to kick your little black head in'. Then they
> put me in the cell. When I was being finger printed, I noticed
> my right hand swolled [*sic*] from being twisted by the [first]
> policeman ... I was let out of the city watch house at 3.30 a.m.
> on 5 December, 1981 and I went home and came back to the
> Adelaide Magistrates Court at 10 a.m. to attend court and
> was released on bail then I went straight to Queen Elizabeth
> Hospital because I knew something was wrong with my hand
> because it was swollen. I had X-rays on my right hand, the
> doctor told me it was broken.[3]

Miller's X-rays showed a fracture of the right, third meta-
carpal (i.e., third finger). But when he went back to the hospital
to get a copy of his X-ray, the administrator of the hospital told
him it was lost. 'X-rays always get lost,' he told John. Maybe the
cops got there before John did.

'It destroyed my life,' says Miller. 'They assaulted me. I
couldn't get jobs because I had a record. That dirtied my name.
That's what they've been doing to all the Aboriginal race, the
white cops. Back in the '80s they were getting the kids before
they turned eighteen and getting them charged. It's still going
on now. They're still doing it. It's been handed down by the
forefathers. They've gotta shut us down so we can't get into
the high places. They're shutting the kids down. I worked that
out a long time ago when they did it to me.'

There were people who wanted to take it up, mount a
case against the police for what they did, but Miller was a bit
scared so didn't go through with it. 'The case should be redone
because they had no evidence,' he says. 'They picked me up
with no charge. I had QCs and all that but I ran away. I lost all
the QCs. The cops got me really quick ... did it in a quick way

in the court. I was convicted. Chuck me in the court, charge me with aggravated assault and resisting arrest, all that stuff.

'That was that. When they broke my hand, I couldn't play. They had to use someone else. Joe [Hayes] had to play. I was in the band for two years. I actually missed the highlight of *Wrong Side of the Road*. I missed the full swing of fame with the band. I missed all that, because I was out.'

~

Before the remainder of the band left Adelaide to go back to Melbourne, Bart Willoughby made Joe Geia an offer. 'Bart said, "Do you want to come on tour with us?"' says Geia. 'And his reason was, "When I play didge, I've got to stop drumming and pick up the didge and play it." I said, "You can keep on drumming and I'll play the didge if that's what you're looking for." Anyway, he spread the news among everybody else and the following week they said, "We're on tour again. You should come as our didge player and percussionist."'

Billy Inda Cummins had already been playing didge and percussion for the band in Melbourne, but adding Geia to the mix gave the band an extra string to their bow. 'Billy was performing with them before I came along,' says Geia. 'There were times where I'd use his cabasas or shakers or tambourine. He was the one with the congas. He had a pair of congas on stage. There were times when I'd just dance and play the didge now and then.' Geia also brought his songs and an extra singing voice.

But the immediate and pressing issue was the vacant bass player position for the upcoming Melbourne support to Ian Dury and the Blockheads. Ricky Harrison decided to ring someone he knew in Morwell, Joe Hayes.

'I grew up with Rick as well,' says Jean Morgan. 'We know the same people. Joe and I got married on my nineteenth birthday. Three months into our marriage Joe got a call from Ricky ... yeah it was Ricky, because John John had left the band. Because they knew that Joe knew all the bass lines and everything.' Hayes joined on bass.

The new line-up didn't have much time to rehearse. 'The first time I performed, it was the Morelands Hotel, in Melbourne, that was one gig,' says Joe Geia. 'The next night or something like that, we were at the Festival Hall, supporting Ian Dury and the Blockheads. I thought, "Wow, what a giant step!" CASM went right out of my mind!'

'Joe Geia was really good,' says Ross Gardiner from Rough Diamond Records. 'Even though he wasn't necessarily leading the songs or leading the band, he had a tremendous presence. And he gave a lot in terms of instrumentation, backing vocals and just good vibes and presence in a live performance. Sort of like early rap style or something. He was very good, I thought, very good for the band at the time.'

'The thing was, I would just focus on "dance to the music",' says Geia. 'And once someone's on the stage jumping and dancing and shaking the tambourine, we noticed it would move the audience. And that's all that band really needed, somebody jumping and enjoying their music. I used to portray that on the stage. Being a land rights activist, lover [of that] sort of thing, I thought all their songs were fantastic. It was for the people. It became a moving band, there were some actions. The next band that did that was Yothu Yindi because they had all those corroboree dancers. I just thought that was my job.'

'That's when we started to put the swing in the reggae,' says Bart Willoughby. 'Because Joe had the swing. Or that thing that Island people have, they just naturally have this rhythm. You play cricket against them and you can't get them out. Like blackfellas in the bush. You grab a rock and try to throw it at a can. Most European people miss. Them fellas, they'll hit it, and hit it in the same spot. They are really accurate. Anyway, he just had this natural rhythm that we needed. We were clap stick people. He was the didge man. Where I come from, we don't have the didgeridoos. That's not our instrument.'

~

Duckie Taylor was at Festival Hall as sound engineer for No Fixed Address on the night of the Ian Dury support. 'We've done the gig with them, everything turned out fine, both sides,' he recalls. 'They saw us and we got invited back to their party.'

'Ian Dury and the Blockheads, they were fantastic,' agrees Maxine Briggs, who was doing lights with No Fixed Address. 'The Blockheads crew were so accommodating; they pretty much let our crew have what we wanted, production wise. Ian and the band invited us all back to their hotel after the show for supper. We kicked on for hours with them, talking, eating , laughing, singing. Great fun, good people, excellent musicians, much respect both ways.'

'They hired out one whole floor of this hotel,' says Taylor. 'Ian Dury sat at the end of this gigantic big long table; he sat down with me and Les [Graham] just sculling drinks and all that. And all we can hear is his manager trying to tell me, "Don't let him drink too much," and he would hide behind me and Les and just drink anyway. That was one of the good times and there was just so much food, plenty of grog, anything we wanted.

'I remember one of the waiters there tried to charge me $30 for a bottle of champagne and I told Ian Dury about it and he said, "Well, I'm going to go and see that guy because everything's paid for and he had no right to try and charge you for the bottle of champagne." So, he went and ripped into that guy or got his manager to go and tell him, "You know what, everybody here is his guest and they don't pay for nothing." But yeah, that was one of the things that stood out for me, how he looked after us. And all the time everybody just talked and drank and ate and we finally went our own way. That was the last time I saw Ian Dury until I found out that he passed away.'

For a Melbourne-based band looking to forge a career in the music industry in the early 1980s, most roads led to one man: Michael Gudinski. Gudinski's interlocking business empire included the leading live booking agency, Premier Artists; the most successful independent record label, Mushroom Records; the Mushroom Music Publishing company; and for tours by international acts, the Frontier Touring Company. No Fixed Address manager Mick Pacholli knew Gudinski well and arranged a meeting. But he had some other options up his sleeve too.

'We had an interview with Michael Gudinski about a record deal,' says Les Graham. 'He said, "Keep your music the same but change the lyrics." I was kinda all for that. I was talking to the band and said, "Once you're on top of the mountain you can sing what you want and everyone's gonna listen to you." But they said, "No, you take us how we are." They didn't want to do the deal with him. He said he had interest from America. That was the kick-off. That was gonna be it. Gudinski ran the show back in them days.'

'I've been associated with Premier and Mushroom since I got into the music industry,' says Pacholli. 'Through advertising in *tagg*, my bands, I had rock'n'roll, reggae, bush bands, acoustic duos. I had deals with the t-shirt people there. They knew me. When I got No Fixed Address, it was all brand new. It took two or three years to get the record deal. We got the deal going and I decided, as manager, that Gudinski can't have everything.'

The previous year, when John John Miller was still in the band, Pacholli had organised some recording sessions with producer Lobby Loyde in Sydney. 'We went up to Sydney on tour,' Pacholli says. 'I was with the band. Central Recorders in Sydney, that was Lobby's studio up there at the time. We did about five or six days in there. It was amazing what came out of there but Lobby was having some trouble with his business and, I don't know, but Lobby never came through.' Songs recorded with Loyde included 'From My Eyes', 'Sunrise', 'Pigs', 'Reality', 'Darkness of Day' and 'Harder Today'.

Les Graham, John John Miller and Duckie Taylor all thought the sessions with Loyde were terrific and remain bewildered as to what happened to them. 'Lobby Loyde had actually done the first recording and that sounded excellent,' says Taylor. 'I don't know what happened after that because all the people involved with the band, they were all trying to get their finger in the pie here and there. I really don't know what happened; somehow that recording of Lobby Loyde's disappeared.'

'Yeah, it was in Sydney, in Kings Cross there,' says Miller. 'We recorded a whole album. It was done. We tried to get in touch with him. But we couldn't get in touch with him. He had the masters with me playing. But when they went to use it, he destroyed it so they had to do it again. It was already there. That was the one. That's why I don't understand why there was another album. Because it was already there.'

Loyde's wife later told Pacholli, 'We just taped over it.'

~

With the recordings they'd made with Loyde erased and the band resistant to Michael Gudinski's suggestion to change their lyrics, Pacholli turned to a former flatmate, who just happened to be involved in a new independent record label.

In partnership with Little River Band guitarist David Briggs and Milly Comfort (a former staffer at Virgin Records London and the Robert Stigwood Organisation), Melbourne *Herald* journalist Ross Gardiner had formed Rough Diamond Records in 1980. Through his connection with Pacholli, Gardiner was well aware of No Fixed Address. 'The whole thing about their formation and movie and soundtrack for *Wrong Side of the Road* coming out of Adelaide was known to me, and when they came to Melbourne, I definitely followed them up,' he says.

Gardiner had met David Briggs in Brisbane while covering the Little River Band's 1977 *Diamantina Cocktail* tour. The two became friends and hung out together in Melbourne after Gardiner moved there in 1978. 'I got into the business of scouting new bands,' says Gardiner. 'The long story short is that I got onto this band in Carlton at the Polaris Inn called Australian Crawl, and I met James Reyne and introduced him to David. And we thought, "What can we do with this band?" [Glenn] Wheatley was saying, "I want to be the manager." Briggs was saying, "I want to be a producer."'

By late 1978, Briggs was recording demos with Australian Crawl and when the band signed with EMI, Briggs was tapped to produce their first single, 'Beautiful People', which came out in August 1979.

That same month, Briggs headed to North America with Little River Band to tour in support of their fifth album, *First Under the Wire*. After a punishing 11-week, 64-date coast-to-coast run, Briggs was back in Melbourne in November to continue work on the first Australian Crawl album. As well as gold and platinum records for *First Under the Wire*, LRB brought home a Grammy nomination for Best Pop Vocal Performance by a Duo, Group or Chorus for the Briggs-penned single: 'Lonesome Loser'.

Released in April 1980, Australian Crawl's *The Boys Light Up* was a stunning debut. Yielding three hit singles – 'Beautiful People', 'The Boys Light Up' and 'Downhearted', the album ended up selling 285,000 copies and being certified five-times platinum.

'What happened after that was the band chose a producer from Sydney, Peter Dawkins, who was the A&R for EMI Music, for the second album,' says Gardiner. 'He brought them in to work with him as a house producer. So, David and I felt, "Oh, shit, why would we let EMI do this? We can do this for ourselves." So, we decided to try and do our own independent label.

'David had a building in North Melbourne that he started fitting out as a recording studio. And so, we've got a plan to release a label and we got a commitment of some funding and distribution from Astor Records which was the only independent manufacturer in Victoria outside of Mushroom.'

Briggs announced his departure from LRB in July 1981, a month after completing the band's sixth album, *Time Exposure*. While leaving LRB meant Briggs could devote more of his energies to production, the first cracks had started to appear in Rough Diamond's overall strategy. Astor Records and German-based multinational PolyGram were both owned by Dutch electronics manufacturer Philips. Concerned at Astor's erratic performance, Philips directed PolyGram to assume financial and corporate responsibility for its smaller stablemate.

In November 1981, Philips announced it was closing the Astor manufacturing plant and the facility ceased operations completely on 31 December 1981.[1] The four remaining pressing plants (CBS, EMI, Festival and Powderworks) were all in Sydney. While Rough Diamond had some cover – for a while at least – through its distribution deal with Astor, the plant's closure dealt a serious blow to other Melbourne-based independent operators such as Missing Link, Au Go Go and Raven Records.

By November 1981, Rough Diamond had released a single and album by ex-Perth outfit, The Stockings; had signed ex-Adelaide outfit, Young Homebuyers; and a local Melbourne act, The Orphans. Looking to expand their roster, Briggs and Gardiner caught No Fixed Address live. Les Graham recalls, 'He [Briggs] came to our gigs and he was excited.'

'Yeah, we got out to see No Fixed Address,' says Gardiner. 'They had a portfolio of very powerful songs. Very powerful songs that were really from the heart, that were very deep in their storytelling of the history and injustices experienced by Indigenous people and the kind of importance that they were to these young men, young Aboriginal men. They were the real

Joe Geia, Bart Willoughby, Joe Hayes, Les Graham, Ricky Harrison, Billy Inda Cummins with Jenny Keath, Mushroom Music Publishing, 1982.

Photo by Greg Noakes.

deal, incredibly genuine and totally deserving of everything that could be brought their way.'

No Fixed Address was receptive to the Rough Diamond approach and so Pacholli went back to Michael Gudinski to talk about a music publishing deal. 'I've gone in to speak to Michael about doing the publishing deal,' says Pacholli. 'I've already done the deal with Rough Diamond, through Astor as a third party. In principle. I hadn't signed anything yet. I went to Michael and I said, "Okay. I want to talk to you about publishing." There's the manager of another well-known band chopping out lines and rolling joints next to us. He goes, "Why haven't I got the record deal, Mick?" I said, "You can't own everything, Michael." I said, "You've got every fucking band in Melbourne and you're not owning the Aborigines as well, okay? You can have their publishing." And he goes, "Mick, I want the band." I said, "You can't have them. I've done a deal with David and Ross and Milly." "Oh, all right then, I'll teach you how to get the best deal any third party's ever had. And so, with publishing I've got to get you the best deal anyone's ever had too, don't I?" "Yes, Michael." "If you ever repeat this, Pacholli, you're dead."'

The upshot was the band's two songwriters, Bart Willoughby and Ricky Harrison, signed with Mushroom Music Publishing.

The Clash flew into Sydney from Japan on Wednesday, 3 February 1982. The group held a press conference the following day before jetting across to New Zealand for gigs in Auckland, Wellington and Christchurch.[1] One of the questions to lead singer Joe Strummer was, 'Tell us why you've come to Australia, Joe.' Strummer replied, 'I don't know. Ian Dury's just been here. He said it was great' (*Roadrunner* February 1982).

Perhaps Lord Upminster had put in a good word for No Fixed Address after their boozy après-gig bonding session in Melbourne? Whatever, a black Australian reggae band was always going to be a good fit for a touring outfit notable for their love of reggae and their determination to have interesting and credible supports. For The Clash's run of seven dates at Sydney's Capitol Theatre, No Fixed Address scored the opening night support on Thursday, 11 February and a second spot on Sunday 14th. The remaining support slots went to ska outfit The Allniters (Friday), Spy v Spy (Saturday), The Hitmen (Tuesday), Sardine v (Wednesday) and The Flaming Hands (Thursday 18th).

The Clash's sprawling triple album *Sandanista!* had been released at the end of 1980. British critics scratched their heads before reaching for their poison pens, but the Americans loved it. *Rolling Stone* gave it a 5-star review and it rose to #24 on the *Billboard* chart, three spots higher than the widely-praised *London Calling*. With original manager Bernie Rhodes back at the helm in early 1981, the band's focus turned Stateside. When US record label Epic refused tour support for a mooted 60-date campaign, Rhodes activated plan B and booked a run of shows in May and June at a tacky former disco on the corner of Times Square and Broadway in New York City. The initial eight nights at Bond's International Casino was extended to seventeen after the New York Fire Department imposed an audience cap of 1750 (it was estimated that only 900 of the first night crowd of 3,500 would have made it out in the case of a fire).

In *Redemption Song*, his definitive biography of Joe Strummer, Chris Salewicz says the Bond's shows marked a major upward turn for The Clash. He goes further, writing: 'The career of The Clash was definitively pre- and post-Bond's: the Top Ten US success of *Combat Rock* the following year can be traced back to this springboard.'[2] Pleased with the experience of a run of nights at a medium-sized venue, the band repeated the New York exercise in Europe, with seven nights at the Théâtre Mogador, Paris in September followed by another seven at the Lyceum, London in October. In their one and only trip to the Far East, they couldn't quite organise seven nights at one venue in Tokyo (four at the Sun Plaza Hall had to do), but seven nights in the faded glory of a former art deco picture palace in Sydney's Haymarket was a fitting way to round off the conceit.

David Langsam, a *Roadrunner* contributor from Melbourne, was staying with *Roadrunner* Sydney editor Stuart Coupe when The Clash returned from New Zealand. Coupe was invited to a CBS drinks night for the band and asked Langsam if he wanted to come along. 'Back in those days, free food, free drinks? Yeah, of course I'd be there,' says Langsam. 'I went along and I was young and a bit irascible, a bit stupid and I had a couple of drinks and I started quoting Keith Richards bagging record companies for, on the one hand, recording music and ripping off artists and being shysters, on the other hand also being invested in nuclear weaponry and killing innocent civilians and being corporate mugs of the worst order. And Stuart was sinking into his seat, thinking, "Oh, what the fuck have I done? Who is this guy I've brought along?" Stuart is very amenable to the people he has to work with but I'm not that clever. And I pretty much alienated CBS on the spot. But Kosmo Vinyl, the Clash's tour manager, and Joe Strummer could hear me and they adopted me very quickly and I ended up down their end of the table. And then back at their hotel in Kings Cross [the Sebel Town House] and we got on like a house on fire.

'I hung out with The Clash for the next day or two. I said to them, "With the *Sandinista!* album, you put Sandinistas on stage in New York and caused huge amounts of consternation by giving them space. You should have an Aboriginal activist get up with you on stage here in Australia." They said, "Yeah, we've been thinking about that – do you know anyone?" I said, "Let me make a call or two." I used their phone and I called Gary Foley's number in Melbourne. A woman who was not very happy to talk to me gave me a number in Sydney and another woman there screened it and I said, "I'm looking for Gary Foley because I'm here with The Clash." Foley could obviously hear it because he grabbed the phone off her and said, "Where the fuck are ya?" I knew him from about 1976 or so. He said, "Where the fuck are ya? I've been trying to get in touch with The Clash." I said, "Well, I'm with them. Do you know anyone who's an Aboriginal activist who'd like to get up on stage and express Aboriginal views with The Clash?" "Agggghhhh – where are ya?" And he was down at the hotel about thirty minutes later.'

~

At the time, Gary Foley had been deeply involved in political, social and cultural activities to advance the cause of Aboriginal rights for more than a decade. He had helped set up Aboriginal legal services in New South Wales and South Australia; he was part of the Black Caucus, the Sydney Black Power collective that established the Aboriginal Tent Embassy on the lawns of Parliament House Canberra; and he had been a director of the Victorian Aboriginal Health Service.

Andrew McMillan wrote an exhaustive account of The Clash's Sydney sojourn in *RAM* titled 'The World's Last Rock'n'Roll Band'. This was his description of Foley's appearance with the band:

During the second encore, the band slips into 'Armagideon Time'. Slides of refugee children plaster the back wall while Strummer sings: 'A lot of people won't get no supper tonight. Justice tonight ...'

It's an excellent version that swings along. The pace is relaxed but Strummer's vocal is bitter. While Mick Jones wiggles his bum and cracks a couple of syndrums next to his amp, Strummer motions to the side stage.

From the shadows a lightly bearded [A]boriginal in a Rock Against Racism t-shirt emerges. He wanders across to Strummer's mike.

"My name's Gary Foley! I'm a black Australian! I'm here to tell you tonight a little bit about what's happening to [A]boriginal people in this country!

"Our brothers here from The Clash said we could tell you a little bit because, this is not just a night for music: this is a night for understanding people who are oppressed!

"And in this country, it's [A]boriginal people who are oppressed!"

His every word is crystal clear and the band continues to play along behind him.

"Our people lived in this country for 50,000 years, and everything was cool until some bloke by the name of Captain Cook came out here ... Now 800 million [A]boriginal people lived and died here before any white man came to this country. When you arrived – when white man arrived in this country – they shot the blacks, poisoned their waterholes, slaughtered them right, left and centre! And those that were left were rounded up like dogs and cattle and stuck in these places called Aboriginal Reserves, which were nothing less than concentration camps! And there they stayed until recently.

"It's only 14 years since you people gave us the vote in this country, and we still have not got the land to give us economic independence. We need land, right! And we need it now!

"It's not good enough just to come and listen to music. If you people can afford the time to come to a Clash concert then you can afford the time, sometime soon, when [A]boriginal people march in this town, for their land rights, then you should be there!

> "I've got one last thing to say ... In October, there's going to be a lot of [A]boriginal people going up to Queensland to protest at the Commonwealth Games! And the reason we're there is because ... in Queensland [A]boriginal people still are under the thumb of Joh Bjelke-Petersen; still have the same law that existed against us in this state! We want black people in Queensland to be free! To have land rights! We want black people all over Australia to have land rights! And we want your support in Brisbane against the Games! Thank you!"
>
> As Foley retires, The Clash increase the volume, surging with the cheers from the audience. Strummer returns to the mike. 'Justice tonight!'[3]

'That was the essential thing that was needed at that moment,' says Foley. 'The opportunity that Strummer and them gave me. I took that opportunity to do that. What I was trying to do was rally up the troops to get as many people as possible to Brisbane, and that provided the perfect opportunity. Even though the audience weren't exactly the kind of people you would normally see at a land rights march, there were a lot of them there in the Brisbane protest. Any time you get an opportunity to talk into a loudspeaker you may not normally have, then you take it, to get the message out there. It's a lifelong thing. People will be doing it after I'm dead because nothing's going to fucking change. But that's life, says the old cynic coming out of me again.'

Maxine Briggs was doing lights for No Fixed Address on The Clash shows. 'The opening night was packed,' she says. 'There were many musos in the house that night. It was a big night. There was a bit of tension, a bit of aggro before they went on. I don't know what was going on, but it made for a really spirited show. I knew the Australian crew that were working on the Clash show and they were really impressed with No Fixed – Les in particular. They just wanted to hit him with follow-spots the whole time. He took some screaming solos. They really owned that stage that night. I think they blew a lot of people away.'

Jean Morgan remembers the great reception No Fixed Address received on the opening night. 'They had two nights supporting The Clash,' she says. 'What was interesting was the first night, the audience, when No Fixed Address played, the crowd just went crazy for them. They all rushed towards the stage and were trying to get close to them and everything. On the next night, the security, they had guard railings up so people couldn't get to the stage. They weren't expecting people to be so rapt in the support act.'

'The Clash gigs were just electric,' says Briggs. 'No Fixed and Gary Foley; Gary just shoved a few home truths down their throats, people who hadn't experienced someone like Foley before. No Fixed Address, kicking arse and spitting some truth like no-one else. And then there was the Clash; loved their music and their politics, a great live band, the bass player just killed it.'

~

In between their two Clash supports, No Fixed Address made a couple of other Sydney appearances. On Friday, 12 February 1982 they were at The Tivoli in George Street, middle of the bill with headliners Men at Work (riding high in the charts with their debut album, *Business as Usual* and the single 'Down Under') and inner-city darlings The Particles. The next night they headlined an all-black band line-up at Selinas in the Coogee Bay Hotel with local outfits Un Tabu and King Cobra.

Men at Work had played with No Fixed Address at a Rock Against Racism show at Northcote Town Hall in Melbourne as far back as July 1980. Men at Work lead singer Colin Hay remembers it being quite a big night. 'It felt very important at the time,' he says. 'And indeed, I'm sure it probably still is.' How aware was he of land rights and other Aboriginal issues back then?

'As much as anyone who leans to the left was aware of whatever was going on,' he replies. 'You're always aware that there seems to be this deep vein of racism that goes through the country, and on the other side of the coin there is this feeling, that I had anyway, about the Australian character being one of hopefulness. In the sense that on the other side of the coin you often find incredible openness and benevolence and empathy and compassion. You get that as well. It's really more a question of who's going to win in the end. It's still a very turbulent state. Like here in a way [Hay has lived in Los Angeles since 1990]. The experiment of the USA is still turbulent and is still to be defined. Whether you can make America great for everybody, instead of what it's been. It's still yet to prove what it claims to be. It's the same in Australia, where I came to as an immigrant when I was fourteen from Scotland. To me it was just an incredibly exciting place to come to. It just felt so different under my feet. I was always aware I was in someone else's place, you know.'

Hay admits his memories of those heady days are very vague ('I gave myself quite a hammering for fifteen or twenty years,' he wryly observes) but he does remember No Fixed Address. 'I think they were a band that was of their time,' he says. 'I was going to say, some people would say they were before their time, but they really weren't. They were exactly what was required at that period of time for many different reasons. I remember a lot of things obviously but there's a lot that's gone. But I remember Bart. He was many things. He was a great drummer. He played ... he had his own thing going. He had his own groove that went through him. And he had his own way of singing. The songs were great and they had melody and they were everything songs should be. And he was kinda like a sexy guy and everything. Joe [Geia], I remember a bit too. But mainly Bart had a big impact as far as I was concerned. If I just think back, it's his face that springs to mind.'

After a final Sydney show on Monday 15th at the San Miguel in Cammeray, No Fixed Address left town, heading down the Princes Highway and over the Victorian border for a show the following night at the Gippsland Institute of Advanced Education in Churchill. Then it was on to Melbourne and news of a prospective Western Australian tour to coincide with the Perth premiere of *Wrong Side of the Road.* In addition, the recording contract with Rough Diamond Records was almost ready to be signed. It was a giddy time.

On the morning of Friday, 26 February 1982, the members of No Fixed Address, accompanied by manager Mick Pacholli, assembled at the Rough Diamond office in North Melbourne to sign a recording contract. The contract, initially for a term of six months, required the band to record sufficient tracks for – and for Rough Diamond to release – at least one mini-LP. It was a big step. But for Joe Hayes' wife Jean Morgan, something didn't feel right.

'They got the boys pretty tanked up,' she says. 'We're in the offices up there at Rough Diamond Studios in Queensberry Street. And yeah, to me they got them … they had the Crown Lagers out and everything and they were pretty tanked and then they pulled out the contracts. We'd only just seen them, and you need lawyers to look at those things with you and explain certain things. None of us were lawyers. I didn't let Joe sign straightaway.

'It was just the way they conducted it all. We got there and we were there for about half an hour to an hour before they pulled the contracts out to be signed. And by that time, the boys had already had a few. Some had had a few joints as well. Everybody's happy and everybody's friendly and, young as I was, I could see there was something a bit funny about it all.'

Nonetheless, Bart Willoughby, Les Graham, Joe Geia, Joe Hayes and Ricky Harrison (under his other name of Chris Jones) signed the contract. Billy Inda Cummins was not included. All signatures were witnessed by Jenny Keath from Mushroom Music Publishing. Was it a good move? Not according to some. 'The worst mistake they ever fucking made was they signed with David Briggs and Ross Gardiner at Rough Diamond,' says Pacholli.

~

The following week, Rough Diamond Records issued a newsflash announcing that No Fixed Address had signed a world-wide deal and had commenced work on their debut release for the label. Producer for the sessions was David Briggs, who was recording the band as the first act at his 'recently updated 24-track Production Workshop in Melbourne'. A single and mini-album were tentatively slotted for May release.

The recording was done in about a four-week period, Gardiner recalls. 'It was done Monday to Friday during the day over four weeks and it was slotted and my memory of going in there every day and listening to what was happening ... it was a good session. It wasn't a session where everyone was fighting and arguing and all of that. It went down a lot smoother than that.

'The first week the bass and drums and rhythm tracks were done, including rehearsing the songs. Then the second week, they started doing the guitars and voices. The third week, other instruments like didgeridoo and clapsticks and bongo drums and all the rest of it were all in, backing vocals and so on, and then the final week was mixing it. So, it was done in one month. It was pretty fast to do.'

Writing in *The Age* in 1984, Adrian Ryan opined that the Rough Diamond sessions 'did not do much to capture the distinctive energy of No Fixed Address'. Bart Willoughby told him, 'On that record it was as if we were robots being told what to do by the producer'.[1]

Graeme Isaac notes David Briggs was merely following the conventional recording approach of the day in assembling the recording track by track – but it was a very different approach to that employed on the *Wrong Side of the Road* recordings. 'In the Adelaide recordings they were recorded pretty much live with selective overdubs after,' Isaac says. 'That was partly a function of necessity – there wasn't the separation in that little 8-track studio to do things differently. But also, this has always been a better way to record "roots" music and "feel" music.'

~

No Fixed Address

From My Eyes recording line-up, 1982. Back row: Joe Hayes, Joe Geia, Ricky Harrison. Front row: Les Graham, Bart Willoughby, Billy Inda Cummins.

Photo by Rough Diamond Records.

When *Wrong Side of the Road* was released in November 1981, its Perth season was earmarked for the Perth Institute of Film and Television (PIFT) in March 1982. PIFT was the Western Australian cog in a loose network of Australian cinemas that focussed on screening independent films. Based in the former Fremantle Boys School, it operated a main cinema as well as the smaller Cinema 16. David Noakes, who was on the board of PIFT and ran Cinema 16, had a bright idea. 'Why don't we get them [No Fixed Address] over?' he thought.

Noakes contacted Mick Pacholli in Melbourne and pitched the idea. 'I said, "We're going to do this screening and we're going to bring people and we can also do a gig that night.

Whaddya reckon?" I think that's what started the ball rolling.' Pacholli contacted Perth promoter Kenn McMillan and they started putting together a tour schedule for Perth and regional Western Australia, based around the premiere of *Wrong Side of the Road* at PIFT on 6 April.

~

Just before No Fixed Address headed to Perth, Billy Inda Cummins was asked if he would reprise his didgeridoo playing on 'Solid Rock' for Goanna's debut album. There are a number of versions of how this transpired. Mick Pacholli says he arranged it after a request from Goanna manager Ian Lovell. Pacholli also says he organised for Joe Geia to go to the recording session when Cummins became indisposed. Ian Lovell strongly disputes this. Joe Geia and Shane Howard each have their own versions too.

'We had to pick up a reverb unit from a place,' Geia says. 'It was the studio where Goanna was recording. And we were parked outside waiting for someone to go in and get the reverb unit. Then somebody come out and said, "Hey, Joe, your cousin's inside there." It was Billy. He was playing the didge. He was doing some recording with people. Billy sees me and says, "Hey, this fella here, he can play didge too. Get him on there." It was like, "Okay." And they put me in the recording area and I put about two tracks down on didge.'

Shane Howard says, 'What happened was, Billy didn't feel capable of the fancier aspects of the didge playing once it got under the microscope in the studio. And he said, "I've got a brother here in Melbourne, I could call him." About an hour or so later this guy walks in to the studio: Joe, Joe Geia. I hadn't met Joe before.

'All those early connections for me were Queensland, the Murri connection. And have remained very strong throughout my life. So, yeah, they both are on that recording. We said we needed a contact for payment and credits and Joe said, "Just say my brother did it." Of course, Joe went on to join No Fixed as well. That year was a pretty eventful year for both of us. We both released albums. I always say to people that No Fixed were playing ... Bart was playing didge in No Fixed before Goanna were, but I wouldn't have seen that. So, it was Billy; it was the Murris that brought the didge to our world really. There was such a lovely synchronicity happening around that time. An incredibly fertile time. That explosion of Aboriginal music and culture and the music coming from South Australia with No Fixed Address, but this culture and the dance and the traditional song coming from North Queensland with Billy Cummins and Joe Geia and all that. They're all relations.'

'Solid Rock' was released as a single in September 1982 and was a big hit, reaching #3 on the Australian Kent Music Report. 'We were in the truck going somewhere,' says Geia. 'I thought I'd roll a joint. And as I was rolling a joint, I leaned over and put the radio on and "Solid Rock" come across the air. And it was, "Hey, that's me, playing didgeridoo. That's the same song we were blowing didge on the other night!" So, it was on the highway that "Solid Rock" came across the radio and I realised that was my didge playing. Anyway, we lit up the joint and listened to the song.'

~

After the No Fixed Address recording sessions with David Briggs were completed, the band members and crew loaded up their equipment truck and piled into two cars for their debut tour of Western Australia. The touring party included Mario Mottct (tour manager), Duckie Taylor (sound mixer), Maxine Briggs (lighting), Edward Love, known by his nickname Woody (stagehand), John Parker, known to all as Car John (vehicle manager and mechanic) and Jean Morgan.

En route, the Adelaide Festival of Arts was in full swing and on the afternoon of Sunday, 21 March, No Fixed Address played a free show in Elder Park with Us Mob. Presented by the Adelaide Festival Centre community arts program in association with the Adelaide Festival of Arts and CASM, the event featured soloists, dancers and musicians both contemporary and traditional.

But before the first engagement over the Western Australian border, things started to go off the rails. The truck broke down, causing the cancellation of the Wednesday gig in Esperance. With the truck fixed, the band played Thursday night in Albany, but as the convoy rolled into Busselton on Friday came the news that many of the gigs that had been booked for them in Perth had been cancelled when venue owners realised they were an Aboriginal band.

In March 1982, Wendy Slee had just turned 22 and was working at the Commercial Hotel in Busselton. 'The Commie was the big old pub on the corner as you drove into town and was the place where all the action unfolded each weekend,' she says. 'Loud rock bands, lingering parties in the carpark, drunken brawls, you name it – of all the four hotels in town, this one had the reputation and delivered the entertainment.

'I remember when No Fixed Address arrived after a long drive, to set up for their first gig. There was no surprise to see they were Aboriginal. My boss Margaret Colthart, the licensee, was an older Scottish lady, a tough resilient woman who knew the industry and did not even bat an eye. Totally unfazed, she just welcomed the boys (and partners and crew) in and showed them the rooms upstairs.

'Looking back, there seemed to be no fuss, no comments made, no raised eyebrows. No-one really took any notice that the entertainment for the weekend was an all-black band. We were all just looking forward to new live music. I did not realise at the time how big an issue it was at other venues or the story behind this particular band. We had bands come through the pub regularly to play, and when these guys rocked up this day I thought, "Oh cool, an Aboriginal band. This is a bit different." There was no problem with them playing at our hotel, no problems with the owner. But when I learned what their history was with racism in towns and venues, I was so glad that Busselton welcomed them. And they were far better than most of the other bands we'd heard playing live at local venues. Their music was so good – that was what defined my first impressions!'

'We absolutely loved Busselton,' says Maxine Briggs. 'It was like a long cool drink. After coming across the Nullarbor and some of the things that happened on the way.'

Originally booked in for just Friday night, the band also

ended up playing Saturday night and the Sunday afternoon session in Busselton. Saturday night had been pencilled in at the Bussell Motor Inn up the road in Bunbury, but it was suddenly 'booked out'.

'I remember being stunned by just how good their music was,' Slee recalls. 'It was both angry and defiant with its very loud message, but also a cry to be heard that pierced the heart (and the conscience, I hope). Whether the audience took on board the message, they certainly picked up on the energy and passion. The dance floor was alive and people sang along.

'Because I worked at the pub, I got to chat to many who were in the band and crew. I especially developed an affinity with Jeannie, the wife of band member Joe, and Maxine who was part of the sound and lighting crew. They were bright and vibrant young women and I was drawn to the idea of a life on the road with music by witnessing their spark. I think though, again being very naïve, I had no idea of the downside to such a life!

'After the pub closed many people would "kick on" – go to someone's house for a party. I recall seeing these Aboriginal visitors amongst the white locals, sitting around drinking, laughing, and chatting, no doubt smoking some weed. It was totally inclusive. For me it was a duality – the shallow gathering to consume alcohol, get a little wasted, to laugh and muck around, but also woven through, the deeper experience sharing and getting to know about the music and the people behind it … the acceptance. So clearly, I recall sitting on the floor leaning against a wall, beer in my hand, and Les sat down beside me with his guitar and played the Beatles classic "Lady Madonna" – like a sensory snapshot, the feelings and memories of that moment have remained with me all my life. Heart wide open! I think the irony is, that I fell in love with these people, yet was both drawn to and shattered by a new reality of the underbelly to their journey, their music, their suffering. But being young, it was first and foremost that I loved the music.'

~

Jean Morgan (left) and Maxine Briggs, Perth Institute of Film and Television, 6 April 1982.

Photo by Wendy Slee.

The front page of Perth's *Sunday Independent* on 28 March screamed 'ES [Eastern States] rock group black banned', with a lead paragraph that ran, 'A race-hate film starring a black rock group has come to life in Perth – for the group who starred in the prize-winning movie'.[1] The paper had a full-page story inside detailing the whole sorry saga. It included an interview with David Noakes, the organiser of the Perth premiere of *Wrong Side of the Road*.

Singled out for criticism by Noakes was Perth nightspot Adrian's. 'Adrian's in James Street offered us two Saturday nights when they heard the group had made an album and there was a film about them,' he said. 'And that clinched the deal. But the club pulled out when the owner found they were Aborigines. They reneged on it.' The paper reported other nightspots to turn the band down included Eagle 1, The Cat and Fiddle in North Perth, Shenton Park Hotel and Victoria Hotel, Subiaco.

~

Cold Chisel were in Perth that weekend. Back in Melbourne, manager Mick Pacholli contacted their management agency, which offered No Fixed Address the support spot on their Monday night show at the Embassy Ballroom.

'Cold Chisel were touring at the same time,' says Pacholli. 'I get on the phone, straight onto Dirty Pool in Sydney, Chisel's management. They said, "Jesus, er, look, we'll bring 'em on, they can support us, okay? We'll look after them and everything else, so your budget will come together." I've gone, "You're kidding." They've gone, "No Mick, let's do it." Wow. Now that is generosity of the heart. And it wasn't Jimmy Barnes. The band will go, "Aw, Cold Chisel were so great." It wasn't anything to do with the band. It was the management that did all this.'

'It was a nice feeling to have that sort of support,' says Maxine Briggs. 'It felt very ... personal and not so much a charitable act. Like they were two Adelaide bands. No Fixed Address played many shows with Cold Chisel on the east coast, and they knew each other from back home. That's how I felt, that their act of camaraderie sort of helped bring that situation together for us in a way. I'd reckon Chisel would have known what was happening with the No Fixed tour.'

Duckie Taylor was mixing live sound on the tour. 'We were booked out for two weeks, and me and Les were the first two to get over there [Perth] and we went to the motel where Cold Chisel was staying. I remember when we got to [Jimmy] Barnes' room, which was downstairs near the pool, all the band members were sitting outside. I remember them saying, "You're game going in there, because he don't like no-one to disturb him until he gets out of bed." I remember me and Les going in the bedroom, into his room, and Les grabs him on the foot and he just flew up. He's seen it was us two and said, grog's in the fridge and the *yarndi* [marijuana]'s on the top, if you want any. So, he got up and started talking and in about ten minutes time, all the boys, the rest of the band outside must have thought it's safe to go in, he hasn't screamed at them or anything. Then we were telling them about our conference meeting and how they cancelled our gigs.'

~

By Tuesday the Perth *Daily News* was reporting that many of the gaps in the band's agenda had been filled.[2] Blazes nightclub in North Perth had booked the band on Friday, 2 April and they were headlining a Sunday afternoon concert presented by Aboriginal Radio 6NR at the Lake Gnangara Aboriginal Cultural Complex on 4 April. They also scored a spot at the Herdsman Hotel on Monday, 5 April.

Tour manager Mario Mottet was interviewed in the *Daily News* and said, 'You have to keep your head high and try not to let it worry you. It is certainly not a new thing for us. Hopefully the tour will turn out better than was expected in the weekend. It just goes to show what happened in the film isn't make believe. We aren't just singing for the black people of Australia. What we want to do is cut down these barriers to racial discrimination that we often run into.'

The issue of the cancelled gigs was compounded by Bart Willoughby breaking his arm in Perth. 'We had to get a replacement drummer,' says Noakes. 'We put the word out and we found this guy in Perth, Reg Zar. He was amazing. He wasn't the fittest guy in the world and he was older than them and he worked his arse off. Keeping up with them was really hard for him. But he was incredible. And he became really good friends with them. Bart couldn't drum so he just did the vocals. So, for the first time we had Bart up the front and the drums at the back. It was just such a bloody rollercoaster, that whole thing.'

No Fixed Address had made quite an impression on Wendy Slee. Not being required at the pub in Busselton, she headed up to Perth. 'I wanted to hear more of their music,' says Slee. 'I had a few days off, so I decided to go to Perth with them as they continued their rather fragmented tour. By then I had heard about the cancellation of their other shows, and the constant battle they faced with acceptance for themselves and the music due primarily to their race. I was also aware that they were promoting the movie about their story, with the opening night at PIFT in Fremantle and I wanted to be there for that. So, I drove to Perth and stayed at the Shaftesbury Hotel [in Stirling Street, Northbridge] where they were staying. It meant I could hang out with the girls and spend more time with all of them. And of course, hear their music while I still could. I remember that I wrote out their set lists for them, which made me feel included and useful. But the big one was the opening night for their movie at PIFT. This was the big one they had travelled to WA for.'

~

PIFT was in the former Fremantle Boys School. The schedule for the opening night included two screenings of *Wrong Side of the Road* (at 6.15 and 8 pm) followed by a concert by No Fixed Address at 9.30 pm in the former school assembly hall. On top of everything else, the concert was to be recorded by ABC-TV for its new late-night music show *Rock Arena*. The first series of the program was produced in Perth by Ian Parmenter.

'When I was based in Perth, I put it to the ABC that there were opportunities for programs for people who had been through *Countdown,* who had grown out of *Countdown*, but who still had a serious interest in music,' says Parmenter. 'I

Les Graham, Joe Geia, Reg Zar, Bart Willoughby (in cast), Joe Hayes and Billy Inda Cummins, Perth Institute of Film and Television, 6 April 1982.

Photo by Wendy Slee.

---

had friends in the record industry in Perth and they had racks of 2-inch tapes in their offices of concerts by brilliant people. I said to the ABC, "I've got access to all the concerts by these top people that have never been seen. It's not going to cost you anything to put this show on." That really rattled all the right cages over there in Sydney. They said, "Okay, fine, go for it." Once I'd got it going, I thought there are opportunities here to do things with bands that are coming to WA or are in WA.

'I had contacts with PIFT, and I'd been involved with putting music on TV for a long, long time. When the No Fixed Address visit came up, I said, "Look, it'd be great, I'll do it as an entire broadcast for one edition of the program." So, what happened was, I got in touch with their management and then I arranged that we would have a soundcheck during the afternoon at PIFT so we could rehearse the band. And they said, "Oh yeah, that'll be fine." So, I turned up with the crew and the band didn't. "Oh, okay, fine." It was fine.'

'They were still flat-out doing rehearsals because Reg was just learning everything,' says David Noakes. 'That was all that day. And at the same time, the ABC were bumping in with all their scaffolding and lighting.'

Parmenter continues: 'We'd already been building up the profile of this band by saying this was, at the time, Australia's only all-Indigenous band and so that's what we were expecting. When they eventually appeared, without a soundcheck, their lead singer, who was also their drummer, had his arm in a sling so he couldn't drum. They had on drums, somebody I actually knew, called Reg Zar, who was white [laughs]. He'd never played with them before.

'Here I was with a national program, unrehearsed, three cameras, which is all we could manage, and an audience and the concert went ahead. And somehow, we managed to cobble a program together out of it. That was my memory of it. It was something of a catastrophe [laughs]. But it all finished up okay. I haven't seen it since, but God, it took years off me.'

~

The following night, the band played at the Shaftesbury to pay for their accommodation. According to Maxine Briggs, the gig didn't end well. 'It turned into a battleground. There were huge fights in the crowd and it ended up out on the street. The whole street was fighting. I think they shut the gig down. That's how I remember it anyway. I don't know what caused it.'

Wendy Slee was blissfully unaware at the time but heard all about it later. 'There was a special below-ground area of the hotel,' she says. 'You could go downstairs to a basement room where people could party after the hotel had closed, everyone hanging out drinking and chatting. Apart from one other person who was on their crew, I think I may have been the only other "white" person there. Many years later, a friend of my family, who had been in the police force, was chatting with our family and something came up about that night and he looked shocked and said, "Oh my God, girl, if I'd known you were in that pub on that night I would have gone in and kicked your arse and dragged you out and sent you home."

Slee continues: 'Apparently, there had been a lot of violence going on outside the hotel; the police were there in full force and, given the level of unrest, he was stunned to think I was there. And I said, "Well, there was nothing going on inside. We were just sitting around eating and having drinks." It was a fairly ordinary "party", just people sharing music, drinks and banter, and good times. Sure, a bit of weed got smoked, but it was minimal, and there was nothing sinister or negative. But yeah, apparently out in the street – Stirling Street – the atmosphere was very different with mob violence and fights and all kinds of stuff going on.'

After leaving Perth, No Fixed Address played two nights in Kalgoorlie over the Easter weekend. 'I vividly remember the night we were in Kalgoorlie,' Jean Morgan recalls. 'We were staying at the Railway Hotel. We'd been there for a night or two. The band invited some of the locals up to our rooms after the gig.'

'They were the Broad Arrow Road mob,' says Maxine Briggs. 'That was the mission down the road. Good people. They really embraced us. The hotel people were not that keen in having the locals in their pub. They were always there on the nature strip outside the pub, drinking. They weren't allowed in the pub. So, the whole time we were there ... that's why we invited them in that time. To show them respect.

'A bit of a fight broke out. A fight broke out between a member of the band and a member of the crew. Nothing to do with the Broad Arrow mob. They just got the blame for it.'

In Perth, No Fixed Address had been using a local roadie, Angelo DiCarlo, at their performances. When it came time to leave town, DiCarlo asked if he could come with them. Sure, was the response. 'He asked the promoter in Perth for a reference,' says Ricky Harrison. 'In the letter they called him a roustabout [laughs]. Angelo came back with us. I remember we were in Kalgoorlie and he's standing up against a wall, talking and eyes blinking, frothing at the mouth, going a hundred miles an hour. We were all drunk and next minute Joey Geia turned around and said, "Shut up, Angelo." And Angelo just kept going and he must have just opened his eyes at the moment Joey took a swing at him. He ducked and Joey busted his hand on the wall. Punched the wall [laughs]. The manager came out and Joey put the charm on then, to the old girl. "Never mind, it'll be okay, I'll look after you." He charmed her for a while there.'

Geia's charm had worn off by the following day. The hotel's proprietress, Miss Nancy Hall, instructed Kalgoorlie legal firm

Evans & Bennett to contact tour promoter Kenn McMillan to register a 'very strong complaint' about the conduct of the band and their guests. The letter sought payment of $1000 'from future earnings and other receipts' for a broken bedroom door, blood stains on new bedroom carpets, badly soiled mattresses and bedcovers, missing hotel property and a hole in a masonry wall 'caused it is alleged by a beer bottle being thrown'.

'And the thing was, we'd already loaded up the truck and all of that,' says Briggs. 'So, everything was set to go in the morning, when we'd be taking off. Unfortunately, this incident happened. All this screaming started, the manager got all upset, people were saying not very nice things to each other, so we just thought, "Aw, we're all packed up, let's just go. We can't stay here."'

And that is why the three-vehicle No Fixed Address convoy, two cars and an equipment truck, was motoring across the Nullarbor Plain at one thirty in the morning when it encountered a car coming in the other direction.

Duckie Taylor was driving the rear car in the convoy. 'We pulled into Norseman,' he says, 'filled up the two cars and the truck and we headed out and we just went past the fruit fly inspection. About five minutes, maybe ten minutes up the road, a car came.'

'We should have been sound asleep,' says Briggs. 'Ours was the only truck and theirs was the only car on the Nullarbor. Oh my God, that situation was frightening. We were in the car ahead of the truck. Rick was driving, I think. We could see the other car coming towards us. He was weaving all over the road. So, we all just shut up and watched. It went past and then Rick said, "Oh, fuck." We all spun around and we could see the truck in flames behind us. Just [groans] incredible, incredible moment of just pure panic, we thought we'd lost them all: Les, Woody and Car John.'

Les Graham says the men in the car had been drinking. 'They drank all the way across the Nullarbor. All the roadhouses knew them buying cartons.' He also says someone in the car threw a bottle at the truck.

'The bottle came in the driver's window. That bloke who threw that bottle, he must have missed his coordination. He was going to throw it at the truck to fuck us off. For a bit of fun, because they were pissed. He was probably saying, "Watch this." The bottle came through the window first. I think that's what he was doing, lining us up to throw that bottle at us. His judgement was wrong and he's come straight into us and underneath us and blown us up.'

In the rear car, Duckie Taylor had a grandstand view of the crash. 'They hit the truck, almost hit me in the back and the truck just went straight up on its roof. There was about a hundred and twenty grands' worth of sound equipment and stage equipment in the truck; lost all that.

'I raced back to the fruit fly inspection place, told them that we've just had a big accident and we need the police and ambulance and fire brigade because the side of the road was catching alight. And I let them know and I got back to the accident and we pulled a couple of guys out of the car onto the side of the road. And about an hour later, the police decided to roll up and that was only ten minutes out of town, but they were at a party and we could smell ... they'd being drinking wine. We could smell the wine on them. And about half hour after the police got there, the ambulance decides to roll up and one of the fellows that hit us ended up dying on the side of the road waiting for the ambulance to get there. The driver had his arm torn off, and when the cops came there, I actually helped. The driver of the car, his foot was stuck under the brake pedal and like his chest was slit open. Well, I actually helped the police to get him out of the car. Yeah, not a nice sight. Part of his arm and hand were just lying in the middle of the road. And I think that freaked a lot of the band members out.'

The driver of the car was John Richard Sullivan, aged 27, late of the Base Supply Depot barracks (single men's quarters) in Mount Isa, Queensland. The post mortem determined his cause of death as 'shock due to multiple injuries'.

The two male passengers, Tony Szabo, 25, and Stephen Leslei Revell, 27, were seriously injured. Szabo and Revell, both unemployed miners from Queenstown, Tasmania, were taken to Kalgoorlie Regional Hospital by St John's Ambulance. Szabo was the owner of the car – a 1977 maroon Holden Premier sedan with Tasmanian plates. He had severe lacerations to his right leg and was also suffering from shock and minor abrasions. He was eventually discharged from hospital on 1 May 1982. Revell had a suspected fractured skull and severe lacerations to his right hand and arm. He was not discharged from hospital until 16 May.

The police report on the accident noted the Holden had rolled and come to rest in the west-bound traffic lane facing back the way it had come. The weather at the time was fine, the road was dry with good bitumen surface and visibility was good for driving. A mechanical check of the Holden, which was a complete wreck, failed to find any defect that may have contributed to the accident.

Edward Love (Woody), who was driving the truck, suffered minor back and hand injuries and was taken by ambulance to Norseman District Hospital but was not detained. 'We were pretty bruised up,' says Graham. 'I was real badly bruised because everyone landed on top of me when we rolled over. The hospital reckoned I was just bruised but I suffered for years and years with back problems.'

'We were all taken to the hospital for the night, for observation,' says Jean Morgan. 'I remember there were spirits or something, Aboriginal people outside the hospital, singing and playing didge and that. Like as if to say, we're looking after you. It wasn't anything scary.'

Maxine Briggs agreed. 'Yeah, some actually saw them and some just heard them. It was a very spiritual experience that one. Yeah. Amazing.'

~

The band's Ford D series truck and everything in it had been destroyed and the insurance situation was ... complicated. The truck had been purchased by the band in early 1982. A comprehensive insurance policy on the vehicle had been taken out by Danny Haveron and Lawrence Byrne. Haveron had been the band's first manager in Adelaide, and Lawrence Byrne was the uncle of Haveron's business associate Kym Byrne. In a statement dated 1 October 1982, Mario Mottet said Lawrence Byrne had defaulted in paying the premium and the policy had lapsed (only $136 of the $600 premium had been paid).

This meant neither the truck nor anything it contained was covered by the comprehensive insurance policy. The truck itself was valued at $6000 and the contents were a mix of equipment owned by the band, equipment on hire purchase via a loan from the Aboriginal Development Commission (ADC) and other hired equipment. The amounts were eye-watering.

Of the equipment owned by the band, guitars lost included a Martin acoustic (valued at $1000), a Gibson SG 1962 ($1000), a Fender Telecaster ($750) and a Fender bass ($850). Money was still owing on the latter two instruments. A Music Man amplifier ($1200), JBL speakers ($500), a Morley Fuzz Wah guitar pedal ($350), an echo chamber ($250) and four didgeridoos also went up in flames. Personal effects to the value of $900 were lost plus tools worth $1000 owned by Car John.

The equipment on hire purchase with the loan from the ADC comprised a Rogers drum kit, two Fender amps and a Martin electric guitar (total $6086).

And the big ticket items were those on hire. Lights from Lazer Lighting were valued at $7420, an acoustic amp from James Music was $1225, a drum from Billy Hyde was $400, and last but certainly not least was the PA from Troy Sound Reinforcements. Mario Mottet estimated the value at $8000, but admitted it could have cost $70,000 new. The PA was insured separately through Alan Kenyon Insurance, which eventually paid out $34,500 to Troy for its loss.

The *West Australian* (14 April 1982) said the band would try to reach Alice Springs where they had been booked to appear at a concert on Thursday. 'Members now hoped to use borrowed equipment for the show. Three band members hoped to fly out of WA today while the others would try to reach the Northern Territory by car.'

'Nobody wanted to go on by car, so they ended up flying,' says Duckie Taylor. 'I mean, me and Les and the two cars, we ended up going ahead with that.'

'Some of us ended up flying to Alice Springs,' says Jean Morgan, 'but some of the boys still drove up, because I remember when they got up there, they had red dirt all over them, in their hair and everything.'

Maxine Briggs didn't go on to Alice Springs. 'I flew home after that crash,' she says. 'It was over and out for me really. I was a little bit older than everybody. That was enough adventure, I think. When I came back to Melbourne I started working on the other side, event management. I worked at the Koori Information Centre in Fitzroy. Part of my job was putting on the Rock Against Racism concerts and doing research into traditional Victorian Aboriginal culture. Took me off on the next bit.'

~

No Fixed Address played twice in Alice Springs: firstly at the Federal Sporting Club on Thursday, 15 April and then an open-air concert for the Central Australian Aboriginal Media Association at Traeger Park Oval on Saturday, 17 April, with Reg Zar again on the drum stool. Then the band, crew and partners straggled back to Adelaide and from there on to Melbourne.

Maxine Briggs moved on but didn't forget. 'These guys mean a lot to me,' she says. 'It's just cemented in me. I was at the point where I was starting to feel a bit lonely and isolated out in the mainstream and I was so pleased when they turned up. Especially when I realised there was a Victorian in the band as well. The thing about No Fixed Address is I was really feeling like I was out on the frontier, no other blackfellas in sight and I was kinda craving that. By the time we met, it was time. And I was ready so they brought me back home, to country, to people, to culture. So, they'll always be important to me personally. But their music and their songs, their words all came together to express what a lot of blackfellas were feeling but in a blackfella way and in a way that was also digestible for so many others.'

'We were making a lot of money until the accident came,' says Bart Willoughby. 'Then we were falling. Because we had an $80,000 debt. I think from that accident is when things started going bad.'

Once the news broke about the truck crash, the Australian music community stepped up to offer assistance. First out of the blocks were Perth bands The Motors and The Reserves. Rival promoters Brian Davidson (who looked after The Motors) and Kenn McMillan (who handled The Reserves) put their heads together to organise a benefit night at the Herdsman Hotel in Wembley on Tuesday, 20 April. Jamie Harries, guitarist with The Motors, told the Perth *Daily News*, 'It's really sad. They're a very good band and for something like this to happen isn't too good. Everyone seems to turn their backs on them so we just thought we would like to help out. It won't be a great deal of money but it will help. I believe similar things are already being organised in the east'.[1] The benefit raised $1608, which was duly forwarded to Mick Pacholli.

Things were indeed happening in the east. 'After the truck crash I organised the fundraiser here in Melbourne at The Venue,' says Pacholli. 'I walked in. Joey and I are mates, Joe Gaultieri who ran the joint. I said "Joey, did you hear about No Fixed Address? About the truck blowing up? Can I have The Venue for a charity concert?" He says, "Yeah, sweet." As I'm walking up the stairs, there's Russell Deppler, Men at Work's manager. I said, "Russell, I've just spoken to Joey. I want to put on a charity gig, a fundraiser here for No Fixed Address." "Mate, we're in. We'll play second fiddle. No Fixed Address headline, all right?" I said, "Sweet." So, Russell's in, right? The manager from Young Homebuyers, I forget his name, was the next person I saw on the steps on the way up the stairs. And he's gone, "Mick." The news of this had gone so quick around The Venue it was insane. He's gone, "Mick, we're in. Young Homebuyers. Because we're in the same stable." So, they opened the night. As I went further and turned the corner, there's Ian Lovell, manager of Goanna Band. "Mick, Mick, can Goanna play on the bill?" "Yes, Ian." So, I had the full fucking thing. No Fixed, Men at Work, Goanna and Young Homebuyers was the largest gig The Venue ever had.'

~

In the month after returning from Alice Springs, the band hardly stopped working, although to one member it felt like they were just running on the spot. On the day of the benefit concert, the Melbourne *Herald* (21 May 1982) ran an interview with Joe Geia. Food had been a luxury since the crash – usually just one meal a day, he said. And the band members literally had no fixed address. 'I've been sleeping on floors or lounges – from sleeping anywhere, I've got bronchitis.'

The same day, *The Age* also ran a piece promoting the concert. 'Tenacity holds No Fixed Address together,' Pacholli told the paper. 'They aren't prepared to see things go down the drain because of something that looks like an act of God.' Pacholli said the music industry in general had given the band strong support, but there was no way they alone could raise the $80,000 to replace the equipment.

'Everyone was just big supporters of the band,' says Men at Work's Colin Hay. 'That's all that I can remember from back then was that ... they were a great band anyway, no matter where they're from, or black or white or whatever. But what often happens in the rock'n'roll business, especially when you're starting out, things can go wrong and they have a habit of happening one after the other and sometimes it can be just devastating. So, I think that might be what happened to those guys.'

Hay agrees that the Melbourne music community came together to help them in a time of need. 'Absolutely, yeah. No doubt about it,' he says. 'I think that's one of the great things about playing in bands, especially around that time. Not that you consciously think about this when it's happening. It's more a retrospective thing. Everyone's doing the same gigs. Everyone's going around trying to attract an audience. So, everyone understands, to a degree, what everyone else is going through. Whether you like that particular band or whether you don't, or whether you're known as being this or known as being that; it's a thing that stays with you and lasts. What you remember more than anything is that if you did run into people, there was a sense of camaraderie, or there was a sense of awe. If all of a sudden, you're playing on the same bill as Midnight Oil or something you think, "Wow, this is another level." Some bands were nice to you and some bands weren't nice to you; it doesn't really matter, it's just the experience of it all. I'm still lucky enough to be banging away on some level which seems to be working for me and the people that come to see me. It's a continuing line if you have the love of it.'

At the time of the benefit concert, Men at Work were riding high. Their first two singles 'Who Can It Be Now?' and 'Down Under' had both topped the Australian singles chart, and *Business as Usual* had been the #1 album for nine weeks. It says something that they and a bunch of others were willing to reach down and offer a helping hand to a young up-and-coming band. 'I have memories of the fact that around that time we sensed what was about to happen to us,' says Hay. 'There was a tour we did just after that that was probably the best Men at Work tour that ever happened, if you like the band. It was better than any of the tours we did after we were very successful and very known around the world. It was the tour we did just before we left Australia to go to the other side of the world, to tour Europe and the United States. Around the time we were still playing Melbourne shows. We were playing a lot of the places we had played before. You do have a sense of this community. You have a sense of what's gone before and what still exists and what's to come. No Fixed Address seemed definitely to be the thing that was to come.'

~

On the day of the truck crash, Mick Pacholli had written to David Cooke, promotions coordinator at Brisbane public radio station 4ZZZ, with the idea of a short tour based around the

Queensland premiere of *Wrong Side of the Road*. A week of gigs was put together for the last week of May and the first week of June, with *Wrong Side of the Road* to screen on 1 June at the Schonell Theatre at the University of Queensland. 'It was pretty easy,' Cooke recalls. 'Being ZZZ, we had access to venues and there was a market because obviously we'd been playing the soundtrack album. And the station was very keen to support Indigenous music, even though there wasn't a lot around at the time. We were promoting the premiere of the film as well. It was quite a big thing.

'The first gig on the tour was at Gatton. So, I drove out there to meet them. The strongest recollection I have was that the guys were quite concerned, even a little bit frightened that the cops would try to stop them from performing. Because Queensland cops had a shocking reputation for racism and everything else. They were really worried that something could happen. When I first met them, we introduced each other and I said, "Where's so and so?" and they said, "Oh, he couldn't make it so the roadie is going to play bass."'

The crash had precipitated the end of the road for bass player Joe Hayes, with sound mixer Duckie Taylor stepping into the role. 'They weren't getting paid properly,' says Hayes' wife Jean Morgan. 'I'd only just gotten married; my husband wasn't getting paid properly. I was just getting sick of it, I suppose, and I think I talked him into leaving. I think that's when we left. With all the gigs and everything, how come the boys were always broke? The boys were always doing it hard, I remember. I know that because my husband was one of the boys and I was part of him, so I was doing it hard too. They were being exploited to the max. I've always been one, from a young age, when I see injustice, I call it out. Even way back then I was a bit like that. I got upset because I could see ... the boys didn't get to eat flash meals; we lived on hamburgers and fish and chips.'

The band needed a sound mixer for the Queensland dates and local sound engineer Michael Fisher put his hand up. Fisher

WRONG SIDE OF THE ROAD
4ZZZ presents
WRONG SIDE OF THE ROAD
WRONG SIDE OF THE ROAD
NO FIXED ADDRESS
Thursday 27th May
GATTON CIVIC CENTRE
Friday 28th May
Q.I.T. CAMPUS CLUB
Saturday 29th May
Unconfirmed, but WATCH OUT!
Sunday 30th May
THE PLAYROOM, Gold Coast
Tuesday 1st June
lunchtime: Schonell Theatre, UNI
evening: Schonell Theatre, UNI
with: Queensland Premiere of
"WRONG SIDE OF THE ROAD"
Wednesday 2nd June
Schonell Theatre, UNI with
"WRONG SIDE OF THE ROAD"
Thursday 3rd June
NEWMARKET HALL, Newmarket
Road, Newmarket
Friday 4th June
JOINT EFFORT, Qld. Uni. Refec.
with: THE DUGITES
Saturday 5th June
THOMPSON'S HOTEL, Mooloolaba
GOING HOME!

had moved from Canberra to work with Brisbane's Popular Theatre Troupe, an ensemble whose output, according to Queensland academic Paul Makeham, 'was forged in the great traditions of leftist agitational performance: popular, didactic, aggressive'. Tour manager Mario Mottet was impressed with Fisher's sound mixing skills and offered him the position.

'He provided production at a couple of the gigs,' says Cooke. 'And when they left town, he left with them.'

'The reason I was with No Fixed Address is because I went "Oh my God, I've just found my calling,"' says Fisher. 'And I soon realised, they can't pay me anything!'

By the end of the year, Fisher would be managing the band and would go on to mix their live sound for the next three years.

~

The final night of the tour, Saturday, 5 June, was originally scheduled for Thompson's Hotel, Mooloolaba, but when that fell over Cooke needed to find a replacement. Local outfit The Black Assassins were playing their final gig at Souths Leagues Club and was asked if No Fixed Address could come onto the bill. 'We said, "Yes, please,"' says Assassins guitarist Andy Nehl. The Black Assassins, a 'very political' punk outfit, according to fellow Brisbane musician John Willsteed, was more or less a 4ZZZ house band. Andy Nehl was the afternoon announcer, bass player Tony Collins did breakfast, Steven Stockwell worked at the station and Tony Biggs was a volunteer. The band was calling it a day as Nehl and Collins were about to relocate to Sydney.

'We liked No Fixed Address,' says Nehl. 'We'd been playing the *Wrong Side of the Road* album on the radio since it came out. They were a fantastic band so we were very happy to do that. It was a fantastic night. There was a fantastic vibe in the room. The venue was really full. There was a crowd of people outside trying to get in. There was really great energy in the room from the first support band 3B2, who were a high-energy

Detroit-influenced powerpop type band. Then Black Assassins played. We had a lot of fun. We had a lot of guest musicians from Brisbane come and play single spots with us on different songs. John Willsteed came and sang on a Judy Garland song, "Zing Go the Strings of My Heart", just to be perverse because it was not the type of thing we would normally do. Bruce Anton, who'd been the drummer with The Survivors came and drummed on one song. Charlie Owen came and played guitar on one song.

'We had a few different guests play and did our usual theatrical Black Assassins performance that ended with a lot of letting off fireworks inside and outside the venue, which probably displeased the venue owners. That was lots of fun, and then No Fixed Address came on and they were just fantastic. The whole room was moving, swaying. Really great, fantastic vibe night, the whole night. Also had a lot of Indigenous people there. A lot higher proportion of Indigenous people at the gig because of No Fixed Address. Everyone was just absolutely loving it, dancing up the front to No Fixed.'

While this eventful burst of touring had been happening, Rough Diamond had been making arrangements for the release of the *From My Eyes* mini-album. The idea of doing a mini-album rather than a full album was reflective of the times, according to Ross Gardiner. 'It was just a cost-effective way of sampling the artist to the market,' he says. 'And it worked with the budget and it was working with the marketplace. It was launched for $4.99, right? Now, five dollars, if I'm remembering correctly, was actually a sweet spot for people passing money out of their wallet to buy music. Ten dollars is maybe too much. So, it was about trying to have something that people would buy.'

The plan was to build on the release of the film and the soundtrack album, and for the mini-album to take things to the next level. 'There was definitely a buzz about the band,' says Gardiner. 'It was out there, it was known, the name was there, people found the name very interesting. They saw pictures of the band, they thought, "Wow, this is very cool." And then when they heard the music ...'

Gardiner felt the record launch should be a big deal and had a prominent person in mind to do the honours. 'Yeah, it was done deliberately and this is actually my idea,' he says. 'I did know Bob Hawke and family personally. I had a personal connection with them.'

'The record company took full effort,' agrees Mick Pacholli. 'I was sharing a flat with Ross, in Toorak, in Mathoura Road. And his two best friends were Rossy [Roslyn Hawke] and her sister [Susan].' Pacholli had a large obscene political cartoon of Bob Hawke pinned on the wall. 'I'm living there with Ross and being the mad publisher I am, I had this cartoon of Bob Hawke on the wall. Seriously, it's a big poster on the wall and Rossy and her sister have walked in and gone, "Fuck, that's dad." Yeah, well. I said, "I like him. I reckon he's the best thing." I just thought this was hilarious. They pissed themselves. But that's his [Ross Gardiner's] connection to Bob Hawke, through the daughters.'

Gardiner put his idea to the members of the band. 'So, I said to the band, "Okay, I can talk to Bob Hawke and see whether he will launch this album for us. Are you okay with that or not? If you think it's a bad idea, we drop it right now, we'll never speak about it again." And it was, "No, no, no." In their eyes Hawke as a politician had credibility toward Aboriginal people. So, they were not dismissive of it. And of course, he's a *balanda*, he's a white guy … so the same level of suspicion towards any white person that you'd expect from an Aboriginal Australian. But I know they had respect for him, and they did see that he offered some vision of hope for Australia at the time. And so, they were quite okay.

'What we did was we took the album down to his place and spoke about it and played it to him, and he read the lyrics and all that, and he said, "Yeah, okay, I'll do it." He totally, instinctively got what it was about. He got the importance of it and why it was important to not only Indigenous audiences, but also younger people in Australia generally. That this was a great vehicle for a very important story if it got out to young people. It could become more towards the mainstream of the fabric of Australian life, rather than on the fringes. And so, he was totally into that and understanding of that and happy to wear his heart on his sleeve and do that. The only thing I think he possibly, at the time, had an issue with was the song "Pigs", about the police. "They'll kick you in the head/until they leave you dead."

'For a major politician in this country, it was difficult to stand up publicly and say I support that. From a political perspective. Whether or not it may be true, half-true, or believed by a majority of people in Australia that it had some truth behind it perhaps? Yeah, that was one … I think someone in the media asked him a question about it. He was a skillful politician. He knew that Aboriginal people have had a terrible experience at the hands of the police … and on the other side he also knew that you need to keep the police on your side and working with you if you're ever going to make any progress on these issues.'

Ricky Harrison recalls Hawke saying, 'It's a really great album, *From My Eyes* and all that, but not every man or woman in a blue uniform is a thorough bastard.' Harrison remembers thinking, 'Is he talking about my song?'

Hawke, who was then Labor MP for Wills in the Federal Parliament and Shadow Minister for Industrial Relations, launched the mini-album at the Melbourne Hilton on 28 June 1982. The event generated enormous media coverage.

'It was fabulous,' says Gardiner. 'National TV, nightly news, huge coverage, national, regional, country, country radio, all the various forms of ABC. It was everywhere.' Hawke posed with the band's bass guitar, prompting the caption, 'Play that funky music white boy.'

Hawke warned the media he was not disclosing another facet of his character as an expert on reggae music. 'Like a lot of us oldies, I received an education through my children,' he said. 'I believe those of us in public life should do what we can to help those in the community who are under-privileged and discriminated against. There is no doubt that Aborigines are under-privileged.'

~

The *From My Eyes* mini-album was an arresting package. On the cover, by Palm Island artist Johnny Cummins, the band's name was hand-painted in white across a representation of the black, gold and red Aboriginal flag. The top right featured a colonial-era photo of a group of Aboriginal men standing in front of a building. All had chains around their necks. A white policeman in a white helmet stood to their right holding one end of the chain. On the gold and red of the flag was a brick pattern, evocative of a jail cell. In the bottom left, tears flowed from the eyes of a red spirit peering out from behind the wall. 'They were looking for an Aboriginal political cover,

'Play that funky music, white boy.' Bob Hawke launches *From My Eyes*, Melbourne Hilton, 28 June 1982. Back row: Billy Inda Cummins, Ricky Harrison, Bart Willoughby. Front row: Duckie Taylor, Hawke, Les Graham.

Photo by News Ltd/Newspix.

for the vinyl,' says Joe Geia. 'I knew Billy Cummins had an older brother, Johnny Cummins, who was an artist. I said to the boys, "Yeah, I know an Aboriginal artist. It's Billy's big brother, Johnny. Johnny Cummins." They got Johnny down from Palm Island to Melbourne to do the artwork for the *From My Eyes* album. It was Johnny Cummins who did that painting.'

At the top of the back cover was the slogan *Tungu-inginyi* (all people come together), which was also the title (spelt slightly differently) of the CASM newsletter *Tjunguringanyi*. The six tracks were listed above and below a stylised logo for the group. On one side of the inside sleeve were lyrics to all the songs, on the other, album credits and a band photo. In an echo of the front cover photo, the six band members were lined up in front of a brick wall. But in this case, it was a pan-Aboriginal line-up – two Nungas, two Kooris and two Murris – wearing urban clobber (sneakers, jeans, trackpants and jackets).

When the needle hit the groove it's fair to say reactions were mixed. Roger Crosthwaite in Sydney's *Daily Telegraph* noted the album was: '... balanced between the thoughtful anguished songs ("We Have Survived", "Stupid System", "I Can't Stand and Look" and "Pigs") that deal directly with the problem of being an Aboriginal in Australia and the gentler songs ("Sunrise" and "From My Eyes") that soothe rather than disturb.' He praised the band's musicianship, writing, 'Their playing is damned good – reggae without cliches is the description that springs to mind, a fresh approach to an easily messed up music.' Arch Brown in *Roadrunner* wrote, 'White oppression of the Aboriginal people is mixed with reggae, country, mid-70s guitar riffs and didgeridoo. A rare instance of a successful mix of music and serious politics.'[1]

Ross Gardiner says the intention was to produce a raw and energetic recording, but to some within the band's orbit the result fell short of the aim. 'Sadly, in my opinion, David Briggs "Little Rivered" them,' says Mick Pacholli. 'I listened to the finished product and I said, "David, that's a bit too shiny, that's a bit too crisp."'

The band's live sound engineer at the time, Duckie Taylor was not a fan of the recording either. 'I think with my style of mixing, I didn't try and make it sound anything they weren't. I tried to make their sound come out as if you were talking to them, singing without microphones, gave them the raw natural sound. But when they did the other recordings with David Briggs … see, to me, I really hated that mix. I even told the band I wouldn't have gone out and bought that record.'

'Briggsy was the hot producer,' says Greg Williams from Rough Diamond labelmates Young Homebuyers. 'But as it turned out, the way he heard records was not good. He's a very AOR [Adult Orientated Rock] kind of guy and he'd point to the thing on the wall and say, "Look, there's my Grammy." And I would say, "But it's a shit record."

'The [No Fixed Address] record sounded weird and he was too much of an intervener and he often played parts and that made the record sound more like him. We had the same complaint, that it didn't really sound like us. His thing was, "Well, you're not good enough to make it sound like that." It was the '80s and everything was done with separation, single tracks and lots of overdubs and that makes no sense for rock'n'roll, really.'

Michael Fisher felt a major problem was that the studio was not up to scratch. 'The studio space was far too live,' he says. 'And it was small. It was a couple of small rooms in a terrace house. The surfaces were really hard. It just didn't sound good in the first place. I think it's all Les's playing, but I think they put an effect on it so his guitar has got a delay thing in one speaker in all the verses of "We Have Survived". It's like, "What is this noise going on?" I think it's Les but I think they've put some really unfortunate effects on his playing. It's just turned into this annoying clatter that is masking so much.'

~

I for one also found the results disappointing. The opening track, 'We Have Survived' was a re-recording of the standout song on the *Wrong Side of the Road* soundtrack album. Starting with a snatch of didgeridoo and clapsticks, the music faded in to a busy, cluttered version in which the vocals were swamped by percussive effects, thereby muting the power of the lyrics.

Crucially, instead of leading the song as it did in the original, the bass merely trotted along with everything else. Not an auspicious start.

'From My Eyes', which was released as a 7-inch single, was a jaunty little number with a clean, poppy treatment that was jarringly at odds with the subject matter of the song – being locked up in solitary confinement in juvenile detention. Once again, the vocals were mixed way back behind rather irritating percussive effects.

If the intent had been to create a raw, Clash-type sound, 'Stupid System' was the closest yet. But the tempo seemed rushed, the bass was missing in action again and the lyrics were not waving but drowning as the guitars washed over everything.

Side two opened with a new song. 'I Can't Stand and Look' was a toe-tapper that featured an acoustic guitar bridge into a slower section with vocals for once clear and distinct. 'Sunrise' was a lovely love song marred by an overly intrusive guitar. To my ears it exemplified the problems resulting from the songs being arranged and produced by a lead guitarist. 'Pigs' rounded off the album with a blast, the driving rhythm and searing guitar for once actually complementing the angry lyrics.

~

Rough Diamond made a film clip for the single 'From My Eyes'. It was filmed at the Old Melbourne Gaol and Hanging Rock, a sacred place for local Indigenous people in Victoria's Macedon Ranges. 'We would have done "From My Eyes" in a one-day shoot,' says Ross Gardiner. 'We booked, paid for, used the Old Melbourne Gaol, the Ned Kelly jail so, we could do that kind of emotive imagery, prison, for Aboriginal people. And then the top of Hanging Rock as the sun set. But that song was a song of hope. That people could actually sit together and talk and learn and go forward, which is a highly noble sentiment from my understanding.'

At the time the biggest promotional vehicle for bands was an appearance on ABC-TV's *Countdown*. After some hesitancy on the part of host Ian 'Molly' Meldrum, a snippet of the 'From My Eyes' clip was played on 11 July and No Fixed Address appeared on the program (prerecorded on Friday, 16 July) that went to air on Sunday, 18 July 1982.

Ricky Harrison remembers being woken up, hungover, on the Friday morning by Les Graham knocking on the door and saying, 'Come on, we're taping *Countdown* today.' This was news to Harrison and bass player Duckie Taylor, who were both staying at Mick Pacholli's place. 'Anyway, we got there,' says Harrison. 'Tina Turner was hosting the show and we had a bit of a chat beforehand about how she would introduce us. She said, "I hear you're the best black band in Australia," and we said, "No, don't introduce us like that." But when she introduced us, she said, "Here's a band who call themselves the best black band in Australia." Ross Gardiner was in the audience with all the young girls and Tina and Molly were sitting off to the side. Ross was trying to give Molly a copy of the album to show and Molly kept refusing to take it.'

'One of my ambitions was to be in an Aboriginal band that went on *Countdown*,' says Les Graham. 'And we did it. It was Tina Turner that got us on that show. Molly Meldrum said we shouldn't have been on the show, because we were too political. We weren't political – we were singing the truth. Then he came and apologised at that fancy hotel in Toorak where we were staying, Macys. And he invited us to a party.'

'We were fortunate to find a guest host in Tina Turner akin to our struggles as black musicians,' Bart Willoughby later told the ABC. 'It seems she specifically asked for an Indigenous act, which is most likely how we got a guest spot on the show.'

'There was a lot of people who turned their noses up at us for working with an Aboriginal band,' says Gardiner. 'But for me it was an absolute badge of honour. If I was to look back on my entire career, I would say it was the greatest thing I have ever done personally, because of the lasting message that it got out there, which will endure. From a personal level, doing the whole thing and making it blow up big and having Michael Shrimpton [executive producer of *Countdown*] from the ABC saying, "I have to have this band on here," was all worth it for me.'

~

The *From My Eyes* mini-album sold something like 15,000 copies on its first release, according to Gardiner, but only reached a peak of #77 on the Kent Music album chart. 'It did sell a lot around all over Australia, and it did sell out,' says Gardiner. 'It just didn't get played because the mainstream media was too afraid to play it. It's probably the point that it exposed.'

The 'From My Eyes' single received some commercial radio airplay in Adelaide and Perth, but not in the major markets of Sydney and Melbourne. One reason was the conservatism of the commercial radio industry. The new commercial FM stations that began broadcasting in 1980 had been a disappointment to the record industry, choosing playlists that largely mirrored the existing AM music stations. It was left to the ABC's triple J in Sydney and public radio around the country to give a glimpse of what was happening outside the mainstream.

The other reason was a dispute between the record industry and FM radio over performance royalties.[2] The introduction of commercial FM radio prompted the Australian record industry to seek (for the third time) performance royalties from radio stations for the recorded music they played. The record industry's two previous attempts ended in failure when the impact on sales of AM radio airplay bans forced it to settle for free ads in place of royalties. Radio's position was that the promotion it gave recorded music should absolve it from the obligation to pay royalties. In response to the record industry move, by mid-1982 AM and FM radio stations in Sydney and Melbourne were moving to ban airplay from record companies on a rotating basis. The first labels to be affected were PolyGram (home of Rough Diamond) and WEA.

While 1981 had seen a blossoming of independent labels, there was concern about the prospect of a boom-and-bust scenario. 'There are a lot of new independents out there who just don't know what they're doing,' Mushroom Records boss Michael Gudinski told *Billboard*. 'These people record poor product with poor artists and clog the market for people who know what they're doing. They will fail in the end but not before they do a lot of damage to Australian music.'[3]

Looking back at 1982 a few years down the track, *Billboard* concluded it was the year 'the arse fell out of the Australian music industry'.[4] Sales of singles dropped by more than 30 per cent and album sales fell by almost 20 per cent. 'The other thing was of course Australia had had a huge economic recession where interest rates got to 17 per cent,' says Ross Gardiner. 'And so, timing was not exquisite.'

Things would only get worse for Rough Diamond in 1983.

Three days after Bob Hawke launched the *From My Eyes* mini-album, No Fixed Address was in Adelaide for two weeks of performances and a meeting with prominent members of the local Aboriginal community. Since heading to Melbourne eight months previously, the band had been on a dizzying ride. Mick Pacholli had landed them a recording contract and a music publishing deal, and they had agreements in place with the country's two largest live booking agencies, Premier Artists in Melbourne and its Sydney sister, the Harbour Agency. But Pacholli had also sent them to the wild west without insurance cover. Having lost their truck and all its equipment, then facing the daunting task of paying off the enormous debt that resulted, the band turned back to the community that had nurtured them, looking for some structure and support.

'I did the first tour around Australia,' says Pacholli. 'I set that up from Melbourne. Then we cracked up. They dumped me. For Mario, the road manager. After I'd got them all this stuff, the guitars and everything. Dumped me for Mario.'

Intriguingly, it appears the wheels were set in motion to depose Pacholli on 27 May 1982, just three days after the benefit concert he had organised at The Venue in St Kilda. On that date, the South Australian Corporate Affairs Commission issued a certificate of incorporation for No Fixed Address Pty Ltd. The initial paperwork had been drafted in November 1981, with the band's first managers, Danny Haveron and Kym Byrne as directors and Haveron as company secretary. The shareholders in the company were Haveron and Byrne, plus Les Graham, Bart Willoughby, Ricky Harrison, John John Miller and Duckie Taylor.

'Danny was there from the beginning,' says Harrison. 'Danny was the contact in Adelaide. Pacholli was part of the whole drug deal sort of thing. So, we were being managed by drug dealers basically. It was the only way we could get anywhere really. At that stage we were pushing for jobs and people were there trying to rip us off. So, I guess in a way that's what Les saw as our protection. Les ran everything back then. He got us mixed up with these people.'

'We were major pot dealers at the time,' says Pacholli. 'It was the fucking pot dealers of Australia that were the ones that broke Aboriginal acts, Aboriginal art, music. Just blokes interested in the right thing being done.'

'I started disliking Danny because they were putting pressure on us in the end,' says Harrison, 'about doing shows and stuff. I wasn't really too happy with their attitude towards the rest of us, to the rest of the members. Towards me, towards Bart. They were running a business, but their business wasn't our business. They were doing something different. In the end we worked it out, because we were smoking a lot of their drugs. Danny was getting like an angry dad. He was always angry about stuff.'

'When you're a songwriter you don't really worry about this sort of thing,' says Bart Willoughby. 'You're just performing and have a smoke every now and then. Then going to the next gig.'

'Perspective here,' says Pacholli. 'Bart is what you might call a living legend, but he wasn't the leader of the band. Apart from being the singer and the drummer, Bart had fuck-all to do with any of their success. Les is the man who drove that band, managed that band. Looked after them like a father. And he's the same age. Les was always the leader. He was the man. He was the one who dealt with all of the managers.'

~

All six band members, plus wives, girlfriends, road crew, sound mixer Michael Fisher and tour manager Mario Mottet attended a meeting organised by the Adelaide Aboriginal community on 1 July. Three people well-known and well-respected by the band – Veronica Brodie and Leila Rankine from CASM, and Mulla Sumner from the Aboriginal Sobriety Group – were among those who constituted themselves as a 'caretaker committee'. Sumner undertook to tell anyone concerned with No Fixed Address about the new arrangements.

After some preliminary discussion, Veronica Brodie cut to the chase: 'Do you intend to be rock stars or fight for the Aboriginal struggle?' she asked.

'We're stuck in the middle,' said Graham.

'Yeah,' agreed Willoughby, 'we're caught in the middle.'

When reminded of the exchange, Ricky Harrison says, 'You've got Auntie Vonnie there talking about do we want to be pop stars or a bloody community band for Aboriginal rights and all this. Basically, from what I saw we were a rock band, writing songs. We weren't any land rights group or anything like that. That was never my thoughts about the band, being anything like that. It was just we were writing these songs about ourselves; what we went through. All that other stuff was just part of the whole thing. I hadn't realised that the songs were part and parcel of that whole era. I guess that's why Bart and Les said we were caught in between. I thought the same thing too. We're in between. We're in the middle. Because we never saw ourselves as anything other than a band. Not as a pressure group or a group that was fighting for Aboriginal rights. In the end it all ended up that way. We came to the realisation, "Aw fuck, we've become this without realising it."'

After the meeting, Mick Pacholli was informed of the decision to dispense with his management services. He responded with an account of the expenses owed to his company by No Fixed Address. The sum was $6668.47, comprising money paid out personally by Pacholli, plus commissions on gigs and telephone bills.

Mottet and Sumner, with the help of others at the Aboriginal Community Centre, set about the laborious task of working what was owed to whom. The process was complicated by the various insurance claims that were flying about in the aftermath of the crash and would ultimately take months.

Following the meeting, Michael Fisher took on the role of tour manager and the band was quickly back on the live circuit – playing Adelaide, Melbourne (including their one and only *Countdown* appearance), Canberra and Sydney – when an offer arrived to headline a proposed Rock Against Racism concert in Brisbane in the lead-up to the Commonwealth Games. They didn't hesitate.

Billy Inda Cummins told the Adelaide *News* (September 1982) the concert would bring the Aboriginal struggle into the open. 'For too long the rest of the world and a great many white Australians have not realised the plight of the Aboriginal,' he said. 'Hopefully the concert will attract members of the world media who will be in Brisbane for the Games. We want the concert to be peaceful but powerful.'

~

The 1982 Commonwealth Games was seen by Indigenous activists and their supporters as a great opportunity to bring the issues of land rights and the living conditions of Aboriginal and Torres Strait Islander people in Queensland to national and international attention.

Queensland's *Aborigines Act* 1971 and *Torres Strait Islanders Act* 1971 were the the last surviving examples of 'protectionist' legislation in Australia. Under protectionist Acts, Indigenous people could be forcibly removed from their traditional lands to live on reserves and missions. While this was under the banner of 'protection', the key concept of the reserve regime was control.

Since Queensland's first protectionist law in 1897, the racist state legislation had been amended several times. But in 1982, the Acts still placed onerous restrictions on Aboriginal and Torres Strait Islander people. Entry to reserves was regulated, and on reserves cultural customs were banned, reading matter censored, relationships controlled, work devalued and movements monitored.[1]

The Federal Labor government had attempted to override the worst aspects of the Queensland laws with the passage of the *Racial Discrimination Act* 1975 and the *Aboriginal and Torres Strait Islanders (Queensland Discriminatory Laws Act)* 1975. But when it tried to establish recognition of Indigenous land rights in Queensland, the state government used its power over land law to stymie the change.

There was plenty for the Indigenous community to protest about, and in 1982 a call to action spread quickly around the country by word of mouth, meetings, street gatherings, and through alternative media of all kinds. Gary Foley's message to the audiences attending the concerts by The Clash in Sydney was but one example.

Peter Gray, one of the organisers of Sydney's Rock Against Racism concerts, was involved with promoting protest activities in the lead up to the games. 'In Sydney, Mandy King proposed making a video documentary to highlight the plight of Indigenous Australians in Queensland,' recalls Gray. 'I jumped on board the project as a co-producer. I helped provide facilities, did the camera work, and later helped with distribution and exhibition. I remember proposing the name *The Whole World Is Watching* for the project. It later became one of the chants used during the protest activities in Brisbane.

'At some point during this period, I got the idea to do an outdoor Rock Against Racism concert to help draw people to Brisbane and also provide an additional focus for protest activities at the games. I contacted the RAR Committee in Sydney which gave the go-ahead. I was to work under the supervision/guidance of Aboriginal activist/elder, Ross Watson who was based in Brisbane. It was an important principle for RAR that all activities be Aboriginal controlled and directed ... and we always respected that fundamental principle.

'As soon as the editing of the video was finished, we jumped in my little red Mazda wagon and road-showed the video to Aboriginal communities in key centres in Queensland between Brisbane and Cairns/Kuranda. We did screenings for communities and community leaders, and handed out VHS copies along the way.

'When I returned to Brisbane from road-showing the video, I probably only had about three weeks in which to organise the concert. I decided to have an outdoor event during the day on the main South's football oval followed by an indoor concert at night in the South's clubhouse. The day-time show attracted a general audience (mainly whites), while the night-time concert attracted mainly Aboriginal patrons. The clubhouse was absolutely packed to the gills and there was a real energy in the air that evening. The two stages complemented each other rather well, as it turned out.

'I worked with the Sydney-based promoter, Michael Chugg, to get some additional headline acts for the day-time show. At the last minute, Chugg came up with Redgum and Hunters and Collectors who agreed to play for free. But of course, the main headliner was No Fixed Address together with a very strong Aboriginal line-up.'

~

The Rock Against Racism concert in Brisbane's West End was held on 25 September 1982, five days before the start of the Commonwealth Games. All proceeds were used to support the protest activities during the games. The outdoor stage featured six bands, starting with Bapu Mamoos, Screaming Tribesmen and Mantaka, and concluding with the big names of Hunters and Collectors, Redgum and the headliners, No Fixed Address. The evening show in the clubhouse saw three Aboriginal bands play: local outfit Dennis Conlon and the Magpies; Bapu Mamoos (again); and all the way from Broome (via CASM in Adelaide), Kuckles.

Madeline McGrady was there to try to capture the event on film. 'We drove up from Sydney and just sort of set ourselves up,' she says. 'It was like me trying to fly to the moon. I was trying to get the gear together really quick. It was hard, but we had some money from the Film Commission, to be able to hire a couple of cameras and stuff. So, I had my young crew there and Maureen [Watson] and them had a crew over the other side. So, we were in different places at the same time.'

'I don't remember how I pulled it off, everything is just a blur now,' says Peter Gray. 'Janie Conway helped with the bands backstage, which is so important for a smooth-running event. Tiga got in a fist fight and was badly beaten up, so he wasn't much help that day. There was a certain amount of luck in that everything went relatively smoothly.'

'It was just a great time to see those bands,' says Madeline McGrady. 'I think it was a real karma, but it was also the first chance for our mob to see the bands. I was just so excited about the fact that No Fixed Address were there. There were other bands there as well and they had other bands doing music at night time just to settle everybody down – for the next day session of fighting!

'It was just amazing and those songs ... it was the appropriate time to do it. We were just surrounded by all these police. And yet those guys stood up there and just sang those songs. It really resonated with everybody. It just gave you a lift to know that these guys wrote these songs at that time. It just fitted in with everything that was happening. There was a lot of people there, from all over Australia, but other places as well – New Zealand and Tasmania and everywhere. It was a big mix. There were a lot of people. There were a lot of journos from overseas and everywhere. There were a lot of non-Indigenous people there to support us as well. I thought that was great. We had a good time. So, they were certainly talking about it for a long time after that one as well.'

With music by No Fixed Address, Bapu Mamoos and Kuckles, *We Fight* (also known as *Guniwaya Ngigu*) was the documentary about the protests that emerged from the footage. Directed by Madeline McGrady and produced by the Black Film Unit (Maureen Watson, Tiga Bayles, Johnny Bayles, and McGrady), it was possibly the first documentary directed and produced by Aboriginal Australians. 'I think of all the films

Rock Against Racism handbill, Brisbane, September 1982.
Artwork by John Willsteed.

I've been involved in, that one was the best,' McGrady says. 'In terms of what came out of it and what happened, it was just fantastic.'

~

Being managed by Tiga Bayles and having performed at Rock Against Racism concerts in Sydney, one might have expected Us Mob to be in Brisbane for the protests. They weren't because they had broken up.

'We were doing a trip, a tour up through northern NSW – Moree and Brewarrina,' recalls guitarist Pedro Butler. 'A lot of out-of-the-way places that a lot of bands would never go to. And we ended going up through to Alice Springs and then got through to Darwin.

'We had a bit of a run-in with the management over funding. Money and stuff. We were trying to get money and we were being told there was no money available and we said, "Hang on, we've just been on the road for nearly two and a half months, three months, doing all these shows." We couldn't figure out why we had no money. Where's all our money? We decided we weren't going to continue on if we can't be told what's happening; be told the truth about what's happening with our finances and stuff. We refused to play anymore shows. And it basically fell to pieces from there. By the time we got back to Sydney … Ronnie [Ansell] refused to go back to Sydney. Wally [McArthur], Carroll [Karpany] and myself went back and then we decided to call it quits. Came back to Adelaide, Wally, Ronnie and myself. We disbanded the band before we went back to Sydney and we were going to get back together in Adelaide. But unfortunately, that never occurred.

'We lost Wally; he took his life. And after that happened, I didn't want to do anything else after that. I was devastated. And then Ronnie. That really capped it off completely. I went into, I don't know what state you'd call it. I didn't want to do anything anymore after that. Although I did start playing in bands again later. But that blew me away. Took the wind out of my sails completely.

'It was just a combination of disorganisation and not being told the truth all the time. We had fires over there in Sydney. We lost equipment. We had no insurance and all this sort of stuff. At the end we said, nah, this is just ridiculous. We can't keep on going like that.

'It's a shame. My personal opinion is we could have gone on; we could have made it in the mainstream. I have no doubt about that. Like a lot of bands with management and stuff like that. Even No Fixed Address, they went through things like that.

'It was a very hard road. It was a heart-breaking road too, from my point of view. We had so much to offer. It was a struggle, all the way through. Nothing came easy for us. We had to prove ourselves all the time too. It wasn't a matter of just walking in.'

After the Rock Against Racism concert in Brisbane on 25 September 1982, things started to get hectic. Like, *really* hectic. No Fixed Address drove back down the coast to Sydney for three gigs, then back up to Queensland for two shows on 8 and 9 October with Cold Chisel. Billed as The Black and White Parity Ball, the shows at Brisbane's Her Majesty's Theatre (which included Goanna as second support) were timed to coincide with the closing of the Commonwealth Games. The title and the line-up were Queenslander Don Walker's 'fuck you' message to the Queensland government – a message the rest of Chisel fully endorsed.

Arriving in Queensland on Wednesday, 6 October, the band played the Surfair Hotel on the Sunshine Coast that night. On Thursday they were at the Gold Coast Playroom, then on Friday and Saturday they did the two shows with Cold Chisel. To make ends meet, after each of the Chisel supports No Fixed Address played a late show. On Friday they went back to the Playroom (where they had played the previous night) and on Saturday they went on to the Prince Alfred Hotel in Ipswich. On Sunday they played a 4ZZZ gig at the New York Hotel in Brisbane.

The band then embarked on a punishing schedule of performances that pushed things to breaking point, and beyond. Hitting the road south, they were booked to play at the Doyalson RSL south of Newcastle on Tuesday the 12th. Michael Fisher was driving the equipment truck, a Ford F350, fully loaded with PA and stage gear. About 50 kilometres north of Doyalson, he heard the wheel nuts on the back wheels starting to pop. After pulling over, he and roadie Angelo DiCarlo flagged down another truck. Fisher asked the driver if he could take him down the road to find a mechanic. 'Sure,' said the driver. Then Fisher had an idea. The truck that had stopped was empty. 'How would you like to make some extra money?' he asked.

'So, we loaded the gear off our truck, loaded it onto the empty truck, drove to the venue, unloaded, and I left Angelo to begin setting up. We found a mechanic and I gave the driver $40 for his trouble. Me and the mechanic went back to our truck where the mechanic welded studs onto the back wheels and I drove it back down to the venue.'

That wasn't the end of the drama; not by a long shot. After the Doyalson gig, Fisher was driving the truck down to Sydney when he fell asleep at the wheel and the truck scraped the guard rail at the side of the road. He woke with a start, adrenalin pumping.

Sometime in that period, word reached percussionist Billy Inda Cummins that his baby daughter had fallen from a swing, struck her head and was in a coma. Cummins left and went back north to Queensland.

~

Les Graham's first cousin Ricky Lovegrove (who went by the name Eric Maher at the time) was on the tour as part of the No Fixed Address road crew. When everyone got to Canberra the following day for the gig at the Stakeout Tavern, Lovegrove started drinking. When the show was over, Fisher and Lovegrove were loading out and, while taking a heavy rack of PA amplifiers down some stairs, Lovegrove lost his grip.

'In Canberra, Rick got a bit pissed,' says Graham, 'and Fisher said, "Don't handle the equipment when you're pissed; it's valuable stuff."'

The next thing Fisher recalls is being in the back of the truck, wedged in between amps and speakers, and Lovegrove throwing a metal conga drum stand at him. Fisher jumped out of the truck and confronted Lovegrove.

'They started arguing,' says Graham, 'and Rick picked up a lighting pole, like a spear, and chased him down the road, saying, "I'm gonna fucking kill you." We sacked Rick from that job, on that night. We really couldn't afford to put up with anyone like that, cousin or not. I had to be strong, so I sacked him. I said, "Look, brus, take a walk."'

Fisher says they drove around Canberra trying to find Lovegrove and Joe Geia the following morning, but couldn't locate them. They had to leave without them. That night at Riverina College in Wagga Wagga, local boy Richard Burgman, guitarist for Sunnyboys, came backstage after the show to say hello. Realising the band was a roadie short, Burgman gave them a very welcome hand with the load out.

The road seemed never-ending as the band and crew climbed wearily into their vehicles for the 560 kilometres, six-hour trek to Mildura to play a town hall fundraiser for the Mildura Aboriginal Education Committee. The committee subsequently wrote a letter of complaint about the performance, saying the band members appeared 'tired and confused'.

The wheels were coming off and the scene was set for a showdown with manager Mario Mottet, who had organised the tour remotely from his office back at the Aboriginal Community Centre in Adelaide.

~

Joe Geia rejoined the band a week later at Melbourne's Billboard night club. He stayed for a couple of weeks but didn't accompany the band when they travelled to South Australia for another series of meetings with the local Aboriginal community. By this stage, the band's original managers, Danny Haveron and Kym Byrne, were out of the picture, having resigned as directors of No Fixed Address Pty Ltd on 6 October 1982. Mario Mottet and Mulla Sumner took their positions, with Mottet replacing Haveron as company secretary.

At a meeting held at Sumner's Elizabeth Downs home on the evening of Monday, 8 November, Les Graham complained that no-one had organised any gigs for the band while they were in Adelaide for what was proposed to be a three-week break. Mottet responded that he had tried to book some gigs but: 'a lot of people he had booked them with had turned around and said they didn't want the band, that they weren't appropriate.' Michael Fisher suggested the band work for two weeks in Melbourne and then one week home. The band countered that they wanted a break. Ricky Harrison's first child was due at the end of November and he said he wanted to be with his wife. It was suggested that Ricky's wife go with them to Melbourne. Harrison said he would check and let everyone know the following day.

Fisher said if the band wanted to work and make money at the same time, they would have to move to Melbourne. They could not survive if they stayed in Adelaide. He took Sumner and the band through the books he had been keeping for the previous ten weeks. These showed earnings of $33,466.15 against outlays of $32,058.09 (comprising expenses of $18,722.09, wages of $10,104, repaid debt of $3182 and $50 stolen). This meant a surplus of $1408.06 for the ten-week period. In that time the band had played 52 gigs at venues in Melbourne, Sydney, Canberra, Taree, Brisbane, Toowoomba, the Gold Coast, Port Macquarie, the Sunshine Coast, Ipswich, Doyalson, Wagga Wagga, Mildura, Swan Hill, Lorne, San Remo, Ballarat, Geelong, Mount Gambier and Millicent.

~

The band was invited to speak to a group of 'concerned Aboriginal people' at the Aboriginal Community Centre in Wakefield Street, Adelaide, on Wednesday, 10 November. The group included Mulla Sumner, Leila Rankine and Veronica Brodie. Two representatives from the Aboriginal Development Commission also attended. Mario Mottet and Michael Fisher joined for the second part of the meeting.

The wide-ranging discussion ran for almost four hours and covered matters such as the attitude of the band, responsibilities, communication, alcohol and drugs, business management and debts. But ultimately it was clear that many of the well-meaning suggestions made by the community members didn't fit with the reality of operating a touring band in the Australian rock scene. The truck crash had been a stroke of ill-fortune, but the hard fact was that they were carrying significant debt. It was also obvious that there was not enough work in Adelaide to sustain their ongoing existence and begin to pay off those debts.

After the meeting Fisher said, 'We've got two weeks guaranteed work in Melbourne through Premier. Let's go to Melbourne and manage ourselves.' There seemed little choice. It was decided to retain Sumner to help manage the debt repayments and insurance claims.

'Les ran everything back then and when Fisher came in, things started to change,' says Ricky Harrison. ' I think it opened Bart's eyes up a bit as to what was going on and who was really in charge. I think he came to the realisation that if he [Bart] wasn't with the band, there wasn't going to be a band. And Les was losing his control. That's why they had the meeting, to try to pull everything back in.'

~

Duckie Taylor indicated he didn't want to tour anymore. What to do about a bass player? The phone rang at Nicky Moffatt's place in Morwell. 'Ricky Harrison rang me up,' says Moffatt, 'because he and I are first cousins. He said, "We're looking for a bass player. Are you interested?" I said, "Am I interested? Of course I am!"'

The band persuaded Duckie Taylor to sit in for a couple of gigs back in Victoria while Moffatt got up to speed. Moffatt had hung out with the band in Melbourne and was very familiar with their material. 'I'd been to numerous gigs,' he says. 'It was good. It was exciting to see an Aboriginal band getting that recognition. At the time they were at their peak, so I was fortunate enough to come in then. Joe Hayes had been playing. He's an uncle from Morwell. Then Duckie Taylor. I came in after Duckie.'

Moffatt took the stage for the first time at the Welshpool Hotel in South Gippsland on 18 November and played with the band in Melbourne and regional Victoria through December and January.

'Okay, there is one other thing,' says Fisher. 'We ran the band as a cooperative. I was effectively a band member. We were all on the same pay, $120 per week which was almost twice the dole at the time, and the band paid for other necessary expenses on top of our pay. That was different from other band management approaches and everything we did was transparent. Getting the message in the songs out to as many people as we could was the aim, and being interactive with the communities wherever we were. It was a mission – not a capitalist enterprise. That's the really different thing about No Fixed Address. Most bands don't have a mission, or a community whom they are involved with.'

Over that summer the members of No Fixed Address settled into the Melbourne scene. Ricky Harrison, his wife Lise and new baby daughter Sandi initially stayed with Maxine Briggs and her partner Louis McManus at their house in Carlton, then moved into a flat in Elwood. Bart Willoughby and his partner Sherrie were just down the road. Les Graham and Joe Geia were around and Nicky Moffatt was travelling up from Morwell. Michael Fisher was doing the sound and the books, and the band was getting regular work through agent Frank Stivala at Premier Artists. After the tumult of the year, things seemed to have stablised.

It was the calm before the storm. Within six months, after a bewildering succession of line-up changes, the band would be down to a three-piece of Harrison, Willoughby and Moffatt. Oh, and putting together a plan for a UK tour.

After an appearance at an Australia Day/Invasion Day concert at the Melbourne Concert Hall, the band was booked on an east coast tour. At the last minute, Nicky Moffatt decided he wasn't going to go.

A distress call went out to Duckie Taylor back in Adelaide. 'I gets the telegram one morning asking me if I could play in Canberra, like tonight,' he recalls. 'The same night. So, I said yeah, and I had a tape of one of the gigs so I just went out the back with my acoustic guitar. I just practised the bass lines for about a couple of hours and then jumped on the plane to Sydney, then jumped on the plane to Canberra; like straight to the gig, straight on stage.'

After a double-header in Sydney the following night, Narara 1983 was next up. Billed as a three-day celebration of Australian music, the festival was held at Somersby, NSW over the January long weekend and featured the crème de la crème of Australian pub rock. Headliners included Cold Chisel, The Angels, Rose Tattoo, Australian Crawl, INXS, Divinyls, Dragon, Mental as Anything, The Church, Men at Work, Goanna, Jo Jo Zep and Mi-Sex. Rather incongruously, No Fixed Address were slotted into the Monday afternoon line-up with blues/funk outfit Rupert B, country rockers Bullamakanka and traditional Oz folkies the Bushwackers.

Strangely (as one of the cars on tour was his), Les Graham wasn't on the drive up to Queensland that followed but instead flew from Sydney to Brisbane. The first Queensland shows were on Thursday, 3 February, a lunchtime show at the Queensland Institute of Technology's Campus Club in Brisbane followed by an evening show at the Cleveland Sands Hotel. Shortly after the band took the stage in Cleveland, Graham freaked out, began smashing his guitar on the stage then walked off.

'I really had a nervous breakdown,' says Graham. 'Just the whole thing with rock'n'roll and trying to keep it together. I was always the only one that had a set of wheels. Anyway, I ended up cracking up and saying that's it, I'm leaving.'

Duckie Taylor said he had had enough as well, but agreed to hang around until a new bass player was enlisted. The band were staying with friends and supporters Lionel Fogarty and Cheryl Buchanan who put the word out to the local Aboriginal community. By the time they left Brisbane they had two new recruits, Peter Meredith on guitar and Billy Gorham on bass. Because Graham had taken his car when he left, Cheryl Buchanan drove the band down to Sydney.

'I'm not sure what was going on with him [Graham]', says Ricky Harrison. 'He was much the same, the same old Les. Angry young man I suppose. But he was also involved with himself. With band members, not so much. Not doing the right thing by band members. He had his own agenda. In the end he left because he didn't have our support, I suppose. Because we worked out he's not really there for us, he's there for himself. He saw himself ... I don't know what he saw himself as. It certainly wasn't a good thing for anybody.'

A rock star? I suggest.

'I think he saw himself as a god [laughs]'.

A rock god?

'A rock god, that's it [laughs]. That's what he would talk about, rock gods. I think he had that idea in his head that he was the main actor. The big god of rock'n'roll. The main man in the band. All he was, was a lead guitarist, nothing less nothing more. I mean, the real star was Bart. That was it. Everybody knew that, except Bart [laughs]. I think Fisher woke him up to the fact. "You know, Bart, it wouldn't be a band if it wasn't for you." People related more to his songs. Mine were more angry and in your face. They freaked a lot of people.'

While former manager Mick Pacholli always considered Graham to be the leader of the band, Michael Fisher had a different perspective. 'I do think about bass players who came and went. The difference between a bass player who doesn't write a song and someone like Bart or Ricky, is that they're just the bass player. They're not a songwriter. It's not their band. They're in the band, but it's not their band. And the fact that Les moves on as well. And when you're the songwriter, you want to get your song out and this is the way you do it. And so the commitment from a bass player or a lead guitarist is not the same as a songwriter.

'Bart always wrote out the set lists. He was the one who spoke to the audience. He wrote and sang two-thirds of the songs. To me, it was Bart's band.'

~

With Duckie Taylor and Billy Gorham alternating on bass, the band played some shows on the NSW mid-north coast organised by Manning Valley public radio pioneer Rob Meaton then a couple of Sydney gigs. After Taylor flew back to Adelaide, the new line-up bedded down with an outdoor Rock Against Racism concert at Narrabundah Oval, Canberra, and a run of college gigs in Melbourne and surrounds in late February and early March.

While the band's schedule of live bookings remained healthy, on the recording side things had taken a decided turn for the worse. By mid-1982, Rough Diamond's distributor Astor Records had been subsumed by PolyGram. In November 1982, PolyGram sacked 40 staff and retired the Astor brand. Then shortly afterwards, Rough Diamond got the chop. 'What happened was that PolyGram said they're not going to fund the label anymore in 1983,' says Ross Gardiner. 'They decided that they were going to run their own aggressive A&R and they didn't need an independent label for that. David [Briggs] said unless we can find somebody else, I'm out. I'll just run my studio or write my songs; or be a session guy.'

~

In early 1983, Gardner told Michael Fisher that Briggs was no longer involved with Rough Diamond. The third partner in the label, Milli Comfort, also appeared to be no longer involved.

'Ross said he was running Rough Diamond by himself,' recalls Fisher. 'He said he wanted to record some more No Fixed Address songs but only had limited funds. I think he was self-funding the recordings. I was under the impression that we were just going to make demos for him to use to gain major record company backing for Rough Diamond.'

Fisher had a number of conversations with Gardner early that year and put his name on the door for a No Fixed Address gig at the Central Club Hotel, Richmond, on 26 February. Gardner hadn't heard the new line-up with Peter Meredith and Billy Gorham, but was obviously happy with what he heard, and the recording session went ahead at Platinum Studios, South Yarra on the evenings of 1 and 2 March.

'On the first evening Karen Hewitt, who went on to engineer some huge hits with Stock, Aitken, Waterman among others, did the recordings,' says Fisher. 'She had some trouble with the equipment and Ross was getting annoyed that the recording was not progressing as quickly as he had hoped. I think he was anxious as he had limited funds for the recording. Ian McKenzie, a partner in the studio, came in and fixed the problem, and he and Karen jointly engineered the recording the next evening.

'I specifically recall that Joe Geia's song, "Ngi Gu Binnahl", which was part of the live set at the time, was recorded. I recall it sounding pretty good coming through the speakers in the control room. Ross was really excited about this song. It was funky and it was in the Aboriginal language of Joe's mob.'

Three other songs, Bart Willoughby's 'Greenhouse Holiday', Joe Geia's '40,000 Years' and Ricky Harrison's 'Stand Up', were recorded on the second evening.

'The recordings were of the band playing live in the studio to which were added a few overdubs,' says Fisher. 'This is a quick and hence inexpensive way of recording a band who play well live. It is also a good approach to capturing the magic of No Fixed Address as playing live is what they do best.'

Nothing from the sessions was released until ten years later, when Gardiner fished three of the demos out of the bottom drawer ('Greenhouse Holiday', '40,000 Years' and 'Stand Up') and licensed them, together with the masters from the *From My Eyes* mini-album, to Mushroom Records for a CD release in its Midprice Masters series. (By then Joe Geia had released new versions of 'Ngi Gu Binnahl' and '40,000 Years' on his 1988 debut album *Yil Lull*.)

'It is disappointing that the Mushroom Records CD does not credit anyone other than David Briggs, who is incorrectly credited as producer of the entire album,' says Fisher. 'It would have been good if everyone was fully credited for their contribution, including Peter Meredith and Billy Gorham for their performance on the three additional songs, and Karen Hewitt and Ian McKenzie for engineering and producing them.'

Fisher notes there are significant differences between the two sets of recordings. Of the three additional songs he says, 'Other than some vocal overdubs, the only overdub appears to be an additional rhythm guitar on "40,000 Years" and "Stand Up". Peter's lead work is similar to Les' playing, or at least my recollection of it. I am pretty sure I gave Peter a cassette of one of my live sound mixes with Les playing guitar for Peter to learn the songs from. Although Peter's playing is similar, he uses far less guitar effects than Les, for example, there is no wah wah on this recording of "Greenhouse Holiday". Also of interest is that there is no additional percussion on these recordings; it is all just Bart on drums. At the time, Joe had been playing percussion instruments such as congas, tambourine, and cabasa when the band performed live, so it is curious that his percussion doesn't feature.'

The release of the CD left the band members perplexed. 'When we signed up with Rough Diamond, we did the mini-album *From My Eyes*, then the company went bankrupt,' says Les Graham. 'Left us in the lurch. Gudinski bought the company. I still don't understand this. When he bought the company, he bought the rights to us.'

Billy Gorham, Joe Geia, Bart Willoughby, Peter Meredith and Ricky Harrison, Melbourne, April 1983.

Photo by Carol Ruff.

~

In early March 1983, Fisher forwarded a copy of the band's Premier Artists weekly worksheets to Mulla Sumner. In the covering letter Fisher wrote, 'Les is okay but he really doesn't know what he is going to do with himself.'

Graham was in attendance at Bendigo's Foundry Arms Hotel on 11 March when guitarist Peter Meredith had a fit on stage. 'He had an epilepsy problem,' says Joe Geia. 'They put the blue light on him one time. The strobe light. It was right next to him. When it came on, he fell down. They thought it was part of the act [laughs].' Meredith was okay, but was unable to continue. Graham offered to step in. The band accepted and completed the set. Graham received $20 for the spot.

Later that month, No Fixed Address played a couple of support slots with Jamaican reggae legend Peter Tosh. There wasn't much of a connection forged between the Australian band and Tosh on the two shows they did. 'It's funny,' Bart Willoughby told Clinton Walker later, 'we didn't quite know how to communicate with each other.' Could it have had something to do with the cloud of green smoke backstage? 'The air was pungent,' Michael Fisher recalls. 'I think they might have been burning Haile Selassie incense as well. It was a stoned religious experience.'

~

Both Joe Geia and Peter Meredith opted to leave the band in early April. In the week prior to their departures, they had played a People for Nuclear Disarmament concert at Sydney's Domain attended by 30,000 people and the second Peter Tosh support at Sydney's Capitol Theatre. Meredith had decided his constitution was not up to the rigours of a touring life and went back to Brisbane. Geia almost immediately formed a new band, Nya Nunga, with members of Sydney-based Un Tabu.

'People were trying to whisper in Joey's ear, "Come with us,"' says Willoughby. 'His people. Maybe the Island thing, being caught in the middle. Melbourne's a hard place. Being an Island fella, I think it was a little bit difficult for him in Melbourne. And for blackfellas there to accept him as a blackfella. So, he was getting it from the whitefellas and the blackfellas. They literally crucified him. Plus, he also had diabetes. He used to crack and do some really, really bad stuff which he couldn't control.'

The band missed Geia's material when he left. 'They were all kick-arse songs,' says Willoughby. '"Kwanji" – about his father, uncle, the struggle, what he done. Another one was "Uncle Willie". From Joey's side they were tropical; the icing on the cake, that little spark that you need for it to swing.'

~

One of the reasons tour manager Mario Mottet had hired Michael Fisher as live sound engineer back in June 1982 was

Tiga Bayles, Ricky Harrison and Billy Gorham, People for Nuclear Disarmament rally, The Domain, Sydney, Palm Sunday, 27 March 1983.

Photo by Juno Gemes.

his proficiency in creating a dub sound. With the band as a three-piece, this skill came into its own.

'No Fixed Address sounded better live than they ever did on record,' says Fisher. 'Certainly *From My Eyes* did not capture them properly. When they did *Wrong Side* … the performers were still fairly young. They weren't really strong tough players at that stage. It had a beautiful sound, but the strength in their playing wasn't there in the very early stages, not like what it developed into. By the time I met them, they were pretty damn good players. And then they got better.

'Nicky and Ricky had been playing together since they were kids. And Bart was incredibly commanding. If you did the wrong thing on stage, there would be a cymbal crash in your ear. "Get your act together." Bart ran it on every gig. He commanded the stage. And they very rarely made mistakes. It was always incredibly tight.

'When we didn't have a lead guitarist, we had to make up for that with a lot more dubby. A lot more effects had to go on to make it bigger. A lot of what you call flanging and phasing. I guess I was a fan of the Police and the Cure and I had an appreciation of what a simple three-piece could do. Andy Summers [of the Police] was not the greatest guitarist in the world. He was a simple guitarist in many ways but still they managed to make a sound that was big and it was drums, bass and kinda that reggae thing and I guess I had that in my mind. And I'd listened to a lot of dubby stuff as well.

'I had a couple of effects machines and I would use them heavily. I would use them on the drums; I was ahead of my time in making the drums have different sounds. I could choose to put an echo on a snare drum or extra reverb on a snare drum. It wasn't just done in a static way. It was all dynamic, with the beat, whatever.

'I would use them on the vocals and the guitar. For example, with the vocal echo, I would be riding that constantly, so on certain things it would push out a little bit more, particularly on Bart's voice. And Bart played with it because Bart heard it coming back. Bart learnt what from I did last night and said, "Oh, he's going to do this again tonight and I will play with that." There was a feedback thing that was happening. When you listen to live recordings of Bart, he's making all these noises. He's making clicks, he pops. He'd know when the echo was there and he'd just work with it and make a noise into it to trigger that. Clicks and pops he would do. And grunts. Bart sings far better behind a drum kit. I feel like the whole motion, his whole way of being when he's playing drums is like the breath worked with the beat.

'Without a lead guitarist you've got to get Ricky's guitar to do something – change its tone as it's going along or every now and then do a little echo. So there were lots of little things I would do to make that three-piece sound bigger.

'I wouldn't use anything on the bass. I kept the bass fairly tight. I just basically tried to make everything bigger. And make it really big bass-wise in particular. So the PAs that we would hire, we would usually ask for extra bass bins so we could get that bigger sound. We would typically have a double four way with a quad bottom end. I don't think most sound engineers would have gone to that dubbiness. I was ahead of my time in being dubby.'

One of the musicians who experienced Fisher's dub magic was Ken Gormly, later bass guitarist with The Cruel Sea. 'They were playing at a place called Surfair, down the coast a bit near Mooloolaba [on Queensland's Sunshine Coast],' he recalls. 'We could see it from miles away, rising up alone on a deserted flat stretch of scrubby coast, all Twilight Zone with its red sign lit like a beacon to all the dumbness of the '80s to come. It was cutting edge Gold Coast Faux Modern in style, basically a new white concrete high-rise dunny block, with a crap bunker beer garden, now caged and overpowered with an oversized PA and choked by monolithic black stacks built on monstrous W bins of frightening tonnage.

'No Fixed Address were truly fuckin' amazing. So fat they kinda stopped the world and changed everything about live music for me. I was utterly swept away by their dubby bounce and swing through those big-arse bins and the natural cool and vibe of their mob thing and their rock star good looks. And they could really play. It was one of the great cathartic gigs for me; it made a deep impression and pointed me toward what was to come with music and my approach to playing bass. And it began my long fascination with them and Bart Willoughby, who I got to know a bit down the road with Mixed Relations who were on Red Eye and toured with The Cruel Sea.'

~

The stage presentation also took on a new dimension under Fisher's watchful eye. 'The whole visual look evolved from being a band that just turned up in whatever environment and the environment set the thing, to something that was very different,' he says. 'We dressed the stage. It was a full-on look. The flag dominated. We just used to call it the land rights flag. We didn't call it the Aboriginal flag back then, because it was the flag of the land rights movement. And it didn't have the official recognition that it has today.

'It was a huge flag. It was enough to fill the back of the stage. The sun was about two metres wide so it was big enough to encircle Bart. Bart would normally be on a drum riser and the sun would be directly behind him. Because the bottom of the flag is red, a lot of the dressing underneath the amplifiers and around the drum riser was all done in red, to match the flag. That was all cotton fabric. When Angelo would do the lighting, the lighting was very much red and yellow as well.

'That was the look and when you'd rock up to a show, you'd have someone at the door selling our merch, which was our posters, badges, bumper stickers, etc. And had Polygram been a bit nicer to us, we would have had an album to sell. But they weren't prepared to do it on consignment. We would have done better selling cassettes. I believe the sale of the cassettes was greater than the sales of the vinyl.

'It was a very strong image. It was very defined.'

~

In mid-March, Michael Fisher was approached by a group of people in Melbourne with the intriguing idea of sending No Fixed Address on a British tour. The group, which would incorporate itself under the rather unwieldy name of the Australian British Cross-Cultural Development Association (ABCD), comprised four members. Australians Richard Micallef and Sally Dawes had been friends living in London, where Micallef had founded a community organisation, Brixton Music Development. Micallef was visiting Dawes, who had moved to Melbourne, and they had been chatting with Doug Gaudi, an old friend of Micallef's who knew Debra Weddall, a director/producer of independent films.

'The plan was to get a grant from the Aboriginal Arts Board,' says Fisher. 'Richard was going to be in England and the other three were here. They would support with the admin to make it all happen. It was a really attractive proposition. Let's join forces and see how we go. People were willing to do this for nix. They're actually motivated to do this. I went, "Wow. This is pretty fabulous." They had different skills. Deb was really keen to do a video. Sally was pretty good on the press release thing. Richard was on the ground to set it up. We discussed the figure and how much we would need to do it.'

Fisher wrote to Aboriginal organisations seeking their support for a grant application by ABCD. He received positive responses from the Koori Information Centre (Hartley Briggs); the Adelaide Aboriginal Community Centre (Mulla Sumner); the Central Gippsland Aboriginal Co-op (John Gorey); the Gippsland and East Gippsland Aboriginal Co-op (Ian Dunkley); the Centre for Aboriginal Studies in Music (Ben Yengi); and Murri Jama Music Company (Tiga Bayles).

Clyde Holding, the federal Minister for Aboriginal Affairs, was on board from the start. Holding wrote to Barry Cohen, the Minister for Home Affairs and Environment, indicating his support for the grant application and asking this be conveyed to the Aboriginal Arts Board. 'So, we got community support; we got political support,' says Fisher.

~

In late May 1983, Billy Inda Cummins rejoined on percussion. Despite not liking the cold southern winter, he stayed on with the band until late August. Two weeks later, after almost a hundred performances with the band, Billy Gorham decided the touring life was not for him and returned to Queensland. 'He was a lovely man, very sensitive,' says Fisher. '"You know what I love about you guys?" he used to say to us. "You don't call me green eyes."'

Gorham had grown up at the Cherbourg mission north-west of Brisbane and in later years became a police liaison officer there. When he left, Nicky Moffatt came back into the line-up on bass guitar.

'It was wonderful having at least three voices,' says Fisher. 'That was one of the real strengths with Nicky Moffatt. He was a really good harmoniser. And his voice sounds really sweet against things. And Ricky also benefited from having Bart doing backing on him as well.'

Also in June, Louis McManus began guesting with the band. 'A smile the size of Australia,' says Willoughby. 'A genius talking.' Proficient on fiddle, mandolin and guitar, McManus, who had previously played with The Bushwackers and Matchbox, added a spicy lead guitar to the mix.

No Fixed Address was invited to support Midnight Oil at the opening of the Sydney Entertainment Centre on 16 September. The concert was being filmed by the Oils and for an additional $500, Fisher got the crew to also film No Fixed Address. His thinking was that a live performance video would be a useful tool in his quest to secure a new recording deal on the proposed UK tour. McManus accompanied the band to Sydney for his only performances with them outside Victoria.

To make the trip work financially, the band's Sydney agent Colleen Ironside crammed ten gigs into the week, including a late spot at Blacktown Soccer Club after the Oils support. 'Because we were playing a second gig, we didn't help the Oils crew load in or out; we paid them a fee instead,' says Fisher. 'As a result, the Oils crew were missing in action on the mixing desk and the sound (and lights) were terrible.' Only one song was captured in decent quality, the final number, 'Pigs', which featured a scorching extended guitar solo from McManus.

The prospect of getting a recording deal with an overseas company was being seriously entertained because the band's deal with Rough Diamond had expired and, in spite of their enduring live popularity, nobody else in Australia seemed interested.

'After the record [*From My Eyes*] came out, for the first few months there was a bit of support,' Fisher says. 'It was in the shops, it was selling; they [Polygram] could have been a lot more helpful. They had the contact with us and the opportunity to pursue us further and they didn't. Same with Mushroom. I had regular contact with Jenny Keath [Mushroom Publishing] and she wasn't saying: "Mushroom would love to do you." They had no problem in their booking agency, Premier Harbour. We weren't getting that interest [in recording]. It was like, you guys do it and we'll take the publishing. They weren't proactive. And it was a shit publishing deal. They were creaming off 50 per cent. They could have done a lot more for their money. We did the rock and they got the roll. It was a gravy train for them.'

~

The band had been demoing new songs on the road all the way through. 'We were looking to do an album,' says Fisher. 'We had almost enough songs. They [Willoughby and Harrison] don't write fast. They write slow. There were so many great songs. Some of them ended up as Mixed Relations songs.[1] And Bart's resurrected some of them for his solo albums as well. "Reality" and "Revolution" are both wonderful, wonderful songs. They were tough, they were good. Songs would not survive in the live set if they weren't good.'

The band was averaging five gigs a week, but Fisher says they were usually doing another day a week of rehearsal. 'That might sound crazy for a band that was playing all the time but it was because there were new songs coming through that needed to be worked out and they were worked out in the rehearsal room.

'Looking back, the amount of work they did seems insane, but they had no problem in doing it. No problem with the energy whatsoever. So, to do interviews, do a gig, and do some other things all in one day was, "Yeah, no worries." And jump in the car and drive back down to Melbourne the next morning. Then have a sleep and the next day go and rehearse or go and do a demo. We had the energy for it. It wasn't a slog. If it was a slog, we would have put up our hands and said, "Oh, no, this is all too much, we can't do it." We basically just kept doing it with enthusiasm. We were having a good time. There was a lot of energy, an amazing amount of energy.

'I look back at my diary and I think, "How, in a day, did I go through all those phone calls, no mobile phone, go to all those places, pick up this gear, pick up some posters and pop them in the post to a new venue that we're playing in a couple of weeks' time and go to the shop and pick up some strings and some drumsticks?" Then we'd do a load-in, set up everything, do a soundcheck, have a little bit of time then it was show time, then you'd pack up. And repeat. I'm thinking this is just insane. This is just an insane amount of work. But that's what we did. And I'm sure the baton got dropped occasionally but in the whole time, maybe five hundred performances, more than that probably, in all that time there were maybe a couple of late starts. It all ran. It was quite amazing how reliable everybody was in getting there and doing it.'

~

The Aboriginal Arts Board considered the ABCD grant application at its meeting in October. At the time, No Fixed Address was on a 15-date tour up the northern NSW coast to Brisbane and back, finishing in Sydney.

'I remember being on tour, going up the coast, and I knew they were meeting that day to discuss it,' says Fisher. 'I remember pulling up at a phone booth and ringing one of the people who was there and asking, "How's it going? Do they need to talk to me? I'm on the line right now." "No, no, no. We haven't got to your item on the agenda yet." I said, "I'll ring you back in another hour." Further up the coast, another phone box.' Eventually the news came through – the grant of $27,200 had been approved.[2]

The spring tour concluded with two notable performances in Sydney. The first was at Paddington Town Hall, with the Murri Jama performers and Warumpi Band. Part of the Independent Music Expo, the show came hot on the heels of the Warumpi's debut single 'Jailanguru Pakernu (Out of Jail)', notably the first rock song released to feature an Aboriginal language (Luritja). For the Butcher brothers and George Rrurrambu, it was their first time into the big city. 'They were a bit wide-eyed,' says Fisher, 'and No Fixed were, "Okay, well, this is how the big city works."'

The following night the two bands played at the Clifton Hotel, a black pub on Botany Road, Redfern. Around midnight, just after No Fixed Address finished their set, the shit hit the fan. Big time.

'The gig was packed and was going really well, nearly everyone was dancing and singing – it was perfect,' Michael Fisher recalls. 'It would have been some time after 11:30 pm, maybe during the encore or just prior to it when suddenly the power to our equipment was turned off and the fluorescent house lights came on. I remember asking the manager what was going on with the power and the lights. He said the police were here and they had done it. He said they didn't want us to perform anymore and wanted everyone out. Then lots of police entered the room and opened the doors to the side lane. They told everyone to leave.'

'I was offstage, I think we'd finished playing,' Ricky Harrison remembers. 'There were all these cops there and the manager said he didn't call them and didn't know why they went there. This old lady was holding her mouth. Apparently, the cops hit her in the mouth with a baton and smashed all her teeth. Outside the cops were getting stuck into everyone for no reason. The cops said the manager called them and he said he didn't. Why would he? He was making a lot of money and everything was working out really well.'

'I certainly do remember that night,' says Nicky Moffatt. 'It was a real big eye-opener, coming from a small country town to the city. The coppers were told they weren't permitted on the premises before midnight. Then they came in and started creating havoc. There was wall to wall coppers in riot gear. So, we took off. Taxis were going past and wouldn't pick us up. Me,

Bart and Ricky were hiding in bushes and Michael flagged a taxi down and bang, we jumped in. The taxi driver freaked out a bit and we said, "No, no, we're heading back to Bondi."'

According to the *Sydney Morning Herald*, the trouble began just before 11.30 pm when a local man and two men from Moree started fighting on the pavement outside the hotel. The hotel's night manager told the *Herald* it was the type of fight the management let the parties settle themselves. He didn't call the police.[3]

At 11.45 pm, a police car was passing the Clifton when a small object was thrown at it. The police stopped and noticed a scuffle at the side of the hotel. They called for back-up. By midnight cars from Redfern, Darlinghurst, Regent Street and Phillip St (Sydney), Waverley, Maroubra, Sutherland, North Sydney, Balmain and Campsie police stations were either in attendance or on their way. Witnesses estimated there were 30 cars, eight vans and around 80 police on the scene. In the ensuing disturbances, 34 people (all Aboriginal) were arrested. All were released the following morning without charge.

That same morning Fisher and the No Fixed Address road crew retrieved the band's stage equipment from the pub and, leaving the chaos behind, drove north to Doyalson for the first date of a nine-date tour of country NSW and Victoria with Goanna. Drama never seemed far away, however, and five shows into the tour Ricky Harrison suffered an injury in Swan Hill, Victoria, that required hospitalisation. Goanna frontman Shane Howard suggested he deputise for Harrison for the next few gigs. Goanna guitarist Ross Hannaford, a long-time fan, volunteered his services as well. Fisher recalls Howard and Bart Willoughby emerging from a motel room with the news and a light-hearted suggestion they adopt the name Mixed Relations for the line-up. The four-piece (with Nicky Moffatt) played the next four shows (Swan Hill, Moama, Albury and Wangaratta) as support to Goanna. When Harrison recovered, No Fixed Address completed the tour at the end of November with gigs in Warrnambool, Wonthaggi and Croydon.

Willoughby was the next to suffer a stroke of bad luck. After a gig at the Caledonian Hotel, Wonthaggi, on 3 December, he was offered a lift back to Melbourne with Denis Walker and his girlfriend Lyn. Walker, an Aboriginal activist who co-founded the Australian Black Panther Party in 1971, crashed the car and Willoughby's right foot was broken after it got stuck under a seat. The band's gigs for the rest of the year were cancelled. Thus, another eventful year drew to a close.

33   A FITTING SEND OFF

The idea of the Aboriginal community in Melbourne mounting a Rock Against Racism concert had been bandied around between Michael Fisher and Maxine Briggs for a while. While Fisher could have organised a concert himself, he felt it would be more beneficial for the community to do it itself, with his assistance. One of Briggs' cousins, Julie Andrews, was part of the circle around No Fixed Address, and Fisher and members of the band would sometimes end up at her place in Northcote to unwind after a gig. Out of the casual conversations there, the idea evolved.

Andrews pays credit to Briggs for introducing her to the band. 'She became like a guiding light to us,' she says, 'as a black woman and our cousin in the music industry. I remember seeing them in Collingwood when Maxine was doing the lighting. It was amazing seeing her standing up there and working lights for a band. Max brought No Fixed into everybody's lives really. She always downplayed her role. If it wasn't for Max, I wouldn't have followed No Fixed.'

For the wider community in Melbourne, it was *Wrong Side of the Road* that heralded the band's arrival. 'When the movie and the record came out, that attracted a lot of people's attention over here,' says Andrews. 'It was a double whammy. You could see a visual story and all their personal stories in that movie and everyone connected to them because of that movie. Me and my cousins, all us girls, we only listened to No Fixed. Us Mob were heavy metal. They never came to Melbourne. It was always No Fixed.

'Those stories of the band members in the film resonated with me and they aligned with the songs and the music. You saw the film was quite badly made but the community events where No Fixed played, the opening scene, that was really good. It really was raw but relatable to mob here in Melbourne.'

Importantly for Andrews and her circle, both the *Wrong Side of the Road* soundtrack album and the *From My Eyes* mini-album that followed included song lyrics. 'The thing with their albums, because me and my cousins bought all of them, they had the words there. So, you knew the songs. You wouldn't just be playing it and walking away, especially if it was Aboriginal message songs. You'd sit down and read the words with them and get involved with the music. And you'd be all sitting around with your cousins listening to it. Having the words and the vinyl ... and it was affordable. We didn't have much money at that age. That was the thing about No Fixed Address, they were accessible, they were affordable and they were meaningful to us. And the other thing was, they dressed like us. That was very much an extension of us. When you hear the word "mob", they were our people and our community. They never had an arrogant attitude about them. They would come in quietly. And they're still like that today.'

While the film and the albums were great, it was the live setting that provided the best experience. And it was pubs like the Aberdeen Hotel in North Fitzroy that provided a culturally safe space. 'When I first saw No Fixed Address. I was leaving that teenager/high school/sport and all that and going into pubs or places where you can see music as an audience member,' says Andrews. 'I would never go to a festival. It was not the place for black people to be. I would always feel threatened as a black person. Even growing up I would feel threatened going to a football match. We couldn't afford a ticket anyway but we would stay locally based, in our community, and watch our own mob play footy. It was always that space where you felt unwelcome, when you were growing up as a teenager. The racial abuse you would cop if you were in public spaces. Or on a tram or a train. Walking down the street.'

Because there were pockets of different groups, even within the Aboriginal community the entertainment options for young Aboriginal women like Julie Andrews were limited.

'We didn't have a place to go,' she says. 'In Melbourne, even before the '80s they had talent nights, Aboriginal band nights. There were pubs that were secured to have Aboriginal groups in there but for our age group – unless you liked country and western which was the big thing with Hard Times and Stray Blacks – for our age group, anything from eighteen up, we had nothing. So, No Fixed was our band. And it was reggae. That was our kind of music. Just like hip-hop and rap is today.

'The politics in our community was against each other at the time. Like with Hard Times – I wouldn't have gone out of my way to see them, to tell you the truth. It was BYO dances back then, with Hard Times. BYO grog. No security or anything. You just turn up and hope for the best that you get out without a fight or getting bashed up. It was community hard times. If you go to the pub, it was totally different. When you went to No Fixed Address, you didn't worry about that. You didn't feel like that. You could enjoy yourself. There were security guards there. You pay for your drink. There was a start and finish time. There were plenty of after-parties where you catch up with everyone. And you'd always be waiting for someone from the band to turn up. And someone always would. It was a good time to be around the music scene, the pub scene in Melbourne.'

A deep connection grew between No Fixed Address and their Melbourne audiences. 'If you're standing in the audience, you really feel a part of the audience and the band, or you feel like an observer on the side,' says Andrews. 'When it came to No Fixed, you never felt you were observing, you always felt a part of it. That was the connection you had with No Fixed Address and the audience. It was a different connection. When Bart would stop and play the didgeridoo and then the guitars would start and then Bart would say, "Fight, fight for your rights" ... it wasn't like a frenzy, it was more like reflecting on your life.

'A lot of their songs let people reflect on their life. And it gave you encouragement to continue on, because they were message songs. They were talking about what it was like to be Aboriginal. And you wouldn't get that on the radio back then. And I did see them on *Countdown* and *Hey, Hey It's Saturday* and the audiences couldn't relate to them. That was the difference with No Fixed. They knew who their audiences were. And that's because their songs always addressed that audience. Us, Aboriginal people.

'I like their songs because it's all about an individual. And then it comes back to being all one together. That's how it feels. They're telling a story about something that happened to them and they don't know why. "Stupid System" is a fantastic song by Bart Willoughby. "We were here first" and "We're the victims of the stupid system". Now that is brilliant for a young person on the dole. Or someone in jail. It gives that political understanding and voice to an individual that otherwise might be feeling wretched and lonely and on their own. Those things they did showed us that we're not alone, you're not alone. This is how I felt, this is what the situation is, this is why it is like it is.

'My mother and my aunts, they never really knew anything about them. It was an underground movement for us as young black people. It was very much about identity culture, politics, self-determination, decolonising. I think a lot of their songs were about decolonising ourselves and being aware of what had happened to us and why and be proud of who you are. Be black and be proud. And they didn't stand up out the front and roar up the crowd, like Freddie Mercury from Queen. They didn't have to. Their music did it for us. And it was culturally a lovely place to be.'

~

After No Fixed Address returned from a January 1984 tour of North Queensland, Andrews and Fisher put their heads together and decided to press ahead with the idea of a community-organised Rock Against Racism concert. The first of a series of planning meetings took place at the Koori

Information Centre (KIC) in Gertrude Street, Fitzroy on 13 February. As well as Andrews and Fisher, those involved included Maxine Briggs, her brother Hartley (who ran KIC) and Andrews' cousin Leanne Miller. Robbie Thorpe, who ran the Aboriginal Health Service next door, and his partner Frances were there and a solicitor from the Aboriginal Legal Service was brought in for legal advice. Central Hall, round the corner in Brunswick Street, was quickly identified as a venue. Owned by the Catholic Archdiocese of Melbourne, the hall was best known for hosting the T.F. Much Ballroom in the early 1970s, when it played host to bands like Spectrum, Daddy Cool and Captain Matchbox Whoopee Band.

~

Meanwhile, plans for the No Fixed Address UK tour were starting to take shape. Richard Micallef had contacts with a number of festivals scheduled for the English summer. The earliest was the Elephant Fayre in Cornwall on the last weekend of July, so that became a benchmark.

Part of the grant from the Aboriginal Arts Board was to enable No Fixed Address to make recordings. 'Since the demise of Rough Diamond, the band had no record company to fund recordings and we were in search of a new record contract,' says Fisher. 'The idea was to fund new recordings using the grant money and these recordings would be used to help secure a new recording contract. The original intention was to make the recordings while on tour in the UK in collaboration with producers in the UK. However, the plan changed during meetings with ABCD in Melbourne.

'Debra Weddall convinced us that she could make a film clip for a single, which we'd be in control of, that we could use to promote No Fixed Address and get a new record contract. It was then decided that the funds would be used to record a single and an accompanying film clip in Australia. We wanted to use a song that would present a strong message and had previously not been released as a single. We felt that the best song we had for this was Bart's song "We Have Survived". Although it had been recorded twice before, we felt that the current performance of the song was far better than the recordings on *Wrong Side of The Road* and the mini album, *From My Eyes*. We also believed the sound could be greatly improved, compared with the previous recordings, and the song would be perfect for a strong story about Aboriginal people's survival in a film clip.

'We thought the film clip might involve dance, and specifically the Aboriginal and Islander Dance Theatre who were based in Glebe, Sydney. Debra knew Paul Elliott, a Sydney-based cinematographer who had shot music clips such as Cold Chisel's "Saturday Night". He indicated that he'd like to be involved and so did some people from the Aboriginal and Islander Dance Theatre. We had a planning session with Debra in Melbourne on 1 May and the next day headed off to Sydney for a few gigs. Part of the purpose of that trip was to meet with Paul Elliott and people from the Aboriginal and Islander Dance Theatre. Debra came up to Sydney to join us for the meetings and to plan with Paul how the filming would work in Sydney.

'A few days after our return to Melbourne, we had a meeting to develop the story board for the clip based on having the dancers involved and filming at Botany Bay in Sydney. The story developed was one of survival. The basic idea of the film clip was there were to be spirits of the band members within the film in addition to their modern-day selves and these spirits were to be played by the dancers.

'The story board for the film clip begins with Bart, as a traditional Aboriginal man, witnessing the arrival of Captain Cook along with his spirit (played by a dancer) and other spirits (also played by the dancers). Bart's spiritual self is then surrounded by the invaders who are represented by other dancers dressed in white with white masks. The invaders are attempting to suppress his spirit. The spirits go on to fight battles with the invaders who bear guns and crosses. This leads to the modern day, where the spirits, in modern-day clothing, fight with the invaders who are also in modern-day clothing. Through this scene walk the band members, each with the Aboriginal flag on their chest. The final film clip also includes real footage of Aboriginal people fighting back during the protests at the Brisbane Commonwealth Games. The battle culminates in a simulation of a nuclear explosion in the desert which flashes in the band members' faces. This part of the story comes from Bart. Bart has relatives from the Maralinga area of South Australia where seven nuclear bombs were detonated in the 1950s and '60s. In the aftermath of the explosion, which results in the death of many of the spirits, the spirits of the band members reunite with the modern-day band members in a celebration of survival.'

Fisher tapped sound engineer Tony Buettel to work on the track and booked three days of recording/mixing time at Melbourne's Richmond Recorders starting on Monday, 28 May. Fisher had been impressed with Buetell's work on Goanna's 'Solid Rock'. 'He was a drummer as well as a sound engineer and got great drum sounds. He was keen to do it when I approached him.'

Fisher produced the track himself and had a very clear idea of what he wanted. 'I wanted to capture the very direct sound of the song as it was played live at the time with my mixing effects. I wanted to capture the strong signature bass and drumbeat, almost a tribal sound, with reverberant guitar at the beginning followed by the clear guitar theme played by Ricky. It had to have a big drum sound with the tough snare and a clear bass guitar, for other than vocal line, it is the bass guitar riff, played by Nicky, that defines the song. The snare was to sound like a punch. The vocals were to be up front with a little echo and the choruses thick. The sound was to be triumphant like the song itself. Louis had a ripping guitar solo and this great idea of creating a chorus of bent guitar notes at the end of chorus lines, using lots of guitar overdubs, to create an effect which was perfect for the triumphant sound we were creating.'

The result was a 24-track recording with several guitar and vocal overdubs, with the lead vocal sung by Bart Willoughby accompanied in the choruses by everyone. 'There were also overdubs of congas played by guest performer, the late Douglas (Dougie) McDonald. We used the reverse-gated reverb effect on the drums, particularly strongly on the snare drum to make it punch very hard without splashing and obscuring anything else in the sound. Listening to it in retrospect I think we achieved exactly what we wanted – it sounds strong and triumphant.'

The striking video for 'We Have Survived', done for a bargain basement $2800, was shot in Sydney on the weekend of 2 and 3 June 1984. Robina Beard, an actress, dancer and choreographer who had been doing work with the Aboriginal and Islander Dance Theatre, came on board to choreograph the dancing. 'I recall when we met her that she looked familiar,' says Fisher. 'The reason was she played the role of Madge the manicurist in the iconic and long-running television commercial for Palmolive dish-washing liquid – it was hard to separate that image sometimes when talking with her!'

The filming of the arrival of Captain Cook, the attack on Bart's spirit and the battle between the spirits and the invaders was done in Palm Beach on the Saturday morning. The filming of the modern-day fight, the aftermath of the nuclear explosion and the reuniting of the band's spirits with their modern-day selves in celebration of survival were all filmed at Botany Bay on the Saturday afternoon. Additional filming of the nuclear explosion flashes in the faces of the band members was done in a warehouse space on the Sunday.

'The film editing by Paul and Debra was completed shortly after filming,' says Fisher. 'We were all very impressed with what they had produced. We thought we had something really good, and this would really help us get a record deal and the film clip would be seen by many. The song and the film clip spoke for the band so well. Everyone involved in making the clip had done so without any payment. Everyone was motivated by something else, which may have been simply the desire to make a statement about Aboriginal survival.'

~

It was touch and go as to whether Louis McManus would be joining the UK tour as a special guest artist. At the last minute, he opted out. He had gone to England with The Bushwackers in 1976 and starved. Despite Fisher assuring him they had the grant and all the dates were booked, he couldn't be persuaded. A discussion followed about whether the band should take a second guitarist or faithful roadie Angelo DiCarlo.

Fisher would do the band's live sound and wanted to take DiCarlo, according to Ricky Harrison. 'He needed somebody there who could help him with the side mix. Somebody who knew the band and was pretty competent at what he was doing. He didn't want to get somebody who didn't know the band to come along in England. We all thought, yeah, we can do this three-piece. We'd been performing three-piece for a while. We had a good idea of what we were doing. It would have been good to take a lead guitarist, but then we would have spent some months rehearsing. Because if Louis wasn't coming then we would have to get Selwyn [Burns] or someone else.'

Fisher arranged to fly out of Melbourne on 6 July, with the band and DiCarlo to follow on 19 July. The two weeks in London would enable him to make sure everything was in place for the band to hit the ground running. About a month before he was due to leave, Fisher bumped into a documentary filmmaker in a Carlton pub. His name was John Tatoulis.

'I can't remember how we got chatting,' says Fisher. 'He said, "I'm going to Greece. I'm making a documentary for SBS about an Australian bouzouki player who is going back to play in Greece. We could come over and do a bit on you guys." I said, "That'd be great!" Some things fall into your lap.'

~

By mid-May, the Rock Against Racism concert had been locked in for 7 July at Central Hall, and quotes were being obtained for posters and production. 'Our way of communicating in the community was very different,' says Julie Andrews. 'We didn't have phones. So we communicated with posters. No Fixed Address posters were how we knew they were coming and where they were going to be. They would be on the billboards and pubs like the Aberdeen. You'd go to see a band at the Aberdeen and you'd see a poster that No Fixed Address were coming. There was always word of mouth being passed around the community.'

The final line-up was Hard Times, Mantaka from Queensland, Warumpi Band and No Fixed Address. 'You should have seen that concert, Don!' exclaims Andrews. 'It was all black. There were blackfellas everywhere. And it was like they were stunned. It was a big hall. It was the Catholic Hall. You've got the Australian Catholic Uni there now.

'I had nothing to do with the sound, the lighting or any of that. It was more about keeping everyone together. That's what Max said. "We'll do this, we'll do that," and I said "What am I gonna do?" and she said, "You can just keep us all together." Max will never give you a title.

'On the night I remember George [Rrurrambu] on the stage with the boomerangs and all that. I walked downstairs and there are all these Fitzroy fellas, Bruce McGuinness and all of them smoking dope. And I went, "What the fuck?" And it was like, "How do they find these bloody little holes that they can crawl into?" There were all these blokes and I went, "Oh, I'm getting out of here." And Bruce McGuinness could see I was freaking out, as one of the organisers and he said, "Okay, we'll close the door." And I went, "I'm getting out of here."

'Back then Rock Against Racism was all around Melbourne but there was no access point for us as black people to be involved. We took that on ourselves and we did a damn good job. And it was all for our mob.'

Reflecting on those times, Andrews says No Fixed Address

were trailblazers and inspired others. 'Everyone of that generation that was around No Fixed Address at that time excelled somewhere in their lives in terms of arts, education or politics. It just gave us a foundation to work from. My cousin Leanne Miller just walked into SBS Radio and was involved in studio recording and booking studios and then a journalist. And my other friend, Janina Harding who was on the RAR organising group with me and Michael, she went into RMIT and got a media degree and now she's director of Cairns Indigenous Arts Festival. These are the women that ... we were all going out watching No Fixed Address together. It was so admirable that they got out there and did that, laid the groundwork for that. Laid the pathway for more people to do it.'

Andrews, who these days is Professor Julie Andrews, Yorta Yorta/Wurundjeri/Wiradjuri (BA Hons, PhD), Director (Indigenous Research), Co-Chair Aboriginal Studies Indigenous Strategy Committee and Convenor of Aboriginal Studies at La Trobe University, feels the lessons from those days continue to reverberate down the years. 'It seems to be that music seems to work as a black and white space to me. I think music has become for our country a space where we can communicate to each other in a non-threatening, culturally safe way. But it's also about reconciling black and white.

'People like Michael Fisher and all those people that supported them – look at Michael. He's still friends with them. Nothing fazes Michael. You can be a blackfella and Michael's not going to run away screaming and terrified, like the *Hallowe'en* movies. I think he's got resilience. And he's got respect for black people. It's truth and integrity. I know a lot of white people that just can't cope with the violence, the horror stories, the alcoholism, the drugs, the incarceration, all that stuff around Aboriginal people and families. They feel themselves first before they think of anything else. Michael, I can't believe that bloke. They're the kind of people we need.'

~

When Michael Fisher arrived in London, he bunked down with Richard Micallef at his council flat. 'There was a hell of a lot of setting up,' he says. Work permits had to be organised, a business name registered, a bank account opened, equipment and truck hired – oh, and somewhere for the band to stay. 'What are we going to do with them all?' Fisher asked Micallef. Through friends of friends, a squat at 125 Kings Avenue, Clapham South was suggested. 'We went round and they were very welcoming of us,' says Fisher. In a fine example of just-in-time management, the squat was secured the day before the band arrived.

With Fisher in London and everything arranged, it seemed nothing could go wrong. Or could it? After Fisher left, Ricky Harrison (aka Chris Jones) received notice of a court appearance. It was addressed to Ricky Harrison. But he hadn't gone under that name for almost two years.

'When we got in there the police had the thing for Ricky Harrison,' he recalls. 'The magistrate turned around to the cop and said, "But this person is Chris Jones. He's not Ricky Harrison. Why have you brought him before us?" And the cop said, "If we can just take him down the station and get his fingerprints, we can prove he's Ricky Harrison." The magistrate went red and said, "I'm not having this," and told him to get out and dismissed the case. So, I was free to go and off I went. Outside, the cop said, "I'll still be looking for you." Eventually they caught up to me, but it was too late. The charge had expired.'

The charge was for stealing cars in Morwell.

'I was with the band,' says Harrison. 'It was 1979, I think. I guess everyone was going to jail back then, but they didn't catch me. Everyone that was with me in the car got locked up. In Morwell. Cousins.'

Harrison walked free; and went to the airport.

PART 4

OVERSEAS TOURS

(1984–88)

By the time No Fixed Address touched down at London's Heathrow Airport, another black group was well on its way to a record-breaking tour of England. The West Indies cricket team had followed up its innings demolition of England at Edgbaston with a fifth day run fest at Lords to claim the second test by nine wickets. They proceeded to smash England in the final three tests, to become the only touring side to inflict a 5-0 whitewash, or as some wags termed it, a 'blackwash', on the home nation. The sun shone, black was beautiful and large Nike billboards of the West Indies vice-captain Viv Richards (the 'Master Blaster') competed for attention on the streets of Brixton and Notting Hill with those for the summer's movie hit *Ghostbusters*.

Meanwhile up north, a far grimmer and wide-reaching struggle was underway. Determined to change Britain by crushing trade union power and destroying the post-war consensus on State-owned key industries, full employment and the welfare state, Prime Minister Margaret Thatcher had brought the full force of her government to bear on striking coalminers and their families. Cavalry charges on picketing miners by baton-wielding police were its public face, while freezing the mining union's funds and cutting supplementary benefits for miners' families applied the squeeze on the home front.

~

Once the touring party cleared immigration at Heathrow, they loaded their gear into Richard Micallef's station wagon and he drove them to Brixton for a hearty English breakfast and then onto their London accommodation – the squatter's house in Kings Avenue, Clapham. In 1970s and '80s England, squatting (the occupation of empty premises) was for many young people a pragmatic solution to the problem of urban homelessness. Under English law, it was not a criminal offence to take possession of an unoccupied dwelling – rather, it was a civil matter between the owner and the new occupants. In practical terms, once squatters had occupied a vacant property, they could change the locks, apply to have electricity, gas and water connected, and claim it as their home address.

'It was a three-storey house with a basement and a nice garden in the backyard,' recalls Ricky Harrison. 'There were three ladies that lived there and two guys. There was Sarah, big blonde woman. There was an Irish girl, Sue. She did most of the cooking. She was going out with this guy who looked like Catweazle [the time-travelling medieval wizard from the British TV series of the same name]. Dave was with Julie. She was from Sydney. She'd only arrived there a couple of weeks before we did. I remember having an argument with Julie. She was going on about the band. "Aw, you come over here and run-down Australia," some shit like that.'

'On the first day I bought sleeping bags and pillows,' says Michael Fisher. 'It had reasonable mattresses. We all chipped in for food and expenses. There was all this gear in the basement: a PA, mics, video dubbing gear. We had accommodation, a rehearsal room downstairs and someone was cooking for us – could we have done better?'

The band's home away from home was located a stone's throw from the West Indian enclave of Brixton, the scene of serious clashes between the police and local residents just three years previously. The disturbances took place during a UK-wide recession in an area blighted by poor housing, 50 per cent youth unemployment, a higher-than-average crime rate and oppressive policing – in particular the increased use of stop-and-search.

Brixton was where the band used to go to get beer and other supplies. 'We would only get 75 pounds a week,' says Harrison. 'We were getting the same as the dole back home, but things were a lot dearer. It was hard for us to go out anywhere. We had enough for smokes, a bit of *yarndi*, some grog and not much for anything else. Down the road was where all the black people were. All you had to do was pull up in front of the flats and all these West Indians would converge on the car. "Whaddya want, geezer?" "Just wanna get ten pounds [worth] ..." of whatever it was, a block of hash. They'd pull out their knife and they'd have a big block of hash and they'd cut off a piece of hash for you.'

~

The band's first UK performance was at the Tropical Palace, a former art deco cinema turned reggae nightclub in Kensal Rise, North London. John Tatoulis was there filming the gig. Tatoulis had interviewed Bart Willoughby and Angelo DiCarlo sitting on the Singapore Airlines 747 at Melbourne airport before take-off, and conducted other interviews during the early weeks of the tour as well as capturing a number of performances. The documentary, *No Fixed Address on Tour*, was screened on SBS on 14 September, while the band were still in England. The Tropical Palace gig was notable for being the first time Willoughby and Nicky Moffatt played didgeridoos together on stage. The didge duet happened during 'Black Man's Rights', with Harrison playing clapsticks in the background. The crowd was transfixed.

On the morning after the Tropical Palace gig, Tatoulis and crew were at the Clapham squat filming the members of the band still sleeping, then loading equipment into their hired van for the drive to the second gig of the tour. 'When friends back in Australia saw the doco they said, "Sleeping on the floor? Couldn't you afford a big hotel?"' says Fisher, laughing.

~

Elephant Fayre in Cornwall was an early 1980s rival to the later-to-be-world-famous Glastonbury Festival. Held in the grounds of the stately home Port Eliot, adjacent to the village of St Germans, the 'fayre' had an alternative bent and included experimental theatre and media in addition to rock, punk, folk and reggae music. The headliners in 1984 were The Fall,

Jonathan Richman and the Modern Lovers, John Martyn and on the Friday night (traditionally reggae night), Linton Kwesi Johnson & the Dennis Bovell Dub Band. No Fixed Address were billed as 'Australian Aboriginal band'.

'We were driving along this real bumpy road,' Harrison recalls. 'It was an old Roman road. Next thing there's a naked woman walking up the road. I'm going, "What kind of festival is this? [laughs]."'

No Fixed Address performed at sunset and Tatoulis captured the set and the crowd reaction. About 2,000 people were gathered in front of the stage when the band began. By the end the audience had swelled to 8,000 and the band was called back for several encores. 'The whole crowd was dancing,' says Harrison. 'They really spun out on the didgeridoo. I'm not sure whether they'd seen the didgeridoo played before. It really had a big impact on a lot of people. They were really emotional about it. They were going wild.'

UK music weekly *Sounds* (11 August 1984) also singled out the didgeridoo in its review of the evening.

> There's a healthily gritty quality to the group's playing and in drummer Bart Willoughby's lead vocals, although they could perhaps do with an additional instrument to brighten up the overall musical framework. But where they do stand out is when Bart plays the didgeridoo – a long wooden pipe – from which he produces an astonishing number of notes and distorted vocalising. Apparently his two colleagues perform on the instrument as well and it would be fascinating to hear more of this authentic aboriginal expression.

Richard Micallef had locked in a few dates, but other gigs were booked as the band went along. Through Micallef's colleague Henry McKenzie, No Fixed Address secured a spot at renowned London rock pub Dingwalls on Tuesday, 7 August. Keen to check out the venue, on the evening before the gig the band members headed over the Thames to Camden Lock. Jonathan Richman and the Modern Lovers were the headline

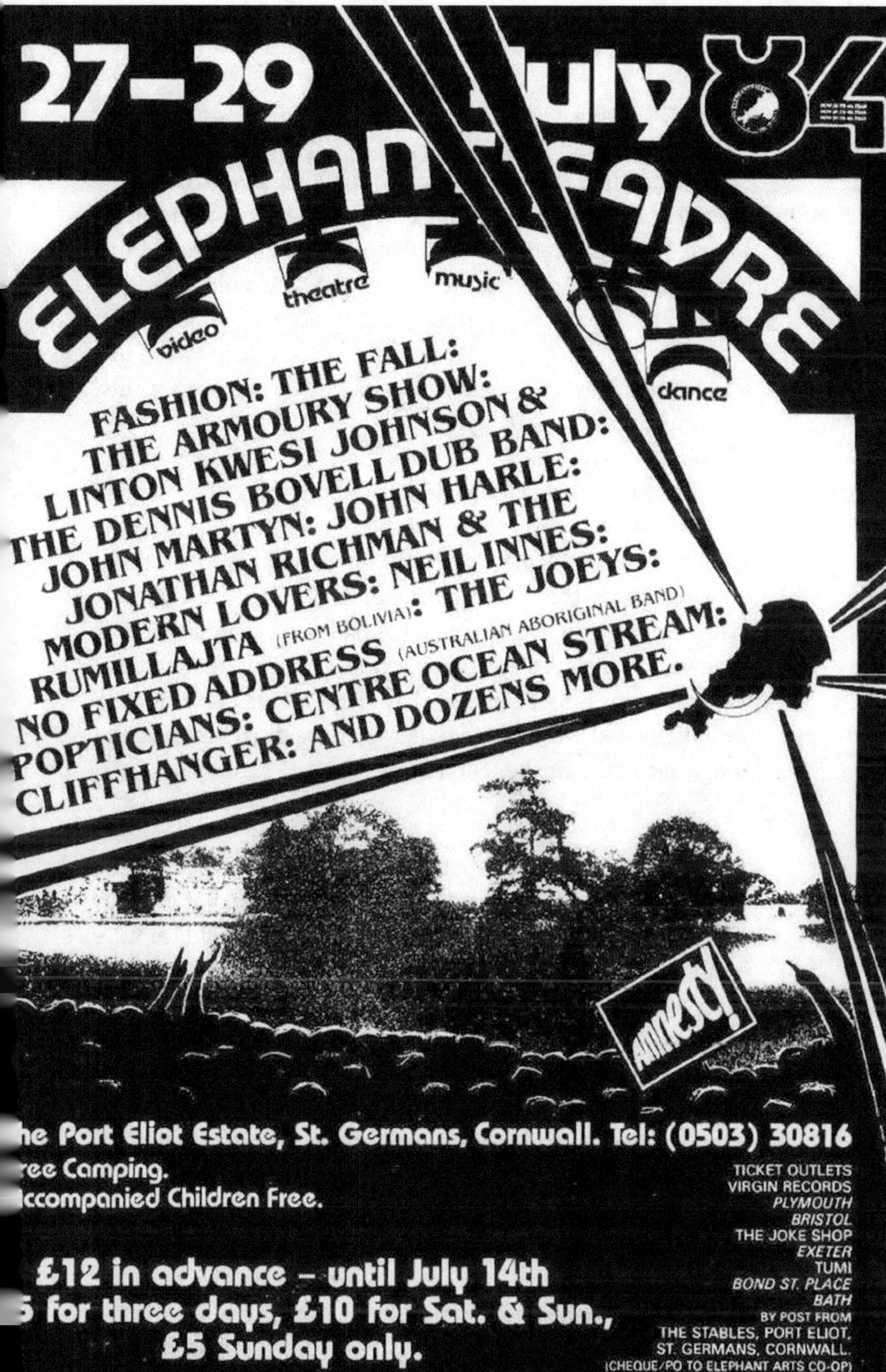

27-29 July 84
ELEPHANT FAYRE
video   theatre   music   dance

FASHION: THE FALL:
THE ARMOURY SHOW:
LINTON KWESI JOHNSON &
THE DENNIS BOVELL DUB BAND:
JOHN MARTYN: JOHN HARLE:
JONATHAN RICHMAN & THE
MODERN LOVERS: NEIL INNES:
RUMILLAJTA (FROM BOLIVIA): THE JOEYS:
NO FIXED ADDRESS (AUSTRALIAN ABORIGINAL BAND)
POPTICIANS: CENTRE OCEAN STREAM:
CLIFFHANGER: AND DOZENS MORE.

AMNESTY!

The Port Eliot Estate, St. Germans, Cornwall. Tel: (0503) 30816
Free Camping.
Accompanied Children Free.

£12 in advance – until July 14th
for three days, £10 for Sat. & Sun.,
£5 Sunday only.

TICKET OUTLETS
VIRGIN RECORDS
PLYMOUTH
BRISTOL
THE JOKE SHOP
EXETER
TUMI
BOND ST. PLACE
BATH
BY POST FROM
THE STABLES, PORT ELIOT.
ST. GERMANS, CORNWALL.
(CHEQUE/PO TO ELEPHANT ARTS CO-OP)
SELF ADDRESSED ENVELOPE

act, but it was a rather more famous face that caught Nicky Moffatt's attention.

'We got the opportunity to meet David Bowie there,' he says. 'He'd just done that song with the Aboriginal Islander Dance Theatre, "Let's Dance". I spotted him and he had this big lounge roped off and these bodyguards came towards us and I said, "No, we're Aborigines from Australia," and he said, "Open the bar, let 'em in." He let us in to his little area. We had a good chat. He was a really down-to-earth person. It was just like whoa, starstruck [laughs].'

John Tatoulis needed a good quality recording of the band's songs for his documentary soundtrack. Up popped Phil Roberts, the co-producer of the music featured in *Wrong Side of the Road*. 'Somebody got in touch and asked if I could do a recording there,' recalls Roberts. 'So, I got a hold of a mate of mine who had a mobile 16-track. We recorded them at Dingwalls, which is a good rock venue. I didn't take it and mix it, I just made sure it came in okay.' The various performances Tatoulis filmed were cut together over the music recorded at Dingwalls in the final documentary.

~

This was basically the pattern of the tour. Most of the performances were around London (many of them at one-day outdoor festivals) but periodically the band would venture from their base to play a night or two in the provinces. There were two performances at the International Garden Festival in Liverpool; overnight trips to Manchester and Bristol; and a three-night jaunt down to Devon. 'When we played Barnstable, there were some Aussies in the audience,' says Harrison. 'Surfers. They had a little following themselves. We met a few English people, but it was more about educating them.'

Bart Willoughby was doing most of the press interviews and found English journalists happy to be educated. As he told Sheryl Garrett from *City Limits*, 'We're trying to get international recognition, to bring our case to the world. The songs are about how we've been treated – or mistreated – and how we still are. The struggle for our land. We're here for our music *and* our Aboriginality, the politics are inseparable, they're what started it off.'[1]

The sympathetic press coverage alerted the Australian expatriate community to the band's presence in England. 'The Aussies were very supportive and great to catch up with,' recalls Harrison. 'They'd never met Aboriginal people before; most of them anyway. Being from Australia they felt more comfortable coming up to us over there than it would be for them when we were here. They were the ones that made the loudest noise and were the proudest ones [laughs]. It was like the crowds we got back home. Once they heard the music and got to listen to the words, they saw that there's nothing sadistic about us at all. Just a band performing and doing songs that meant a lot to us. We had the balls to go out and say things. They really appreciated that we were doing our own stuff that was really different. They really enjoyed the music, music they could dance to and relate to being Australians. "Yeah, this does happen in Australia. Yeah, you're right about that." When we spoke to some of them after the shows, they didn't really talk about that. They talked about where they came from and what they were doing. They'd miss being back home. They'd talk about themselves. It was good because we knew what they were talking about. It was good to have conversations with other Aussies over there.'

~

The 1984 Notting Hill Carnival, the annual celebration of British-Caribbean culture, was hailed at the time as the best ever. Perhaps it was the gorgeous weather, but more likely it was the absence of oppressive policing. London bobbies, along with colleagues from across the UK, were deployed in force in the country's mining areas where they were engaged in increasingly violent clashes with picketing coal miners. No Fixed Address played at the carnival on the afternoon of

Sunday, 26 August at Portobello Green in the shadow of the Westway. In front of a crowd of around 3,000, the band's performance impressed the British music press, with Adam Isaacs in *Melody Maker* writing:

> There was a large Australian contingent for No Fixed Address, an Australian Aborigine band who played a dynamic combination of rock/reggae/ethnic music. They've surfaced previously as the single best group on a music video titled 'Australia Now' and drove the crowd wild with what I presume was a genuine didgeridoo – whatever, the lengthy piece of wood tubing produced eerie moaning sounds that were highly effective! Holding it all together was a charismatic drummer/lead singer and the band as a whole pulled no punches lyrically or musically.[2]

and Mat Snow in *New Musical Express* opining:

> Aborigines who play reggae must be few, those who add a country tinge (the Waylon Souls?) even fewer. NFA do both and snort their furious indignation at the treatment their race has had at the manicured hands of the white race. No designer label clobber, no comforting covers.[3]

Carnival headliners Aswad were also impressed. So much so, they offered No Fixed Address the support spot on their upcoming 25-date autumn tour. Under the 'pay-to-play' arrangements common to UK tours, the band did not have the required funds and had to regretfully decline the offer.

~

Opposite above: Bart Willoughby blowing didge and blowing minds, Notting Hill Carnival, London, August 1984.

Opposite below: Ricky Harrison and Nicky Moffatt, Notting Hill Carnival, London, August 1984.

Photos by Manwel Tabone.

CARIBBEAN
TIMES
STAR

After creating waves on the London live circuit, No Fixed Address were invited to participate in a series of benefit concerts for the striking miners. Organised by London Miners Gala, *5 Nights for the Miners* ran from Monday 3 to Friday 7 September at the Royal Festival Hall. Performers included the Style Council, Van Morrison, Christy Moore, Bert Jansch and Loudon Wainwright III; plus comedians Ben Elton, Rik Mayall, Nigel Planer and Alexei Sayle.

Things were slightly chaotic backstage on the Wednesday night – reggae night – and Ricky Harrison was trying to tune his guitar when a naggingly familiar face hove into view. 'This guy walked in and said something and I looked at him and I thought, "I've seen you somewhere before. I know you, but I don't know you." He walked over and he was trying to talk to Bart. And it was Jimmy Page from Led Zeppelin. And Bart said, "No, no, I'm busy." He was sticking water down the didgeridoo trying to tune it up, to get it into the right key. It dries out and it goes to a different note. He had to put water on it. I think it changes the acoustics in it. From an open, like a hall sound to a studio sound. If the wood was wet it absorbed the sound more. He was able to change the note, so by the time we got on stage it was in the right key.'

'I brushed him off, but I didn't know who he was,' Willoughby confirmed at No Fixed Address's induction into the South Australian Music Hall of Fame in 2016.'

But Page wasn't the only famous personage lurking backstage. 'My favourite band was playing that night,' Willoughby says. 'Misty-in-Roots. They had a dressing room a couple of doors down. I went down to check them out. I opened this door and there were two guys sitting there. They turned around and I waved. They waved back. That was Billy Bragg and Nick Cave. I went to the next door and I heard this big noise. I opened the door and a big gust of smoke came out. There were about fifty blackfellas in there getting warmed up to perform.'

~

Nicky Moffatt, Ricky Harrison and Bart Willoughby beside the Thames, Wapping, London.

Photo by Bleddyn Butcher.

Two days after the final gig of the tour, at the Greater London Council Thamesday free concert at Jubilee Gardens on 15 September, Harrison, Moffatt and Angelo DiCarlo flew home. Fisher and Willoughby stayed on as Fisher continued doing the rounds of British record companies, seeking a recording deal. He had a three-video package to show them: the Rough Diamond video for 'From My Eyes', the live version of 'Pigs' from the opening of the Sydney Entertainment Centre; and the new version of 'We Have Survived'. However, Fisher got no bites. A trip to New York failed to elicit interest either.

'We had hit the pinnacle, says Fisher. 'We had tried our best. That is what we'd done. We got that grant and we had a vision. We were going to go there; we were going to blow them away. It was all going to happen. And the live gigs went well. The press was good. Everything was going right but no record deal came from it.'

The film clip for 'We Have Survived' was screened on SBS TV and other channels in Australia, on *The Tube* in the UK, on Rock America in the USA and supplied to Aboriginal organisations in Australia. It was also used by promoters in England and Germany and used extensively to promote No Fixed Address to dozens of record companies.

'Despite its impressive quality I can see, in retrospect, that it was just too political for anyone to touch in terms of securing a major recording contract,' says Fisher. 'I recall the words of a major record company executive in New York, one of many I had meetings with. He seemed to like the clip when I showed it to him but said to me quite frankly, "MTV will never play this."'

~

Perhaps the reaction wasn't surprising. The musical trends were not in favour of the political rock'n'reggae that No Fixed Address was offering. In the UK, the summer charts had been dominated by the massive Trevor Horn-produced synthesised beat of Frankie Goes to Hollywood's 'Relax' and 'Two Tribes'; the plaintive sophisto-funk of Prince's 'When Doves Cry'; the hip-hop of Grandmaster and Melle Mel's 'White Lines (Don't Do It)'; and the mellow tones of Sade's 'Smooth Operator', Spandau Ballet's 'Only When You Leave' and the Kane Gang's 'Closest Thing to Heaven'. In the US, Prince reigned and the new school of hip-hop, typified by Run DMC and LL Cool J was making waves. Drum machines were making drummers redundant everywhere.

Before leaving English shores, No Fixed Address scored a coveted feature in the country's premier music weekly *New Musical Express*. Bart Willoughby didn't hold back about the plight of his people back in their homeland. 'We're in a terrible state,' he told Danny Kelly. 'The blacks in the cities are freaked out on drink and drugs. Those in the country have their lands taken from them, their ancient tribal lands ruined.' The issues of land rights, including mineral rights, and preservation of culture were inextricably linked, Willoughby said. 'It's not just a belief or a religion. Our culture is land, moon, rivers and sun … If you treat the land badly, it will get back at you. We had harmony with the land for tens of thousands of years; for two or three ice ages. Now look at it … bushfires and hurricanes. And what about the uranium? If you let the snake out, the world's gonna blow up.'[4]

When Bart Willoughby and Michael Fisher returned from overseas in late 1984, rather than going back on the road, No Fixed Address decided they would be more discerning about the shows they played and use the downtime to write more songs for the album they still wanted to make.

The band only played twice before the turn of the year – firstly at the Sky to Earth Confest, at Daylesford, north-west of Melbourne on 7 December and then at an old haunt, the Central Club Hotel in Richmond. For both shows, the band was augmented by Selwyn Burns on guitar. There was a third show booked, at Warrnambool on 28 December, but it was cancelled when Nicky Moffatt broke his leg in a motorbike accident. The band stopped playing. But Fisher was dreaming big.

'After a few gigs in Australia, I realised what I really needed to do was tap into the international indigenous network more,' he says. 'We would try to get more arts funding, more cultural stuff, align more with that. In our naivety we had thought if we waved our flag, someone might take us up. "Here we are. This is out latest and greatest." But the reaction everywhere was, "Oh, it's too indigenous, it's too left-of-centre." No Fixed Address was not going to be a mainstream band, ever. That was my big realisation – we needed to change our approach.'

In the week before Christmas, Fisher spoke with Men at Work's manager Russell Deppler about the possibility of No Fixed Address supporting the Men on an upcoming US tour. Deppler was receptive to the idea, but cautioned, 'The band is shaky'. Indeed, after coming back together after a year off, Men at Work were wracked with arguments about songwriting and management, and when it came time to record their third album, drummer Jerry Speiser and bass player John Rees found themselves 'not required'.

Fisher mapped out an ambitious program for the year ahead. In March the band would record 'a modern dance song

Selwyn Burns, Monty Lovett, Bart Willoughby and Ricky Harrison, Phoenician Club, Sydney 27 January 1985.

---

based on the didgeridoo' followed by a video in April. In June/July they would tour the USA with Men at Work, followed by a tour of the UK, France, Holland and Germany in August/September, then finish with their own October shows in the USA.

In the first week of January, Fisher contacted the organisations that had written letters of support for the 1984 UK tour, asking if they would offer their support for the 1985 program. A grant application was fired off to Gary Foley at the Aboriginal Arts Board on 10 January 1985.

With Nicky Moffatt still sidelined with his leg injury, Monty Lovett was drafted in on bass for a Radio Skid Row Survival Day concert at the Phoenician Club in Sydney on 27 January. Originally from Western Victoria, Lovett had been at CASM in a soul rock band called All States and played in the *Indulkana Suite*, CASM's multi-media urban corroboree that toured nationally in 1983–84.[1] Selwyn Burns again contributed lead guitar.

In an interview in the week leading up to the show, Bart Willoughby was looking forward to the year with optimism. 'With what I know now, and with the band as it is now, I can't see nothing stopping us. Not making it to the top, but going around the world, making music, making money. We've been around the world. We're going around the world again. Still independent.'

Despite this bravado, Ricky Harrison and Nicky Moffatt, both married with young children, were struggling. Moffatt was preoccupied with family issues back in Morwell, and Michael Fisher wrote to a friend in England that 'he doesn't seem interested'. Harrison was living at Moorabbin and driving a cab for Eastmoor Taxis.

The grand plan started to unravel. Gary Foley advised Fisher that the Aboriginal Arts Board at its March meetings had deferred consideration of the No Fixed Address grant application. Men at Work's third album *Two Hearts* was released in April to largely negative reaction, and their proposed US tour was cancelled. Things looked brighter in Europe, however. In early April, Fisher was contacted by Birger Gesthuisen from Exile, an intercultural non-profit organisation based in Duisburg, West Germany, that organised tours for musical groups. Gesthuisen had received material about No Fixed Address and was keen to help the band come to Europe if there were any plans. While that news was being digested, there was another gig to organise. And it was quite the logistical challenge.

~

In September 1984, the Australian Broadcasting Tribunal had granted the Alice Springs-based Central Australian Aboriginal Media Association a special interest public radio broadcasting licence, the first awarded to an Aboriginal organisation. CAAMA built a studio and transmission facilities at Little Sisters, a renovated former Catholic convent on the southern outskirts of Alice Springs. The convent was next to a town camp also called Little Sisters. The radio station, 8KIN-FM, began broadcasting to Alice Springs, and on relay to communities in Ali Curung, Hermannsburg (Ntaria) and Santa Teresa, on Friday, 26 April 1985. It was an auspicious occasion, although the official launch on the Friday afternoon didn't quite go to plan. CAAMA director Freda Glynn [known at the time by her married name, Freda Thornton] told the *Centralian Advocate*: 'We had a large yellow, black and red flag with pulleys on it, so the whole community could open it. But the flagpole collapsed when everyone, including children, were pulling the ropes!'[2]

CAAMA mounted a big weekend concert to celebrate the launch. At CAAMA's request, Michael Fisher had organised the production for the event. A PA, lights and two crew were hired from Concert Sound in Adelaide. A truck from Showfreight was filled with the equipment, put on the Ghan and sent up by rail from Adelaide to Alice Springs.

The concert took place on a stage in front of the new station. CAAMA had invited numerous Aboriginal bands, choirs, solo artists and traditional dancers from communities throughout Central Australia to attend. Friday night's performances were purely traditional and ran from sundown till midnight. On Saturday the music began at 1 pm and again ran till midnight, with everything broadcast live-to-air. Headlining the Saturday show were No Fixed Address, with Monty Lovett on bass and new recruit David Osborne on lead guitar. Coloured Stone, whose 'Black Boy' had been the first single released on CAAMA's Imparja Records the previous year, were the other major act on the bill.

On the Sunday after the concert, Ricky Harrison and Monty Lovett went to watch a game of Australian Rules football. 'I remember we went to some footy oval the next day. They had a footy match on. Monty wanted to go so we drove out there,' says Harrison. 'I remember we pulled up next to this car and it was playing the *From My Eyes* album. And it was like, "Oh!" They turned around and looked at us and a big smile came over their faces. "We're playing your music here, man."'

When it came time to pack up and leave the Alice, Bart Willoughby asked Michael Fisher if he would leave the drum kit behind. Willoughby said he wanted to play with his cousins Buna Lawrie and John John Miller, who were both now in Coloured Stone. 'Sure,' said Fisher.

~

Fisher had been having discussions with the Aboriginal Artists Agency about releasing the version of 'We Have Survived' recorded the previous year and recording an album of new songs. The agency had established a record label, Yinura, and its first release, Warumpi Band's *Big Name, No Blankets* had been a critical and commercial success.

Some of Bart Willoughby's songs that would have been the core of such an album included 'Our Mother', 'Revolution', 'We Go Back', 'Living In The City' and 'Reality'. All had been extensively road tested in the band's live set.

'These are all environmental songs,' says Fisher. 'The whole lot. They're all about how the land is being treated. "Our Mother" was about the land. "Revolution" is about looking after nature. Realising that nature is in trouble and stop being so selfish. Something needs to change. "We Go Back" is talking about the depth of Aboriginal history. "Living In The City" is about losing yourself and not being in connection with the land. And "Reality" is about the reason I am in the city is because I've got to face up to the reality that I've got to change things here.'

Other songs in the mix included 'Jack's Back', 'Affection' and 'My Song'.

'These are little bit different,' says Fisher. '"Jack's Back" is about a guy from Warrnambool. About getting back to your Aboriginality. "Affection" was the second love song that Bart had written to that point. And "My Song" was about how he sees things and why he's doing what he's doing.'

And there was also one of the new songs Willoughby had written in this period, 'Message for Young and Old'. Performed live for the first time in Alice Springs, it is a song Fisher considers one of Willoughby's finest.

'One of the reasons we didn't sign anything with the Aboriginal Artists Agency was there wasn't enough money to record,' says Fisher. 'So what was the point? They were happy to take "We Have Survived" the way it was. This was Martin

Hardie. In July, Bart and I flew up to meet with Martin. Went to see Gary Foley but he was away that day. We went to the Northern Beaches and met a dude from Powderworks and we went to the Aboriginal Arts Board. But they weren't going to give us money.'

Negotiations got to the point of exchanging contracts but then petered out.

~

With no album in prospect and No Fixed Address off the road, Ricky Harrison and his family moved to Adelaide and Bart Willoughby went to Alice Springs where he formed a scratch band with John John Miller and guitarists Selwyn Burns and Mackie Coaby. The band was called Mixed Relations.

'Mixed Relations started getting our first gigs on a Monday night at the Stuart Arms, a musos night,' Miller recalls. 'We used to go there and jam, me, Bart, Mackie and Selwyn. One day Bart went down to the pub and he came back and said, "Shane Howard's in the Stuart Arms!" Shane Howard was a broken-down man and he was in the pub in Alice Springs; in the Stuart Arms.'

After the success of the album *Spirit of Place* and its hit single 'Solid Rock', Goanna's lead singer Shane Howard and manager Ian Lovell had travelled the globe trying to put together a worldwide deal for a follow up. The band was on the verge of signing with CBS, when their original label made an offer. Goanna re-signed with WEA Australia and spent much of 1984 recording a new album with Little Feat's keyboard player Billy Payne producing. Already struggling financially with the overheads of their home base (Goanna Manor in St Kilda) and the cost of the fruitless overseas trips, the band added to their problems by insisting on financing the second album themselves, to ensure 'creative freedom'.

Oceania was released in April 1985 and, while the band toured relentlessly in its support, the debts stubbornly refused to go away. In September 1985, an exhausted Shane Howard went 'walkabout', and the band was reportedly forced to cancel $20,000 worth of bookings.

'I disappeared into Aboriginal Australia,' says Howard. 'It was restorative. It saved my life – that's not an exaggeration. There was nothing more for me in the white man capitalist music industry world. I saw into its dark heart and there was nothing there, other than commerce. I got to see America. Ten trips to America. I got to see that whole world and found it pretty wanting. They are big choices. You have to make a choice between whether you want to be an entertainer or an artist. You have to do deals. Australia is a tough country. In America you can be a fringe artist and still appeal to a great number of people who will support you. In Australia you have to connect with the mainstream or you will not have a following. It's a tricky old situation. This country's a tough country if you want to be an artist.'

'It was a Monday night,' says Miller. 'We got him out of the Stuart Arms and we took him on tour with us, to the bush. He did a couple of numbers, "Solid Rock" and all that stuff, and we backed him up. That was Mixed Relations.'

'They took us out bush for a week to Tennant Creek,' Howard told the *Canberra Times* in 1986. 'And we ended up a month later in Broome having played many outback places.'[3]

'We were four bands in one,' says Miller. 'We were Shane Howard's band, Mixed Relations, NFA set one hour, then Coloured Stone set, three hours. Me, Bart and Selwyn, we played six, seven-hour shows. We had blisters on our fingers but they got harder.'

After that, somehow Mixed Relations morphed into a new version of Coloured Stone. Bart Willoughby played drums, which allowed songwriter and drummer Buna Lawrie to move out front and concentrate on vocals. 'When we had Mixed Relations, Buna came in and took over,' says John John Miller. 'We had this magic band and Buna came along and ... we got shanghaied there. We went back to Coloured Stone.'

'We were doing a lot of covers,' Willoughby recalls. 'Selwyn was just starting to write his own songs. We weren't doing any of my songs. I was only helping. I was like a soldier of fortune. The unsung hero.'[4]

~

In Melbourne, Michael Fisher's discussions with Birger Gesthuisen about a Western European tour for No Fixed Address had been continuing, despite Willoughby's extended absence. Fisher now had a man on the ground in West Berlin in the person of Peter Gray. Fisher knew Gray from the 1982 Rock Against Racism concert in Brisbane and had run into him again in London during the No Fixed Address tour.

In September, Gray made contact with Elke Bitterhof, the International Coordinator of Freie Deutsche Jugend (Free German Youth, the youth wing of the East German Communist Party) about the possibility of No Fixed Address appearing at the Festival des politischen Liedes (Festival of Political Song) in East Berlin. The festival, first staged in 1970, showcased the international left-wing singer songwriter scene and became big cultural business in the German Democratic Republic. Bolstered by funding from the FDJ, it ran for a week each year in February and included 30 events in a dozen venues.[5]

Meanwhile, in Adelaide things had been brewing that would have a destabilising influence on Fisher's plans. In early 1985, founding No Fixed Address member Les Graham had formed a new band with his cousin Ricky Lovegrove. Aroona, from an Aboriginal word meaning 'dawn', featured Graham and Lovegrove on guitars and a non-Indigenous rhythm section, Tony Sarno (drums) and Victor Mowett (bass). Aroona played around Adelaide, toured interstate and recorded a ten song self-titled cassette for Imparja Records. The group's manager was Mulla Sumner, administrator for Adelaide's Aboriginal Sobriety Group (ASG).

The ASG received financial support from the Aborigines Advancement League of South Australia Inc., a body established in the 1930s which by the 1980s had become, in effect, a foundation that granted non-governmental funds to worthy Aboriginal causes. The secretary of the league was Ron Hall, whose wife Bev Hall was secretary of the SA branch of the Australia–German Democratic Republic Friendship Society. The Halls were both active members of the left wing of the Australian Labor Party and Mulla Sumner was a family friend.

The news that No Fixed Address had the possibility of an appearance at the Festival of Political Song in East Berlin set channels humming between the German Democratic Republic (GDR) and South Australia. One of Bev Hall's close contacts in the GDR was Professor Fred Rose, an anthropologist. A former member of the Communist Party of Australia, Rose had left Australia for the GDR in 1956 after coming under intense scrutiny by the Petrov Royal Commission and ASIO. In a letter to Rose on 10 October, Hall seemed confident Aroona would be heading to the East Berlin festival.[6]

'We are arranging for Aboriginal band to come in February,' she wrote. 'No Fixed Address have left their white manager and some have formed with the original group to form a new band called Aroona so they have been invited by Bulgaria and some Western countries so they are really excited. We had problems trying to explain why the group's name changed to Festival people so we hope they understand. They are really good and very political with a very good Aboriginal manager. The white ex-manager received invitation and we understand has legal right to name so this is why group changed name but can have old name in brackets.'

In East Berlin meantime, Elke Bitterhof had been receptive to Peter Gray's pitch and wrote to Michael Fisher on 29 October, formally inviting No Fixed Address to attend the 1986 festival. The plan was for the group to play at least three concerts in East Berlin in the week 16–23 February. Following Gray's meeting with Bitterhof, Birger Gesthuisen wrote to Fisher proposing the period 5–23 March for Western European dates. As well as West Germany, he hoped to get gigs in Austria and Switzerland, a couple of radio broadcasts and an appearance on *Rockpalast* (Rock Palace), the live music show on West German television station WDR.

Fisher approached the Aboriginal Arts Board and the Department of Foreign Affairs for financial support. Gary Foley replied in late November, advising the AAB had no money available till February 1986; too late for the proposed tour. The Department of Foreign Affairs eventually responded on 31 December, offering $3000 towards expenses.

~

On 6 December, Gesthuisen wrote to Fisher with news of an alarming rumour circulating in Germany. The rumour was that No Fixed Address had split, although Gesthuisen thought the rumour might be a matter of 'bad wishes'. Gesthuisen called Fisher who reassured him that the band was Bart Willoughby, Ricky Harrison, Monty Lovett and David Osborne (the line-up that had played in Alice Springs in April) and that Fisher would not think of attempting the project without Willoughby or Harrison.

The rumour had also reached East Berlin, and on 13 December Peter Gray had a crisis meeting with Elke Bitterhof east of the Berlin Wall. It emerged that she had received a letter from the Australia-German Democratic Republic Friendship Society. 'It seems rather clear to me,' Gray wrote to Fisher on 14 December, 'that there are forces originating from Aroona that are trying to sabotage the proposed N.F.A. tour so that it will be possible for Aroona to go to the Music Festival in East Berlin instead.'

Bitterhof wanted to be reassured – in person – that the band with Willoughby and Harrison would be the one coming to Berlin in February. Fortunately, she seemed willing to accept Gray's assurances and Gray advised Fisher that 'all negotiations seemed back on course'.

~

Things might have seemed back on course in Europe, but they were about to go seriously off track in Australia. While letters had been going back and forth between Melbourne and Berlin, Harrison and Lovett had been biding their time in Adelaide and Willoughby was gigging with Coloured Stone in Darwin. Lead guitarist David Osborne was also on standby if sufficient funds could be obtained to get him on the plane. Fisher had been keeping Willoughby abreast of developments and the plan was for him to leave Darwin in mid-January for a few weeks of rehearsal in Adelaide before everyone left for Berlin.

In early January, Harrison was offered a scholarship to go to university in Adelaide. Willoughby then tried to persuade Fisher to include Buna Lawrie and Mackie Coaby from Coloured Stone in the No Fixed Address line-up. Word of this reached Birger Gesthuisen in Germany. Peter Gray wrote to Fisher on 10 January 1986: 'I'm not sure why you didn't get to Birger first, but when he heard about the line-up changes he totally freaked out. He has a demo cassette of Coloured Stone and Birger hates country and western music. Birger is worried that the music from the new line-up will be shithouse because country and western musicians can't possibly learn how to play convincing reggae in the space of a month or so.'

Gray managed to reassure Gesthuisen by saying he had faith in Willoughby's ability to put together a good band. Elke Bitterhof took the news calmly and was okay with the developments, provided Willoughby was still coming.

When a couple of days later Harrison agreed to defer his scholarship, the line-up was back to the three-piece of Willoughby, Harrison and Lovett. Fisher rang Willoughby in Darwin on Thursday, 16 January 1986 to ask which flight to Adelaide he wanted to take the next day. All seemed well, and Fisher booked the flight, but two hours after he had hung up the phone, Willoughby left Darwin for Port Keats (Wadeye) with Coloured Stone. It later emerged that Willoughby had been under heavy pressure from Lawrie and Coaby to take them with him to Europe – or not go at all. In a last desperate attempt, Fisher made arrangements to fly Willoughby back from Port Keats – it was 400 kilometres and a 12-hour drive from Darwin via a dirt road – but could not contact him.

In despair, on 22 January Fisher made the decision to cancel the tour. Willoughby's decision to pull out of the European tour that he and others had laboured so long to put together was a breaking point. He took Willoughby's decision as more than just opting out of a tour, but as a decision to quit No Fixed Address as an on-going project.

~

Two days after Fisher pulled the pin, Mulla Sumner was on the phone from Adelaide wondering if Aroona could step into the breach. Fisher wrote to Sumner on 26 January, magnanimously offering to help in any way he could. He enclosed a rough budget for the tour and contact details for Bitterhof, Gesthuisen and Gray.

When Aroona arrived in Berlin there was a bit of controversy because the festival wasn't expecting an Aboriginal rock'n'roll band. 'They were expecting more traditional stuff,' says Les Graham. 'The only thing we had that was traditional was the didgeridoo. But we pulled it off. I think we went over for five shows. It wasn't many shows that were booked for No Fixed. We ended up doing thirty-six gigs. Within nine days, we were doing three, four, five gigs a day. We were in demand. Aroona was a very, very tight band. It was against apartheid; it was against racism. It had two Aborigines, one Italian, one Australian. The band had a lot of potential. It had a lot going for it. In the East, we were set up in motels with our own spaces. When we went to the West, we were all put in a matchbox. We had to live together, smell each other's jocks and socks. We wore each other's company out; started bitching.'

The band broke up on their return to Australia.

In November 1986, Bart Willoughby and John John Miller had parted ways with Coloured Stone and were back in Adelaide. Les Graham and Ricky Lovegrove were also free agents. Graham got in touch with Willoughby and Miller and, after a couple of practices, they approached Ricky Harrison about getting the band back together – the original line-up of No Fixed Address.

'Les and Ricky came around to my house,' says Harrison. 'I'd completed a year of my studies at university. I wasn't really interested in getting back in the band. Les said, "We're going over to Europe. Do you want to come with us? John John's back in the band too." Les had been playing with Ricky in Aroona. They were first cousins. They were always hanging around together. I knew Ricky from college. I said I just want to stay and finish university. I said, "Why don't you just take Ricky instead?" So, that was settled then.

'The reality was that I didn't want to perform with Bart anymore and be let down like last time. But eventually I realised that it wasn't only about Bart, but about working with all the original band members, and performing before people who loved the band. It didn't matter how I felt about shit. We had some unfinished business, but there was still a lot of shit going on between band members back then.'

With Lovegrove on guitar, the reformed No Fixed Address started to rehearse at Graham's house in Christies Beach, south of Adelaide. 'We started doing new songs,' says Graham. 'Ricky Lovegrove was an unbelievable guitarist and songwriter. With some of his stuff I had to slow him down and shorten the songs because they went too long. But we got it together.'

The new line-up set off on a national tour in February 1987. In Sydney, Bart Willoughby told *Tribune*, 'We believe what we're doing is right. People will see what sort of talent we've got. We'll just get stronger and stronger, that's why we got together. First off, we were like little kids mucking around. Halfway through it's like toddlers getting a bit better at it. Now we're still at the halfway mark, but we're more experienced. Our destiny is guiding us. We've just got to believe in that.'[1]

Mick Thompson was recruited to do the band's live sound. Thompson had worked at Murri Jama Music Productions in the early and mid-1980s. The Redfern-based company set up by Tiga Bayles had a PA system and crew for hire to local bands and bands visiting Sydney. Thompson was sound engineer for Us Mob, who were managed by Bayles, and did a couple of tours with them. He also mixed bands that came through to Sydney from the Northern Territory (including Warumpi Band, Yothu Yindi and Saltwater Band) and other Aboriginal bands such as Coloured Stone, Pigram Brothers and Scrap Metal.

'I was also working at triple J for a while, about three years,' says Thompson. 'As a producer/director. I was working at Studio 221, recording bands like Midnight Oil, Jimmy Barnes, with another guy called Alan Parsons. He was chief engineer at triple J.

'When I wasn't working with Murri Jama and No Fixed Address were in town, it was a blessing. I loved No Fixed's music. I always wanted to be around their music. In their music was a message and the message is foretold ever since. What they have written now is still happening to this day. It's really magic music. It's a story been told long ago and it's still to this very day happening. It's like a time-warp.

'Bart ... it's like he's been here before. And he's travelled forward in time. And he's brought back something that was in his head and written it back then and it's happening now. Crazy.

'Ever since then I've studied him. And the boys in the band, what they did individually in their music. I started to feel what No Fixed Address were. I started to want to put that feeling I had into their music, through mixing. More or less to help bring out the story of what their music was about. The rhythm. The magic of the rhythm of No Fixed Address – you never hear this rhythm anywhere in the world. There's only one No Fixed Address and only one music No Fixed Address had. That grew on me and grew on me and really started getting into my head.'

~

In 1987, the Murri Jama truck with the PA inside was stolen and Thompson was out of a job. 'My heart was broken,' he says. 'I'd put everything into that PA. I knew everything about that PA, every screw. It never turned up again.'

One day Thompson got a call from Willoughby in Adelaide. 'Bart said he was going to get No Fixed Address back together again. "Do you want to mix?" I said, "Yeah." They got back together. A new line-up. Bart, Leslie, John John and Rick Lovegrove. We started playing the circuit. It was my chance to put my thing in, that I had in my brain.

'I was always drawn to the bass, to make sure it was tuned perfect. I always said the bass and the kick, the drum kick, are the pump – they are the heartbeat of the music. When Bart hits the kick and at the same time John John hits the string, and everything else just falls into place. The snare was always a little bit softer than the kick. Everything else sat just a little bit under. The first two things I used to do was the kick and the bass. That was the most important thing to me. And everything else I just folded in and balanced it all out. And then the vocals was above that.

'They made me a part of everything. They were the band and I was the sound engineer, but they didn't see that. With No Fixed Address I wasn't just the sound engineer; I was a band member. I played an instrument but it was electronically done – the sound. What I was doing, even though I wasn't on stage, was the speaker boxes. They said, "You had the bigger part of the sound because you played all of us. You made us come out of the speaker boxes as one." So, I'm the fifth member of the band. That to me, was an honour. It was a pleasure, and it turned into a devotion.'

~

As the 200th anniversary of the European invasion of Aboriginal Australia approached (26 January 1988), Indigenous people were considering how to mark the date.[2]

The election of the Federal Labor government in March 1983 had prompted a burst of optimism among Aboriginal people. The success of the Aboriginal-led protests at the 1982 Brisbane Commonwealth Games had brought the position of Aboriginal people and the issue of land rights to national and international attention. Appreciating the momentum for change, the land rights policy the Labor Party developed and took to the election specified five basic principles: Aboriginal land to be held under inalienable freehold title; protection of Aboriginal sites; Aboriginal control in relation to mining on Aboriginal land; access to mining royalty equivalents; and compensation for lost land to be negotiated.

It didn't take long for Labor's bold stance to start unravelling, however. The mining industry launched a hysterical advertising campaign against the policy, while Western Australian Labor Premier Brian Burke lobbied Bob Hawke and his federal colleagues to water down the proposed legislation, claiming it would cost him the upcoming WA state election.[3]

In the Hawke government's 'preferred model' released in February 1985, four of the five basic principles were dumped. The sense of betrayal among Aboriginal land rights campaigners and their supporters was profound. Almost 40 years on, Gary Foley is unrelenting in his contempt for Bob Hawke. 'The worst prime minister of Australia in terms of Aboriginal stuff,' says Foley. 'They didn't call him dodgy bodgie for nothing. And in addition to all of that, class traitor.'

Fearful that the government would water down the existing Northern Territory Land Rights Act to bring it in line with the preferred model, Aboriginal leaders in the NT called on support from Aboriginal groups across the country. The Federation of Land Councils organised a large demonstration at Parliament

House, Canberra in May 1985. The *NT Land Rights Act* survived, but relations between Aboriginal organisations and Labor had been 'poisoned'.[4]

The connections made between organisations and communities across the country from the Commonwealth Games and the national land rights protests provided the basis for a coordinated national response to the bicentennial. Building on the strengths of the Federation of Land Councils, a broader body called The National Coalition of Organisations formed in 1986. It included representation from Aboriginal legal services, medical services and childcare services as well as the land councils. Membership was open to all Aboriginal organisations that were community, rather than government initiated and controlled. The coalition provided a forum for the discussion of a wide range of ideas, but the aim was to reach consensus and speak with one voice. One of the things to percolate to the top was the idea of a Makarrata, a treaty.

The plan that emerged to mark Invasion Day was for Aboriginal people from communities across the country to go to Sydney, where they would be welcomed and accommodated. According to Patty Anderson, director of the Darwin Medical Service, 'it was a conscious decision not to make it just a protest, but rather to make it a celebration of who we are and that we're here'.[5]

~

With an eye on the upcoming bicentennial, in September and October 1987, No Fixed Address mounted *We Have Survived ... 200 Years*, described by the Adelaide *Advertiser* (1 October 1987) as 'a powerful new show, constructed as a cabaret performance'.

'We are touching on new issues, looking at the gap between young and old people and the attitudes of young and old,' Rick Lovegrove told the paper. 'Some people grew up in the country with a racist attitude and they don't even know why. It's a big problem and we're not trying to lay the blame anywhere; we are just saying there has to be a better way. If people begin to think about the problem, we have made an important first step.'

'The performance takes an unashamedly political stance,' the *Advertiser* wrote, 'with the Aboriginal band addressing issues directly affecting the social and political situation of Aboriginal people on the eve of the Bicentenary celebrations.'

Once again, Adelaide proved to be a less than practical base for a national touring band, and when their old manager Mick Pacholli held out the offer of recording some demos, No Fixed Address relocated to Melbourne. Pacholli had an office at Richmond Recorders, a studio in East Richmond. The studio had recently been taken over by members of the band Painters and Dockers and their manager Lobby Loyde.[6]

'Pacholli grabbed hold of us,' says Les Graham. 'He put us in Richmond Recorders. I'd really like to know what happened to those recordings. They were fucking unbelievable. Lobby Loyde was there, but he wasn't the engineer. I don't know what happened to the masters. No-one had the cash to go on with it.'

Graham briefed Pacholli on Aroona's experience at the East German Festival of Political Song and his desire to take No Fixed Address back there in the bicentennial year. Pacholli started planning an outback tour for the band towards the end of the year and turned his mind to extending the scope of the overseas visit. An agreement on cultural cooperation between Australia and the Federal Republic of Yugoslavia had been in force since 1977 and JAT Yugoslav Airlines had started flying from Melbourne to Belgrade in 1987. It seemed promising. And it was.

'Just before we did the second tour, up through Darwin and around, Les and I had been up to Lisson Grove, Hawthorn to the Yugoslav Consulate,' says Pacholli. 'I've done the deal with the Yugoslav government and JAL the airline to fully sponsor the band on a cultural exchange.'

Bev Hall wrote from Adelaide to Professor Fred Rose in

East Berlin on 10 October about the band's plans. 'No Fixed Address are coming about the 12th of February for the Political Song Festival. There will be 7 altogether plus a film crew of 8. There is going to be a film made of the tour which will cover Nicaragua, Cuba, then Berlin after which they go to BRD [West Germany] then Moscow, Bulgaria and Yugoslavia. All in all 6 months. Les is the band leader. The band has become the best Aboriginal band in Australia and will be doing an Australian tour before leaving for Cuba end of December. They are making a record to take with them also. They wish to take the opportunity to promote Aboriginal culture and so will be taking advantage of media everywhere, being 1988.'[7]

Hall followed up with more details in a letter to Rose on 28 October. 'The band leave here Dec 27th for Nicaragua, etc. and arrive in Berlin Feb 12th for the Festival. They then tour Europe including Moscow, Sofia, Yugoslavia and Canada (July) so all in all 6 months taking an exhibition of arts/crafts and selling Aboriginal Rights shirts, etc. They are bringing the film *Wrong Side of the Road* with them, and a film crew is accompanying them to make a film of the band's tour. They have composed a song for the Aboriginal women to have as a theme for their International conference called 'Aboriginal Woman'. For the Festival in Berlin, they have composed a special song for Peace and respect for the Environment called "Greenhouse" and the tour is called the Greenhouse tour. They have letters of support from the Ministers. Les and Rick want to see you when they are there, and are really excited to meet up with former friends again.'

~

The outback tour set up by Pacholli as a lead-in to the overseas trip was massive. Starting in Adelaide, it would head north to Darwin, take in the towns along the north-west coast of Western Australia, then wind up in Perth. Pacholli contacted the Perth-based Brady Drum Company about making one of its handcrafted Australian hardwood drum kits for Bart

On the desert run: the Dignity tour, 1987

Willoughby to take to Eastern Europe. It would be a promotional exercise for Brady's, which was looking to expand its business internationally.

'After we did the recording, we did do an Eastern States tour, followed the old tracks,' says Les Graham. 'Then he sent us on a fucking desert run. There was this fucking drum kit that Bart wanted in Perth. A Brady's kit. We should have left it there. I don't know where the fuck Pacholli's brain was. Anyway, he started setting up this tour and he had a mate with a semi-trailer. We got sponsored by Trucklines. They let us use their warehouse to respray the truck. Put containers on it and put the equipment in it and all this stuff. Logo on the side there. 'Dignity – No Fixed Address'. It looked like the circus coming into town. The truck was a crowd puller.'

Pacholli's mate with a semi-trailer was Neil Trcin. 'I chose Neil because he was Yugoslav, had a semi and was huge, and a very hard, highly intelligent ex-criminal who could stand up for them,' Pacholli says. 'I had a 40-foot prime mover, a white prime mover painted black, and we put two containers on in Adelaide. One had a huge rainbow serpent painted all the way down one side of it. One opened up at the front so they could get in there and live. It was set up like a bit of an apartment. And the back one was the equipment. Forty-foot tray. Two 20-foot containers. Arse to arse. With a giant fucking rainbow serpent painted down both sides. This one toured around Australia before they went to Yugoslavia. I had all that done for free, for sponsorship. We did so much work for that band. They had no idea what went into it. Everything was going well and they decided they were going to go with someone else again. And I didn't talk to them for twenty fucking years.'

The Dignity tour might have looked solid on paper, but the distances were vast and the weather was often torrid. Even 35 years on, soundman Mick Thompson's memories are vivid. Over to you, Mick.

'From Sydney, to Adelaide, one gig,' he recalls. 'Then from there to Port Augusta, did a gig there. Packed up the car and then we drove to straight through to Alice Springs. We were in this old brown Valiant Safari station wagon. No air conditioning.

'It was summer. It was really hot. We were going across the plains in this bloody car and we came to this rest area. We were bathing in this water. It had a water tank. The water was pumped up by a windmill. Later on, when you were driving you had salt on you. That salty freshwater, that's what it was.

'Around the side we found all these flagon bottles, and Les says, "Fill 'em up." "What for? Can't drink it." "Nah, fill 'em up. We'll use 'em to cool down." We filled up about twenty-odd bottles and put them in the back of the station wagon, where the spare wheel is. We were driving along the highway and these bottles are rattling away in the back. And Bart started tapping his hand. And as the bottles are rattling, he's tapping his hand. And then he's starting to hum. I think, "This guy's making music out of the sounds of the bottles and he's tapping his hands." He's tapping away. He says, "I don't know the song." We only drove about a hundred kilometres down the road and he had a song. That's how clever he is. He's very smart. He's the rhythm man. He can make music out of the sound of bottles clanging. What was that song? I don't think we even played it.

'Everyone took a turn at driving. As we were going along, we were opening the bottles of water and tipping them onto ourselves. Inside the car. The heat that was coming through the window had heated the bottles up and it was like hot water.

So, when you tipped it on yourself it was scalding. When the wind hit you, that was good, but within two minutes you were dry. We worked out a way, after a while, to wind down the window at the back. And we would sit down there and hold on to the rack that was on the roof. The two boys in the back seat of the car would grab the bottles and empty the bottles out. They would hold the bottles to the rear passenger window and the wind would suck the water out of the bottle. And the water would hit you in the back. And you'd cool right down. It was beautiful, it was like aircon. And you'd have turns. We ran out of water about half way down the road. The heat started to get to you so you'd have a little sleep. We woke up and Bart's driving. And we said, "How the bloody hell did he get in the driver's seat?" Bart doesn't drive. He's never had a licence in his life, that bloke. When I opened my eyes and looked out the window, things were just flying past. "Hey, how fast are you going, mate?" He said, "Aw, 60 kilometres an hour." Well, the speedo wasn't in kilometres, it was in miles. But when I looked over his shoulder at the speedo, he was sitting on 110 mph. I say, "Hey, you're not doing 60, you're doing 110. Hey boys, he's doing 110." "What? Hey Bart, slow down. He can't even drive." He said, "Well, I'm driving now."

'We're all freaking out in the car. So, everyone's staying awake watching him. He drove and drove and we swapped over. We'd driven all night and all day to get to Alice Springs. We finally arrive. Grab guitars. Walk straight into the pub. Walk over the pool – because the stage is built over the pool. The boys got up. Plugged in their guitars, I said, "Right?" They said, "Yes." I walked over to the desk and we played. We arrived dead on time. No soundcheck, just played. And played all through the night. We got there at 7 o'clock and that's what time we played. After the gig, we had something to eat, slept there in Alice Springs that night and then drove to Katherine.

'You've seen *Wrong Side of the Road*? You know that little part where they get to the pub where they're supposed to play? And the publican says, "No, we've got someone else playing here tonight"? And they say, "No, we're the band, we're No Fixed Address." At the Katherine Hotel, the publican did exactly that. It was the same thing as the movie. I said, "Hey, hang on – we're not shooting a movie here, are we? Bart, are we making a movie?" "No." We said, "We're playing here tonight." And the publican says, "No, I've already got this guy here, a band playing tonight." And I say, "Oh, I thought No Fixed Address were playing here tonight." And he says, "No, No Fixed Address are not playing here tonight." And I said, "How come you've got our posters up on the wall? And written out there on the blackboard – 'No Fixed Address playing here tonight'?" And he says, "Aw, no, they're not booked here." I said, "We are booked in the motel here?" He said "Yes." I said, "So you do know No Fixed Address?" So, we got our rooms and everything.

'That night we were swimming in the pool. Then we heard the band playing. I jumped out of the pool and I ran over to the door and I looked inside. It was not a band. It was just this fella sitting up there with a microphone and his guitar, singing. He got one of his mates to come and play that night. People came and said, "Is No Fixed Address playing here?" "Oh, no, they're not playing." The people just walked right back out the door. There was hardly anyone in the pub.

'We never got no money out of that one, so that was a hole in our pocket really. Because we needed that money to get fuel to keep going to Darwin.'

After shows in Darwin and Broome, the next gig was Exmouth. 'We were driving along, wondering when we were going to get there,' says Thompson. 'We've seen these red lights on the horizon. We thought, "Oh yeah, that must be the American base." We were going to the American base. They hired us to play there, where the submarines go. Top secret spot.'

The Naval Communication Station Harold E. Holt is a joint Australian-US facility at North West Cape, six kilometres north of Exmouth. Established as a US military base in 1963, the town of Exmouth was built to house the families of US Navy personnel who worked there. The base serviced the US Polaris/Poseidon nuclear-powered ballistic missile submarine fleet and became a joint facility under the Federal Labor government in 1974.[1]

'We were getting closer and closer and as we were getting closer there were more red lights,' Thompson recalls. 'And they seemed to rise. Go up. By the time we got there, these red lights were way up in the air. We didn't know what it was. We couldn't see what it was because it was night when we got there. We played that night. They put us up in the motel there that night. That was a good gig. Met a lot of American defence force men and women. Had a good talk to them about our music. They were very excited about our music. Bart was full-on asking questions.

'We woke up in the morning and walked outside, still dreaming about what these red lights were up in the sky, wanting to see what was going on. Walked out and there were these great big bloody aerials. They must have been over a thousand feet high. They were huge. The biggest aerials I've ever seen in my life.'

There are 13 radio towers at the base. The tallest, called Tower Zero, is 387 metres (1270 feet) tall, and for many years was the tallest structure in the Southern Hemisphere. Six towers, each 364 metres (1194 feet) tall are placed in a hexagon around Tower Zero and a further six towers, each 304 metres (997 feet) tall sit in a larger hexagon around Tower Zero.

After Exmouth, there was a show in Port Hedland, then driving south to Carnarvon at night and being mindful of local conditions, the band's station wagon was tucked in behind the semi-trailer. 'We were thinking if we hit a kangaroo, the truck would hit it and we'd be right,' says Thompson. 'But that wasn't the case. We were driving down the road and all of a sudden, this bloody roo ... it jumped between the truck and us. And the old Valiant hit it and it busted the radiator. Put a big hole in it. The fan went through it. I had a CB radio in the car, so I could talk to the truck. Because there were no [mobile] phones in them days. I called the truck with the CB. I said, "We hit the roo. And Bart's gone." They said, "Where?" "He's gone after the roo. It bounced off into the bush. And Bart's gone." "What did he do?" "He told me to pull up. I pulled up. He grabbed the knife out of the glove box and he took off." Pitch black. He's gone into the bush chasing the bloody roo. I got a torch and where is he? The next minute in the long grass I see Bart's head jumping up and down. The next thing, he disappeared. I yelled, "Bart! Where are ya?" No answer. "Bart!" Nup, still no answer. Then I seen him coming out and I said, "Brother, did you want a hand from us? I thought something happened." He was coming out of the bush with the kangaroo tail over his shoulder. I said, "What did you do?" He said, "You think that kangaroo was gonna get away that easy? Nup." I said, "Where is it?" He said, "Over there but this is the only good part I could get off it." So, he cut the kangaroo tail off. He chucked it in the back of the station wagon. We hooked up to the truck and he pulled us all the way into Carnarvon.

'The place we stayed had a big charcoal coal burner. Bart's already gone and got wood and he's chucked it in there and he's burning it up and I said, "What's that for?" And he said, "I've got the tail here," and he chucked it in. He said, "We're gonna have a feed." We had that kangaroo tail for lunch. What a lunch that was. It fed all of us. That roo that hit us, it would have stood over the car, about seven foot high. He was huge. The roo was buggered. When you hit a roo, the skin goes like crystal. When you push on it, it crackles. That's poisonous, so you can't eat it. But he kept the tail and that was alright. All the rest of the meat was no good. The shock, the adrenalin, spoils the meat, but he cut the tail off before it got to it.'

Les Graham takes up the yarn. 'When you're talking distances of travelling, you're talking about 1200, 1500 kilometres. And he [Pacholli] never gave us enough time to travel. We hit kangaroos and all this shit. From Broome to Port Hedland, to Carnarvon, Geraldton. Then we went down to

Perth and we hit skid row because we were broke. I still don't understand it. I guess you're feeding everybody and you're going along the track, money does go quick.

'Bart goes down to get his Brady drum kit. That was the main objective – to get to Perth, to get the drumkit, get back to Sydney. When he picked the drumkit up, he brought it back. I looked at it and I said, "Is this it? Is this the fucking drumkit?" It was only the shells. There was no metal on it at all. They could have sent that by courier, it would have been cheaper. It cost us $20,000 to go and get it!

'We were stuck in Perth with this drum kit. What happened is, Don Walker rang up and asked Bart and me if we wanted to be in a film clip for one of his songs.'

After almost five years away from the game following Cold Chisel's break-up in 1983, Don Walker had signed with WEA Records and was recording under the name Catfish. The clip was for 'When You Dance', which was released in April 1988 as the first single from the album *Unlimited Address*. Graham and Willoughby play the parts of a guitarist and drummer in the clip, directed by Kimble Rendall and shot in a Glebe warehouse, although neither played on the record or as part of a live line-up.

'He flew us over there to Sydney to do this film clip,' says Graham. 'Don was up front singing. He really wanted us to join this band. We said, "We don't want to disappoint you, but we're dedicated to No Fixed." He's a beautiful man, but ... anyway, Bart and I were in Sydney so that gave a bit of relief for the other blokes, more room in the car. They jumped in this station wagon and put the drums on the roof, tied everything down and shipped it over to Sydney. They drove from Perth to Sydney and met us in Sydney.

'We did a couple of gigs and then I ended up going down to Canberra, to see Charlie Perkins [Secretary of the Department of Aboriginal Affairs] about this tour to Europe and how do I go about getting some finance for air tickets and that? He said, "This is a very special offer for you blokes. I one hundred per cent support it. Give me your details and how much it costs and mum's your word." I said "Okay." He passed the details on to his administration and they gave us $10,000 to get everything together.[2] The drumkit was still there. Because he was sponsored, Bart insisted we take the drumkit. We should have left it in Australia. It cost us $1500/$2000 to get this sent over to Europe.'

After the Dignity tour ended in a shambles in Perth, the band parted ways with manager Mick Pacholli. 'We said, "Fuck you, bro'. You're sending us on a fucking desert run,"' says Graham. Despite Pacholli's exit, road manager Neil Trcin was still keen to go to Europe, but the band was casting around for some management support. 'When we got back to Sydney, through Neil we met this guy, Lou Scholer. He was in the film business. He's got one of the reel-to-reels of *Wrong Side*. He used to run some sort of documentaries on surfing. He had a lot of contacts and he knew a lot of people with a lot of money.'

With the support from the Department of Aboriginal Affairs and a contribution from the SA branch of the Australia–German Democratic Republic Friendship Society, the budget for the European tour eventually came together.

~

While No Fixed Address had been on their desert run, Aboriginal people from all over Australia were busy making preparations to travel to Sydney to mark Invasion Day. The gathering was given the name Long March for Justice, Freedom and Hope. As it became apparent how many people were going to come, fundraising – for travel costs, food, bedding and other support – became a priority. Reviving the Rock Against Racism model of the early 1980s, a small group set to organising a concert, both as a way of welcoming the incoming travellers but also as a means of raising funds.

Under the banner Building Bridges, a concert of Aboriginal performers was held on the afternoon of Sunday, 24 January at Bondi Pavilion on Bondi Beach. The line-up included Roger

Knox, Coloured Stone, Yothu Yindi and Black Lace. It was $5 to get in, but there were so many people, for safety reasons the organisers threw the doors open and went round collecting donations with buckets.

Andrew Belletty was playing drums for Yothu Yindi that day. 'I think it was one of the last shows I did with them,' he says. 'Bart [Willoughby] was there as well. It was the very first Survival Day at Bondi Pavilion. I drummed with Coloured Stone that night as well. We were down in Sydney doing some recording. When we got to the Bondi Pav there were thousands of people. They were just hanging off the rafters. It was this massive gig. I did play with Coloured Stone that night, but I know Bart was around and was hanging out with us. It was the very first one. We had these three great traditional singers and they really captivated the audience.'

On Tuesday, 26 January, around 40,000 Aboriginal people and non-Indigenous supporters joined the largest march in Sydney since the Vietnam moratorium in the early 1970s. The busloads of Aboriginal people from other states and rural and remote communities who had arrived at La Perouse south of Sydney in the preceding days made their way to Redfern. They formed up and marched to Belmore Park on the northern side of Central Station. Gathered to meet them there were the Sydney-based marchers.

Patrick Dodson, who had travelled from Alice Springs, later recalled what they saw as they came through the railway tunnel to the east of the park. 'We came through the tunnel there ... and we'd talked about what we were going to do; we were going to have a rest at this park, you know, sit down and have a drink and everything. And then we couldn't even get into the park, hey. They were all standing there – clapping. We just couldn't stop crying, because we didn't expect it. We didn't expect anyone there. We thought we were just doing it ourselves.'[3]

The protesters marched through the streets of Sydney chanting for land rights. Yothu Yindi led the way. 'Milkay

[Mununggurr] had his massive yidaki with him so he was playing this throughout the park, Belmore Park, where the march started from,' recalls Belletty. 'We ended up being in the front of that whole parade.'

The march ended at Hyde Park where Gary Foley was among the speakers. 'Let's hope Bob Hawke and his government gets this message loud and clear from all these people here today,' Foley said. 'It's so magnificent to see black and white Australians together in harmony. This is what Australia could and should be like.'

Patty Anderson thought the action did make a difference. 'I think our lobbying against 1988 was one of the most positive things we've done because it really did take all the "oomph" out of that "celebration of the nation" they were planning. There were non-Indigenous Australians really stumbling on the word "celebrate" ... And I think it's made them ... at that time at least, a little bit more thoughtful. It seemed to me that after 1988, we heard them say more often: "the time of the invasion" and "the first inhabitants". So the language kind of changed a little, it shifted just a bit.'[4]

On 11 February 1988, the *Advertiser* proudly claimed that Adelaide's No Fixed Address was leading the international assault by Aboriginal rock bands. 'This week the four-member band embarked on a five-month tour of Europe taking in Russia, Yugoslavia, Czechoslovakia and East Germany,' wrote entertainment reporter David Sly. 'The invitation to perform behind the Iron Curtain was initiated by the Soviet government as part of its widening cultural exchange program.'[1]

Three days earlier, under the headline 'Aboriginal band off for Eastern bloc tour', *The Age* (8 February 1988) had reported, 'As Aborigines continued to protest against Bicentenary celebrations, Les Freeman [aka Les Graham], the leader of No Fixed Address, left with the Aboriginal band yesterday for the Eastern bloc countries to spread the word. The tour is one of the first human contact steps since the PM Mr Hawke visited Moscow last year. After East Berlin they will tour the USSR, Bulgaria, Yugoslavia, Czechoslovakia, Holland and Greece.'

The scope of the tour appeared to have expanded significantly from the cultural exchange negotiated earlier by Mick Pacholli with the Yugoslav consulate in Melbourne. Relations between Australia and the USSR had warmed considerably since the ascension of Mikhail Gorbachev to the Soviet leadership in 1985 and cultural exchanges were ramping back up following Gorbachev's moves to withdraw Soviet military forces from Afghanistan.

Graham told the *Advertiser* that he re-established links with European audiences in 1986 when he travelled to Berlin with Aroona for the Festival of Political Song. The enthusiasm for Aboriginal rock music at the festival encouraged him to organise another European tour for No Fixed Address.

'We consider performing overseas as a very responsible job,' he said. 'We represent our country and our people. We sing about the truth ... of people and opinions. I don't think that's particularly political, but a lot of people seem to think it is. People will form an opinion of Australia from what we do and say. It's a fabulous position to be in.'

~

By the late 1980s the music on offer at the Festival of Political Song had expanded from its folk roots to include a range of styles, from rock to jazz to world music. As well as East and West German performers, the line-up in 1988 included veteran folk singers Ewan MacColl and Peggy Seeger, the African-American a cappella group Sweet Honey in the Rock, plus a clutch of Latin American and southern African performers.

No Fixed Address's traditional instruments caused a bit of stir at East German customs and immigration. 'I was carrying a didgeridoo,' Mick Thompson recalls. 'Rick had his didgeridoo. When I got to customs, they were wondering what it was. They thought it was a weapon. "No, it's an instrument." They looked at me and I said, "Instrument." I grabbed it and I started playing. You should have seen the looks of amazement on their faces. Then Rick grabbed his and started playing and we were talking to each other didge to didge. They were amazed. One of the customs people had a look and said, "It's hollow. How do you make sound?" He had a go but he couldn't do it. We told them we were guests here and they said, "Yes, you are ambassadors. Ambassadors from Australia." We were all ambassadors. The Australian government made us ambassadors to go over there and represent Australia. We just wanted to represent ourselves. We had certificates from the government saying we were ambassadors.'

~

There was almost a week before the band's first performance. Time to settle in and get acclimatised. The seven-strong touring party (which included tour managers Neil Trcin and Lou Scholer) had come from the Australian summer to the East

German winter and according to Thompson it was 'stinkingly cold'.

The day after they arrived, festival organisers organised a photo session with local photojournalist Gabriele Senft. She took Thompson and the four band members to the snow-covered Alexanderplatz in the centre of East Berlin. Cloaked in their full-length Driza-Bone riding coats, they staged a snowball fight in front of the plaza's famous world clock.

'We were throwing snowballs because we had never seen snow in our lives,' says Thompson. 'Apparently, you wasn't allowed to do that in that country but they never bothered us, because we were guests of their country. By their government. We got away with a lot of stuff over there. The police said it was okay for you to do it.'

Along with the band's guitars and didgeridoos, the Brady drum shells had made it to East Berlin, but Bart Willoughby had to go over to the West to buy the rest of the kit. 'This is probably why we had no money,' laughs Graham. 'He had to buy cymbal stands, road case, all the skins. But when he put it together, that drumkit was fucking unbelievable.'

~

The Festival of Political Song ran for a week, from Sunday 14 to Sunday 21 February. Match-fit and battle-hardened from the rigours of the outback Dignity tour, the first performance by No Fixed Address at the Palace of the Republic on Tuesday the 16th went off with a bang. In fact, you could say they hit the audience with both barrels.

'We were the last band to play and just before we were going to go on, I peeked through the curtain,' says Thompson. 'I saw the auditorium, what it looked like. All I could see was people. This thing was packed. Really, really full right through. I pushed the curtain back and walked back over. "How many people there?" "Aw," I said, "a couple. There's a few there I reckon." Bart said, "You go first."

Bart Willoughby, Ricky Lovegrove, Les Graham, John John Miller and Mick Thompson in the snow, Alexanderplatz, East Berlin, February 1988.

Photo by Gabriele Senft.

I said, "Nah, you go first. You've got to go to your drum kit." He said, "No, you go first, because you've got to go and play your didge." I said, "Ahhhh, no, you go first!" Then John John came over and said, "What's the matter, Mick?" I said, "Come and look." Then John John looks and he says, " Waaah! What the ...?" I said, "Yeah, eh? Man, I'm going to freak out. I'm not gonna play didge." Bart says, "Nah, you're playing didge." I didn't wanna. There wasn't a soundcheck. I did it on the go. I had no choice. The desk, I'd never seen one like it in my life.

'It came to the stage where we had to go out,' Thompson continues. 'Bart walked out first. All I saw was his head just go left, go right, up and down. And then he looked at me and I'm laughing my guts out. And he goes, "Come on." So, I said,

"Right." Me and Rick had radio mics put onto the didge and I started playing before I'd even walked down to the front and as I was playing, I walked down. Rick went over and plugged his guitar in. His didge was there already on a stand. He didn't have to hold it. I walked out and I walked straight down the front and I was playing didge. John John and everyone else was plugging in and getting ready. I did my calls and then Rick started playing the didge. And we started talking to each other through the didge. Then I said, "What do we want? Land rights. When do we want them?" And he said, "Now." But we were blowing and at the same time talking. It was a technique we learned from Joe Geia. I listened to him and he used to do it all the time.

'We started playing and I gave the signal for John John to start "We Have Survived". And then Bart started. And then Rick. And Rick stood back from his didge and he was playing his rhythm, picking up the rhythm for "We Have Survived". Then I did my last call. Then I put my didge down on the stage and I walked straight up the centre to the desk. Everyone looked at me. "Where are you going?", y'know? I walked up to the desk. Mixed straight up. Went EQ, EQ, EQ, then did the gains, and then bang! Half way through the first song, we were pumping. Because I'm so used to No Fixed Address, I can do these sorts of things. I only need half a song. What I can do with this band, it's not hard for me to do. I've never had trouble doing sound for this band.

'We played that gig, blew them all out. I think we did five songs. Wasn't many. I don't how many encores. They were so blown away by our music. It wasn't just a clap; it was this roar. The sound. The whole auditorium was like a roar. Every song, when we finished, there was this applause and yells and Bart had to keep going, "Next song, next song", to keep 'em quiet. Otherwise, they would have gone for too long. Bart was amazing at that gig. He had everything going. Like he gets off on how people come at him.'

~

In many respects, No Fixed Address performing in the German Democratic Republic was a contradiction. On the one hand, their trip was officially sanctioned and partly funded by the Australian government, through the Aboriginal Arts Board. Yet the lyrics to the band's songs were strongly critical of both the historical and contemporary Indigenous experience in Australia. The festival journal and daily newspaper were unequivocal: 'Colonialism was brutal and predatory and had catastrophic effects for Aborigines'.[2]

But there was also a contradiction in the attitude of the GDR government. While it was comfortable to provide a platform for No Fixed Address to criticise Australia's policies towards Indigenous people, it would not tolerate criticism from its own citizens.

In January 1988, the GDR government imprisoned more than a hundred people who had been demonstrating for human rights. The demonstrators were part of an annual march in East Berlin to commemorate the 1919 murders of German socialists Rosa Luxemburg and Karl Liebknecht. Some held signs quoting Luxemburg: 'Freedom is also the freedom of those who think differently'.

Historian Tony Judt wrote in *Postwar*, his history of Europe since 1945: 'Communism depended on control – indeed, communism was control: control of the economy, control of knowledge, control of movement and opinion and people.'[3] So, when Mikhail Gorbachev set about reforming the moribund Soviet economy with a policy of *glasnost* (openness) – as a precursor to *perestroika* (restructuring) – the slight easing of control proved to be a breath of air that unleashed the winds of change.

Flush with subsidies from West Germany, confident of Moscow's backing and at liberty to export to the West its more troublesome dissents, the hard-line East German regime initially seemed impervious to any change. The GDR's 75-year-old leader Erich Honecker publicly praised Gorbachev's perestroika while studiously avoiding its implementation at home.

~

No Fixed Address had brought a considerable amount of Aboriginal artefacts, supplied by Adelaide's Overway Centre and the Queensland government, to present to European politicians.[4] During the festival a group called 'Support group for native people' organised a small exhibition about the Aboriginal bicentennial protests in Australia that displayed the artefacts. At the conclusion of the festival, No Fixed Address took part in a one week-tour across the GDR. Anke Bornschein accompanied the tour with the exhibition in tow and acted as interpreter. Photographer Gabriele Senft also came along. Six weeks had passed since the incident at the East Berlin march, but the authorities were still twitchy and on the lookout for any signs of public dissent – as the touring party discovered.

'We went from Berlin to Rostock,' says Bart Willoughby. 'Took us about seven or eight days. Stopped in every town. It was done professional. Western way. Three buses. There were three bands, there was us, there was one from Madagascar [Rossy] and there was a Cuban band [Moncado].

'We couldn't speak to the other guys because they spoke French or they spoke Spanish. So, we had our own buses. No, the Spanish had their own bus and we were with the Madagascans. Some of them spoke a bit of English. Then we had another bus with all the roadies and a truck with the equipment. Anyway, we're happy to all take off to go on this tour.'

Opposite above: Les Graham with members of Cuban band Moncado, East Germany, February 1988.

Opposite below: Marie-Josephine Rasoarimalala of Madagascan band Rossy with Bart Willoughby, East Germany, February 1988.

Photos by Gabriele Senft.

Performances from the Festival of Political Song had been broadcast on the East German television service DFF. Audiences on the regional tour had seen the three bands and it soon became clear who their favourite was. 'The first two gigs on the tour, we were the first act then the Madagascan band would play after us and then straight after that the Cubans,' says Willoughby, 'because they were spectacular. They didn't have a drummer but the percussion was just going berserk. And the singing was just amazing. After the second gig, the organisers saw that there was a big line around the building. They would see us play and then they would get up and leave. The organisers went, "Wow. They're not here to see the Madagascan band or the Cuban band. They're here to see No Fixed." The organisers came up to us and said, "You play last." So when we did, the crowd would stay.'

Just after midnight on 27 February, the whole entourage was detained by the East German police. 'We stop in a town,' says Willoughby, 'and one of the organisers said, "It's such and such's birthday so we all have to stand in the square and light a candle." So, we all got off the bus, about a hundred of us and we all lit a candle. The next minute, the Russian army came and surrounded us and escorted us to the police station. Because they'd had a demonstration the week before, a few people got killed or something, so it was pretty full on.'

The town was Wismar, on the Baltic Sea about 250 kilometres north-west of Berlin. 'We came to this town and we pulled up in this square,' Mick Thompson recalls. 'It had cobblestones and a statue in the middle. It was stinking cold, middle of the night. Someone pulled out a popper cracker and it went boom! All lights in the sky. Then we all jumped back on the bus and the convoy was going down the highway and we got pulled up by the cops. They were waiting down the road for us. After pulling up all the buses, I remember Anke saying, "Everything's alright, they just want to take us back to their headquarters." And I said, "Oh yeah?" And I started getting ideas in my head about, "What's going on here?" So,

Mick Thompson, East Germany, February 1988.

Photo by Gabriele Senft.

---

the convoy was taken back to this headquarters. I remember it being a two-storey building and it was surrounded by a high fence. And we drove in and they told us to get off the bus and head upstairs. All these guards were standing around us like we were prisoners. That's what it felt like.

'We were there for about two hours and then the police came in and said we could go. Apparently, they rang up their boss and their boss was a bit angry about them pulling us up because we were something to do with their government. We were guests. They got blown up. That's what we heard anyway.

'We got back on the bus and the police gave us an escort, lights flashing. We were cruising along the highway then. They took us all along the highway to the next town, to Rostock. Took us to the big hotel where we were staying.'

In Rostock, the mayor had organised a reception for the touring bands. 'We did a TV show in Rostock, not the other two bands, just us,' says Willoughby. 'An interview. Then we went to the town hall. The other two bands were still on their way. The mayor and all the delegates from Rostock, they saw us coming up. They all rose and put the beer towards us and said, "We really appreciate you being here. We don't really like the other two bands but we really love your band." We just went, "Oh, thank you." That's when we started to notice that all the gigs we had done at the festival, it had been filmed and been shown around Germany. We were starting to become the favourite band of the whole festival.'

After each of the festivals, the organising committee produced a compilation album of live recordings by the featured artists. Introduced by some fluid lead guitar from Les Graham and underpinned by John John Miller's jaunty bass, Bart Willoughby's 'Aboriginal Woman' was No Fixed Address's contribution to the 1988 edition. Even with its reggae swing, it's the closest track to mainstream Western rock on the record, which includes a wild variety of styles; from the Anglo-Celtic folk offerings of Ewan MacColl and Peggy Seeger and the Sands family from Ireland, to the world music of Rossy and Zimbabwe's Stella Chiweshe, to a barnstorming rendition of the renowned Argentinian protest song 'Solo le pido a dios', by female singers from Nicaragua, Mexico, Brazil and Peru.

~

The entertainment programs on DFF were also popular with viewers over the border, particularly in West Berlin. So, when No Fixed Address performed at a big multi-band concert at the Deutschlandhalle, it was apparent a lot of people had seen the band's performances broadcast from the East.

Originally built as an indoor arena for the 1936 Berlin Olympics, the Deutschlandhalle (with a capacity of 16,000) was the major concert hall in West Berlin, hosting concerts in the mid-1980s by acts such as AC/DC, Elton John, Queen, Prince, Rod Stewart and Supertramp.

'They had all these bands from everywhere,' says Willoughby. 'It's chock-a-block. We're the tenth act. The first band plays, everyone is sitting down, listening. These guys are a really cool blues band, kicking arse. Everybody's sitting down, clapping. Then a heavy metal band from Czechoslovakia, then a band from Holland, but everybody's sitting down, clapping. As we turn up, a couple of seconds after we started playing the whole crowd got up and rushed to the stage. Each song we did, they were freaking out, whistling, we're going, "Oh, oh," but we just keep playing. Because we had songs that were joined together too. Bang, straight into the next song. We let the music talk for itself. Then as we got up to walk offstage, back to our band room all we could hear in German was 'NO FIXED ADDRESS!' All the people yelling out our name. The organisers came back to our room and said, "You've got to get back up there. We'll take time off the next act." So, we went back up and did a couple of songs. By then we knew there was something going on in Germany and they really loved what we were doing.'

'The biggest gig we ever had was in the Deutschlandhalle, the skating rink for the Berlin Games,' says Thompson. 'It had two stages, one behind the other. It had a circular PA. The sound was just amazing in there. Dangerous that one, as Bart would put it. It was a roar again. I'd never experienced that, with that many people.'

How did the band react to that kind of audience reaction?

'I asked them. Bart said he saw everything on the stage. It was like he was out in the audience looking back at himself. It was the sound and the people reacting to the sound. I was freaking out because I'd never mixed in that kind of environment with that many people. He said it was like the stage was alive. They were up on the stage and he was down on the ground watching himself.'

~

While they were part of the official program, things were *organised*. 'It was quite busy over there,' says Thompson. 'We didn't have a day when we weren't doing something. Interviews, TV stations. It was organised to a T. We had our own bus.

'Before the regional tour, we were taken to a concentration camp, where they murdered all the Jews. We said, "We don't want to go there." Driving past on the bus, being spiritual people, we could feel the people there. Like the deaths that had occurred there. We asked Anke to take us somewhere else. We ended up at these castles around a lake.'

When the officially-sponsored activities were over however, things started coming apart.

The Australian duo managing the tour, Neil Trcin and Lou Scholer, were an intimidating pair, says Bart Willoughby. 'Neil, you might as well say, he's a gangster. Grew up hard. In prison. Saw people murdered in front of him in jail. And Lou was a bouncer for the Triads in Japan. Lou knew how to handle himself. He was about six foot six. And Neil was about six foot two and just muscles. Whereas Lou was just overwhelmingly big and didn't need muscles.'

In the changeover in management from Mick Pacholli in Australia, it seemed some things had fallen through the cracks. 'The tour that we were on, it was Germany, Romania, Czechoslovakia, Hungary, Yugoslavia and Bulgaria,' says Les Graham. 'There were invitations from the governments of those countries, inviting us there to play. Lou never went to this meeting with all the contact people so they didn't think we were interested. So, the tour got cancelled. Over there, they don't promote you till you're sitting on their doorstep, especially if you're coming from Australia. A lot of Australian bands don't get there because they haven't got the money.'

~

Unfolding alongside the collapse of the grand touring scheme was a subplot of the disposition of the tour finances. Shortly after arriving in East Berlin, Graham spent the evening of Thursday, 11 February 1988 at the home of Professor Fred Rose, whom he had met on Aroona's visit to the Festival of Political Song in 1986. Graham told Rose about the Aboriginal artefacts the band had brought with them and Rose thought the Museum für Völkerkunde in Leipzig, where he held a position as a researcher, might be interested in purchasing some of the material. He rang a colleague, Birgit Scheps, who spoke with Graham and the East German tour supervisor, Matthais Müller. The next morning, Scheps rang Rose and said she could come to Berlin the following week to sight and possibly purchase some of the artefacts. Although it was forbidden to take currency out of the GDR, Rose told Scheps, 'On the question of payment, I discussed with the manager the possibility of spending GDR money on binoculars.'[1]

On Tuesday, 16 February, Scheps and two of her colleagues came to Berlin to view the collection. Scheps later told Rose it included batiks, textiles, decorated shields, 12 bark paintings of 'a really fine quality', necklaces, boomerangs, fire sticks, clapsticks, and carvings from Central Aust or Ernabella in SA. Scholer was at the Soviet embassy all afternoon trying to sort out visas for the band to tour the Soviet Union, but Scheps met with him that evening after No Fixed Address had played at the Palace of the Republic. Scholer's price for the collection was 30,000 DDR Marks (the rough market equivalent was 7500 West German Marks, or US$4250).

This was the museum's entire annual acquisitions budget, but the director gave the go-ahead and so two weeks later, after the band's regional tour, Scholer and Neil Trcin came to Leipzig and handed over the collection. The museum paid them and they explained that, because they couldn't export the money, they had to buy things they could sell in Australia to give the money back to the Aboriginal communities that gave the artefacts. They told Scheps that they wanted to use the money for community houses in SA and Queensland. Scheps told Rose, 'So we had to find out what goods are available here and possibly this will be pianos.'[2] The plan was for the band to return to Leipzig after the completion of their tour in the Soviet Union, the Czechoslovak Socialist Republic, France and Hamburg to play a big open-air concert at the museum. And presumably to collect and arrange the export of the goods for resale in Australia.

Rose had left Berlin on 19 February for a visit to Australia and wrote to Scheps from Canberra on 21 March, telling her he had received a couple of calls from Bev Hall in Adelaide.

'While they were still in Berlin,' Rose wrote to Scheps, 'he

[Scholer] rang BH [Bev Hall] saying that he had no more money and asked her to get more from the Dept of AA [Aboriginal Affairs]. Her answer was to the point as she pointed out there would have been no need to spend any money in the GDR as all costs would have been met by the organisers of the FdpL [Festival des politischen Leiden].'[3]

~

After the GDR regional tour, Scholer and Trcin set up themselves up in West Berlin, while everyone else was in a motel in the East. Consequently, Mick Thompson and the band were frequent users of Checkpoint Charlie, the main border crossing in the Berlin Wall. 'I think we went through thirty times or something,' says Thompson. 'Going through Checkpoint Charlie was like going through a maze. It never went straight. It went left, then right, then left, to this other door. When you got to the door, you pushed this buzzer and went into this cubicle. Then pushed another buzzer. It was a bloody X-ray machine. Then another maze to an office where they stamped your passport.

'In West Berlin, we stayed in a squat for a couple of nights. We went up to the top of a castle and saw all these domes. This was on the western side. We asked what they were – they were silos with nuclear missiles. They were all over the place.'

~

On 28 March, fellow Aussies AC/DC were at the Eissporthalle in West Berlin as part of the Blow Up Your Video world tour.

'When I was in East Berlin, this journalist from Finland, she took me over to the West, to an AC/DC concert,' says Graham. 'I was talking to the manager. He said, "Bicentennial year of Australia. We got an Australian band and an Aboriginal band – whaddya wanna do?" I said, "Are you for real?" and he said, "Ja, ja. We'll do this as a thing for Australia in the bicentennial year. Two Aussie bands – AC/DC and No Fixed Address." They started steering me down to the big boss and this and that ...

"You can talk to Angus but they're all hyped up. You can go and say hello," but I was a bit shy.

'Lou didn't know about my meeting with AC/DC. We were going to perform in England probably. They guaranteed us US$50,000. Plus, there was a tour set up with another guy too. To play with AC/DC, you've gotta pay them that kind of money. Sting wanted to have something to do with us. I ended up going to France from Germany. I left the boys for about a week or so. These people that took me wanted them to come. They should have all got in that car. That was Sting over there, he wanted to take us on. A lot of these people in Europe, these rock stars, wanted to get a taste of us. The doors started opening.'

In West Berlin, Scholer put a proposal to the band but was knocked back. 'That guy was all for him,' Graham says. 'He was a headstrong bloke. If it wasn't his way, it was the highway. He wanted us to sign a contract. We would have got five per cent. Not even ten per cent. We said, we just got out of a contract with the same sort of deal where we ended up with fuck-all. He said, "Aw no, I'll pay for everything." He wanted to take us to Japan. Maybe we should have signed that and went there.'

~

At the song festival in East Berlin, the band had met a Hungarian musician called LaVin Virag. He told them if they came to Budapest, they could stay with him and he could find them some places to play.

With all other options having fallen over, the band decided to take the plunge and bought train tickets from East Berlin to Budapest. When the train reached the border between East Germany and the Czechoslovak Socialist Republic there was a problem, however. 'Lou was supposed to take care of all of our travel documents,' says Thompson. 'Visas and all of that. Well, we get to the next country and we had to go through all these checkpoints on the train and because we never had the visas, we got hauled off the train.

'The guards were walking through the train with their

machine guns – it was like watching a James Bond movie, but it was real life. They had huge mounds at the train station. That was the border. And if you tried to go over that mound you get shot. When we got to the station, we could see the guards going along with torches, looking underneath the train. These other guys were walking through the train checking travel documents. They came to our carriage and John John was sitting next to the door. They opened the door and started asking us for the travel documents. This guy walked in, he looked like SS. And behind him was this soldier with a bloody machine gun. Where John John was sitting, the machine gun was pointing straight at him. I see him leaning back. I'm sitting beside him. I said, "Why are you leaning back?" And I looked over and I see the gun pointing at me! I thought. "Oh, shit!" I started leaning back too! Anyway, they took our passports and documents and when they came back, they said we had to get off the train.

'We got off the train with all the band equipment. We had guitars and Bart's drum kit. That thing weighed a ton. It was made from jarrah wood. It was beautiful, but it was heavy. And we were lugging this thing around. The kick drum weighed a ton. These drum kits were just pieces of wood all slapped together, spun on a lathe till they were round on the inside and the outside. You can imagine what they looked like. They were like half an inch thick. They were pretty heavy, very solid.

'We got put in a little waiting room and had to wait for the next train to come to take us back to Berlin. Train came, went back to Berlin, got our visas, jumped on the train and came back the same direction.'

With the correct visas to transit the Czechoslovak Socialist Republic, the touring party made it to the historic town of Komárno on the Danube. The Hungarian city of Komárom lay across the 415 metre Elisabeth Bridge on the south side of the river. But once again there was a problem. Thompson, Miller and Graham have various, sometimes conflicting, memories of the eventful night.

'They wouldn't let us across the border,' says Thompson. 'Because we never had a visa again. That bloody manager stuffed up again. He spent some of our American dollars and gave it to the guards so they would let him across. So, he goes to Hungary to get our travel documents done.'

'We had to hang around this bridge,' says Graham. 'I was glad to get out of there. It was pretty hairy, guys wandering around with AK-47 machine guns, pointing them at us. They were as scared of us as we were of them.'

Thompson takes up the story: 'But overnight, while he's gone, there we are staying at this place at the border. The checkpoint. We're inside the checkpoint, nice and warm. Then the police say we can't stay there. They kicked us out, so we were out in the cold. We walked back to the city. As we were going, this van came across the border and pulled up and gave us a lift into the city. We loaded all the band equipment in there and he took us into the town. I remember being in the street. We took all the band equipment out and there was this little stairway. We were all sitting in there. Made a little area to break the cold wind and made ourselves warm sitting there huddled up. And next to it was sort of a nightclub that we didn't know was there. It was like a pub, but when you looked at it, it was nothing. Like an underground shelter ... a bunker, that's it. And all these people came walking out. Where did they come from?

'A couple of blokes came up to us and one of them started talking to us and he said he'd been to Australia and he talked English all right. He said, "What are you doing here?" We told him we were a band and we were on tour in Europe. And we were stuck there because the manager had stuffed up with the visas to go to the next country, Hungary. He stayed there talking to us for a while. We hadn't eaten or anything. He asked us if we wanted to go to his place and stay there. It would be nice and warm for the night. We all said, "Yes, please." We were going to say no, but we're Aboriginal people and not used to the cold. He took us to his place. He helped us carry the bloody drum kit and everything. He couldn't get over how heavy it was. He said, "Do you guys carry this around?" and we said, "Yes." We ended up in this place. I remember walking up the stairs. He opened up the door. He had a wife and a couple of children. She welcomed us in and made us feel comfortable. It was nice and warm in the house. He fed us and everything, this guy.'

John John Miller's account adds some more details. 'We had to busk on the corner of a place,' he says. 'We had no home. We had nowhere to go. It was snowing and we were standing outside a pub and the border was there. Like Port Augusta – you've got that bridge and the border is in the middle of the bridge. We're standing outside the pub, we didn't know it was a pub, and this bloke walks out drunk. We had all our stuff. He seen the baggage. I had an Australian flag on my backpack. And I had my guitar and I had Australia with a Nunga flag. An Australian map with a Nunga flag on it. He's looking and he goes, "Austra-lia! ... Austra-lia – good people!" He says, "You know George? Melbourne, George?" His cousin George lives in Melbourne, see? "Yes, George in Melbourne, pizza bar, Melbourne there." "Ah, good people, Australia." Anyway, he says, "Play 'Johnny B Goode'. I give you money." We needed that money to get over the border. So, I said, "Ricky, brother, play "Johnny B Goode", brother. I'll back you up, c'mon. "Down in Louisiana close to New Orleans ..." "No Particular Place to Go". We were No Fixed Address. We played it. He pulled out $100, their money. I don't know what it was, but I tell you what, that $100 of theirs got us a taxi to the border and paid our visa to get over there and he even took us back to his house. He was in a three-storey apartment. He was on the top floor, very squashy.'

'We were busking in the street to buy pizzas and get a feed,' confirms Graham. 'This bloke said his brother lived in Sydney. "You must know my brother." "I guess so." He let us stay in his place. Let us sleep in the lounge. They were very nice people. He opened a couple of bottles of wine. We were buggered. We stayed the night there. We gave him some Aboriginal artefacts that we had. Didgeridoos and boomerangs. An Australian flag and a Nunga flag. He was overwhelmed that he got that stuff.

'Then I'm thinking, "Fuck, we walked a long way last night, carrying that fucked-up drumkit. And we've gotta do it again." To get back to the bridge, to the border, to get on the Hungarian train. Anyway, this horse and cart was coming down the road. Took you back, twenty, thirty, forty years. It had car tyres on it. There's Bart up there with this old fella [laughs]. "Throw the stuff on here," he said. So, the bloke gave us a ride. I think he got a didgeridoo too. That was a blessing because we didn't have to carry the drumkit again.'

'The checkpoint was right on the Danube,' says Thompson. 'On the other side of the bridge was the train station that took us to Budapest. The manager came back and he had all the documents stamped and we were allowed to go through the checkpoint. As we walked along there was this guy on the other side and he had a van. A big truck it was. And he offered to take us to the train station for nothing. We loaded all the stuff in there, went to the train station. We booked our tickets, jumped on a train and went to Budapest.'

Graham takes up the story again. 'We go on the train. We get into Budapest. Get all our stuff, get off the train. There's all these other cops there with their AK-47s. We showed them we had a visa and they were happy. Ricky Lovegrove left his passport on the train, and the train took off. I just cracked up. "Fuck me. We're in a foreign country and that's your only ticket! And you have to fuck up and leave it on the train. Why did you pull it out your pocket?" And he said, "I got sick of pulling it out of my pocket. Because every five minutes they're asking for your passport." It was all cool, they let us through and told us to go to the police station to report the passport.

'So off we go to the police station and they got this bloke in to talk English and he said, "Bullshit. You're not Australians. There's no black people in Australia. Who the fuck are you fooling?" He was saying, "You guys are terrorists. You're fucking Arabs." Anything but Australian. They never heard of black people in Australia. For us, listening to that, I felt like hooking the bloke. Let's make history.

'At the same time, this other cop walks in with Rick's passport and gives it to that cop. He looked at it, and looked at Rick and said, "Australian". Rick said, "Yeah, and I'm an Aboriginal." The cop said, "What's an Aboriginal?" Everywhere we went, they didn't know about Aboriginal people. At all the borders they'd give us a hard time, because there was all this terrorism happening with Palestinians and Arabs and dark-skinned people blowing people up and shooting people. It was all happening. It was pretty crazy.'

~

LaVin Virag was rather taken aback when the Aboriginal band he'd met in East Berlin two months previously arrived on his doorstep. 'LaVin said, "Come to my place,"' says Bart Willoughby. 'When we turned up, he was shocked. Because he didn't think we would turn up. He only had a flat. Me, John John and Rick, we all slept on the floor. For like, two or three weeks.'

The arrival of No Fixed Address in Budapest coincided with the opening of a club called Fekete Lyuk, ('black hole' in Hungarian. LaVin Virag was part of the alternative artistic and musical community that established the club. Fekete Lyuk provided a home for new wave and alternative music, and gained a following among young intellectuals, punks and skinheads; but it also quickly became a symbol of nonconformity and rebellion. Its establishment was a signal that political and administrative controls in Hungary were relaxing. In the club, bands could present alternative views of life and art, views which included criticism of the communist system.[4]

No Fixed Address started playing at Fekete Lyuk. 'It was a bunker,' says Thompson. 'And when we played, the bloody dust was coming down from the ceiling. It freaked us out how deep down they were. It was nice and comfortable. Like a club.'

'We could smoke dope there,' remembers Willoughby. 'This was still behind the Iron Curtain. Lots of drinking. We'd play the Lyuk and we'd get money. One time, I woke up one morning and Lou comes in. "You spent $500?" Because I was shouting everybody a drink. It was on a tab. "You spent $500 on drinks?" But I was his favourite so he didn't really crack up.'

One of the people in the Fekete Lyuk scene was Péter Ivan Müller. Considered one of the defining personalities of Hungarian alternative culture, at the time Müller was fronting a band called Sziámi (Siamese), but also worked in TV, radio and theatre. With Müller directing, No Fixed Address made a video clip in Budapest for a song called 'Gurukangaroo'. The clip is available on Facebook with a description in Hungarian. The English translation reads:

> The Australian indigenous rock band No Fixed Address toured Europe, led by Bart Willoughby (drummer of David Bowie), (they performed with us a few times) - we wrote this song with him. Do you know what "kangaroo" means indigenously? (Incidentally, we invented the kangaroo caterpillar and rummaged through the entire Váci Street). We cut the clip in the first serious Hungarian studio, trying out all the digital tricks that the technology of the age allowed … it all happened back in 1988. The cassette has now been unpacked. Worth to share! Dancing especially! Kangaroo! KANGAROO![5]

'We're just playing this gig, the Lyuk, and LaVin has some sort of big name in Hungary,' says Willoughby. 'We're getting all these people coming to the gig and next minute we're on TV, next minute we're recording. So, we're breaking it in Hungary. The people are loving us. It's weird.'

Then Lou Scholer disappeared.

'Yeah,' says Willoughby. 'He took off. Left me hungry in Hungary. But we weren't really. We were eating every day and we were making money every night.'

~

The band had been unhappy with Scholer for a while. 'He mucked up a lot of things,' says Willoughby. 'Neil, he's starting to ... he gets it, hanging out with us. He's learning that we're actually brothers. Lou's not thinking that.'

Bev Hall later told Fred Rose that from the time Scholer left the band in Hungary, they were ringing her constantly about the money paid for the Aboriginal artefacts in Leipzig. In the end, the band didn't return to the GDR so the fate of the 30,000 DDR Marks was not uncovered until after everyone had returned to Australia. To help them out, Bev Hall contacted various people they knew and these sent money to them – $2500 altogether.

'The arrangement I made with the band before they left,' she wrote to Rose, 'was that any currency they had left over they could leave with you or a mutual friend and I would give them the equivalent here, because I could use it to buy materials for our society. Instead I ended up with a $2000 phone bill all their expenses, reversed charges and Aust Embassy reversed charges on their behalf, but I then suggested not to worry the money the band thought was left in Leipzig would cover this or some of it anyway.'[6]

Still reeling from Scholer's sudden departure, the band copped another blow. Mick Thompson received an ultimatum from his wife back in Australia. 'She said, "If you don't come back this week, I'm going out to look for another bloke,"' says Willoughby. 'So Mick, you could see he was worried. Couldn't sleep.'

'He didn't wanna go,' says Miller. 'I had to tell him. I said, "Brother, your family is the most important thing in life." I said, "Go home, there's no chains holding on you here. We need you but we can get somebody else."'

'He said, "Look, guys, I'm going. You wanna come back? Nothing's going to happen,"' says Willoughby. 'There's this one day Les and Rick caught me and John John and Mick scheming to fly back. There was a big talk and Bulgaria pops up. They say we've got a big tour. We'll do these cities all the way from Sofia to the Black Sea. I think about nine gigs. But the money's really good. We all decide to keep going but Mick decides to fly back.'

~

From Budapest, the band headed south to Yugoslavia. Mick Thompson flew back to Australia and the band played a few gigs in the Yugoslav capital before heading to Bulgaria. 'The band was really sharp and shiny in Belgrade,' says Graham. 'We went from Hungary to Yugoslavia and we were opening up nightclubs there too. When we went there the embassy had to give us US$100 each. To help us out, to get accommodation because that bloke from Foreign Affairs didn't do anything about the tour that we went there to do.'

Lou Scholer had gone but Neil Trcin stayed. 'He started hanging out with us,' says Willoughby. 'He's actually from Yugoslavia. And he was blown away that he was back in his motherland.'

Things could get volatile on the road. Willoughby recalls Ricky Lovegrove getting into a fight with Neil in Belgrade. There was only going to be one winner. 'They smashed up the house we were staying in and we had to hide all the broken bits when the owner came back. I'd stand in front of this thing that was smashed so when he's talking to me, he can't see that its smashed. Same as John John. We're all standing in front of something that's smashed. But he can't see it.

'It was all smashed because Neil and Rick had a big fight. Neil didn't punch him or hit him. He just chucked him and Rick went through the air and hit this cupboard and it would smash and then a table got smashed because he got chucked on the table. Everything got smashed that Rick got thrown towards. Rick would get back up and run towards him. Rick was drunk.'

~

After the trials and tribulations of Budapest, thankfully the Bulgarian tour was well organised. 'When we first turn up in Bulgaria, we get off the plane, meet our driver, put all the equipment in the bus and this is our tour bus all the way from Sofia to the Black Sea and back again,' says Willoughby. 'The organisers are there and they actually saw the Berlin festival on television. It went all through Eastern Europe. So, the people know of us. So everywhere we're playing, we're playing to packed houses.'

Bulgaria's Communist Party had spent years trying to suppress and eradicate Western rock music. While by 1988, the official stance had mellowed slightly under the influence of Mikhail Gorbachev's glasnost policy, No Fixed Address discovered that some sounds were still beyond the pale.

'We were in Bulgaria and we done "It's a Long Way to the Top" in a soundcheck,' says Graham. 'And we had didgeridoo playing in place of the bagpipes. The police came to us. They were going to take all our stuff off us. It was amazing. AC/DC was completely blacklisted. You weren't allowed to play any of it. We said, "That's not our song." We shut up and we turned down and we played our own music. That was just the soundcheck. We didn't do it on the night, it was taboo. We thought we were going to get clocked in the head with a hammer. But now you can do it. All the crowd there was calling out for AC/DC, "Australia, Australia." I think Angus knows about that and he was anxious to hear it but we never got to record it. We had to stop playing AC/DC or we were going to get thrown out of the country.'

Willoughby remembers another incident when Graham was not quite so accommodating to the authorities. "We did a concert in the top hills of Bulgaria. The whole town was marched to the concert, by the guards. A couple of thousand people. Outdoors in a quarry area and at the back is an old arena that looks like it was for gladiators. And I remember me and John John and Rick were going [wondering whisper], "Gladiators were here." We get out and start performing, and Les is a bit drunk, he's had a few. We start playing and some people get up and start to dance. The soldiers come with batons and started hitting them really hard to sit down. Les saw this and said very loud on the mic, "What the fuck is going on? You can't hit people like that, you cunts!" And everyone just turned around and stared at him [laughs]. Even the fellas with the batons, they stopped. And people were allowed to get up and dance. The soldiers went back and the people cheered and got up and danced. That was the best yell and reaction I've ever seen.'

'We toured around Bulgaria then we went back to Yugoslavia,' says Graham. Like the other East European Communist states, Yugoslavia was heavily indebted to the West. But whereas the response in Budapest and East was to keep borrowing foreign cash, in Yugoslavia they simply printed more of their own. Through the 1980s the country moved steadily into hyper-inflation. 'The economy was that bad, to buy groceries you had to have two wheelbarrows of money,' recalls Willoughby.

There was mounting civil unrest in Belgrade too. Newly appointed Serbian President Slobodan Milošević was making a bid for power in the vacuum that had followed the death of Yugoslavian President Tito by arousing and manipulating Serbian national emotions. Milošević began openly encouraging nationalist meetings at which the insignia of the wartime Chetniks was on display for the first time in 40 years. The reminder of the ethnic cleansing carried out by the Chetniks in the Second World War was calculated to arouse disquiet, among Croats and Muslims in particular.

In Belgrade, the band was staying with a local called Domenico. 'He had a house he called "Cave", because there was no electricity,' says Willoughby.

'He told us about the Serb soldiers,' says John John Miller. 'Don't walk around, the soldiers will kill you. It was already brewing there.'

'Me and John John experienced this twice when we went out one night,' says Willoughby. 'We bumped into the Serb army. I thought they were going to kill us. We only went out once and twice we bumped into fellas we thought were going to kill us. And this is just before the war breaks out.'

Despite their precarious situation, Les Graham was keen to explore the opportunities Europe was offering. 'We started doing other gigs,' he says, 'and this bloke said to us, "Listen, guys, I've got two BMWs. We can all get in them and go to Sweden. Because there's interest in you guys there." And I said, "Come on, boys, let's get in the car and fucking go. We're here." Their idea was to go back to Australia, mellow out and come back. I said, "Where are you gonna get twenty grand to come back?" We ended up getting on the plane and coming back.'

'We had to leave the big $10k jarrah drum set that the sponsors gave us from Perth,' says Miller. 'They gave Bart a big 10-piece drum set, jarrah wood to promote their drum kits. We had to leave it over in Yugoslavia, Belgrade, because we never had no dollars to put it on the plane.'

~

Reflecting on the Eastern European experience, Graham says, 'That tour was worth the effort. There was lot of energy put into it.'

'There you start to see things,' says Willoughby. 'Yeah, we've got something. So, if I come back to Australia, people say, "Well, look at you" ... well, you've got all this energy inside and they really don't know what they're mucking with.'

'The gigs over there ... like when we played in Germany, the whole crowd got up and stood up and clapped,' says Miller. 'And I said, "What are they doing that for?" It was because they respected us. Because the music that we sing and the words that we say is true. And the truth stands on a foundation that doesn't break. But when you build on a lie, it's just like Australia is now. They think that's it's their land but it's all crumbling beneath them.'

40   AFTERMATH

As soon as the members of No Fixed Address touched down back in Australia, they went their separate ways. A breaking point had come in Bulgaria.

'Me and Les had a couple of fights,' Bart Willoughby recalls. 'This fella invited us to his place when we were in Bulgaria. He was going with this woman whose mother was organising the trip. Invited all these girls around. It was the most weirdest party I've ever been to. I don't go to parties where men can't speak English. Les got drunk on wine. I wasn't having a drink. He started talking shit. I had this spoon in my mouth with this egg thing. "Pfft." He was straight across from me at the table. It hit him in the face. His face turned red. The fella whose house it was, he'd invited us there, we were only there for about one hour and this big fight breaks out. "Right fucker, downstairs!" And I'm downstairs yelling out, "Come on, you fuckhead!" Lights turn on and people are saying, "Shut up, they'll ring the cops." That was one bad incident. There were heaps.'

Ricky Harrison recalls Graham telling him about another altercation. 'I only got Les's version of what happened,' says Harrison. 'They got on this bus somewhere. Les had his guitar out and he was playing guitar to this couple. Bart walked over to Les and said, "Look, this fella's married to that woman there." And Bart was going off his head at Les about this. And Les said, "No, look man, I'm just playing guitar here. We're just having a bit of a singalong and that's it." Bart wouldn't have it. He thought Les was trying to come on to this guy's woman [laughs]. Serenading, yeah. Something happened and Bart went for Les. Les jumped up and they all jumped in between them. Bart's trying to punch Les and Les is trying to punch Bart over this couple. Les just likes grabbing his guitar as far as I know and just sits there and plays it. They're swinging punches. Bart's trying to punch Les over the top and Les is trying to punch Bart over the top and then Les thought, "Oh,

hang on, I'm going to hit this fella in the ribs in a minute." He
went to hit him in the ribs. He ducked down and he's thrown
a punch really hard towards Bart's ribs. But Bart had the same
idea. But he put his head right where Les's fist was coming.
And it knocked him out. So that was the fight that changed
everything.'

'When we got back to Australia, me and Les were arguing,'
says Willoughby. 'Les went down to Adelaide. Rick Lovegrove,
who's passed away now, he went to Perth. That's where his
girlfriend was. John John, he was sick of playing. He caught a
bus or train to Adelaide.'

~

Eventually tour manager Lou Scholer also returned to
Australia. Bev Hall conveyed the news to Fred Rose in a letter
of 8 September 1988. 'His report condemns strongly the
Eastern European [*sic*] particularly DDR. It was badly and
untidily written and the band was furious when they read it.
The band is bitter as it now has caused them to break up and
they are being pursued again for "outstanding" debts. None
can play again anywhere as a result and their music is lost. Les
is seeking legal action because of these added problems.'[1]

Rose replied on 9 November. 'I emphasise again that I know
absolutely nothing officially but I keep my ear pretty close to
the ground. In this way I learnt that there is something over
M9,000 [DDR Marks] in the GDR left over from the M30,000
[DDR Marks] paid for the artefacts.'[2] He suggested getting a
solicitor to write to the museum director in Leipzig through
the GDR embassy in Canberra, advising Scholer was no longer
the manager and claiming the residual amount to the credit of
Les Graham as leader of the group. And there the money trail
goes cold.

~

Bart Willoughby stayed in Sydney and took time out. Eventually,
he sought out Mick Thompson in Redfern. 'When they got back,

3 6 9

I was in the studio working on my own stuff,' says Thompson. 'I had a studio through Radio Redfern. Bart walks in and says, "What are you doing?" I say, "I'm doing some work on my own stuff here." He says, "Don't worry about that. I've got something for us to work on together." I said, "Bart, you always do that. You always disturb me when I'm doing something." He says, "Oh man, this is wild. This is dangerous." So, I said, "Righto." And we started working on this stuff.

'When he did it, it was this new style of music that he did with Mixed Relations. It was totally different to No Fixed. We'd done four or five tracks when Joe rang up and said he needed us. We were going to tour with Joe Geia. Bart was going to play bass and I was going to mix the sound.'

'I got a phone call from Joe Geia, from Darwin,' Willoughby confirms. 'He goes, "Bart, whatcha doin'?" "Nothing." "You want to come up to Darwin and play bass?" "Yeah, okay." So, I went to Darwin. Took about three days to travel by bus. Anyway, I was on Melville Island. Beautiful little island. I spent about three days there deciding whether I wanted to play bass with Joe Geia. Joe Geia had a gig in Darwin and that night his band just kicked arse. It was the most amazing concert I've been to in Australia. He was just like Mr Slick in his happiest hours. Then I got a tap on my shoulder and it was the manager from Yothu Yindi, Adam James. He was a nervous little fella, because he'd never been in the business. He goes, "Do you want to play drums for Yothu Yindi in America?" I said, "Yep." His face just changed. He thought I was going to say no.'

~

Yothu Yindi had been recording their debut album in Sydney in late 1987 and early 1988, and had three major events booked for the second half of 1988. First, in August, there was the Festival of Pacific Arts in Townsville. Then in September, the Olympic Arts Festival in Seoul, South Korea. Both of these events provided opportunities for Yothu Yindi's traditional performers to strut their stuff. To cap off the year, Yothu Yindi had been invited to support Midnight Oil on a full-on six-week North American tour starting in the first week of October.

Andrew Belletty had been the drummer in the Swamp Jockeys and Yothu Yindi. Belletty had pulled the pin midway through 1988 and the band was without a drummer for the upcoming Midnight Oil tour. 'After we did the recording and a series of shows, I'd had enough,' he says. 'I really didn't want to do it anymore. I had already lined up some work in Sydney. By June, I'd come back to Sydney and I started working in the film industry. I just changed because I couldn't physically do that and I really didn't want to do it. Psychologically either. It was doing my fucking head in. Those mob were just too … the sound of a beer can at 7 am being cracked, people drinking and smoking … it was just horrific. Even in those days, Manda [Mandawuy Yunipingu] was drinking more than a carton a day. He ended up [drinking] three or four cartons a day. It was a pretty horrific time. You either join in with that or you cut out of it and I couldn't do it anymore. I pulled out in the middle of the year.

'They continued but there was no way I was going on a junket for three months on a bus. That was probably the decider for me. I knew what it was going to be like. I knew who the mob were who were going to be on tour. And I thought, "This sounds like three months in hell." They just had these roughnut ex-Midnight Oil production crew … because Midnight Oil were winding down at that point. It was just this horrible environment, this really toxic environment and I just thought, "I don't want to be any part of that."'

Belletty remembers Bart Willoughby hanging out with Yothu Yindi while they were recording in Sydney. 'I know that Bart was in Sydney,' he says. 'And *yarndi* had a lot to do with the connection. There was a huge smoking culture in those days. There was a lot of smoking and drinking. I was on the back of that trying to get out of the whole rock'n'roll thing. I'd had enough. Bart and Manda and Stu [Stuart Kellaway, bass] and the boys, they used to really hook in. We would bump into him all the time, and we got on really well. And as a bunch, we would sit around and have these really big sessions.'

It was a big call for Willoughby to accept Yothu Yindi's invitation. As well as the bass spot with Joe Geia, there was an offer for another overseas tour for No Fixed Address on the table. West German promoter Birger Gesthuisen had set up a two-month tour beginning in October 1988 – a total of 36 concerts across West Germany, Austria, the Netherlands, Belgium, England and France. All the band needed to do was get themselves over there. But the Eastern European experience had ruptured a key relationship within the band.

'I had problems with Les. That's why I left,' says Willoughby. 'At that time, I had a choice to go with No Fixed and do a world tour with Sting, or go with Yothu Yindi in America. This was my choice. So, I chose to go with Yothu Yindi because there were a lot of things weighing on their side that allowed me to go that side. That tour with Sting would have skyrocketed No Fixed because we had good-looking guys in the band, the lead guitarist. Not only that, we were on the right track.'

~

There's still more than a tinge of bitterness in Les Graham's recollection of the missed opportunity. 'I think that was going to be our big take-off,' he says. 'The big break. It was going to be just totally amazing. But anyway, what happened is, Bart signed a contract with Yothu Yindi and we were on the phone to them saying, listen this is what's happening with us. And we were talking to Bart. He ended up going to America with Yothu Yindi and Midnight Oil. They paid him session rates and a good wage and all that, but then when they got back to Australia, they said, see you later. And kinda left him. It kinda ... well that there did fuck us right up.'

'Les came back to me,' says Ricky Harrison. 'He said, "Look, ah, Bart's left the band" [laughs]. And he said, "We're supposed to go back to Europe." He said, "Can you come back with us? We'll grab a drummer and do some songs just to fill in." Probably just like Aroona did, I suppose. He got in contact with Birger, but Birger said if Bart's not coming, he wasn't interested. So that was the end of that. I was going to go the second time. But it didn't happen.'

'We just thought, no; we'll throw the towel in,' says Graham. 'We couldn't do that to Bart anyway. He can think himself lucky. No Fixed could have been up there in the lights. He feels bad now, he threw the towel in at the wrong time. We could've been sitting on top of the world. We could've been doing anything now to help our own people. Promoting Indigenous music – that was my objective. That was Bart's too. We got half way up then we fell over a cliff. That's how I see it. It's pretty depressing but it happened.'

~

In late September, Yothu Yindi flew out of Gove in the Northern Territory to Hawaii and then on to New York. Surfing on the success of the *Diesel and Dust* album and the US top 20 single 'Beds Are Burning', this was Midnight Oil's second international tour of the year.[3] As well as Yothu Yindi, the tour included Native American Indian band Graffiti Man, fronted by John Trudell, a Santee Sioux Indian and former leader of the American Indian Movement.

From the opening date on 4 October in Baltimore, the tour crisscrossed the US/Canadian border before winding its way down the US west coast to the final night in Los Angeles on 12 November. The bands played 32 cities in 38 days. A film crew followed Yothu Yindi throughout the tour, and director Ned Lander (who directed *Wrong Side of the Road*) made a documentary about the experience titled *Into the Mainstream*.

'So, I'm working with Yothu Yindi and the music's just good rock'n'roll to me,' says Willoughby. 'They asked me just to work on little things that they'd never had a chance to work on. So, every show I gave my all, because I understood that. I've been on stage a hundred trillion times and these fellas hadn't. I'd have to roar it out to give these fellas confidence. They'd never been in this situation. I had to explain a lot of things.

'At the same time there was this Indian band on, led by John Trudell. He was an activist, like Lionel Fogarty or David Gulpilil, but more dangerous. He has had things done to him, and lived to tell about it. A been-there-and-done-it fella. He had this band and they kicked arse. There was this Indian band, then Yothu Yindi then Midnight Oil. After playing about the third concert, they [the Indian band] all walked out and just left this lead guitarist, and he was quite amazing. Brilliant guitarist. Anyway, they asked me to play drums for them. So, it was just drums and guitar while this Indian fella spoke and these two other Indians chanted.

'So, all through the tour, the rock stars weren't going to see Midnight Oil or Yothu Yindi, they were going to see this icon, John Trudell. He was an icon. So, all these people came. Jackson Browne and Daryl Hannah, Kris Kristofferson. The guitarist from the Bruce Springsteen band, Miami Steve – he was a weird fella – aw, heaps. Anyway, when they came to my room, I'd get them in and take them round to Yothu Yindi's room. They'd freak out, get their photo taken. I was in a weird position. I'm hanging out with one of the cores of American society and I'm with a traditional band from Australia and the feature is Midnight Oil, the number one act.

'I get to meet the two Indian blokes. Every morning ... you could get dope, not much smoke ... I'd go round there every morning and just before I had a smoke those two Indian blokes would want me to sing, "Aboriginal Woman". They really loved it. I didn't understand it. I just thought I was skinning for a smoke. I would just sing it as quick as possible so I could get a smoke.

'Then one day, I think we were in Quebec, and we're meeting all these Indian people. And Mandawuy's talking to them and he goes, "We have a song in Australia that Bart will want to sing. Bart, you sing it." And he's talking about me singing "We Have Survived". And everyone's there, even the other band. I'd never sung "We Have Survived" to these other fellas, just "Aboriginal Woman". I played it. I just played it the way I always play it. By the time I finish, I think there was silence for about a minute. Maybe twenty seconds. A long time. I think it hit the right situation. It was accepted by whoever was there. And I remember the lead guitarist from the band, from the Indian band, who was an amazing guitarist, he goes, "There's a bit more to you, isn't there, Bart?" In other words, he saw it too.'

When the tour was over, Yothu Yindi returned to Australia and Willoughby decided he would start his own band. 'Yothu Yindi's on the way' he recalls. 'Mandawuy would come round and would say, "Oh Bart, it's not going to happen." I'd say, "Mandawuy, you have grabbed the rock and you have chucked it in the middle of the pond and the waves have already started." And when I said that I could see him look and understand what I was talking about. He understood exactly what I was talking about, like when he started the whole thing off. It started off a long time ago. It was embedded in him. It gave him the confidence to accept this thing.'

By the time Mick Thompson got back to Sydney after the Joe Geia tour, Willoughby was back from America and ready to start work again. 'We worked in the studio for about a month and a half,' says Thompson. 'Then he said, "Let's get a band together." Then he formed Mixed Relations and we rehearsed in the studio. That band went through to 1994. I did the live sound and all the sound effects. This music is made up of jazz, blues, classical, you name it. The sax player would play jazz. The bass player would play a mixture of reggae and blues. Bart was playing rhythm – I call it the 'sore-hand' rhythm. You know when you hit your hand with a hammer and you're waving it round? That's how Bart was hitting the strings.'

~

In 1989, Andy Nehl was station manager at triple J as the ABC's Sydney-based youth radio station prepared to go national. He recalls one of the questions being asked was: "What is the first song we're going to play on triple J as it goes national in each city?" Because famously the first song that was played when Double J launched in Sydney had been Skyhooks' 'You Just Like Me Because I'm Good in Bed', a track that was banned on commercial radio across Australia. 'I wanted it to be an Indigenous band; Indigenous music to signify some commitment to that,' he says.

Nehl had been a fan of No Fixed Address from when he first heard the *Wrong Side of the Road* record at 4ZZZ, but particularly from the gig at Brisbane's South's Leagues Club in 1982 when No Fixed Address played at the farewell gig of his band, the Black Assassins.

No Fixed Address had disbanded but Mixed Relations were up and playing around the traps. Nehl asked Bart Willoughby if he could come up with a song for the launch of the radio network. One of the numbers Mixed Relations was doing was a song that Willoughby had written and performed with No Fixed Address on their 1984 UK tour. 'Bart put forward his song "Take It or Leave It" by Mixed Relations as the song for that,' says Nehl. 'We recorded that in Studio 221 at triple J's studio up at Forbes Street, up the back of triple J when it was still based on William Street in Darlinghurst.'

'Take It or Leave It' was the first song played on triple J in Melbourne, Perth, Adelaide, Canberra, Hobart, Brisbane, Newcastle and Darwin when the station went national over the next couple of years. The track was later included on the Mixed Relations album *Love*, released in 1993.

Nehl subsequently involved Mixed Relations in a big live music simulcast of Indigenous music on triple J and ABC-TV. 'That's a whole other story,' Nehl laughs. 'Basically, David Hill, managing director of the ABC, had been up in Hall's Creek on a weekend and he sees a young Aboriginal band play. Kids, maybe eight, ten, twelve, fourteen, playing in this band. Thinks they're fantastic. That year they had major concerts for the Melbourne Symphony Orchestra and the Sydney Symphony Orchestra planned as big simulcasts for the ABC's

60th birthday. Then David Hill sees this band of Aboriginal kids play in Halls Creek and thinks, "Wow, we should have a big concert of Indigenous music and culture from somewhere out in the bush as well as having the Melbourne and Sydney Symphony Orchestras." So, he rings up the head of ABC Radio that weekend and says, "This is what I want, make it happen." And I'm late into work at triple J the next morning, about 10 am on the Monday morning, and I get a message from the station secretary saying, "Andy, the head of radio wants to see you straight away." And I think, "Oh yeah, what are we in trouble for now?" And I was late because, coincidentally, I'd been out seeing Mixed Relations play till about 3 in the morning the night before. So, I go in and he says, "Andy, David Hill wants a big concert of Indigenous music on TV and radio from somewhere out in the bush. Make it happen." I go, "Great – how much money have we got for this?" "None."

'I hunted around, found a suitable festival, went up and chatted to the Aboriginal people in Broome who were very keen, and we worked collaboratively. We worked closely with the Aboriginal community in Broome and managed to create a much bigger festival than they were going to have.

'That was a huge logistical exercise between triple J and ABC-TV and the Aboriginal community in Broome. I ended up flying over and lobbying the WA government to put money into it. They put about $100,000 into it out of the State Lotteries. ABC-TV in those days ... couldn't do it now because everything's totally costed to an inch and you need a budget code to approve things ... we pulled staff out of the ABC around Australia. We had a radio mixing truck drive up there from Perth or Adelaide, I can't remember which. ABC tried to do a deal with the air force to give us a Hercules to transport the four tons of OB gear and equipment and sixty people to Broome. That fell through and Australian Airlines did a deal for us where they gave us free excess baggage and we put four tons of gear on Australian Airlines to Darwin. We couldn't fly into Broome because at that time Broome had a tiny airport with only propeller planes going in. And then hired a truck and a bus in Darwin. We had a truck accompanying us and a whole lot of TV gear underneath the bus as well as some ABC people and people from Mixed Relations and the Warumpi Band and Coloured Stone and Kev Carmody, all on this bus across to Broome for it. Twenty-two hours, including Bart taking us to some secret swimming hole he knew when we stopped on the bus somewhere between Katherine and Hall's Creek, which was a lot of fun.'

Stompen Ground '92, the first Kimberley Aboriginal Arts and Cultural Festival, was held in Broome over the September 5–6 weekend. More than 40 different acts took part, including Yothu Yindi, Mixed Relations, Scrap Metal, Coloured Stone, Kev Carmody, Tiddas, Warumpi Band, John Albert Band and Fitzroy Express. 'We put that on as a seven-hour live national simulcast of music on ABC-TV, triple J and regional radio for the ABC's 60th birthday,' says Nehl. 'It ran over two days and we recorded half the acts on the Friday night and we did the simulcast on the Saturday night and we used the recordings we'd shot on the Friday night to go in between when the bands changed over on the Saturday night. It was fantastic.'

Yothu Yindi's 'Treaty' finally broke the colour bar on Australian commercial radio in the winter of 1991, reaching #11 on the singles chart. It went on to be the Australasian Performing Rights Association's Song of the Year and an international dance hit across Europe and North America.

And Stompen Ground '92 was living proof across the national airwaves that thirteen years after No Fixed Address stood on stage in Taperoo and played an original rock'n'reggae song called 'Vision', Australian Indigenous rock had truly come of age.

EPILOGUE   **NO FIXED ADDRESS LANE: 25 MARCH 2021**

Walking west from Pulteney Street down Adelaide's Rundle Mall, after about a hundred metres you come to Twin Street. Running south off the mall, it was the home of the Cellar Blues Club in the late 1960s and early '70s, and also Modern Love Songs, the go-to import record shop for punk and new wave (and birthplace of *Roadrunner* magazine) in the late 1970s. Just a few metres on, again on your left, is the entrance to the city's grand old dame of shopping, the heritage-listed Adelaide Arcade. Directly opposite, on the northern side of the mall, is the Richmond Hotel, where No Fixed Address played during their early years in Adelaide. Continuing west, you pass the more recent, and now rather rundown Regent Arcade on your left, and Bert Flugelman's Mall's Balls sculpture in the middle of the mall. Then, again on the south side and flanked by fashion outlets Uniqlo, Lorna Jane's and Sussan, is the newly minted No Fixed Address Lane. At the far end of the lane, past Remy's Deep Dish Pizza & Bar, is the entrance to the Rundle Place shopping centre car park. The back half of the lane is partially covered, with lights embedded in the underside of the roof that juts out from the western wall.

The lane launch was scheduled for 11.30 am. I arrived about 30 minutes beforehand and joined the small group at the far end. On the western wall a stunning ground-to-ceiling mural loomed over the scene. Its main element was a painted rendition of the iconic black and white photo of the five-piece version of the band. The photo, by Ian de Gruchy, had accompanied my story about the band in the August 1980 *Roadrunner*. I exchanged pleasantries with the band members, met their former manager Michael Fisher and was introduced to Mick Thompson, who had flown down from Cairns to mix live sound at their performances. Les Graham had suffered a bout of pneumonia over the summer and I noticed his breathing was still strained. At one point, John John Miller was sitting down and quietly weeping. I asked his wife Davinia if he was okay. 'It's Veronica,' she said, pointing to the image of the late Veronica Rankine on the mural. 'He's sad that she isn't here.'

The ceremony got underway with Elizabeth Close, one of the mural artists, describing how she and her two colleagues (Shane Mankitya and Thomas Readett) had approached the artwork. She concluded by saying, 'We are deeply honoured to have been able to create this work and would like to thank the band for being so generous with your time and energy and for placing your trust in us. Thanks to Rundle Place for your support in helping us to realise this vision and the City of Adelaide for driving such an important project. It's our hope that we have in some small way contributed to ensuring that the legacy of No Fixed Address is an enduring one.'

While Close was speaking, Jack Kanya Buckskin arrived to do welcome to country. 'Sorry,' he said, to chuckles from the crowd. 'It's a bit hard to find the place when it's got no fixed address.' Buckskin is the Kaurna Language Coordinator and Teacher and Cultural Educator at Tauondi College. Promising his address would be 'short, sharp and shiny', he gave the welcome in language and played a brief passage on the didgeridoo.

Grayson Rotumah, lecturer at the Centre for Aboriginal Studies in Music, then spoke. 'It's an honour to talk about these people,' he said. 'Coming down to Adelaide many years ago I was just empowered by the legacy they left behind. Coming down from my community on the Gold Coast and seeing how people can use music as a very powerful spearhead to create opportunities for our future generations.

'The end of the 1970s heralded the beginning of an important era of development in Aboriginal music. Bob Marley's visit to Adelaide in 1979 had invigorated the popular music of Aboriginal Australia and gave a platform to propel our culture onto the international stage with a musical spearhead. No Fixed Address emerged out of CASM and were a catalyst for this spearhead. They were pioneers in this new movement and led the way for many other Indigenous artists from CASM such as Coloured Stone, Joe Geia, Jimmy Chi, Stephen Pigram, Stephen and David Page and of course Zaachariaha Fielding from Electric Fields.

'The arrival of the members of No Fixed Address at CASM and the songwriting that followed also had a transformative effect on the approach to Aboriginal music and education at the University of Adelaide. CASM shifted from a classical approach in the early 1970s to an emphasis on storytelling and contemporary Indigenous music making and song. And in doing that, gave a kickstart to a new vanguard of musical pioneers. The legacy of No Fixed Address lives on today through CASM, its teaching and its students and has inspired many Indigenous musicians to pursue university studies.'

Bart Willoughby was then invited to speak on behalf of No Fixed Address. In fact, although it wasn't planned that way, all four members spoke. But Willoughby led off. 'It's actually a real pleasure to be here,' he said. 'We've been together for something like 44 years. I didn't think we'd be here 44 years later having a street named after us, or a laneway. And we're still performing. We should have died years ago but we didn't [crowd laughs].

'But we did look after ourselves on the road. We did care about the music. We didn't know where we were going but we just kept on believing in what we were doing. Also, when you're creating new things, you actually don't know that you're creating new things. You're just following your heart. And I think that was the main thing we passed on to our people. And also, to whitefellas too. Which are our people too. You just follow what you believe in and your love of it is just going to show anyway. I think that's what we handed down. I think the politics were just a kid's reaction. I think our parents had a harder life. We were just young, not naive, but we wanted change. And through people like Bob Marley and other great artists, they gave us the road to travel down.

'Like I said, we've been on that road for over 44 years and

we're still travelling. We're still performing everywhere and I shouldn't say this, but we'll probably be doing it till the day we die. I'd like to hand you over to Les, who is one of the other founding members of the band. And actually Les, after 44 years, brother, I didn't think we'd be where we are now and thanks for asking me to join the band with you.'

Les Graham, his voice cracking with emotion, stepped up next. 'It's a blessing. It's hard. I'm trying not to cry. I want to celebrate this laneway. How would you say it? It's a rock against racism. To bring unity together. To bring all Australians together and we're tired of fighting against racism. And I see this laneway as very important to all cultures of the world. We're Indigenous, we're only three per cent of Australia, which is around 760,000 people, and that's not many people to be Aboriginals. There's not much I can say about that. I thank the mayor and the council and I thank Australia. For putting up with us [crowd laughs]. We've had arguments, you know, racist arguments. We've faced racism everywhere we go. Every time we go do a gig there's a figure of racism, such as catching taxis in Geelong. The band was trying to catch a taxi after a gig and no taxis would stop for them. Because I'm the fairest, they used to put me out on the street and the taxi would pull up. Then when they saw these guys, it would take off [crowd laughs]. It might seem like a funny thing but that was reality. And living that life's not nice. I wish we had been free to jump in any taxi. And things like that.

'In the beginning of No Fixed, it was a lovable, commercial band. We looked up to the Beatles, we looked up at Skyhooks, we looked up to Cold Chisel and we wanted to be in that commercial scene. Then we started getting booked, gigs and they cancelled us. So openly. "That's an Aboriginal band. We don't want them here."

'So, we turned political. When you're talking political, that's singing the truth. So, what's so political about it? We sing the truth of our lives. And it's taken us all the way to a brand-new day, as they say. Now we've got a laneway named after us.

Ricky Harrison, Mick Thompson, Bart Willoughby, John John Miller and Les Graham at the launch of No Fixed Address Lane, Adelaide 25 March 2021.

Photo by Donald Robertson.

So, we've scarred the earth forever. And I love it. Thanks very much for coming and we're playing at the Governor Hindmarsh tonight – I need to promote the band! – and I hope to see youse there. God bless you all and thank you.'

Then Ricky Harrison spoke. 'I'd just like to thank the City of Adelaide for commissioning the artists who painted this magnificent painting. I'd just like to thank ... there were a lot of members that came with the band as well over the years. We won't mention them all but we'd like to thank them for helping us out over the years. Especially all our families, friends and fans and all the people that supported us, especially the local

Nunga community and people here today who've turned up to support us. I'm not really good at doing speeches so ... I'm just, um ... [coughs, pats chest] ... getting a bit old, I suppose. Yeah, anyway, to all the musicians too that we worked with over the years, that supported us, and helped us get around the countryside and around South Australia in particular. And let us do our thing. And with our songwriting and music and stuff and with CASM supporting us at the very beginning and a lot of the people that were there that helped us. It was good to meet up with all of you and we really appreciate the support that we got from everybody. Thanks to the mayor and everybody today, for turning up today and yeah, thank you.'

Finally, it was John John Miller's turn at the microphone. 'I didn't organise a speech, so I'd just like to say, I followed the leader. I was the youngest. I didn't realise what was happening at the time. I was young. What I'd like to say is thanks everybody. Thanks to the mayor, City of Adelaide for putting us up on this wall. To see this – Australia will change. It's changing now. I hope soon that one day there won't be two flags. There will be one flag to make one Australia. I'd like to see that before I leave this world to go to the next world. I'd like to say thanks to my family. That's my foundation of me. I'd like to say thanks to No Fixed Address. Our message will stand forever I suppose. Thank you.'

When the applause died down, The Right Honourable, the Lord Mayor of Adelaide, Sandy Verschoor took to the little stage. 'That's making me cry. Oh dear. What an honour,' she said. Composing herself, she continued. 'To the No Fixed Address band members, it is such an honour to have you here in my city. The City of Adelaide is committed and very proud of our achievement in reconciliation with local Aboriginal and Torres Strait Islander communities. We've worked with a number of supporters on this laneways project over the past three years, including the SA Music Hall of Fame, and they've continued to provide ongoing pro bono support to help choose appropriate locations. We've also been supported by the Adelaide UNESCO City of Music Committee.

'We talk about being the most livable city – I like to think we're the most creative city in the world. And of course, we are the first and only UNESCO-designated City of Music in Australia. That was bestowed on us in 2015 as an acknowledgement of the breadth and depth and vibrancy of Adelaide's music culture, its international reach, its history and of course that includes the history of Aboriginal reggae and rock band No Fixed Address.'

After the plaques had been unveiled and photos taken with the lord mayor and family and friends, a group of us adjourned to Remy's in the lane for a free lunch, courtesy of the city council. After some remarkably glutinous pizza, we bade our farewells, but as I walked away down Rundle Mall, I reflected on what had been a surprisingly moving and emotional ceremony. Nathan Davies in the next day's *Advertiser* summed it up well. 'There was barely a dry eye in the house yesterday at the opening of the city laneway renamed in honour of pioneering Indigenous rock band No Fixed Address.'

~

With the members scattered to the four winds, it had taken a bit of organising to assemble No Fixed Address for the launch of the Adelaide lane. In fact, none of the four lived in Adelaide. Les Graham was closest, living on a property north of Murray Bridge; John John Miller was in Port Lincoln, South Australia; Bart Willoughby was in Melbourne; and Ricky Harrison was in Morwell, Victoria. The band needed to play some gigs around Adelaide to make the trip financially viable. This was challenging enough in normal times, but made more difficult by the Covid pandemic.

A sizable crowd rolled up for the opening show at the Governor Hindmarsh that evening. Prominent in the audience (he is pretty tall) was former Central Districts and Sydney Swans Australian rules footballer Michael O'Loughlin, who dealt generously with a steady stream of young women asking for selfies. When the band hit the stage, the sound – which had been fine at the soundcheck in the afternoon – started misbehaving and Mick Thompson had to scramble to sort it out.

Les Graham sang the opening song, 'Unity' and it was immediately obvious he was having breathing difficulties. During 'The Vision' he sat down, looking completely out of breath. The sound gremlins were eventually sorted out and the band really hit their stride during 'Black Man's Rights', which featured an instrumental break with some dazzling guitar harmonics and effects from Graham. The crowd dancing in front of the stage grew as the band warmed to the task and the songs rolled out like old friends: 'Sunrise'; 'Johnny Too Bad'; 'From My Eyes'; a storming 'Pigs' from Ricky Harrison; and finally, the anthemic 'We Have Survived'.

Without a car, I didn't have the means to get to Murray Bridge and back for Friday's gig at the Longriders Motorcycle Club, but thought I'd try to make it up to Macclesfield for the Saturday show at the Three Brothers Arms. Dave and Joan, two old schoolfriends from Whyalla, had tickets, and I said perhaps we could catch up beforehand. On Saturday morning, I was having brunch in the city with another old friend Collette, when my phone rang. It was Dave. 'Hey Donald, we're in Macclesfield. We were just in the pub where the band are playing tonight and we overheard the manager saying one of the band members has had a heart attack and been taken to hospital.' Shit!

I called Mick Thompson. It went to voicemail. Then I tried Michael Fisher. Voicemail again. Eventually Fisher rang back. He told me Ricky Harrison had felt unwell after the gig the previous night. Everyone was staying at Les Graham's place on a property north of Murray Bridge and Harrison woke up about two in the morning with chest pains and having trouble breathing. When it didn't settle down, Fisher took him to the emergency department at the hospital in Murray Bridge. They did some tests, said it was a heart attack, and sent him in an ambulance to the Queen Elizabeth Hospital in Adelaide, where he was stable.

A little while later Mick Thompson called. He confirmed the details, but added that the Macclesfield gig would go ahead with a replacement guitarist. Wow. Okay.

More recently, Thompson recalled the signs were there, but he just didn't read them. 'The vocals at the Gov ... we didn't know that Rick was having a heart attack on stage,' he says. 'I was wondering why he was singing soft. I had the headphones on and I was listening to him sing and I knew there was something wrong. He was singing soft. The gain on the desk was overboard because all that feedback was coming from Rick's microphone. I had to bring it up. I went up to check the mic. I said, "One, two" and I got a fright. It made me jump. I was just talking the normal way I'd talk into a microphone. I had to do what I wanted with the EQ to bring it back down again.

'He was sick that day. That morning. I went to his room and I said, "You right, my brother?" "Yeah." "Well, we're downstairs waiting." And he said, "I'll come along later." Rick was still in bed when I rang his room to get him up. He came waddling along behind later on. And when we went home from the lane, because I was walking with him, I noticed he was a bit strange. I wanted to go and get a jumper and he said, "Mick, I might just go and have a lie down." He wasn't well.'

I reminded Thompson that Harrison had thumped his chest while he was speaking at the launch.

'He was getting angina. I should have caught on. I had a zipper put on me but I never caught on. He's a bugger for that. He'll play while he feels sick. He's done it a few times while we've been on tour. But that's Rick. His devotion to music, his love of music ... he'll die with a guitar in his hand.'

~

While in Adelaide, I'd been staying with another old schoolfriend, Chris, who kindly lent me a car for the evening. So that afternoon I headed up the South Eastern Freeway into the Adelaide Hills. Arriving at the Three Brothers Arms in Macclesfield, I spied Bart Willoughby out the front. 'Terrible news about Ricky,' I said. 'Yeah,' he replied. 'We think he'll be okay. I had a heart problem myself. Ten years ago. I had a bypass operation.' Willoughby was waiting for his nephew to arrive. Russell Lawrie was the replacement guitarist for the evening. 'He's never played with us before, but he knows all the songs,' he said. At that moment, a car pulled up and Lawrie got out. 'Okay, see you later,' I said, thinking, 'This should be interesting!'

Opening its doors in 1841 as the Goat's Head Inn, The Three Brothers Arms is the oldest continuously trading hotel in the Adelaide Hills. Its performing space is a covered verandah out the back with a stage at the far end. On its open side, the ground falls away to lawns and a tributary of the Angus River.

The gig was quite remarkable. After support acts Warren Milera and house combo the Black Diamond Roots Band, Bart Willoughby performed some solo numbers before Russell Lawrie joined the three remaining members on stage. The sound mix was great with drums and bass creating a confident, springy floor and as Lawrie settled into the set-up, he and the seated Les Graham started trading some jaw-dropping guitar solos, drawing whoops from the crowd. It was hard to believe Lawrie had not played, in fact, had not even rehearsed with the band before. And at times, the music reached out and touched the giddy heights of the band at their magical prime. Michael Fisher got up and sang 'The Vision', but without the rest of Ricky Harrison's songs it was a somewhat truncated set. Given the circumstances however, the crowd was both understanding and deeply appreciative.

As I took the midnight drive back to the city, the full moon was out, there was no-one else on the road and the country was silent and sparkling. I sang the opening lines of 'The Vision' to myself; 'It was a moonlit night over Lake Victoria/I saw some people standing there'. And I thought of Ricky Harrison and hoped he was okay.

~

The next day, I was able to visit Harrison at the Queen Elizabeth Hospital. Michael Fisher was already there when I arrived. Harrison was sitting up; his colour was a lot better and the three of us chatted away for ninety minutes or so. It was reassuring to see him in good spirits. I returned to Sydney the next day.

Harrison had triple bypass heart surgery on 1 April and flew home to Victoria three weeks later. He wrote from hospital, 'Thanks all my family, friends and fans for your well wishes and concern regarding my health. Looks like I've been given a second chance in life. Great surgeons and hospital staff in Adelaide made things a lot easier to endure while sick and away from home. Kura Yerlo staff in particular helped out heaps to ensure that I was okay and able to get the help I needed. Great that the band members and crew kept vigilance over me, love you guys, brothers 4 ever. Back home on Monday, have a few songs to record and finish off. Hopefully the pain will all be gone by the end of the month – or not? Really brus and sisters, the drink and smoke is not worth the pain that you will have to endure if you get caught out. It will knock you on your arse and make you suffer real pain. Don't go there. Not funny being made to feel useless, cause you can't do what you used to doing. Be strong now before it's too late. Love and power to you all.'

 LIVE PERFORMANCES (AND OTHER SIGNIFICANT EVENTS)

1979

March

> *Line-up: Bart Willoughby (drums, vocals), Les Graham (guitar, vocals), Ricky Harrison (guitar, vocals), Tony Mullett (bass), John Newchurch (vocals)*

— Point McLeay (Raukkan), SA. (*Conquest of the Ngarrindjeri* book launch)

April

14 Meyer Oval, Taperoo, SA (Aboriginal Country Music Festival)

16 Kilburn Hall, SA (Nunga Football Club social)

May

5 Port Lincoln, SA (5-11 May, Come Out Festival 1979)

12 Ceduna, SA

July

> *Line-up: Ricky Harrison (guitar, vocals), John Newchurch (vocals), Duckie Taylor (bass), Carroll Karpany (guitar), Wally McArthur (drums)*

21 Port Adelaide Town Hall (with Mr X, Raw Deal, Mickey Finn)

October

> *Line-up: Bart Willoughby (drums, vocals), Les Graham (guitar, vocals), Ricky Harrison (guitar, vocals), John John Miller (bass), Veronica Rankine (sax, vocals)*

19 Norwood Town Hall, SA (supporting The Immigrants)

November

30 SA Institute of Technology, Adelaide (Aboriginal Task Force dance)

December

16 Christmas Hills, Vic (supporting Skyhooks)

— Eltham Hall, Vic (supporting Rueben Tice)

21 Martinis, Carlton, Vic

31 Burnt Ridge Mission, Kempsey, NSW (Children's Free Embassy Teenage Roadshow, with Waldo's Wedding and Transaction)

1980

January

1 South West Rocks Surf Club, NSW (Children's Free Embassy Teenage Roadshow, with Waldo's Wedding and Transaction)

2 Crescent Head Surf Club, NSW (Children's Free Embassy Teenage Roadshow, with Waldo's Wedding and Transaction)

3 Nambucca Heads Surf Club, NSW (Children's Free Embassy Teenage Roadshow, with Waldo's Wedding and Transaction)

4 Coffs Harbour Youth Club, NSW (Children's Free Embassy Teenage Roadshow, with Waldo's Wedding and Transaction)

5 Coffs Harbour Youth Club, NSW (Children's Free Embassy Teenage Roadshow, with Waldo's Wedding and Transaction)

6 Evans Head, NSW (Children's Free Embassy Teenage Roadshow, with Waldo's Wedding and Transaction)

8 Coraki Youth Club, NSW (Children's Free Embassy Teenage Roadshow, with Waldo's Wedding and Transaction)

9 Ballina Mardi Gras, NSW (Children's Free Embassy Teenage Roadshow, with Waldo's Wedding and Transaction)

11 Ballina, NSW (Children's Free Embassy Teenage Roadshow, with Waldo's Wedding and Transaction)

17 Plaza, Canberra City (afternoon)

at last . . .

THE ADELAIDE FESTIVAL OF GRASS

with . . .
- Paul Madigan & The Humans
- Nasty Nigel and the T.H.C.
- No Fixed Address — Street Choir
Street Poets, Actors & A Circus!

FRI., MARCH 14th BURNSIDE TOWN HALL

FOOD, BAR, ETC. A BUMPER CROP

17 Parliament House, Canberra (*It's Coming Yet* ... book launch)

— Adelaide Tavern, Canberra

24 Native Rose Hotel, Chippendale, NSW

26 Mt Druitt Shopping Centre, NSW

— The Jolly Frog, Windsor, NSW

March

9 Rundle Mall, Adelaide (Rocking Nungas, Adelaide Festival of Arts, with Essie Coffey, Us Mob, Black Fire)

14 Burnside Town Hall, SA (Adelaide Festival of Grass, with Paul Madigan & The Humans, Nasty Nigel & The Teenage Hellcats)

15 Elder Park, Adelaide (Adelaide Festival of Arts)

April

3 Tivoli Hotel, Adelaide (supporting The Jumpers)

12 Richmond Hotel, Adelaide (supporting The Jumpers)

17 Scott Theatre, Adelaide College of Advanced Education (Aboriginal Secondary School Students Conference)

May

15 YWCA Hall, Adelaide (CASM concert, with Us Mob, Coloured Stone)

17 Richmond Hotel, Adelaide (with The Jumpers)

June

6 Union Hall, Latrobe Uni, Bundoora, Vic (supporting Mi-Sex and James Freud's Radio Stars)

7 Arkaba, Adelaide (supporting Taj Mahal)

18 Meningie Institute, SA (CASM Noonameena tour, with Us Mob, Coloured Stone)

20 Murray Bridge High School, SA (afternoon, CASM Noonameena tour, with Coloured Stone)

20 Murray Bridge Town Hall, SA (evening, CASM Noonameena tour, with Us Mob, Coloured Stone)

21 The Australian Cultural Association Basement, Hindmarsh, SA (with Bad Poets, The Jump)

27 Richmond Hotel, Adelaide (supporting The Jumpers)

28 Adelaide University Bar (5MMM Rock Off, semi-final)

July

11 John Barleycorn Hotel, Collingwood, Vic

13 Northcote Town Hall, Vic (Rock Against Racism with Men at Work, Lucky Dog, Cassava)

16 Central Club Hotel, Richmond, Vic

17 Martinis, Carlton, Vic

18 John Barleycorn Hotel, Collingwood, Vic

19 Universal Workshop, Fitzroy, Vic

20 Hearts, Carlton, Vic

26 Parks Community Centre, Angle Park, SA (5MMM Rock Off, final)

August

8 Hartley College of Advanced Education, Magill, SA

15 Flinders University Tavern, Bedford Park, SA (ACA Basement Riot Benefit, with The Brats, The Bad Poets and Dennis Aubrey)

— Start shooting *Wrong Side of the Road* (mid-August)

17 Tivoli Hotel, Adelaide (with The Fabulaires)

23 Festival Theatre Plaza, Adelaide (afternoon, with Redgum and Max's Case)

September

11 Tivoli Hotel, Adelaide (with Spanish Holiday)

26 Blackwood Uniting Church, SA (CASM fundraiser, with Us Mob)

30 Finish principal shooting *Wrong Side of the Road*

30 Union Hall, Adelaide Uni (supporting Daniel Viglietti)

October

17   Eureka Bar, Trades Hall, Adelaide
24   Governor Hindmarsh Hotel, Hindmarsh, SA

November

8   Point Pearce Mission, Yorke Peninsula, SA (reshoot concert scene for *Wrong Side of the Road*)

> Veronica Rankine leaves.
> Line-up: Bart Willoughby (drums, vocals), Les Graham (guitar, vocals), Ricky Harrison (guitar, vocals), John John Miller (bass)

13   John Barleycorn Hotel, Collingwood, Vic
18   Central Club Hotel, Richmond, Vic
30   Roundhouse, UNSW, Kensington, NSW (supporting Cold Chisel)

December

13   John Barleycorn Hotel, Collingwood, Vic
16   Family Village Inn, Rydalmere, NSW (supporting Cold Chisel)
17   Australian National University, Canberra
18   Woodfull Pavilion, Melbourne Showgrounds (supporting Cold Chisel)
20   Barr Smith Lawns, Adelaide University (early, supporting Cold Chisel)
20   Arkaba, Adelaide (late)

31   Thebarton Town Hall, Adelaide (5MMM New Year's Eve Party, with Young Homebuyers, Distressed Innocents and Nuvo Bloc)

1981

January

26   Sydney Town Hall (Rock Against Racism, with Us Mob, Black Lace, Un Tabu and others)

February

10   Festival Theatre, Adelaide (SA-FM Summer Search)
13   Governor Hindmarsh Hotel, Hindmarsh, SA (with The Bash)
15   Festival Theatre Amphitheatre, Adelaide (afternoon)
27   Hartley College of Advanced Education, Magill, SA (with The Units and Hurricane)
28   Alma Hotel, Norwood, SA

March

7   Alma Hotel, Norwood, SA
13   Sinatras, Hotel Performance, Adelaide
28   Adelaide University Bar (with The Blessed)

April

3   Governor Hindmarsh Hotel, Hindmarsh, SA (with The Hawks)
4   Alma Hotel, Norwood, SA
11   Alma Hotel, Norwood, SA (with Hard Times)

16   Findon Hotel, SA (with
      The Dukes, The Innocents,
      Session)
18   Shandon Hotel, Seaton, SA
      (with Swanee, Mickey Finn
      and The Others)
19   Port Elliot Football Oval, SA
      (with Vertical Hold, Lounge
      Lizards)
23   Festival Theatre, Adelaide
      (Royal Charity Concert)

May
1   Dallas Brooks Hall, Melbourne
      (supporting Redgum, Margret
      RoadKnight)
8   Central Club Hotel, Richmond,
      Vic (supporting Redgum)
9   Sentimental Bloke Hotel,
      Bulleen, Vic (supporting
      Redgum)
10   Ferntree Gully Hotel, Vic
      (supporting Redgum)
13   Jam Factory, Canberra
22   Alma Hotel, Norwood, SA
29   Sinatras, Hotel Performance,
      Adelaide

June
6   Alma Hotel, Norwood, SA
13   Alma Hotel, Norwood, SA
27   Alma Hotel, Norwood, SA

July
3   Jam Factory, Canberra
16   Jam Factory, Canberra
18   Adelaide University Bar (with
      Hard Times, The Kuckles)

August
1   Mona Vale Hotel, NSW
6   Enfield Boulevard Hotel, NSW

8   San Miguel, Cammeray, NSW
12   Sydney Trade Union Club,
      Surry Hills (with Ward 13)
13   Enfield Boulevard, NSW
14   Comb and Cutter Hotel,
      Blacktown, NSW
15   Manzil Room, Kings Cross,
      NSW
16   San Miguel, Cammeray, NSW
18   Astra Hotel, Bondi, NSW
19   Sydney Trade Union Club,
      Surry Hills
20   Enfield Boulevard, NSW
21   Selinas, Coogee Bay Hotel,
      NSW (supporting The
      Bushwackers)
22   Clifton Hotel, Redfern, NSW
      (afternoon)
22   San Miguel, Cammeray, NSW
23   Paddington Town Hall, NSW
      (supporting The Bushwackers)
27   Enfield Boulevard, NSW
29   Clifton Hotel, Redfern, NSW
      (afternoon)

29   Sonia's, Leichhardt Hotel, NSW

September

16   Regent Theatre, Sydney (AFI Awards)

October

2   Tanelorn Festival, Gloucester, NSW

15   Entertainers Club, Redfern, NSW

20   Trak Cinema, *Wrong Side of the Road*, Adelaide premiere

22   Sinatras, Hotel Performance, Adelaide

23   Governor Hindmarsh, Hindmarsh, SA (with Paramours)

30   Governor Hindmarsh, Hindmarsh, SA (with Paramours and Acrylic Chewies)

30   Sydney Opera House Cinema, *Wrong Side of the Road*, Sydney premiere

November

2   Prince of Wales Hotel, St Kilda, Vic (3PBS live to air)

5   Central Club Hotel, Richmond, Vic

6   Longford Cinema, *Wrong Side of the Road*, Melbourne preview

6   Catherina Cabaret, Barkley Street, St Kilda, Vic

7   John Barleycorn Hotel, Collingwood, Vic

9   Wrong Side of the Road album released

12   Central Club Hotel, Richmond, Vic

13   Longford Cinema, *Wrong Side of the Road*, Melbourne premiere

13   Catherina Cabaret, Barkley Street, St Kilda, Vic

14   John Barleycorn Hotel, Collingwood, Vic

19   Central Club Hotel, Richmond, Vic

21   Civic Hotel, Canberra (with Stray Dags)

22   Sydney Town Hall (Rock Against Racism, with Us Mob, Un Tabu, King Cobra)

28   Tin Sheds, Darlington, NSW (with Ratbags of Rhythm)

December

> *John John Miller leaves. Joe Hayes, Billy Inda Cummins and Joe Geia join.*
> *Line-up: Bart Willoughby (drums, vocals), Les Graham (guitar, vocals), Ricky Harrison (guitar, vocals), Joe Hayes (bass), Billy Inda Cummins (percussion), Joe Geia (percussion, didgeridoo, vocals)*

9   Morelands Hotel, Brunswick, Vic
10 Festival Hall, Melbourne (supporting Ian Dury & The Blockheads)

1982

February

6   Overlander, Shepparton, Vic
10 Manzil Room, Kings Cross, NSW
11 Capitol Theatre, Sydney (supporting The Clash)
12 Tivoli, Sydney (with Men at Work, The Particles)
13 Selinas, Coogee Bay Hotel, NSW (with Un Tabu, King Cobra)
14 Capitol Theatre, Sydney (supporting The Clash)
15 San Miguel, Cammeray, NSW
17 Gippsland Institute of Advanced Education, Vic
19 Morelands Hotel, Brunswick, Vic
20 Central Club Hotel, Richmond, Vic
25 Bridge Hotel, Mordialloc, Vic

27 Central Club Hotel, Richmond, Vic

March

Recording *From My Eyes* mini-album
20 Alma Hotel, Norwood, SA
21 Elder Park, Adelaide (afternoon, with Us Mob)
25 Albany, WA
26 Commercial Hotel, Busselton, WA
27 Commercial Hotel, Busselton, WA
28 Commercial Hotel, Busselton, WA (afternoon)
29 Embassy Ballroom, Perth (supporting Cold Chisel, early)
29 Stoned Crow, North Fremantle, WA (late)
31 Geraldton, WA

April

2   WA Institute of Technology, Bentley, WA (early)
2   Blazes, Perth (late)
3   Stoned Crow, North Fremantle, WA
4   Lake Gnangara, WA
5   Herdsman Hotel, Perth
6   Perth Institute of Film & TV, Fremantle (Perth premiere *Wrong Side of the Road* followed by performance)
7   WA Institute of Technology, Bentley, WA (lunchtime)
7   Shaftesbury Hotel, Northbridge, WA
8   Murdoch University, Perth
8   Cleo's, Perth
10 Railway Hotel, Kalgoorlie, WA
11 Railway Hotel, Kalgoorlie, WA

13   Norseman, WA, truck crash
15   Federal Sporting Club, Alice
     Springs, NT
17   Traeger Park Oval, Alice
     Springs, NT (CAAMA concert)
21   Bendigo College of Advanced
     Education, Vic
22   Prospect Hill Hotel, Kew, Vic
23   Sandringham Commodore
     Hotel, Vic

*Joe Hayes leaves. Duckie Taylor
joins.*
*Line-up: Bart Willoughby (drums,
vocals), Les Graham (guitar,
vocals), Ricky Harrison (guitar,
vocals), Duckie Taylor (bass), Billy
Inda Cummins (percussion), Joe
Geia (percussion, didgeridoo,
vocals)*

24   Pier Hotel, Frankston, Vic
29   Ballarat College of Advanced
     Education, Vic
30   Ferntree Gully Hotel, Vic

May
1   Central Club Hotel,
     Richmond, Vic (early)
1   The Venue, St Kilda, Vic (late)
5   Burwood State College, Vic
6   Monash University, Clayton,
     Vic
7   Eureka Hotel, Geelong, Vic
8   Central Club Hotel,
     Richmond, Vic
11   Da Gamas, Carlton, Vic
12   Sandringham Commodore
     Hotel, Vic
13   Aberdeen Hotel, Fitzroy, Vic
14   Lower Plenty Hotel, Vic
15   Central Club Hotel,
     Richmond, Vic

21   The Venue, St Kilda, Vic (No
     Fixed Address benefit concert,
     with Men at Work, Goanna,
     Young Homebuyers)
27   Gatton Civic Centre, Qld
28   Campus Club, Queensland
     Institute of Technology,
     Brisbane
29   Griffith University, Nathan,
     Qld
30   Playroom, Palm Beach, Gold
     Coast, Qld

June
1   Schonell Theatre, University
     of Queensland, Brisbane
     (lunchtime and evening with
     Queensland premiere of
     Wrong Side of the Road)
2   Schonell Theatre, University
     of Queensland, Brisbane (with
     Wrong Side of the Road)
3   Newmarket Hall, Brisbane
     (Murri community benefit)
4   University of Queensland
     Refectory, Brisbane (4ZZZ
     Joint Effort, with The Dugites,
     Missing Words)
5   Souths Leagues, West
     End, Qld (with The Black
     Assassins, 3B2)
8   Manzil Room, Kings Cross,
     NSW
9   University of Sydney
10   Orana Hotel, Blacksmiths,
     NSW
11   Southdown, NSW
12   Selinas, Coogee Bay Hotel,
     NSW
13   Sonia's, Leichhardt Hotel,
     NSW (early)

13   Governor's Pleasure, Sydney
     (late)
15   Civic Hotel, Canberra
19   Central Club Hotel, Richmond,
     Vic
24   Aberdeen Hotel, Fitzroy, Vic
25   Da Gamas, Carlton, Vic
26   Albion Hotel, North
     Melbourne
28   Hilton Hotel, Melbourne,
     From My Eyes launched by
     Bob Hawke
30   University of Adelaide

July
1   University of Adelaide
2   Hartley College of Advanced
     Education, Magill, SA
3   Alma Hotel, Norwood, SA
4   Adelaide (Rock Against
     Racism concert)
8   Unley High School, SA
9   Otherway Centre, Adelaide
     (Nunga benefit)
10   Alma Hotel, Norwood, SA
11   Governor Hindmarsh Hotel,
     Hindmarsh, SA
14   Lady Bay Hotel, Warrnambool,
     Vic (with Tinsley Waterhouse
     Band)
15   Prospect Hill Hotel, Kew, Vic
16   Countdown, ABC TV, 'From
     My Eyes' (pre-record,
     broadcast Sunday, 18 July)
16   Macy's, Her Majesty's Hotel,
     South Yarra, Vic (with Kevins)
17   Sandringham Commodore
     Hotel, Vic
17   The Venue, St Kilda, Vic (with
     Nicest People, Flying Colours)
23   Modbury Hotel, SA

24   Adelaide University Bar (with
     Speedboat)
30   Italo/Australia Club, Canberra
     (Koori benefit)
31   Hotel Civic, Canberra

August
1   Players, Paddington Green
     Hotel, Paddington, NSW
3   Bondi Tram, NSW
4   San Miguel, Cammeray, NSW
5   Illinois Hotel, Five Dock, NSW
6   Stardust Hotel, Cabramatta,
     NSW
7   Orana Hotel, Newcastle, NSW
8   Rozelle Hotel, NSW
9   Tollgate Hotel, Parramatta,
     NSW
11   Prospect Hill Hotel, Kew, Vic
12   Aberdeen Hotel, Fitzroy, Vic
13   Swinburne Institute of
     Technology, Hawthorn, Vic
13   Chisholm Institute of
     Technology, Frankston, Vic
14   Eureka Hotel, Geelong, Vic
17   Jump Club, Collingwood, Vic
18   Centre Club Hotel, Morwell,
     Vic
19   Aberdeen Hotel, Fitzroy, Vic
20   Fawkner Technical School, Vic
20   The Venue, St Kilda, Vic
21   Sandringham Commodore
     Hotel, Vic

September
1   The Venue, St Kilda, Vic
     (Reggae One Love with Randy
     and The Roots, King Cobra)
2   Aberdeen Hotel, Fitzroy, Vic
3   Prospect Hill Hotel, Kew, Vic
4   Sentimental Bloke Hotel,
     Bulleen, Vic

5   Waterloo Cup Hotel, Moonee Ponds, Vic
8   Players, Paddington Green Hotel, Paddington, NSW
9   Astra Hotel, Bondi, NSW
10 San Miguel, Cammeray, NSW
10 Selinas, Coogee Bay Hotel, NSW
11 Stakeout Tavern, Canberra
14 Bondi Tram, NSW
15 Sydney Trade Union Club, Surry Hills (with King Cobra)
16 Sonia's, Leichhardt Hotel, NSW
17 Astra Hotel, Bondi Beach, NSW
18 Musicians Club, Sydney
21 Royal Hotel, Taree, NSW
22 Homestead Hotel, Brisbane
23 Campus Club, Queensland Institute of Technology, Brisbane
23 Darling Downs Institute of Advanced Education, Toowoomba, Qld
24 Playroom, Palm Beach, Gold Coast, Qld
25 South's Oval, West End, Brisbane (Rock Against Racism, with Redgum, Hunters & Collectors, Mantake, Bapu Mamoos, Screaming Tribesmen)
25 Crossroads, Brisbane
26 Jet Club, Coolangatta, Qld
28 Players, Paddington Green Hotel, Paddington, NSW

October
1   San Miguel, Cammeray, NSW
2   Bayview Tavern, Gladesville, NSW (with The Magnetics)

3   Port Macquarie Town Hall, NSW
6   Surfair Hotel, Marcoola, Sunshine Coast, Qld (supporting Cold Chisel)
7   Playroom, Palm Beach, Gold Coast, Qld
8   Her Majesty's Theatre, Brisbane (supporting Cold Chisel at The Black and White Parity Ball)
8   Playroom, Palm Beach, Gold Coast, Qld
9   Her Majesty's Theatre, Brisbane (supporting Cold Chisel at The Black and White Parity Ball)
9   Prince Alfred Hotel, Ipswich, Qld
10 New York Hotel, Brisbane (4ZZZ gig)
12 Doyalson RSL, NSW

*Billy Inda Cummins leaves. Joe Geia misses next four gigs.
Line-up: Bart Willoughby (drums, vocals), Ricky Harrison (guitar, vocals), Les Graham (guitar, vocals), Duckie Taylor (bass)*

13 Stakeout Tavern, Canberra
14 Riverina College of Advanced Education, Wagga Wagga, NSW
15 Mildura Town Hall, Vic (Koori dance)
16 Swan Hill Town Hall, Vic (Koori dance)

Joe Geia returns.

Line-up: Bart Willoughby (drums, vocals), Ricky Harrison (guitar, vocals), Les Graham (guitar, vocals), Duckie Taylor (bass), Joe Geia (percussion, didgeridoo, vocals)

20 Billboard, Melbourne (with Jo Jo Zep)
21 Prospect Hill Hotel, Kew, Vic
22 Aberdeen Hotel, Fitzroy, Vic
23 Pacific Hotel, Lorne, Vic
27 Westernport Hotel, San Remo, Vic
28 Prospect Hill Hotel, Kew, Vic
29 Aberdeen Hotel, Fitzroy, Vic
30 Ballarat Town Hall, Vic (Koori dance)
31 Waterloo Cup Hotel. Moonee Ponds, Vic

November

1   The Venue, St Kilda, Vic
4   Eureka Hotel, Geelong, Vic
5   Mt Gambier Football Club, SA
6   Civic & Arts Centre, Millicent, SA
13 Tattersalls Hotel, Warrnambool, Vic
17 Aberdeen Hotel, Fitzroy, Vic
18 Welshpool Hotel, Welshpool, Vic
19 Stockade Hotel, Carlton, Vic
20 Pacific Hotel, Lorne, Vic
24 Aberdeen Hotel, Fitzroy, Vic

Nicky Moffatt joins. In a period of transition, both he and Duckie Taylor play part of the set

Line-up: Bart Willoughby (drums, vocals), Ricky Harrison (guitar, vocals), Les Graham (guitar, vocals), Duckie Taylor and Nicky Moffatt (bass, vocals), Joe Geia (percussion, didgeridoo, vocals)

25 Centre Club Hotel, Morwell,
    Vic
26 Eureka Hotel, Geelong, Vic
27 Chapel St Festival, South
    Yarra, Vic (afternoon)
27 Prospect Hill Hotel, Kew, Vic
    (evening)

> *Duckie Taylor leaves.*
> *Line-up: Bart Willoughby (drums,*
> *vocals), Ricky Harrison (guitar,*
> *vocals), Les Graham (guitar,*
> *vocals), Nicky Moffatt (bass,*
> *vocals), Joe Geia (percussion,*
> *didgeridoo, vocals)*

December

1   Lady Bay Hotel, Warrnambool,
    Vic
2   Prospect Hill Hotel, Kew, Vic
3   Aberdeen Hotel, Fitzroy, Vic
    (with No Nonsense)
4   Armadale Hotel, Vic (with
    Short Story)
5   Gippsland Institute of
    Technology, Churchill, Vic
    (Koori benefit)
9   Prospect Hill Hotel, Kew, Vic
10 The Venue, St Kilda, Vic
11 Eureka Hotel, Geelong, Vic
15 Le Tote, Ivanhoe Hotel,
    Collingwood, Vic (with
    Scarlet)
16 Aberdeen Hotel, Fitzroy, Vic
17 The Venue, St Kilda, Vic (with
    Randy & the Roots, Mataqali
    Music)
19 Northcote Town Hall, Vic
    (Rock Against Racism)
22 Westernport Hotel, San Remo,
    Vic

23 Aberdeen Hotel, Fitzroy, Vic
24 Eureka Hotel, Geelong, Vic

1983

January

2   Pacific Hotel, Lorne, Vic
5   Aberdeen Hotel, Fitzroy, Vic
6   Billboard, Melbourne (with
    The Orphans)
7   Central Club Hotel, Richmond,
    Vic
8   Tattersalls, Warrnambool, Vic
9   Pacific Hotel, Lorne, Vic
12 Prospect Hill Hotel, Kew, Vic
    (with Do Be Do)
13 Council Club Hotel,
    Richmond, Vic (supporting
    Goanna)
14 Foundry Arms Hotel, Bendigo,
    Vic
15 Manhattan Hotel, Ringwood,
    Vic (supporting Goanna)
16 Waltzing Matilda Hotel,
    Springvale, Vic (supporting
    Goanna)
19 Stockade Hotel, Carlton, Vic
20 Centre Club Hotel, Morwell,
    Vic
21 Westernport Hotel, San Remo,
    Vic
22 Armadale Hotel, Vic (with
    Scarlet)
23 Pacific Hotel, Lorne, Vic
26 Melbourne Concert Hall
    (Australia Day/Invasion Day
    concert)

> *Nicky Moffatt leaves, Duckie Taylor rejoins*
> *Line-up: Bart Willoughby (drums, vocals), Ricky Harrison (guitar, vocals), Les Graham (guitar, vocals), Duckie Taylor (bass), Joe Geia (percussion, didgeridoo, vocals)*

28 Stakeout Tavern, Canberra (with Russian Roulettes)

29 Bexley North Hotel, NSW (early)

29 Tivoli, Sydney (late, with Johnny Guitar)

31 Narara Festival, Somersby, NSW

February

1 Wingham Town Hall, NSW (with Robert Meaton)

3 Campus Club, Queensland Institute of Technology, Brisbane (lunchtime)

3 Cleveland Sands Hotel, Qld

> *Les Graham leaves.*
> *Line-up: Bart Willoughby (drums, vocals), Ricky Harrison (guitar, vocals), Duckie Taylor (bass), Joe Geia (percussion, didgeridoo, vocals)*

4 Grand Hotel, Brisbane

5 Surfair Hotel, Marcoola, Sunshine Coast, Qld

> *Peter Meredith joins.*
> *Line-up: Bart Willoughby (drums, vocals), Ricky Harrison (guitar, vocals), Duckie Taylor (bass), Peter Meredith (guitar), Joe Geia (percussion, didgeridoo, vocals)*

6 New York Hotel, Brisbane

> *Billy Gorham joins. In a period of transition, both he and Duckie Taylor play part of the set.*
> *Line-up: Bart Willoughby (drums, vocals), Ricky Harrison (guitar, vocals), Peter Meredith (guitar), Billy Gorham and Duckie Taylor (bass), Joe Geia (percussion, didgeridoo, vocals)*

8 Star Hotel, Wauchope, NSW

9 Little Plains Hall, Elains, NSW

10 Tivoli, Sydney (early, supporting Turnaround)

10 Royal Antler, Narrabeen, NSW (late)

> *Duckie Taylor leaves.*
> *Line-up: Bart Willoughby (drums, vocals), Ricky Harrison (guitar, vocals), Peter Meredith (guitar), Billy Gorham (bass), Joe Geia (percussion, didgeridoo, vocals)*

11 Manzil Room, Kings Cross, NSW

12 Family Inn, Rydalmere, NSW

13 Narrabundah Oval, Canberra (Rock Against Racism, with Wailing Cockatoos and Bush Fire)

16 Foundry Arms, Bendigo, Vic

17 Waurn Ponds Hotel, Vic

18 Swinburne Institute of Technology, Hawthorn, Vic (lunchtime)

18 Westernport Hotel, San Remo, Vic

19 Billboard, Melbourne

20 Prospect Hill Hotel, Kew, Vic (supporting Renee Geyer)

22 Footscray Institute of Technology, Vic (afternoon, with Scarlet)

23 Gippsland Institute of Technology, Churchill, Vic (with Exposay)

24 Bendigo College of Advanced Education, Vic (with Dark Side)

25 Rusden State College, Monash University, Clayton, Vic (lunchtime)

25 Ferntree Gully Hotel, Vic

26 Central Club Hotel, Richmond, Vic

March

3 Ballarat College of Advanced Education, Vic (with Psycho Sloth)

4 Monash Uni, Vic

4 Alexandra Gardens, Melbourne (Moomba Festival, with Phantom Band, Liquid Engineers and the Routinos)

5 Prospect Hill Hotel, Kew, Vic (with General Public)

6 Pier Hotel, Frankston, Vic (with Iration)

7 Chisholm Institute of Technology, Caulfield, Vic (lunchtime)

8 Deakin University, Geelong, Vic

9 Aberdeen Hotel, Fitzroy, Vic

10 Aboriginal Advancement League, Thornbury, Vic (Koori benefit, with Hard Times)

11 Foundry Arms Hotel, Bendigo, Vic

12 Armadale Hotel, Vic (with Short Story)

13 Macy's, Her Majesty's Hotel, South Yarra, Vic (with Scarlet)

14 Club Chevron, Melbourne (with Exposay)

16 Aberdeen Hotel, Fitzroy, Vic

18 Thebarton Theatre, Adelaide (early, supporting Peter Tosh)

18 Stagedoor Tavern, Shandon Hotel, Seaton, SA (late)

19 Eureka Hotel, Geelong, Vic

21 Manzil Room, Kings Cross, NSW

23 Carmen's, Miranda Hotel, NSW

24 Royal Antler, Narrabeen, NSW (with Big Five)

25 Musicians Club, Sydney (with Chris Bailey and The Noise)

26 Sonia's, Leichhardt Hotel, NSW (early)

26 Sylvania Hotel, NSW (late, with Beat Detectives)

27 Domain, Sydney (People for Nuclear Disarmament concert)

28 Manzil Room, Kings Cross, NSW

30 Capitol Theatre, Sydney (supporting Peter Tosh)

31 Players, Paddington Green Hotel, Paddington, NSW

April

1 Stakeout Tavern, Canberra

2 Manly Vale Hotel, NSW (supporting Sunnyboys)

Peter Meredith leaves on 3 April, Joe Geia leaves on 6 April.
Line-up: Bart Willoughby (drums, vocals), Ricky Harrison (guitar, vocals), Billy Gorham (bass)

6   Library Lawn, UNSW,
     Kensington, NSW (afternoon)
8   Governor's Pleasure, Sydney
     (with Big Five)
9   Manly Vale Hotel, NSW (with
     Celibate Rifles, Iced Vovos)
9   Goldstein College, University
     of NSW, Kensington (late,
     supporting Young Lions,
     Turnaround, Benghazi)
13   Ambassador Nightclub,
     Newcastle, NSW
14   Illinois Hotel, Five Dock, NSW
15   Blue Gum, Waitara, NSW
     (early supporting Little
     Heroes)
15   Mosman Hotel, NSW (with
     The Gallery)
16   Manzil Room, Kings Cross,
     NSW
18   Dee Why Hotel, NSW
19   Star Hotel, Wauchope, NSW
20   New Royal Tavern, Kempsey,
     NSW
21   The Poplars, Taree, NSW
22   Bellingen Hall, NSW (with
     Struth)
23   Locomotive Hotel, Tamworth,
     NSW
24   Wingham Brush Concert,
     NSW
27   Foundry Arms Hotel, Bendigo,
     Vic
28   Bridge Hotel, Mordialloc, Vic
     (with Iration)
29   Eureka Hotel, Geelong, Vic
     (with Zeroes)
30   Armadale Hotel, Vic (early,
     with An Affair)
30   Billboard, Melbourne (late,
     with The Giants)

May

1   Macy's, Her Majesty's Hotel,
     South Yarra, Vic
6   Prospect Hill Hotel, Kew, Vic
     (with Cyril B. Bunter Band)
7   Central Club Hotel, Richmond,
     Vic
12   Melbourne University
     (lunchtime with Pilot
     Bombadere)
13   The Venue, St Kilda, Vic (with
     Exploding Cats and Randy
     and the Roots)
13   Billboard, Melbourne (with As
     You Like It)
14   Chelsea Hotel, Chelsea, Vic
     (with The Bosch)
18   Village Green Hotel, Glen
     Waverley, Vic
19   Eureka Hotel, Geelong, Vic
20   Central Club Hotel, Richmond,
     Vic (with Scarlet)
21   Melbourne Town Hall
     (supporting Dynamic
     Hepnotics)
25   Caesars Palace, Ipswich, Qld
26   Cleveland Sands Hotel, Qld
27   Grand Hotel, Labrador, Gold
     Coast, Qld
28   Surfair Hotel, Marcoola,
     Sunshine Coast, Qld
29   National Hotel, Brisbane (with
     The Conflict)

*Billy Inda Cummins rejoins.
Line-up: Bart Willoughby (drums,
vocals), Ricky Harrison (guitar,
vocals), Billy Gorham (bass), Billy
Inda Cummins (percussion)*

31   Manzil Room, Kings Cross,
     NSW

June

1 Tivoli, Sydney (with The Cuckoos)

2 Illinois Hotel, Five Dock, NSW

3 Governor's Pleasure, Sydney (with Chris Bailey)

4 Comb and Cutter Hotel, Blacktown, NSW (with Iced Vovos)

5 Sonia's, Leichhardt Hotel, NSW

6 Dee Why Hotel, NSW

7 Manzil Room, Kings Cross, NSW

8 Tivoli, Sydney (with Iced Vovos)

9 Hotel Manly, NSW (with Electric Pandas)

11 Blondies, Rockdale, NSW (with Chris Bailey)

12 San Miguel, Cammeray, NSW

14 Chisholm Institute of Technology, Caulfield, Vic

> *Billy Gorham leaves. Nicky Moffatt joins.*
> *Line-up: Bart Willoughby (drums, vocals), Ricky Harrison (guitar, vocals), Nicky Moffatt (bass, vocals), Billy Inda Cummins (percussion)*

16 Cross Keys Hotel, North Essendon, Vic

17 Pier Hotel, Frankston, Vic (with Eye to Eye)

18 Armadale Hotel, Vic (with Liquid Engineers)

21 Village Green Hotel, Glen Waverley, Vic

> *Louis McManus joins.*
> *Line-up: Bart Willoughby (drums, vocals), Ricky Harrison (guitar, vocals), Nicky Moffatt (bass, vocals), Louis McManus (guitar), Billy Inda Cummins (percussion)*

22 Club Chevron, Melbourne

24 Central Club Hotel, Richmond, Vic (supporting Phil Manning Band)

25 Eureka Hotel, Geelong, Vic

26 Lucknow Hall, Bairnsdale, Vic (Koori benefit)

July

7 Cross Keys Hotel, North Essendon, Vic

8 San Remo Ballroom, Carlton, Vic (early, NAIDOC Ball)

8 Armadale Hotel, Vic (late, with Exploding Cats)

9 Eureka Hotel, Geelong, Vic

16 Chelsea Hotel, Melbourne

17 Macy's, Her Majesty's Hotel, South Yarra, Vic

21 Centre Club Hotel, Morwell, Vic

22 Bombay Rock, Brunswick, Vic (with Eye to Eye and Liquid Engineers)

23 Pier Hotel, Frankston, Vic (supporting INXS)

28 Monash University, Clayton, Vic (with Afrojah and Exilio 73)

August

4 Latrobe Uni, Bundoora, Vic (with Tinsley Waterhouse Band and No Nonsense)

5 Prospect Hill Hotel, Kew, Vic (with E.Q.)

6   Cross Keys Hotel, North Essendon, Vic (with The Exports)

12 Prospect Hill Hotel, Kew, Vic (with Changing Names)

13 Eureka Hotel, Geelong, Vic (with The Exports)

18 Aboriginal Advancement League, Thornbury, Vic (Koori benefit, with Hard Times)

19 Swinburne Institute of Technology, Hawthorn, Vic (lunchtime)

20 Armadale Hotel, Vic (early)

Billy Inda Cummins leaves. Line-up: Bart Willoughby (drums, vocals), Ricky Harrison (guitar, vocals), Nicky Moffatt (bass, vocals), Louis McManus (guitar)

24 Central Gippsland Aboriginal Co-op, Morwell, Vic

30 Prospect Hill Hotel, Kew, Vic (with The Ordinary Men)

31 Club Chevron, Melbourne (with Racket)

September

1   Armadale Hotel, Vic

2   Bombay Rock, Brunswick, Vic (with Metro Jets and No Nonsense)

3   Sandown Park Hotel, Noble Park, Vic (early, with Tour de Force and Racket)

3   Billboard, Melbourne (late, with Gimix)

7   Club Chevron, Melbourne (Survival Reggae Club)

10 Manzil Room, Kings Cross, NSW (late, with The Cuckoos)

11 Avalon Beach RSL, NSW (with
    The Rubes)
13 Wollongong University, NSW
    (lunchtime)
14 Cronulla Workers Club, NSW
    (early, supporting Dynamic
    Hepnotics)
14 Hotel Bondi, NSW (late, with
    Innocent Butlers)
15 Illinois Hotel, Five Dock, NSW
    (early)
15 Tivoli, Sydney (late, with Iced
    Vovos)
16 Sydney Entertainment Centre
    (early, supporting Midnight
    Oil)
16 Blacktown Soccer Club, NSW
    (late)
17 Hotel Manly, NSW (with
    Forever 15)
23 The Venue, St Kilda, Vic
    (with Rupert B Band, Tinsley
    Waterhouse, and Randy and
    Jah Roots)
24 Pacific Hotel, Lorne, Vic
25 Pier Hotel, Frankston, Vic
    (with Allniters, Mother Goose)
28 Westernport Hotel, San Remo,
    Vic
29 Dandenong College of
    Technical and Further
    Education, Vic (lunchtime)
29 Cross Keys Hotel, North
    Essendon, Vic (late)
30 South Mount Gambier
    Football Club, SA

October

1   Mildura Aboriginal Co-op, Vic
5   Prospect Hill Hotel, Kew, Vic
    (with Ordinary Men)

8   Duke of Edinburgh Hotel, St
    Kilda, Vic
12 Palais Theatre, Melbourne
    (supporting Goanna)
14 Eureka Hotel, Geelong, Vic
15 Sandown Park Hotel, Noble
    Park, Vic (with Tony Catz
    Band)
18 Bulga Hall, Elands, NSW
19 Exchange Hotel, Taree, NSW
20 Kempsey Bowling Club, NSW
21 Windsor Catholic Hall,
    Brisbane
22 National Hotel, Brisbane (with
    Conflict)
23 Nambour Showgrounds, Qld
    (4ZZZ concert)
24 Bush Factory, Nimbin, NSW
25 Lobster Pot, Ballina, NSW
26 Lismore Workers Club, NSW
    (supporting Goanna)
27 Laurieton Hotel, NSW
28 Thora Hotel, Bellingen, NSW
29 Scotts Head Bowling Club,
    NSW
30 Taree Showgrounds, NSW
    (afternoon)

November

1   Paddington Town Hall, NSW
    (Independent Music Expo,
    with Warumpi Band and
    Murri Jama Performers)
2   Clifton Hotel, Redfern, NSW
    (with Warumpi Band)
3   Doyalson RSL, NSW
    (supporting Goanna)
4   Royals Rugby Club, Canberra
    (supporting Goanna)
5   Goulburn Valley Hotel,
    Shepparton, Vic (supporting
    Goanna)

6   Ballarat City Hall, Vic
     (supporting Goanna)
7   Horsham Town Hall, Vic
     (supporting Goanna)
8   Oasis Hotel, Swan Hill, Vic
     (supporting Goanna)
9   Rich River Golf Club, Moama,
     Vic (supporting Goanna)
10   Albury Cinema Centre, NSW
     (supporting Goanna)
11   Wangaratta Town Hall, Vic
     (supporting Goanna)
23   Warrnambool Institute, Vic
     (with The Reds and Southern
     Junction)
24   Miners Rest Hotel,
     Wonthaggi, Vic (supporting
     Goanna)
26   Duke of Edinburgh Hotel, St
     Kilda, Vic
27   Dorset Gardens Hotel,
     Croydon, Vic (supporting
     Goanna)

December
2   Prospect Hill Hotel, Kew, Vic
3   Caledonian Hotel, Wonthaggi,
     Vic

1984

January

> *Louis McManus leaves.*
> *Line-up: Bart Willoughby (drums,*
> *vocals), Ricky Harrison (guitar,*
> *vocals), Nicky Moffatt (bass,*
> *vocals, vocals)*

11   Rockhampton Rugby Leagues
     Club, Qld (with Big Five)
12   Emeos Hotel, Mackay, Qld
     (with Big Five)

13   Criterion Hotel, Townsville,
     Qld (with Big Five)
14   Victoria Hotel, Ingham, Qld
     (with Big Five)
15   Kuranda Amphitheatre, Qld
     (with Big Five)
16   Great Northern Hotel, Cairns,
     Qld (with Big Five)
17   Great Northern Hotel, Cairns,
     Qld (with Big Five)
18   Criterion Hotel, Townsville,
     Qld (with Big Five)
19   Airlie Beach Hotel, Qld (with
     Big Five)
20   Prince of Wales Hotel,
     Mackay, Qld (with Big Five)
21   Prince of Wales Hotel,
     Mackay, Qld (with Big Five)
22   Rockhampton Rugby Leagues
     Club, Qld (with Big Five)

February

> *Louis McManus rejoins.*
> *Line-up: Bart Willoughby (drums,*
> *vocals), Ricky Harrison (guitar,*
> *vocals), Nicky Moffatt (bass,*
> *vocals), Louis McManus (guitar)*

3   Miner's Rest Hotel,
     Wonthaggi, Vic
4   Duke of Edinburgh Hotel, St
     Kilda, Vic
8   Prospect Hill Hotel, Kew, Vic
     (with Gothic Farmyard)
9   Eureka Hotel, Geelong, Vic
10   Pinky's Nightspot, Golden
     Valley Hotel, Shepparton, Vic
     (with AK 47)
11   Pacific Hotel, Lorne, Vic
15   Westernport Hotel, San Remo,
     Vic

16 Centre Club Hotel, Morwell,
Vic

17 London Tavern, Caulfield, Vic
(with Dirty Rats)

23 Philip Institute of Technology,
Bundoora, Vic

24 Ritchie's Nite Spot, Preston,
Vic (with Tinsley Waterhouse)

25 Duke of Edinburgh Hotel, St
Kilda, Vic

> *Louis McManus leaves.*
> *Line-up: Bart Willoughby (drums,*
> *vocals), Ricky Harrison (guitar,*
> *vocals), Nicky Moffatt (bass,*
> *vocals)*

29 Melbourne University
(afternoon, with Rhythmatics,
Shane Bourne)

March

1 Swinburne Institute of
Technology, Hawthorn, Vic
(lunchtime, with Spaniards)

2 Village Green Hotel, Glen
Waverley, Vic

3 Alexandra Gardens,
Melbourne (Moomba folk
stage, early)

3 Duke of Edinburgh Hotel, St
Kilda, Vic (late)

7 RMIT, Melbourne (lunchtime)

7 Westernport Hotel, San Remo,
Vic

8 Latrobe Uni, Bundoora, Vic
(lunchtime)

9 Parkview Hotel, North Fitzroy,
Vic

10 Alexandra Gardens,
Melbourne (Moomba folk
stage)

11 Alexandra Gardens,
Melbourne (Moomba
rock stage, with Dynamic
Hepnotics)

13 Manzil Room, Kings Cross,
NSW

14 Mitchell College of Advanced
Education, Bathurst, NSW
(with Total Fire Band and
Stormy Monday)

15 Mosman Hotel, NSW

16 Selinas, Coogee Bay Hotel,
NSW (with Mataqali Music,
Man Friday)

17 Sydney Trade Union Club,
Surry Hills (early, with
Laughing Clowns, The Triffids
and These Cars Collide)

17 Carmen's, Miranda Hotel,
NSW (late, with Blues
Brothers Revival and The
Hurt)

18 Sonia's, Leichhardt Hotel,
NSW

20 Bobin School of Arts Hall,
NSW

21 Laurieton Hotel, NSW

22 Kempsey Bowling Club, NSW

23 Bush Factory, Nimbin, NSW

24 Southern Suburbs Rugby
League Football Club, Ipswich,
Qld (outdoor concert, with
Kashmir, Mop and the
Dropouts)

25 Moree Town Hall, NSW
(Moree Police Boys Club
concert)

30 Collingwood Town Hall,
Vic (Koorie College Health
Workers benefit)

31 Duke of Edinburgh Hotel, St
Kilda, Vic

April

10 Prospect Hill Hotel, Kew, Vic (with Assassins)

13 Troubadour, Canberra

14 Troubadour, Canberra

17 Ballarat College of Advanced Education, Ballarat, Vic (with Sole Twisters)

18 Melbourne State College, Carlton, Vic (lunchtime)

19 Central Club Hotel, Richmond, Vic

21 Pacific Hotel, Lorne, Vic

24 Prospect Hill Hotel, Kew, Vic (with Suburban Prowl)

27 Eureka Hotel, Geelong, Vic

28 Duke of Edinburgh Hotel, St Kilda, Vic

May

3 Newcastle Workers Club, NSW (with Shadow Play and Vulgar Beatmen)

4 Wentworth Building, University of Sydney (with Nya Nunga, Conway's Carnival and Vulgar Beatmen)

5 The Chevron, Potts Point, NSW (with Syrens and Vulgar Beatmen)

6 San Miguel, Cammeray, NSW

8 Prospect Hill Hotel, Kew, Vic (with Coup d'Etat)

11 Duke of Edinburgh Hotel, St Kilda, Vic

12 Caledonian Hotel, Wonthaggi, Vic

18 Eureka Hotel, Geelong, Vic

19 Central Club Hotel, Richmond, Vic (with Mike Rudd)

20 Pier Hotel, Frankston, Vic (with Dance Exponents)

25 Prospect Hill Hotel, Kew, Vic (with Latest Thing From England)

26 Duke of Edinburgh Hotel, St Kilda, Vic

June

8 Box Hill College of Technical and Further Education, Vic (early, with Sole Twisters)

8 Duke of Edinburgh Hotel, St Kilda, Vic (late)

9 Pacific Hotel, Lorne, Vic

10 Central Club Hotel, Richmond, Vic (with X Ports)

22 Pier Hotel, Frankston, Vic (with X Ports)

23 Duke of Edinburgh Hotel, St Kilda, Vic

29 Armadale Hotel, Vic (with Cross Member)

30 Duke of Edinburgh Hotel, St Kilda, Vic

July

6 Central Club Hotel, Richmond, Vic (with Mantaka and Warumpi Band)

7 Central Hall, Fitzroy, Vic (Rock Against Racism, with Hard Times. Mantaka and Warumpi Band)

14 Duke of Edinburgh Hotel, St Kilda, Vic

26 Tropical Palace, London, England

27 Port Eliot, St Germans,
    Cornwall (Elephant Fayre,
    with Linton Kwesi Johnson,
    John Martyn, Jonathan
    Richman and the Modern
    Lovers)
29 Battersea Park, London
    (Tolpuddle Martyrs 150th
    Anniversary Festival)
30 Australia House, London,
    press reception

August

2   Liverpool (International
    Garden Festival)
3   Liverpool (International
    Garden Festival)
7   Dingwalls, London
10 Band on the Wall Hotel,
    Manchester
14 Half Moon Hotel, Putney,
    London
17 100 Club, London
18 Trinity Hall, Bristol
19 Victoria Park, London (Save
    The GLC concert)
20 Queens Hall, Barnstaple
21 Riverside Hall, Exeter
22 Oceans Nightclub, Plymouth
26 Portobello Green, London
    (Notting Hill Carnival)
27 Greyhound Hotel, Fulham,
    London

September

5   Central Independent TV,
    Birmingham (with UB40)
5   Royal Festival Hall, London
    (Gala Evening for the Miners,
    with Misty-In-Roots)
8   Fordham Park, New Cross,
    London (Anti-Racist Concert)

14 Anson Hall, Cricklewood,
    London (Aboriginal Day
    Concert)
14 SBS TV, *No Fixed Address on
    Tour*, documentary
15 Jubilee Gardens, London (GLC
    Thamesday)

December

> *Selwyn Burns joins.*
> *Line-up: Bart Willoughby (drums,*
> *vocals), Ricky Harrison (guitar,*
> *vocals), Nicky Moffatt (bass,*
> *vocals, vocals) and Selwyn Burns*
> *(guitar)*

7   Daylesford, Vic (Sky to Earth
    Confest 84, with Canned
    Heat)
21 Central Club Hotel, Richmond,
    Vic

1985

January

> *Nicky Moffatt leaves. Monty Lovett*
> *joins.*
> *Line-up: Bart Willoughby (drums,*
> *vocals), Ricky Harrison (guitar,*
> *vocals), Monty Lovett (bass) and*
> *Selwyn Burns (guitar)*

27 Phoenician Club, Ultimo, NSW
    (Committee to Defend Black
    Rights and Radio Skid Row)

April

> *Selwyn Burns leaves. David Osborne joins.*
> *Line-up: Bart Willoughby (drums, vocals), Ricky Harrison (guitar, vocals), Monty Lovett (bass) and David Osborne (guitar)*

27 Alice Springs, NT (launch of 8KIN radio station, with Coloured Stone, Ilkari Maru, Auriel Andrews, Isaac Yama)

1986

November

> *Band reforms with line-up: Bart Willoughby (drums, vocals), Les Graham (guitar, vocals), Ricky Lovegrove (guitar, vocals) John John Miller (bass)*

1987

February

6 The Settlement, Chippendale, NSW (organised by Radio Skid Row)
21 Graphic Arts Club, Sydney
— Canberra
— Bendigo, Vic

March

— Melbourne
— Adelaide
21 Paddington Town Hall, NSW (Afrika Nite, with Club Ska, T-Vibes, Charles Euchu, Wanjiku Wa Kiarii)
22 Tivoli, Sydney (supporting Ian Moss)
— Brisbane

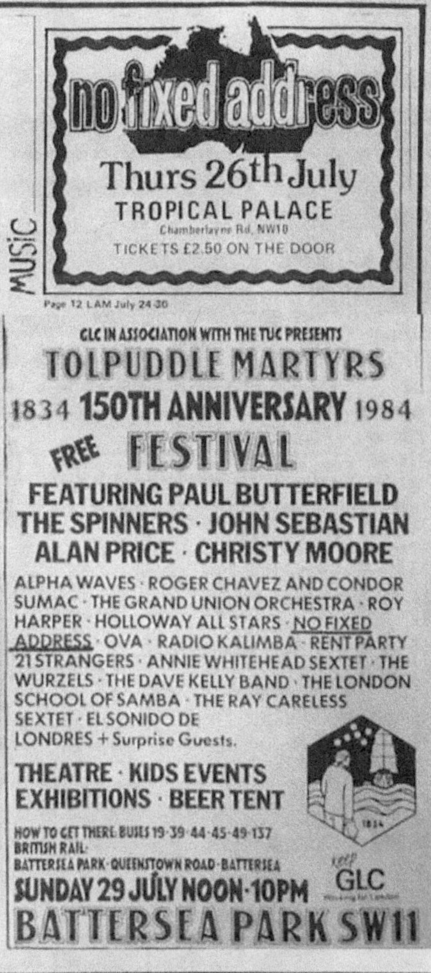

April

22 UNSW, Kensington, NSW

May

2 Living Arts Centre, Adelaide (May Day March and Cabaret)

August

28 Maughan Church, Adelaide (Stand Up for Justice, Stop Black Deaths in Custody)

October

1 Otherway Centre, Pirie Street, Adelaide (We Have Survived ... 200 Years)

2 Otherway Centre, Pirie Street, Adelaide (We Have Survived ... 200 Years)

3 Otherway Centre, Pirie Street, Adelaide (We Have Survived ... 200 Years)

October/November

— Adelaide
— Port Augusta, SA
— Alice Springs, NT
— Darwin, NT
— Broome, WA
— Exmouth, WA
— Port Hedland, WA
— Carnarvon, WA
— Geraldton, WA

December

5 Morelands Hotel, Brunswick, Vic

6 Central Club Hotel, Richmond, Vic

1988

February

16 Palace of the Republic, East Berlin

— East Berlin (Feb 16-21 Festival of Political Song)

— East Germany (Feb 22-26)

27 Rostock, East Germany

March

— Deutschlandhalle, West Berlin

April

— Fekete Lyuk, Budapest, Hungary

May

— Yugoslavia
— Bulgaria

1996

October

> *Line-up: Bart Willoughby (drums, vocals), Les Graham (guitar, vocals), Ricky Harrison (guitar, vocals), John John Miller (bass)*

3 The Stage, Fitzroy, Vic (Koori Kulture Club, with Warumpi Band)

November

22 Thebarton Theatre, Adelaide (Rock Against Racism, with Rough Image)

2008

June

5 Woodford, Qld (Dreaming Festival)

November
15   Killarney, Vic (Tarerer
     Festival)

2011

August
19   Garden's Amphitheatre,
     Darwin (Induction into
     National Indigenous Music
     Awards Hall of Fame)

2013

October
19   Producers' Hotel, Adelaide
     (with Us Mob)

2016

June
3   Goodwood Institute Theatre,
     SA (Induction into SA
     Music Hall of Fame, plus
     performance)

September
29   Lomond Hotel, East
     Brunswick, Vic
30   Marngrook Grand Final Footy
     Show, NITV

2017

January
26   Treasury Gardens, Melbourne
     (Share the Spirit Festival)
28   Governor Hindmarsh,
     Hindmarsh, SA

May
27   Memo Music Hall, St Kilda
     (with Madder Lake)

August
31   107 Projects, Redfern, NSW
     (with Coloured Stone)

2018

February
23   Broome, WA (Saltwater
     Festival)

March
21   Spotted Mallard, Adelaide
23   Marrickville Bowling Club,
     NSW

September
22   Jigamy, Eden, NSW (Giiyong
     Festival)

October
13   Governor Hindmarsh,
     Hindmarsh, SA

2019

August

2   Morwell (GLaWAC Community Treaty Yarn)

9   Forestec, Kalimna West (GLaWAC Community Treaty Yarn)

2020

January

26   Treasury Gardens, Melbourne (Share the Spirit Festival)

2021

March

25   Launch of No Fixed Address Lane, Adelaide

25   Governor Hindmarsh, Hindmarsh, SA

26   Kura Yerlo Disability Hub, Taperoo, SA (lunchtime)

26   Longriders Club, Murray Bridge, SA (evening)

27   Three Brothers Arms, Macclesfield, SA

2022

January

26   Lawns of Old Parliament House, Canberra (50th anniversary of Aboriginal Tent Embassy, with Mop and the Dropouts, Kutcha Edwards)

February

26   Rumbalara Football Netball Club, Shepparton, Vic (Treaty Day Out, with Yothu Yindi, Archie Roach, Briggs, Electric Fields and others)

October

1   Bendigo Showgrounds, Vic (Treaty Day Out, with Dan Sultan, Briggs and others)

Sources include: The Advertiser (Adelaide); The Age (Melbourne); Canberra Times; Centralian Advocate; Chester Schutz archive; Daily News (Perth); Melody Maker; Michael Fisher archive; New Musical Express; The News (Adelaide); Northern Star; Radio Times (4ZZZ Brisbane); RAM; Roadrunner; The Sydney Morning Herald; tagg; Tjungaringanyi; Tribune; The West Australian; Whyalla News.

My thanks to the following people for taking the time to speak with me and share their memories (date of interviews in brackets).

Julie Andrews (4 Aug-22); Martha Ansara (28 Dec-20); Andrew Belletty (20 Aug-21); Matthew Bienstock (1 Oct-20); Maxine Briggs (18 Jun-21); Margaret Brodie (12 Nov-20); Jen Jewel Brown (27 Oct-20); Pedro Butler (6 Jan-21); Janie Conway-Herron (8 Jul-21); David Cooke (25 Jul-21); Ian de Gruchy (13 Nov-20); Margaret Dodd (6 Dec-20, 20 Jan-21); Michael Fisher (10 Aug-21, 28 Nov-21, 30 Nov-21, 9 Dec-21, 16 Dec-21, 6 Jan-22, 7 Aug-22); Gary Foley (24 May-21); Ross Gardiner (12 Oct-20); Joe Geia (3 Jun-21); Sherree Goldsworthy (21 Sep-20); Les Graham (19 Aug-20, 16 Sep-21); Ricky Harrison (17 Aug-20, 29 Oct-20, 19 May-21, 28 Jun-21, 21 Aug-21, 28 Aug-21); Colin Hay (1 Jun-21); Leigh Hobba (4 Sep-20); Shane Howard (7 Apr-21); Graeme Isaac (2 Sep-20, 24 Feb-21); Jean Morgan Kelly (29 Apr-21); Ned Lander (17 Sep-20); David Langsam (8 Oct-20); Madeline McGrady (12 Aug-21); Michael McMartin (22-01-2022); John John Miller (1 Sep-20, 5 Oct-21); Alec Morgan (14 Jan-21); Jean Morgan Kelly (29 Apr-21); Andy Nehl (22 Jul-21); Tim Nicholls (1 May-22); David Noakes (13 May-21); Mick Pacholli (30 Oct-20, 2 Nov-20); Ian Parmenter (13 May-21); Doug Petherick (23 Mar-21); Philip Roberts (15 Sep-20); John Schumann (22 Mar-21); Wendy Slee (11 May-21); Collette Snowden (11 Oct-20); Mary Stutters (6 Nov-20); Duckie Taylor (10 Nov-20); Mick Thompson (13 Jul-21, 14 Jul-21); Mark Thomson (1 Sep-20); Wayne Thorpe (10 May-21); Anthony Wallis (16-01-22); Greg Williams (29 Sep-20, 8 May-21); Rod Willis (25 Oct-20, 26 Oct-20); Bart Willoughby (21 Aug-20, 6 May-21, 12 Oct-21); John Willsteed (28 Jul-21).

Thanks to Ricky Harrison for permission to include the lyrics from 'How Many Voices', 'All Because', 'Stand Up' and 'Pigs'.

Thanks to Bart Willoughby for permission to include lyrics from 'We Have Survived' and 'From My Eyes' and quotes from his interviews with Peter Parkhill in 2000; part of the Parkhill Collection held by the National Library of Australia.

Thanks to Eric Algra, Bleddyn Butcher, Ian de Gruchy, Margaret Dodd, Juno Gemes, Chris Grosz, Eddie Hughes, Leonie Lane, Andy

Nehl, Greg Noakes, Gabriele Senft, Carol Ruff, Wendy Slee, Manuel Tabone, John Wilsteed and Toby Zoates for permission to use their photographs and illustrations.

Thanks to Robert Brokenmouth for permission to use extracts from his review of the No Fixed Address album *Live PBS 106.7FM*.

Thanks to the estate of Andrew McMillan for permission to use an extract from his article on the Clash, "The world's last rock'n'roll band'.

Special thanks to Michael Fisher for sharing the contents of the incredible Michael Fisher archive; to Ian Chambers and Steve Wood for their accounts of the Children's Free Embassy Christmas Tour 1979-80; to Wendy Slee for sharing extracts from her scrapbook of the No Fixed Address tour of Western Australia in 1982; to Peter Gray for sharing material relating to Rock Against Racism, Sydney and the Brisbane Commonwealth Games protests; to Doug Petherick for providing details about the recordings held by the Centre for Aboriginal Studies in Music; and to Nicholas Sparks and Marie Larsen at the Barr Smith Library, University of Adelaide for facilitating access to the collection of Chester Schultz papers and recordings 1974-2015.

Thanks to Eleanor Hogan at the Alice Springs Library, Andrew Piper and staff at the State Library of South Australia; and staff at the State Library of NSW and the National Library of Australia.

Thanks also to people who contributed information either in writing or in conversation including: Chris Bastic, Graham Bidstrup, Anke Bornschein, Robert Brokenmouth, Harry Butler, Pip Chandler, Sally Collins, Murray Cook (the non-Wiggly one), Sean Dempsey, Zev Eisik, Martin Fabok, Ken Gormly, Lyn Griffen, Phillippa Gwynneth, Anne Jones, Ralph Kerle, Ian Lovell, Ian McFarlane, George Matzkov, Philip Mortlock, Dianna O'Neill, Mark Pope, Kimble Rendall, Grayson Rotumah, Clive Scollay, Manwel Tabone, Samantha Trenoweth, Kosmo Vinyl, Rebecca Weaver, Clinton Walker, Don Walker, Anthony Wallis, Bob Yates, Reginald Zar, Michael Zerman and Toby Zoates. And to others who have helped along the way, you know who you are and I offer you my thanks as well.

For their valuable comments on drafts of the manuscript, grateful thanks to Ricky Harrison, Graeme Isaac and Michael Fisher.

I would like to pay tribute to art director Jim Paton. Jim strongly felt this book was an important document and was enthusiastic about working on it. Jim prepared the cover design and selected the typography for the book while undergoing chemotherapy for cancer, but tragically he died in December 2022. I am extremely grateful to his colleague Murray Bennett for taking on the work Jim had done and seeing the job through to completion.

Thanks to Miranda Brown of Miranda Brown Publicity for getting the word out.

Thanks to the South Australian History Trust for a grant from the South Australian History Fund to assist with the costs of design and publicity.

Thanks to Louis de Vries and Anna Blay at Hybrid Publishers for having the belief and for their unfailing courtesy, flexibility and professionalism in producing the work.

And finally, thanks to Di for love and support, and for the happy home where it all happened.

101.   Essie Coffey, Graeme Isaac and Philip Roberts, Greenhill Studios, SA, March 1980 (© Ian de Gruchy, used with permission).

111.   No Fixed Address, Adelaide CBD, 1980 (© Ian de Gruchy, used with permission).

117.   Filming *Wrong Side of the Road*. Bart Willoughby, Ricky Harrison and publican (© Carol Ruff, used with permission).

119.   Filming *Wrong Side of the Road*. Chris Haywood, Pedro Butler and Ronnie Ansell (© Carol Ruff, used with permission).

131.   Supporting Cold Chisel, University of Adelaide, 20 December 1980 (© Eric Algra, used with permission).

137.   Bart Willoughby, Festival Theatre, Adelaide, 10 February 1981 (© Eric Algra, used with permission).

139.   Bart Willoughby with didgeridoo, Festival Theatre, Adelaide, 10 February 1981 (© Eric Algra, used with permission).

143.   Rocking the Royal, April 1981 (© Newspix, used with permission).

149.   Ricky Harrison (© Carol Ruff, used with permission).

163.   Leila Rankine, *Wrong Side of the Road* Adelaide premiere, Trak Cinema, Toorak Gardens, SA, October 1981 (© Ian de Gruchy, used with permission).

165.   Ned Lander and Bart Willoughby, *Wrong Side of the Road* Adelaide premiere, Trak Cinema, Toorak Gardens, SA, October 1981 (© Ian de Gruchy, used with permission).

199.   Joe Geia, Bart Willoughby, Joe Hayes, Les Graham, Ricky Harrison, Billy Inda Cummins with Jenny Keath, Mushroom Music Publishing, 1982 (© Greg Noakes, used with permission).

211.   Rough Diamond publicity shot, 1982. Back row: Joe Hayes, Joe Geia, Ricky Harrison. Front row: Les Graham, Bart Willoughby, Billy Inda Cummins. (Rough Diamond Records, used with permission).

217.   Maxine Briggs (right) and Jean Morgan (© Wendy Slee, used with permission).

221.   Les Graham, Joe Geia, Reg Zar, Bart Willoughby (in cast), Joe Hayes and Billy Inda Cummins, Perth Institute of Film and Television, 6 April 1982 (© Wendy Slee, used with permission).

235.   4ZZZ tour handbill, May/June 1982 (© John Willsteed, used with permission).

241.   Bob Hawke launches *From My Eyes*, Melbourne Hilton, 28 June 1982. Back row: Billy Inda Cummins, Ricky Harrison, Bart Willoughby. Front row: Duckie Taylor, Hawke, Les Graham (© Newspix, used with permission).

255.   Rock Against Racism handbill, Brisbane, September 1982 (© John Willsteed, used with permission).

269.   Billy Gorham, Joe Geia, Bart Willoughby, Peter Meredith and Ricky Harrison, Melbourne, April 1983 (© Carol Ruff, used with permission).

271.   Tiga Bayles, Ricky Harrison and Billy Gorham, People for Nuclear Disarmament rally, The Domain, Sydney, Palm Sunday, 27 March 1983 (© Juno Gemes/Juno Gemes Archive, used with permission).

301.   Elephant Fayre, July 1984 (Roadrunner collection).

305.   Bart Willoughby blowing didge and blowing minds, Notting Hill Carnival, London, August 1984. (© Manwel Tabone, used with permission).

305.   Ricky Harrison and Nicky Moffatt, Notting Hill Carnival, London, August 1984. (© Manwel Tabone, used with permission).

307.   Nicky Moffatt, Ricky Harrison and Bart Willoughby beside the Thames, Wapping, London (© Bleddyn Butcher, used with permission).

311.   Selwyn Burns, Monty Lovett, Bart Willoughby and Ricky Harrison, Phoenician Club, Sydney 27 January 1985 (Mitchell Library, State Library of New South Wales and courtesy SEARCH Foundation).

329.   On the desert run: the Dignity tour, 1987 (photographer unknown).

343.   Bart Willoughby, Ricky Lovegrove, Les Graham, John John Miller and Mick Thompson in the snow, Alexanderplatz, East Berlin, February 1988 (© Gabriele Senft, used with permission).

347.   Les Graham with members of Cuban band Moncado, East Germany, February 1988 (© Gabriele Senft, used with permission).

347.   Marie-Josephine Rasoarimalala of Madagascan band Rossy with Bart Willoughby, East Germany, February 1988 (© Gabriele Senft, used with permission).

349.   Mick Thompson, East Germany, February 1988 (© Gabriele Senft, used with permission).

383.   Ricky Harrison, Mick Thompson, Bart Willoughby, John John Miller and Les Graham at the launch of No Fixed Address Lane, Adelaide 25 March 2021 (© Donald Robertson, used with permission).

Back cover:
Nicky Moffatt, Ricky Harrison and Bart Willoughby beside the Thames, Wapping, London (© Bleddyn Butcher, used with permission).

The core of this playlist is a) songs recorded and released by No Fixed Address and b) songs performed live by No Fixed Address but recorded by others (i.e., Joe Geia, Bart Willoughby and Mixed Relations). It also includes songs by people the band played with, people they met along the way and other significant songs mentioned in the text.

The playlist is available on Spotify, at https://spoti.fi/3FXtY1A

'The Vision', No Fixed Address, *Wrong Side of the Road (Songs from the Motion Picture)*

'Trenchtown Rock', Bob Marley & the Wailers, *Live at the Rainbow, 3 June 1977*

'We Have Survived', No Fixed Address, *Wrong Side of the Road (Songs from the Motion Picture)*

'Dancing in the Moonlite', Coloured Stone, *CAAMA 25 Year Anniversary Compilation*

'Genocide', Us Mob, *Wrong Side of the Road (Songs from the Motion Picture)*

'Greenhouse Holiday', *No Fixed Address, Wrong Side of the Road (Songs from the Motion Picture)*

'Khe Sahn', Cold Chisel, *The Live Tapes Vol 5: Live at the Bondi Lifesaver Feb 29, 1980*

'Black Man's Rights', No Fixed Address, *W'rong Side of the Road (Songs from the Motion Picture)*

'The Last Frontier', Redgum, *Against the Grain (The Redgum Anthology 1976-1986)*

'Uncle Willy', Joe Geia, *CAAMA 25 Year Anniversary Compilation*

'Bran Nue Day (Millya Rumarra)', Kuckles, *Bran Nue Day*

'Wrong Side of the Road', Us Mob, *Wrong Side of the Road (Songs from the Motion Picture)*

'Get a Grip', No Fixed Address, *Wrong Side of the Road (Songs from the Motion Picture)*

'Spasticus Autisticus', Ian Dury and the Blockheads, *Hit Me! The Best of Ian Dury*

'The Magnificent Seven', The Clash, *Sandanista!*

'Armagideon Time', The Clash, *Sound System*

'The Vision (version)', No Fixed Address, *Wrong Side of the Road (Songs from the Motion Picture)*

'Lonesome Loser', Little River Band, *First Under the Wire*
'Beautiful People', Australian Crawl, *The Boys Light Up*
'From My Eyes', No Fixed Address, *From My Eyes* (mini-album)
'Solid Rock', Goanna, *Spirit of Place*
'Sunrise', No Fixed Address, *From My Eyes* (mini-album)
'Down Under', Men at Work, *Business as Usual*
'Stupid System', No Fixed Address, *From My Eyes* (mini-album)
'Brisbane Blacks', Mop and the Dropouts, *Best of Koori Classic (The Early
    Years Aboriginal Collection)*
'I Can't Stand and Look', No Fixed Address, *From My Eyes* (mini-album)
'Talking To a Stranger', Hunters & Collectors, *Hunters & Collectors*
'Where Ya Gonna Run To?', Redgum, *Against the Grain (The Redgum
    Anthology 1976-1986)*
'Pigs', No Fixed Address, *From My Eyes* (mini-album)
'Bow River', Cold Chisel, *The Barking Spiders Live 1983*
'40,000 Years', No Fixed Address, *From My Eyes* (CD)
'Bush Doctor', Peter Tosh, *Complete Captured Live*
'Only the Strong', Midnight Oil, *Scream in Blue Live*
'Stand Up', No Fixed Address, *From My Eyes* (CD)
'Jailanguru Pakarnu (Out from Jail)', Warumpi Band, *Warumpi Band 4 Ever*
'That Summer Feeling', Jonathan Richman and the Modern Lovers,
    Jonathan Sings!
'Making History', Linton Kwesi Johnson, *Reggae Greats*
'Let's Dance', David Bowie, *Let's Dance*
'Roots Rocking', Aswad, *Live and Direct*
'Man Kind', Misty in Roots, *Roots Controller*
'Message for Young and Old', Bart Willoughby, *CAAMA 25 Years
    Anniversary Compilation*
'Black Boy', Coloured Stone, *Best of Coloured Stone*
'Blackfella/Whitefella', Warumpi Band, *Warumpi Band 4 Ever*
'When You Dance', Catfish, *Unlimited Address*
'Ambilahao Zaho', Rossy, *Madagascar*
'Aboriginal Woman', Mixed Relations, *CAAMA 25 Years Anniversary
    Compilation*
'Ngi Gu Binnahl', Joe Geia, *Yil Lull*
'Djapana', Yothu Yindi, *Homeland Movement*
'Graffiti Man', John Trudell, *AKA Graffiti Man*
'Warakurna', Midnight Oil, *Diesel and Dust*
'Treaty', Yothu Yindi, *Tribal Voice*
'Freedom', Kev Carmody, *Bloodlines*

NOTES

Introduction
[1] H Reynolds, The other side of the frontier, UNSW Press, Sydney NSW, 2006.

Chapter 2. Connections
[1] C Horne, 'The Arts', *The Dunstan decade: social democracy at the state level*, eds. A Parkin & A Patience, Longman Cheshire, Melbourne Vic, 1981.
[2] C Fleming & J Tait, *Captain Matchbox & Beyond*, Melbourne Books, Melbourne Vic, 2015.

Chapter 3. Taperoo
[1] L Hobba, I de Gruchy & J Stokes, *Aboriginal Country Music Festival 1979*, Leigh Hobba & Ian de Gruchy, Adelaide SA, 1979.
[2] Bart Willoughby interviewed by Peter Parkhill, 3-4 May 2000, National Library of Australia, ORAL TRC 4571.

Chapter 4. The Adelaide Aboriginal Orchestra
[1] L Barwick, 'Catherine Ellis 1935-1996', *Yearbook for Traditional Music*, 28, Cambridge University Press 1996, pp. xi-xiii.
[2] R Amery, 'The history of Aboriginal languages and linguistics at the University of Adelaide', *A history of the faculty of arts at the University of Adelaide*, eds. N Harvey, J Fornasiero, G McCarthy, C Macintyre & C Crossin, University of Adelaide Press, Adelaide SA, 2012.
[3] S Lindeman, *To the beat of his own drum: the Ben Yengi story*, KADI Australia, Prospect SA, 2009.
[4] C Dow & J Gardiner-Garden, *Overview of Indigenous Affairs: Part 1: 1901 to 1991*, Social Policy Section, Parliamentary Library, Canberra, ACT, 2011.
[5] BG Dexter, G Foley & E Howell, *Pandora's box: the Council for Aboriginal Affairs 1967-1976*, Keeaira Press, Southport, Queensland, 2015.
[6] National Native Title Tribunal, *25 years of Native Title Recognition*, viewed 1 June 2022 <http://www.nntt.gov.au/Documents/Road%20to%20native%20title.pdf>.
[7] G Foley & T Anderson, 'Land Rights and Aboriginal Voices', *Australian Journal of Human Rights*, vol. 12 (1), 2006, pp. 83-108.
[8] 'Notes from meeting held at the University of Adelaide on 16 October 1974 of discussions between tribal and urban Aborigines and officials of the university', Chester Schultz papers and recordings 1974-2015, Barr Smith Library, University of Adelaide, Adelaide SA.
[9] Lindeman.

[10]V Brodie, *My side of the bridge*, Wakefield Press, Adelaide SA, 2002.

[11]L Rankine, 'Looking into the future – 1978', *Tjunguringanyi*, vol 4 no 1, 1978, p.2.

[12]BL Yengi, ' The uniqueness of the Centre for Aboriginal Studies in Music', *Aboriginal Child at School*, Vol. 10, No. 2, Apr/May 1982, pp. 44-50.

Chapter 5. 'Can you take those handcuffs off?'

[1] Bart Willoughby interviewed by Peter Parkhill.

[2] Bart Willoughby interviewed by Peter Parkhill.

[3] Bart Willoughby interviewed by Peter Parkhill.

Chapter 6. Operation Public Disorder

[1] L Rankine, 'Come Out 79', *Tjunguringanyi*, vol 5 no 1, 1979.

[2] M Thomson, 'Wrong side of the road', *Roadrunner*, Vol 4 No 10, November 1981, p.27.

[3] Bart Willoughby interviewed by Peter Parkhill.

Chapter 7. 'I've been hassled by the cops nearly all of my life'

[1] D Dunstan, Speech to Council of Civil Liberties, Sydney, 1978.

[2] J Summers, 'Aboriginal Policy', *The Dunstan decade: social democracy at the state level*, eds. A Parkin & A Patience, Longman Cheshire, Melbourne Vic, 1981.

[3] Summers.

[4] A Woollacott, *Don Dunstan: the visionary politician who changed Australia*, Allen & Unwin, Crows Nest NSW, 2019.

[5] BJ O'Neil, 'Beyond trinkets and beads: South Australia's Aboriginal Legal Rights Movement, 1971-1978', *Aboriginal History* Vol 6, Part 1, 1982, pp. 28-37.

[6] Summers.

[7] Commissioner for Community Relations, 'Report on allegations and appearances of racial discrimination in Ceduna and neighbouring areas, South Australia', Canberra 1978.

Chapter 10. 'Imaginations involves being in dangerous positions'
1 Australians Together, 'The Stolen Generations', viewed 5 April 2022, <https://australianstogether.org.au/discover/australian-history/stolen-generations/>.
2 Australia. Royal Commission into Institutional Responses to Child Sexual Abuse, Final Report, Canberra ACT, 2017, viewed 25 March 2022, <https://www.royalcommission.gov.au/child-abuse/final-report>.
3 Bart Willoughby interviewed by Peter Parkhill.
4 Find and Connect Web Resource Project, 'McNally Training Centre (1967-1979)', 2011, viewed 25 March 2022, <https://www.findandconnect.gov.au/ref/sa/biogs/SE00078b.htm>.

Chapter 11. The Children's Free Embassy
1 Bart Willoughby interviewed by Peter Parkhill.
2 S Britton, 'Teenage Roadshow', *Artlink*, Vol 10 No 3, 1990, pp. 46-48.
3 S Carney, 'Songs of Melbourne', Age, 28 August 2004.
4 M Thomson, 'Aboriginal reggae: No Fixed Address, a young black band on the move', *Roadrunner*, Vol 3 No 3, April 1980, p.11.
5 Bart Willoughby interviewed by Peter Parkhill.
6 Bart Willoughby interviewed by Peter Parkhill.

Chapter 12. Festival City
1 R Moreton, 'My Survival as an Aboriginal', *Australian Screen* website, viewed 21 October 2021, <https://aso.gov.au/titles/documentaries/my-survival-aboriginal/notes/>.
2 I Petke, 'Backroads', *Phillip Noyce*, Pan Macmillan, Sydney NSW, 2004.

Chapter 13. 'We just want to check your indicators mate'
1 M Thomson, 'Aboriginal reggae'.

Chapter 14. On the Melbourne run
1 D Robertson, 'No Fixed Address: original Aboriginal reggae', *Roadrunner*, Vol 3 No 7, August 1980, pp. 12-13.
2 Bart Willoughby interviewed by Peter Parkhill.
3 D Robertson.

Chapter 15. Cookie Monster
1 Bart Willoughby interviewed by Peter Parkhill.

Chapter 16. Cold Chisel's Summer Offensive
1 S Coupe, 'Aboriginal band plays on pride', *Sun-Herald*, 21 December 1980.
2 M Lawrence, *Cold Chisel: wild colonial boys*, 2nd edn, Melbourne Books, Melbourne Vic, 2017.

Chapter 17. Rock Against Racism
[1] A Dunn, '"I was using my camera as a tool against the system": Trailblazing filmmaker Madeline McGrady', NITV, 2018, viewed November 2022 <https://www.sbs.com.au/nitv/article/i-was-using-my-camera-as-a-tool-against-the-system-trailblazing-filmmaker-madeline-mcgrady/5wxfdiwxa>
[2] S Hunter, 'A reason to be humble', *Advertiser*, February 1981.

Chapter 18. Royal Charity Performance
[1] I Richards, 'They're new royal showmen in song', *Advertiser*, 22 April 1981, p. 3.
[2] R Erlich, 'A show that's undemanding', *Age*, 1 May 1981.

Chapter 20. Jury Prize
[1] Bart Willoughby interviewed by Peter Parkhill.
[2] Ninti One Limited, 'Categories of Indigenous homeless people and good practice responses to their needs', viewed December 2022 < https://www.nintione.com.au/resources/rao/categories-of-indigenous-homeless-people-and-good-practice-responses-to-their-needs/>
[3] Bart Willoughby interviewed by Peter Parkhill.
[4] B Wright, 'Rock's vanishing venues', *Sydney Morning Herald*, 14 September 1981.

Chapter 21. Reaction
[1] G Brooks, 'A hard look at a tough life', *Sydney Morning Herald*, 31 October 1981.
[2] J Lapsley, 'Wrong Side of the Road', *Sun-Herald*, 1 November 1981.
[3] D Macdonald, 'Aboriginal view across the rift', *Canberra Times*, 12 March 1982.
[4] M Breen, 'Wrong Side of the Road', *Australian Film 1978-1994*, ed. S Murray, Oxford University Press, Melbourne Vic, 1995.

Chapter 22. The tip of the spear
[1] R Brokenmouth, 'Live PBS 106.7FM – No Fixed Address', i94bar.com, 2018, viewed May 2021, <https://www.i94bar.com/albums/live-pbs-106-7fm-no-fixed-address-no-fixed-address>.
[2] W Birch, *Ian Dury: the definitive biography*, Sidgwick & Jackson, London, 2010.
[3] Quoted in K Hampton & C Mattingley (eds), *Survival in our own land: 'Aboriginal' experiences in 'South Australia' since 1836*, Wakefield Press, Adelaide SA, 1988, pp. 64-65.

Chapter 23. Deals
[1] GA Baker, 'Astor plant closure alarms Aussie indies', *Billboard*, 14 November 1981, p. 98.

Chapter 24. The Clash
[1] G Solis, 'Punk politics, blackness and Indigenous protest: The Clash's Australian tour, 1982', in *Transnational perspectives on the only band that matters*, eds. S Cohen & J Peacock, Bloomsbury Academic, New York, 2017.
[2] C Salewicz, *Redemption Song*, HarperCollins, London, 2006.
[3] A McMillan, 'The world's last rock'n'roll band', *RAM*, 19 March 1982, pp. 17-19.

Chapter 25. Rough Diamond
[1] A Ryan, 'The trouble with Rastafarians in London', *Age*, 21 December 1984, p. 37.

Chapter 26. The West
[1] R Heston, 'ES rock group black-banned', *Sunday Independent*, March 28 1982, pp. 1, 3.
[2] T Robertson, 'Black rock band fills the gaps in tour', *Daily News*, 30 March 1982.

Chapter 28. Back in the saddle
[1] T Robertson, 'Concert will help NFA', *Daily News*, 14 April 1982.

Chapter 29. From My Eyes
[1] A Brown. 'From My Eyes: No Fixed Address', *Roadrunner*, vol 6 no 1, January 1983, p. 59.
[2] GA Baker, 'Aussie labels in row with "pay-for-play"', *Billboard*, 27 November 1982, pp. 1, 64.
[3] GA Baker, 'Riding an international wave', *Billboard*, 12 June 1982, pp. A/NZ 2, 6, 14.
[4] GA Baker, '1985 market surge helps Australia restore status as major rock nation', *Billboard*, 9 November 1985, p. A4, 20.

Chapter 30. The Games
[1] A good account of the prevailing Queensland regime is contained in M Langton & N Loos, 'The Dawn is at Hand', in R Perkins & M Langdon (eds), *First Australians*, The Miegunyah Press, Carlton Vic, 2008.

Chapter 32. Ch-ch-changes
[1] 'Our Mother', 'Living in the City' and 'Reality' appeared on the Mixed Relations album *Love* (1993).

2 Aboriginal Arts Board, *Annual Report 1983-84*, Australia Council, North Sydney NSW, 1984.

3 R Thomson, 'The night the police came to the Clifton', *Sydney Morning Herald*, 4 November 1983, pp. 1, 4.

Chapter 34. *That summer feeling: England 1984*

1 S Garrett, 'Out in Oz', *City Limits*, 1-16 August 1984.

2 A Isaacs, 'Notting Hill Carnival', *Melody Maker*, 8 September 1984, p. 32.

3 M Snow, 'Notting Hill Carnival', *New Musical Express*, 8 September 1984, p. 45.

4 D Kelly, 'Mission', *New Musical Express*, 29 September 1984, p.8.

Chapter 35. *The tour that never was*

1 M Breen (ed.), *Our place, our music*, Aboriginal Studies Press for the Australian Institute of Aboriginal Studies, Canberra ACT, 1989.

2 R Irby, 'Station opens with a blast!', *Centralian Advocate*, 1 May 1985, pp. 1, 2.

3 P Sutton, 'Coloured Stone join Goanna in Canberra', *Canberra Times*, 2 October 1986.

4 Bart Willoughby interviewed by Peter Parkhill.

5 AW Hurley, 'No Fixed Address, but currently in East Berlin: the Australian bicentennial, Indigenous protest and the Festival of Political Song in 1988', Perfect Beat, vol 15 no 2, 2014.

6 B Hall, B Hall to Professor F Rose 10 October 1985. Letter. Series 1: Frederick Rose General correspondence [ca. 1930]-1991. Mitchell Library, State Library of NSW.

Chapter 36. *Dignity*

1 J Stafford, 'No Fixed Address – young, gifted and Black', *Tribune*, 18 February 1987, p. 12.

2 K Cook & H Goodall, *Making Change Happen*, ANU Press, Canberra, ACT, 2013.

3 G Foley & T Anderson.

4 G Foley & T Anderson.

5 K Cook & H Goodall.

6 Recording Studio Living Archive Melbourne, 'Richmond Recorders (1978-86)', 2021, viewed 27 September 2021, <https://recordingstudios.net.au/featured-studios-scenes/richmond-recorders/>.

7 B Hall, *B Hall to F Rose* 10 October 1987. Letter. Series 1: Frederick Rose General correspondence [ca. 1930]-1991. Mitchell Library, State Library of NSW.

Chapter 37. The desert run

[1] K Beazley, 'North West Cape: the joint facility that changed Australian politics', *The Strategist*, 2017, viewed 27 October 2021, <https://www.aspistrategist.org.au/north-west-cape-the-joint-facility-that-changed-australian-politics/>.

[2] Aboriginal Arts Board, *Annual Report 1987-88*, Australia Council, North Sydney NSW, 1988.

[3] K Cook & H Goodall.

[4] K Cook & H Goodall.

Chapter 38. Festival des politischen Liedes: East Berlin 1988

[1] D Sly, 'The Dawn of Black Rock', *Advertiser*, 11 February 1988.

[2] AW Hurley.

[3] T Judt, *Postwar: a history of Europe since 1945*, Penguin Press, London, 2005.

[4] D Sly.

Chapter 39. Hungry in Hungary

[1] F Rose, 12 February 1988. Note for file. Series 1: Frederick Rose General correspondence [ca. 1930]-1991. Mitchell Library, State Library of NSW.

[2] B Scheps, *B Scheps to F Rose* 4 April 1988. Letter. Series 1: Frederick Rose General correspondence [ca. 1930]-1991. Mitchell Library, State Library of NSW.

[3] F Rose, *F Rose to B Scheps,* 21 March 1988. Letter. Series 1: Frederick Rose General correspondence [ca. 1930]-1991. Mitchell Library, State Library of NSW.

[4] Unearthing the music, 'Fekete Lyuk', 2018, viewed 13 October 2021, <http://database.unearthingthemusic.eu/Fekete_Lyuk>.

[5] PS Müller, Gurukenguru, 16 September 2017, viewed 13 October 2021 <fb.watch/b_pOY1UMtY/>.

Chapter 40. Aftermath

[1] B Hall, *B Hall to F Rose*, 8 September 1988. Letter.

[2] F Rose, *F Rose to B Hall,* 9 November 1988. Letter. Series 1: Frederick Rose General correspondence [ca. 1930]-1991. Mitchell Library, State Library of NSW

[3] M Dodshon, *Beds Are Burning*, Viking, Camberwell, Vic, 2004.

INDEX

I N D E X

www.ingramcontent.com/pod-product-compliance
Lightning Source LLC
Chambersburg PA
CBHW061501050726

47593CB00004B/1746